Problematic
Sovereignty

Problematic Sovereignty

Contested Rules and Political Possibilities

STEPHEN D. KRASNER, EDITOR

Columbia University Press NEW YORK

Columbia University Press

Publishers Since 1893

New York Chichester, West Sussex

Library of Congress Cataloging-in-Publication Data

Problematic sovereignty / Stephen D. Krasner, editor

   p. cm.

   Includes bibliographical references and index.

   ISBN 0–231–12178-4 (cloth : alk. paper)—ISBN 0–231–12179–2
   (pbk. : alk. paper)

   1. Sovereignty. I. Krasner, Stephen D., 1942–

KZ4041.P76 2000

327.1′01–dc21

00-064426

∞

Casebound editions of Columbia University Press books
are printed on permanent and durable acid-free paper.

Printed in the United States of America

c 10 9 8 7 6 5 4 3 2 1

p 10 9 8 7 6 5 4 3 2 1

CONTENTS

PREFACE

Ethnic wars, transnational concerns for human rights, the Internet, financial crises, multinational corporations, international trade, and more generally, globalization have given rise to the sentiment that sovereignty as it has been conventionally understood is eroding or even withering away. This conclusion has been reached without much sense of the extent to which the present is different from the past, and without much systematic thought about how the concept of sovereignty might be understood and how the rules of sovereignty have actually functioned in the international environment.

Many recent discussions about the status of sovereignty have addressed economic questions — especially the possible loss of state regulatory capacity. However, this volume addresses different and possibly more consequential issues: namely, the way in which basic rules regarding mutual recognition and the exclusion of external authority, what are termed in this study international legal sovereignty and Westphalian sovereignty, are influencing, facilitating, or impeding the resolution of difficult political and economic issues. The rules associated with sovereignty, like any set of rules, may be more or less functional — more or less able to facilitate the realization of political, economic, security, or ideological objectives that are pursued by actors. The conventional rules of sovereignty — that is, to recognize juridically independent territorial entities and exclude external sources of authority from domestic territory — have been widely recognized at least since the early part of the nineteenth century. These rules, which originated in Europe, have spread to all parts of the globe, displacing other institutional forms such as the Chinese tributary state system or the Moslem practice of dividing the world between Dar al-Islam, the House of Islam or the civilized world, and Dar al-Harb, the House of War inhabited by infidels. For many purposes sovereignty rules have been attractive and stabilizing. They have established the political equivalent of property rights. They have facilitated the conclusion of treaties — contracts among states. They have made it easier to define transgressions.

The contemporary international environment is, however, complex. It would be surprising if one set of rules were optimal for all situations. Problematic sovereignty refers not only to the violation of conventional rules but also to the fact that such rules might not provide actors with the best possible ways to realize their economic, political, and ideological objectives. China, for instance, wants both juridical control over and international recognition for Hong Kong. The major Western powers want fully sovereign states in the Balkans but are at the same time prepared to violate the domestic autonomy of those states to protect and promote the rights of minorities. The leaders of Russia followed the script of sovereignty in supporting the breakup of the Soviet Union but would prefer that at least some parts of their former homeland remain functionally subordinate even if they are formally independent. The leader of Belarus would like the option of becoming the leader of some larger entity that would include Russia. Taiwan wants international recognition but does not want to declare its formal independence from China. Palestinians want a sovereign state but the Israelis will not accept a Palestinian state that has full control over its own security policies.

What happens in cases where the conventional rules of sovereignty do not provide optimal outcomes? Can the rules be bent? Can they be rewritten? Can new rules be invented? These are the questions addressed in this volume. The former Soviet Union; parts of China including Hong Kong, Tibet, and Taiwan; Bosnia; and Palestine all present situations in which the interests of actors might be better served if they could find alternatives to sovereignty. In some cases such alternatives have been developed. In others they have not.

The fundamental conclusion of this study is that the rules of sovereignty are not absolutely constraining. They are not taken for granted. New rules can be written; conventional ones can be ignored. Innovation is, however, possible only if actors can reach voluntary agreements or if some powerful states are willing to engage in coercion. Absent contracting or coercion, conventional sovereignty rules are the default.

This project could not have been completed without the support of the Institute for International Studies at Stanford. The institute, like some of the cases in this volume, defies conventional rules. Its activities involve a number of different substantive issue areas and engage the worlds of both academia and public policy.

My wife, Patricia, in this, as in all things, has been unfailingly loving and supportive despite my complaints about lost references and other more consequential issues.

Stephen D. Krasner
Stanford, California

ABOUT THE AUTHORS

Coit D. Blacker is deputy director and senior fellow at Stanford University's Institute for International Studies. During the first Clinton administration, he served as special assistant to the president for National Security Affairs and senior director for Russian, Ukrainian, and Eurasian Affairs at the National Security Council.

John Boli is professor of sociology at Emory University. A native Californian and graduate of Stanford University, he has published extensively on the topics of world culture and global organizations, education, citizenship, and state power and authority in the world polity. His books include *The Globalization Reader, Constructing World Culture: International Nongovernmental Organizations Since 1875*, and *Institutional Structure: Constituting State, Society, and the Individual.* His current projects include a book on the origins, structuration, and consequences of world culture since 1850, and a longitudinal study of the impact of world-cultural trends on transnational corporations.

Thomas C. Heller is the Shelton Professor of International Legal Studies at Stanford University Law School and senior fellow at Stanford University's Institute for International Studies. He currently writes about and teaches international and comparative economic law, legal theory, and law and political economic development. His principal preoccupation for the past seven years has been the evolution of international environmental regimes, both as a lead author for the Intergovernmental Panel on Climate Change and as a lawyer trying to design mechanisms to encourage the building of cleaner energy systems in the restructuring of the energy sectors of China and India.

Stephen D. Krasner is the Graham H. Stuart Professor of International Relations in the Department of Political Science and a senior fellow at the Institute for International Studies at Stanford University. He has written about American foreign policy, international regimes, and relations between industrialized and developing countries. His recent publications include *Sovereignty: Organized Hypocrisy* and *Exploration and Contestation in the Study of World Politics* (co-editor).

Robert A. Madsen is a fellow at Stanford University's Asia/Pacific Research Center. He also works as an analyst and author for the Economist Intelligence Unit and is the Asia Strategist for Soros Real Estate Partners, a private-equity fund that invests in corporate restructuring around the globe. Madsen writes frequently on the politics and economics of China, Taiwan, and Japan.

Michael McFaul is an assistant professor of political science at Stanford University. He is also a senior associate at the Carnegie Endowment for International Peace and the Peter and Helen Bing Research Fellow at the Hoover Institution. He is the author of several monographs on postcommunist politics and economics. His latest book, *Russia's Troubled Transition from Communism to Democracy: Institutional Change during Revolutionary Transformations*, will be published in the summer of 2001.

Michel Oksenberg is a senior fellow at the Asia/Pacific Research Center at Stanford University. He has taught Chinese politics and Chinese foreign policy at Stanford, Columbia University, and the University of Michigan. He served on the National Security Council staff during the Carter administration and as president of the East West Center in Honolulu. His most recent publications include *China Joins the World* with Elizabeth Economy, *China's Uncertain Future* with Michael Swaine, and "China A Tortuous Path onto the World's Stage" in *The Major Powers*, edited by Robert Pastor.

Condoleezza Rice is a Hoover Senior Fellow and professor of Political Science at Stanford University. She completed a six-year tenure as Stanford's Provost in June 1999. Her teaching and research interests include the politics of East-Central Europe and the former Soviet Union, the comparative study of military institutions, and international security policy. Her publications include *Germany Unified and Europe Transformed* (1995) with Philip Zelikow, *The Gorbachev Era* (1986) with Alexander Dallin, and *Uncertain Allegiance: The Soviet Union and the Czechoslovak Army* (1984). She is a fellow of the American Academy of Arts and Sciences.

James McCall Smith is assistant professor of Political Science and International Affairs at George Washington University in Washington, D.C. He received his doctorate from Stanford University and worked as a Luce Scholar in Hong Kong, China, during 1996–97.

Shibley Telhami holds the Anwar Sadat Chair for Peace and Development at the University of Maryland and is a nonresident senior fellow at the Brookings Institution.

Abraham D. Sofaer is the George P. Shultz Senior Fellow at the Hoover Institution, Stanford University, and professor of law (by courtesy) at Stanford University Law School. He was a United States district judge in the Southern District of New York from 1979 to 1985, and the legal adviser at the U.S. Department of State from 1985 to 1990. He has written extensively in the areas of international law and national security.

Susan L. Woodward is senior research fellow at the Centre for Defence Studies, King's College, London. She was previously senior fellow at the Brookings Institution and professor of political science at Yale University, Williams College, and Northwestern University, among others. She is the author of *Socialist Unemployment: The Political Economy of Yugoslavia, 1945–1990* (1995) and *Balkan Tragedy: Chaos and Dissolution after the Cold War* (1995).

Problematic
Sovereignty

1

Problematic Sovereignty

STEPHEN D. KRASNER

This volume addresses the following question: to what extent do existing institutional arrangements, rules, and principles associated with the concept of sovereignty inhibit the solution to some of the most pressing issues in the contemporary international order? Can these rules be bent? Can they be ignored? Do they present an insurmountable or at least significant barrier to stable solutions, or can alternative arrangements be created?

Any answer to these questions involves a set of prior stipulations about exactly what rules are associated with sovereignty. The concept of sovereignty has been used by sociologists, international lawyers, and political scientists, but not always with the same meaning. For sociologists sovereignty offers a script, a shared cognitive map that facilitates but does not determine outcomes. For international lawyers individual states are the basic building blocks of the international system. These states are sovereign in the sense that they are juridically independent and can enter into treaties that will promote their interests as they themselves define them. What is critical for international lawyers is not the substance of these agreements but rather that they not be coerced. For political scientists sovereignty has sometimes been an analytic assumption, as in the case of neorealism and neoliberal institutionalism, where states are assumed to be rational, unitary, independent actors. For other political scientists, such as the English School, sovereignty is a set of normative principles into which statesmen are socialized, the most important of which is nonintervention in the internal affairs of other states.

This project builds on these existing conceptualizations by recognizing that sovereignty is not an organic whole. It has different components, and having one attribute of sovereignty does not necessarily mean having others. In particular four aspects, or different ways of conceptualizing or talking about sovereignty, can be identified: interdependence sovereignty, domestic sovereignty, international legal sovereignty, and Westphalian sovereignty.[1]

Interdependence sovereignty refers to the ability of a government to regulate the movement of goods, capital, people, and ideas across its borders. Domestic sovereignty refers both to the structure of authority within a state and to the state's effectiveness or control. International legal sovereignty refers to whether a state is recognized by other states, the basic rule being that only juridically independent territorial entities are accorded recognition. Westphalian sovereignty, which actually has almost nothing to do with the Peace of Westphalia,[2] refers to the autonomy of domestic authority structures—that is, the absence of authoritative external influences. A political entity can be formally independent but de facto deeply penetrated. A state might claim to be the only legitimate enforcer of rules within its own territory, but the rules it enforces might not be of its own making.

Control over transborder movements, domestic authority and control, international recognition, and the autonomy of domestic structures do not necessarily go together. In fact rulers have often traded one off against the other. Securing recognition has sometimes involved sacrificing Westphalian sovereignty. Membership in international organizations has required relinquishing control over transborder movements. Establishing effective domestic authority structures and control has not guaranteed international recognition, and not having these attributes, even the attribute of territory, has not precluded recognition.

The specific cases presented in this volume have not been randomly selected. Rather, they have been chosen precisely because they are problematic. Other arrangements that have been widely accepted, but are inconsistent with at least some of the principles that have commonly been associated with sovereignty, are not included. The most obvious is the European Union, whose member states have created supranational institutions that are inconsistent with Westphalian sovereignty.

The cases of problematic sovereignty investigated in this volume have involved questions of authority, not just issues of control. In Taiwan, Hong Kong, Tibet, Bosnia, Palestine, and Belarus the rules associated with one or more of the characteristics associated with sovereignty have not been, or could not have been, followed. As Robert Madsen and Michel Oksenberg argue, Taiwan is problematic because of questions associated with domestic structures of authority and international recognition: Is Taiwan a part of China or not? Can Taiwan secure international legal sovereignty given the ambiguous nature of its domestic sovereignty? Hong Kong is problematic because its economy can function most effectively only, as James Smith contends, if China can credibly commit to providing it with quasi-autonomy, including some form of international legal sovereignty involving membership in international organizations, even though it is formally part of China. Tibet is problematic because, as Michel Oksenberg shows, both Chinese and foreign governments accept it as being part of China, but at the same time the Tibetans are unwilling to accept their present status. Palestine is problematic because, as Shibley Telhami argues, Israel will not accept a Palestinian state that has full Westphalian autonomy even if it is given international legal sovereignty. Bosnia is problematic because, as Susan Woodward suggests, of the tortured and unorthodox character of its domestic sovereignty and the extent to which its Westphalian sovereignty has been compromised by the major powers in an effort, ironically, to create a Bosnian state that would more closely conform with conventional practices. The breakup of the Soviet Union was greased, as Michael McFaul shows, by the availability of a script of sovereignty, but at the same time at least some parts of the former Soviet Union are problematic because, while they enjoy international legal sovereignty and juridical domestic sovereignty, their de facto Westphalian sovereignty is questionable. As Coit Blacker and Condoleezza Rice point out, in the case of Belarus, Lukashenka, the country's leader, signed several agreements that hinted at undermining his country's formal juridical autonomy and international legal sovereignty.

In some of these cases the rules associated with sovereignty appear to have powerfully constrained the options that are available to actors. For instance, in the case of Tibet neither its leaders nor the leaders of China appear willing to embrace a status that would be something in between complete independence on one hand and the status quo on the other. Such a status, the tributary state, was readily available, as Michel Oksenberg shows, in the classical Chinese international system. For centuries Tibet was a tributary state that operated with a high, although varying, degree of independence from Beijing. Michael McFaul shows that conventional international legal and domestic sovereignty, if not de facto Westphalian sovereignty, steered the breakup of the Soviet Union. The republics of the former Soviet Union became juridically independent and internationally recognized states, even those republics, such as Belarus, Uzbekistan, and Tajikistan, that have no history of formal independence and only the most limited consciousness of a national identity.

In contrast, in the case of Hong Kong institutional arrangements that are inconsistent with conventional rules of sovereignty have been embraced. Hong Kong does not have domestic sovereignty; it does not have formal juridical independence. Yet it enjoys international legal sovereignty. Hong Kong's, that is to say China's, Westphalian sovereignty, especially its judicial system, has been compromised. Hong Kong uses common law rather than Chinese law, and a foreign judge has the right to sit on the bench of its highest court. For Palestine none of the participants expect that any Palestinian state that does emerge will have full Westphalian sovereignty; at a minimum, Shibley Telhami suggests, the security options of a Palestinian state would be constrained. There are major impediments to creating a Palestinian state, but the fact that any such state would be inconsistent with the conventional rules of sovereignty is not an insurmountable barrier, otherwise the notion of a Palestinian state would never have been explored in the first place. The Westphalian sovereignty of Bosnia has been compromised by coercion from its immediate neighbors, from other European states, and from the United States. Here, again, conventional notions or rules of sovereignty have not precluded innovative arrangements, even though the ultimate objective of the major powers, Susan Woodward argues, has been to create a more conventionally sovereign Bosnian state.

How can these variations in outcome be explained? Why have conventional rules of sovereignty been constraining in some cases, while being defied in others? The answer suggested by the contributors to this volume is that political leaders can rewrite rules if they so choose. Such initiatives can be the result of voluntary actions, either unilateral or through agreements with other states, or of coercion. Absent coercion or voluntary action, the rules of sovereignty are the default. They are well-understood institutional or social facts. They can easily be invoked because they are so widely recognized. New rules can be developed, and actors can regard them as credible, as has been the case for the European Union and may be the case for Hong Kong, but only if there is time to negotiate and if the rules themselves prove durable.

If, however, conventional rules are violated through coercion rather than voluntary agreement, their durability and robustness will be more problematic. Coercion is an instrument of the major powers. Intervention in the internal affairs of other states, for instance, has been pervasive over the last two centuries in the Balkans and Central America among other areas. But sustaining violations of Westphalian sovereignty has proven difficult because over the long run the costs of intervention have outweighed the benefits. The governance costs involved in sustaining institutional arrangements that would fail in the absence of external support can be substantial.[3] Hence, conventional rules of sovereignty are the default when actors are unwilling to use force or cannot make unilateral or multilateral commitments to different institutional arrangements, and these alternatives are more likely to be durable if they are the result of voluntary initiatives rather than coercion.

Conceptualizing Sovereignty

The concept of sovereignty has been used by political scientists, international lawyers, and sociologists, but not in the same way. As Thomas Heller and Abraham Sofaer point out international lawyers have conceived of sovereign states as analogous to the individual in liberal political theory. Sovereign states are autonomous actors. They have the right and the ability to enter into contractual relationships. These contracts, even though they are promises that may limit freedom of action, are an indication of the sovereignty of the state, not a curtailment of it. Agreements can take any form and deal with virtually any issue area provided they are entered into voluntarily. As Heller and Sofaer suggest, "as understood by legal practitioners, the commitments by which states bind themselves in advance to principles or rules, and their delegations to international and nongovernmental entities of the management of important elements of transnational affairs, do not constitute a surrender of sovereign power, but rather its exercise." They go on to conclude that

> the concept of sovereignty is not a set of established rules, to which states must bend their conduct in order to preserve their capacities. It is instead an ever-changing description of the essential authorities of states, intended to serve rather than control them in a world that states dominate. Hence, virtually anything that states choose to do to enhance their capacity to deal with the complicated problems of a changing world is seen by those engaged in the practice of statecraft as perfectly normal—an exercise rather than a diminution of sovereignty. If states lacked the power to commit themselves in advance to specific policies, or to delegate authority to international institutions or private entities to implement such policies, they would be weaker— not stronger—entities than the sovereign states of today's complex world.

John Boli offers a different view of sovereignty. For Boli, a sociologist, sovereignty is a script whose most important line is that a state has the legitimate right to exercise authority. The state can reject claims of authority and control that are made by external actors. Whether it can actually make these rejections stick is a matter of power, not of authority per se. Scripts are often decoupled from actual behavior. The more vigorous the external threat to the state's effective control, the more forcefully it may assert the script of sovereignty. Intervention, Boli argues, is becoming less legitimate, but at the same time, states are agreeing to share authority in order to preserve their control in the face of economic globalization, claims of universal human rights and citizenship, and the growing salience of transnational norms and policy prescriptions that can undermine domestic control.

Sovereignty has also been a salient concept for political scientists, influencing all of the major approaches to the study of international relations. For neorealism and neoliberalism, sovereign states are the basic ontological given: the actors in international politics are unitary, territorial, autonomous entities; they are sovereign states. The English School, whose most well known representative is Hedley Bull, has also taken sovereignty as a central concept, although Bull and his successors have approached sovereignty from a sociological and historical perspective that understands statesmen as being socialized into a set of common norms.[4] Recent constructivist work has been more sensitive to the problematic nature of sovereignty, arguing that structures and agents are constantly reconstituting each other; neither can be taken for granted.[5]

For most observers, then, some constructivists being a notable exception, sovereignty has been conceptualized as a set of attributes more or less immutably bound up with one another.[6] These attributes include a territory, a population, an effective domestic hierarchy of control, de jure constitutional independence, the de facto absence of external authority, international recognition, and the ability to regulate transborder flows.

Some of the confusion that has been associated with the concept of sovereignty can be dispelled if it is recognized that the different rules and characteristics that have been associated with sovereignty do not necessarily go together. They can be unbundled.

The term *sovereignty* has been commonly used in at least four different ways: domestic sovereignty, referring to the organization of public authority within a state and to the level of effective control exercised by those holding authority; interdependence sovereignty, referring to the ability of public authorities to control transborder movements; international legal sovereignty, referring to the mutual recognition of states; and Westphalian sovereignty, referring to the exclusion of external actors from domestic authority config-urations. These four meanings of sovereignty are not logically coupled, nor have they covaried in practice.

Domestic sovereignty involves both authority and control; interdepen-dence sovereignty, only control; and Westphalian and international legal sov-ereignty, only authority. Authority is based on the mutual recognition that an actor has the right to engage in a specific activity, including the right to command others. Authority might, or might not, result in effective control. Control can also be achieved through the use of force. If, over a period of time, the ability of a legitimated entity to control a given domain weakens, then the authority of that entity might eventually dissipate. Conversely, if a particular entity is able to successfully exercise control, or if a purely instru-mental pattern of behavior endures for a long period, then the entity or prac-tice could be endowed with legitimacy.[7] In many social and political situations both control and authority can affect the behavior of actors.[8]

DOMESTIC SOVEREIGNTY

The oldest usages of the term *sovereignty* refer to domestic sovereignty—the organization of authority within a given state and its effectiveness. Bodin and Hobbes wanted to establish the legitimacy of some one single source of au-thority within the polity. Later liberal theorists recognized that there need not be one single fount of legitimacy; indeed, the Founding Fathers in the United States wanted to divide authority among the different branches of the federal government and between the federal government and the states. The orga-nization of domestic authority within the polity is irrelevant for international legal or Westphalian sovereignty.[9]

International legal and Westphalian sovereignty need not be affected by the level of domestic control that the political authorities within a polity can exercise. What are now termed failed states, essentially domestic governments that are incapable of regulating developments within their own borders, retain their international legal sovereignty. Both the state and its government con-tinue to be recognized. They are members of international organizations, vote in the United Nations, and sign contracts with international financial insti-tutions. The Westphalian sovereignty of such states might, or might not, be compromised by external actors. If powerful external entities were indifferent to the fate of a failed state, then there would be no external efforts to alter its domestic authority structures.

INTERDEPENDENCE SOVEREIGNTY

Many observers have claimed that new technological developments have undermined the ability of states to regulate movements across their own borders with regard to goods, capital, ideas, individuals, and disease vectors. Globalization is seen as threatening sovereignty, but sovereignty here is in the first instance entirely a matter of control rather than authority.[10] The fact that a state cannot govern a particular form of activity does not mean that some other authority structure will be developed or even that the authority of the state in that area, its right to regulate, will be challenged.

High levels of global interaction are not a new thing. Net capital flows were higher in the nineteenth century than at the end of the twentieth, although gross flows have dramatically increased. Ratios of trade to gross national product (GNP) increased from the Napoleonic Wars until World War I, declined in the interwar period, and grew again after 1950, and in some, but not all, countries surpassed the levels of the nineteenth century. In the Atlantic area migration was higher in the nineteenth century than has been the case more recently. Some areas have become more deeply enmeshed in the international environment, especially East Asia; others, notably most of Africa, remain much more isolated. What has changed is not so much the level of international interaction but the scope of government activities, the demands that have been placed on the state, and the range of constituencies to which governments in advanced industrialized countries must respond. In the nineteenth century countries could adhere to the gold standard, which facilitated international flows, because domestic economic performance could be sacrificed to international balance. In the late twentieth century, with the dramatic increase in the franchise, no regime could ignore questions related to domestic growth and employment.[11]

Regardless of whether interdependence sovereignty is more at risk today than in the past, the ability of states to regulate their transborder flows has no logical relationship to their status as independently recognized states, their international legal sovereignty, or their ability to exclude external authority structures (their Westphalian sovereignty). In practice, however, a loss of interdependence sovereignty might lead rulers to compromise their Westphalian sovereignty by entering into contractual arrangements to establish supranational authority structures better able to regulate activities beyond the control of any single state. Such treaties could be concluded only by international legal sovereigns, by political entities that mutually recognized each other's ability to freely enter into such contracts.[12] Heller and Sofaer, and Boli, emphasize this point in their essays in this volume.

INTERNATIONAL LEGAL SOVEREIGNTY

International legal sovereignty involves the status of a political entity in the international system. Recognition of such sovereignty implies that a state has juridical equality, that its diplomats are entitled to immunity, and that its embassies and consulates have extraterritorial status. An international legal sovereign can enter into agreements with other entities.

The basic rule for international legal sovereignty is that recognition is extended to states with territory and formal juridical autonomy. The recognition of a specific government, such as the Communist government of China, has sometimes been separated from the recognition of the state itself. Historically, rulers have also invoked other conditions for recognition, such as the ability to defend territory and maintain order.[13] Recognition has been used as a political instrument; it has been withheld from some governments that met widely recognized criteria and extended to those with only tenuous or even no control over the territory they claimed to govern.

Even entities, as opposed to specific governments, that do not conform to the basic norm of appropriateness associated with international legal sovereignty, because they lack either formal juridical autonomy or territory, have been recognized. India was a member of the League of Nations and a signatory of the Versailles settlements even though it was a colony of Britain. The British Dominions were signatories at Versailles and members of the League even though their juridical independence from Britain was unclear. The Palestine Liberation Organization (PLO) was given observer status in the United Nations in 1974, and this status was changed to that of a permanent mission in 1988 coincident with the declaration of Palestinian independence, even though the PLO did not have any juridically accepted independent control over territory, although as Shibley Telhami points out, the organization did have de facto domestic sovereignty in Lebanon in the late 1970s. Beyelo-Russia and the Ukraine were members of the United Nations even though they were part of the Soviet Union.[14]

Almost all rulers have sought international legal sovereignty because it provides them with both material and normative resources. Recognition facilitates contracting. Alliances can enhance security; membership in the

World Trade Organization can increase access to markets; membership in the World Bank can provide financial resources.

Recognition may also enhance a ruler's domestic support. Recognition as a sovereign state is a widely, almost universally, understood construct in the contemporary world. A ruler attempting to enhance his own position by creating or reinforcing a particular national identity is more likely to be successful if his state or his government enjoys international recognition. In a situation in which domestic sovereignty is problematic, international recognition can enhance the position of rulers by signaling to constituents that a ruler may have access to international resources such as alliances and sovereign lending.

The absence of recognition, however, does not preclude activities that are facilitated by recognition. Lack of recognition has not prevented states from engaging in negotiating and contracting. American officials met their Chinese counterparts before they recognized the People's Republic of China (PRC) as the government of China. When Taiwan was de-recognized, as Robert Madsen elaborates in this volume, the United States took steps to provide Taiwan with something very much like the status that it had enjoyed before 1979. The Taiwan Relations Act stipulated that the legal standing of the Republic of China (ROC) in American courts would not be affected, that Taiwan would continue to control property that had been bought since 1949, and that the American Institute in Taiwan, a nongovernmental agency, would be created to, in effect, conduct the functions of an embassy.[15]

Recognition has not meant in practice that a state will respect the Westphalian sovereignty of its counterparts. The Soviet Union, for instance, not only established the communist regimes of the satellite states of Eastern Europe during the Cold War but intervened on an ongoing basis in their domestic political structures, organizing, for instance, their internal security services and their militaries. Recognition does not guarantee that domestic authorities will be able to monitor and regulate developments within the territory of their state or flows across their borders; that is, it does not guarantee either domestic sovereignty or interdependence sovereignty. Obviously, recognition does not guarantee that a state will not be invaded or even that its existence will not be extinguished. Conquest and absorption is not a challenge to rules of sovereignty but merely a redrawing of boundaries.

WESTPHALIAN SOVEREIGNTY

The basic rule of Westphalian sovereignty is that external authority structures should be excluded from the territory of a state. Sovereign states are not only de jure independent; they are also de facto autonomous. Rulers are always to some extent constrained by the external environment. Other states, markets, transnational corporations, or international financiers may limit the options available to a particular government, but that government is still able to freely choose within a constrained set. Moreover, the government of a Westphalian sovereign can determine the character of its own domestic sovereignty, its own authoritative institutions. Rulers might choose to establish an independent central bank because they believe that this would increase the country's attractiveness for international investors, a choice that would be completely consistent with Westphalian sovereignty. If, in contrast, another state or an international financial institution conditions a loan on the creation of an independent central bank, Westphalian sovereignty would be at risk. If the external actor is able to influence domestic decision-making processes through the appointment of officials or by altering the views of actors within the polity, Westphalian sovereignty would be even more challenged. And if the external actor could dictate the creation of an independent central bank, the Westphalian sovereignty of the state would be nullified, at least with regard to this particular issue area.

Domestic authority structures can be compromised both as a result of the coercive action of other states or through voluntary decisions. Poland would not have had a communist government in 1950 without the presence and threat of Soviet military forces. In contrast, the member states of the European Union have voluntarily created supranational institutions, such as the European Court of Justice, and pooled sovereignty through qualified majority voting, which compromises their domestic political autonomy. While coercion, or intervention, is inconsistent with international legal as well as Westphalian sovereignty, voluntary actions by rulers, or invitations, do not violate international legal sovereignty but can violate Westphalian sovereignty.

While autonomy can be compromised as a result of both intervention and voluntary choice, the former has gotten much more attention. Some observers have regarded nonintervention as the *grundnorm* of the sovereign state system.[16] Weaker states have always been the strongest supporters of nonintervention, which was first explicitly articulated by Wolff and Vattel during the latter part of the eighteenth century. During the nineteenth century Latin American leaders, who governed the weakest states in the system, vigorously defended the notion that coercion was unacceptable. The United States did not formally accept the principle of nonintervention until the seventh International Conference of American States held in 1933. After the Second World War nonintervention was routinely endorsed in major treaties, such as the Charter of the United Nations, although ethnic conflicts in the 1990s prompted Kofi Annan, the secretary-general of the United Nations, to argue at the fall 1999 General Assembly that sovereignty might have to be conditioned on respect for human rights.

Voluntary arrangements that compromise the domestic authority of a state have usually not been regarded as problematic. In part this is because such arrangements are consistent with international legal sovereignty, which requires only that agreements be entered into voluntarily, even if they violate Westphalian sovereignty. Rulers may choose to legitimate external authority structures for a variety of reasons including tying the hands of their successors, securing financial resources, and strengthening domestic support for values that they, themselves, embrace.

In sum, analysts and practitioners have used the term *sovereignty* in four different and distinct ways. The absence or loss of one kind of sovereignty does not logically imply an erosion of others, even though they may be empirically associated with each other. A state can be recognized, that is, have international legal sovereignty, but not have Westphalian sovereignty because its authority structures are subject to external authority or control; it can lose control of transborder movements but still be autonomous; it can have domestic sovereignty, a well-established and effective set of authoritative decision-making institutions, and not be recognized.

Variable Constraints

This volume's contributors come to different conclusions about the extent to which the rules of sovereignty, as they are commonly understood, constrained behavior in the cases they present. Michel Oksenberg addresses this question most directly. He writes: "These concepts, of which 'sovereignty' is central, permit a wide range of choice. They are not very constraining. But adherence to them creates certain tendencies, propensities, or predispositions to accept some solutions more readily than others. These concepts render solutions of the past less viable today and enable solutions of the present that were inconceivable in the past. These concepts weight choice in certain directions, still permitting choice in many different directions but making some choices more difficult than others." In his analysis of the way in which China has dealt with three problematic issues—Taiwan, Hong Kong, and Tibet—he concludes that "the importation of 'sovereignty' in its full meanings—especially the Westphalian notions of territoriality and autonomy and the notion of international recognition as a defining characteristic of nationhood—has had a profound impact on the aspirations of all the actors involved. Because the concept of sovereignty and its associated notions now structure the East Asian regional system, solutions available in the early 1800s are no longer available, while other solutions, inconceivable in the 1800s, are now possible."

The concept of a tributary state consisting of peripheral areas more or less loosely associated with the imperial center was standard practice in the Sinocentric world before the arrival en masse, and with military power, of the West. But the Western powers introduced a new set of institutional rules. The European powers trampled on China's Westphalian sovereignty, fighting the Opium Wars to secure access to China's domestic market and establishing extensive extraterritorial control by the end of the nineteenth century. Nevertheless, before the arrival of the West, the ready availability of China's tributary state system made it easier for Beijing and Lhasa to maintain a loose relationship that served the interests of rulers in both China and Tibet. The disappearance of tributary states as a widely recognized social fact in the contemporary sovereign state system makes it more difficult for the leaders in both entities to accept something other than juridical independence or hierarchical subservience.

In his discussion of the breakup of the Soviet Union Michael McFaul takes a similar position, arguing that the script of sovereignty provided Yeltsin with a salient set of options that allowed him to most effectively pursue his political objectives. Yeltsin could have chosen from a number of strategies. He could have portrayed himself as an anticommunist leader of a new Soviet Union, but this was problematic because of his own past. He could have endorsed capitalism, but capitalism was still a suspect concept in Russia. Yeltsin and other Russian leaders did attempt to create some kind of confederal system, but, McFaul argues, the Commonwealth of Independent States failed at least in part because the "rules of the game regarding sovereignty in today's international system, however, constrained and eventually helped to suppress these alternative models." Declaring Russia to be a sovereign state, and thereby precipitating the breakup of the Soviet Union, was a widely recognized script that offered the best chance for Yeltsin to emerge as the leader of a new regime. McFaul concludes that "the very existence of this concept as a norm or idea of the contemporary international system (sovereignty) changed fundamentally the way in which the revolutionary struggle unfolded in the Soviet Union in the late 1980s."

Susan Woodward also points to the salience of sovereignty in her discussion of the disintegration of Yugoslavia. The country initially broke up along the lines of existing republican units—Serbia, Croatia, Slovenia. There were other options, including the continuation of a federal system, but these failed in part because the script of sovereignty provided the would-be rulers of Croatia and Slovenia with a ready-made appeal to major powers, especially Germany and France, the leading members of the European Community, whose support was critical for their success. In the case of Palestine sovereignty likewise has provided a focal point for aspirations of actors. Shibley Telhami argues that the last half of the twentieth century is "a world made of state actors, and Palestinian interests had no chance of being met without a state of their own."

Both McFaul and Woodward point out that framing the breakup of the Soviet Union and Yugoslavia along the lines of preexisting federal units did not mean that the successor states would have all the attributes that have been associated with sovereignty. McFaul notes that Russia's Westphalian sovereignty, the de facto autonomy of its domestic institutions with regard to external actors, was compromised by international financial institutions. Russia's fragile economic situation, as well as the new government's need to secure support from the major Western powers, initially gave the International Monetary Fund (IMF) considerable leverage. To secure external financing, Russia's new leaders had to accept the IMF's recommendations regarding such basic questions as government expenditures and tax policies. Regardless of the merits of these policies, the collapse of the Soviet economy in 1998 suggests that Yeltsin might, in retrospect, have pursued other options.

The tension between formal juridical independence and international recognition on the one hand and de facto autonomy, or Westphalian sovereignty, on the other is even more apparent in the case of Bosnia. The constitutional structure for the new state of Bosnia was created by outsiders. Woodward notes that the Dayton accord was essentially written by Americans. The participation of representatives from Bosnia itself was limited. European judges have a numerical majority on the Human Rights Commission. Under annex 10 of the Dayton accord, the High Representative who initially has been a European can override local politicians if they undermine the agreement.

At the same time, Woodward argues that the "international community in this case is defying the autonomy principle of sovereignty in order to create an autonomous state. And the level of violation is *increasing* over time. The more the international community has difficulty with the implementation of the Dayton accord, the more it seeks leverage over the parties to gain their compliance." What the major powers want is a Bosnian state that is autonomous and, perhaps more important, stable—an outcome that would allow them to extricate themselves from Bosnia. By according Bosnia international legal sovereignty, they have already accepted the country's formal juridical independence. But in an effort to establish domestic stability they have compromised Bosnia's Westphalian autonomy by themselves creating a constitutional order that has limited domestic support.

The situation in Palestine, like that in Bosnia, also presents a trade-off among the different elements of sovereignty. As Shibley Telhami points out, the Palestinian leadership wants both to establish effective domestic sovereignty, in the sense of both authority structures and control, and to secure international legal sovereignty. The Palestine Liberation Organization has already achieved some measure of international personality. In 1974 the Arab League recognized the PLO as the sole representative of the Palestinian people, and the organization was admitted to the United Nations as a permanent observer. Previously, permanent observer status had been granted only to states that were not members of the UN and to regional organizations. A number of states recognized the PLO and gave diplomatic status to its local office. When Palestine's independence was declared in 1988 the UN changed the designation to the Palestine Observer Mission.[17]

To secure full international legal sovereignty, including the acceptance of a juridically independent Palestinian state by the major Western powers and by Israel, Palestinian leaders will almost certainly have to compromise their Westphalian sovereignty. At a minimum, the Israelis will insist upon limitations on the military and alliance policies that any Palestinian state might follow. There might be other constraints in security-related areas as well. Such constraints could be achieved through treaties and thereby be consistent with international legal sovereignty.

Hence in the breakup of the Soviet Union and Yugoslavia, the script of sovereignty, especially international legal sovereignty, and the concept of juridically independent and internationally recognized territorial entities made it easier to achieve some outcomes than others. The script of sovereignty was available to both individuals and groups within these countries and to decision makers in other states. In China, the cognitive and temporal remoteness of scripts associated with the traditional Chinese international system has made some solutions more difficult. It is easier for Tibet to be either independent or a part of China than for it to be something else, like a tributary state. For at least some issues associated with the former Soviet Union, Yugoslavia, and China, sovereignty is a cognitive construct that facilitates some outcomes and impedes others.

At the same time, however, different elements of sovereignty have been in tension with each other. International recognition and juridical autonomy have not necessarily been accompanied by de facto autonomy or Westphalian sovereignty. International financial institutions have intruded into Russian domestic affairs. Bosnia's Westphalian sovereignty has been violated in an effort to create a state that may eventually have de facto as well as juridical autonomy. Formal Palestinian independence—that is, international recognition—is contingent on its accepting constraints on security policies.

The cases of Belarus, Taiwan, and more clearly, Hong Kong suggest, in contrast, that the script of sovereignty might not be quite so constraining. Belarus hardly seems to have made a serious effort to establish its domestic and Westphalian sovereignty, and its leader has toyed with the idea of relinquishing his state's international legal sovereignty as well. Coit Blacker and Condoleezza Rice write, "Belarusian schools still rely on history and social science texts published in Moscow in the 1970s and 1980s. The country's president, Alyaksandr Lukashenka, speaks in Russian when he addresses the nation, notwithstanding the fact that the national language is Belarusian. Most notably, since 1994 the Belarusian leadership has pressed the Russian government to conclude one agreement after another to accelerate the integration, or reintegration, of the two countries' economies and to forge the closest possible political ties." The two countries signed a Union Treaty, although its exact meaning and consequence is not clear. Lukashenka has been much more enthusiastic about these initiatives than decision makers in Russia, who have not been anxious to assume any responsibility for the moribund Belarusian economy.

Blacker and Rice argue that the most persuasive explanation for Lukashenka's behavior is his own personal ambition: "Those in Russia and in the West who have dealt with the Belarusian leader at close range comment— virtually without exception—on the breadth and intensity of his political ambition. The particular office to which Lukashenka aspires, it seems, is president of a Russian/Belarusian union or commonwealth." Whatever has guided Lukashenka, it is not the conventional script of sovereignty, which he seems intent on ignoring, even to the extent of violating some of the basic rules of international legal sovereignty by displacing foreign ambassadors from their residences.

The situation of Taiwan also confounds conventional notions of sovereignty. Taiwan has prospered in a kind of never-never land where it has many of the attributes of fully sovereign states—territory, population, and domestic and Westphalian sovereignty—but only very limited international legal sovereignty. Moreover, the government on Taiwan has not formally made any claim to juridical autonomy. As Robert Madsen points out, the Taiwanese government has been nervous about the loss of its international legal sovereignty, which has led to some economic costs, such as a decline in investment flows during the 1970s. Taiwan has cultivated a number of smaller countries, providing them with financial resources, in exchange for recognition.

Yet Taiwan has prospered. Its economic growth has been robust, and it weathered the Asian crisis of the late 1990s better than most other Asian countries in part because of its large financial reserves. Moreover, functional alternatives to international legal sovereignty, such as the Taiwan Relations Act of the United States, have worked well. Taiwan has been able to conduct foreign relations, albeit in a somewhat roundabout way.

The possibilities for anomalous institutional arrangements is most evident in the case of Hong Kong, where new structures have been established with the support not only of the Chinese government but of other states and international organizations as well. These arrangements are inconsistent with both international legal and Westphalian sovereignty. As James Smith argues, "The crux of China's dilemma was how to reconcile its long-standing assertion of the right to exercise sovereign control over Hong Kong with its desire to maintain the confidence of local Chinese and foreign residents, thereby ensuring the territory's continued stability and prosperity." But that goal could not be achieved using a conventional script of sovereignty. If China had de jure control of Hong Kong, implying that Hong Kong would not be an internationally recognized sovereign entity, and if China's Westphalian sovereignty were intact, including the exclusion of external authority structures from Hong Kong, then it would be more difficult to maintain the confidence of the international business community. The rule of law is not well established in China itself. The power of the Communist Party is substantial. There have been abrupt shifts of policy. A Hong Kong fully integrated into China with no international personality would be a less attractive place to do business.

The institutional structure that was developed for Hong Kong challenges notions associated with the script of sovereignty. The Chinese were insistent that Hong Kong should be a part of China, that Beijing had ultimate authority over the territory. Chinese leaders never compromised that principle. But in negotiations with the British government that resulted in the 1984 Sino-British Joint Declaration and subsequent arrangements, the Chinese government made a number of commitments with regard to Hong Kong. Smith points out that although "China retains control over foreign and defense affairs, the Joint Declaration and Basic Law provide Hong Kong the specific authority to forge international agreements; participate independently in international organizations and conferences under the name 'Hong Kong, China'; maintain its own currency; set and enforce its own customs regulations as a free port; establish trade or economic missions abroad; and issue its own passports." Moreover, Hong Kong's Court of Final Appeal may invite foreign judges from common law countries to sit on its panels and may invoke precedents from common law countries in reaching its judgments.

The institutional arrangements associated with Hong Kong were the result of decisions taken by the Beijing government. They were not a product of external coercion. China did not, however, embrace conventional notions. If Beijing had followed the sovereignty script, it would simply have taken over Hong Kong in 1997. Britain could not have resisted such an initiative. China would then have declared that there would be a one-country, two-systems policy. Common law, for instance, would operate in Hong Kong but not in the rest of China, just as the legal system of Louisiana is based on continental rather than common law in the United States. Hong Kong would have a separate currency. These would have been decisions entirely consistent with conventional notions of sovereignty, which do not impose any particular stipulations on how the domestic authority structure of a sovereign should be organized. There would have been no international personality for Hong Kong. There would have been no foreign judges on the Court of Final Appeal. There would have been no joint declarations with the British government.

This would not have been an optimal strategy for the Chinese government. As Smith argues, it was essential for Beijing to make its commitments credible. Simple unilateral pledges would not have been the best way to accomplish that. The institutional arrangements for Hong Kong violated conventional notions of both international legal and Westphalian sovereignty. Despite the fact that it lacked formal juridical autonomy, Hong Kong was allowed to be a full or associate member of fourteen international organizations, including the World Trade Organization, in which China itself had been denied membership. Hong Kong could issue passports, conclude visa abolition agreements with other countries, and send trade and commercial missions. All of these activities required the acquiescence of other states. They could not simply be unilaterally enacted by China itself. A passport that no other state accepts has little value. Hong Kong's, which is to say China's, Westphalian sovereignty was compromised by the stipulation that foreign judges could sit on the Court of Final Appeal.

As Smith points out, the position of Hong Kong can hardly be regarded as absolutely secure. China could unilaterally revoke existing arrangements. It could compromise the ability of representatives from Hong Kong to take independent positions in international organizations. It could override the decisions of the Court of Final Appeal by narrowing the court's jurisdiction. The right to interpret Hong Kong's basic law is reserved to the Standing Committee of the National People's Congress in Beijing, not to any entity in Hong Kong itself. Nevertheless the credibility of Beijing's commitments to provide Hong Kong with significant autonomy was enhanced by the creation of new institutional arrangements that were inconsistent with both international legal and Westphalian sovereignty.

Hence, in some of the cases discussed in this book—the breakups of the Soviet Union and Yugoslavia, for example—the script of sovereignty appears to have provided a greased track that facilitated even if it did not determine the final outcome. For Tibet the salience of sovereignty has made quasi-autonomy a less likely outcome. In other cases—for example, constitutional and personnel arrangements for Bosnia and the involvement of international financial institutions in Russia—international legal sovereignty has been embraced but Westphalian sovereignty has been violated. In contrast Taiwan has had Westphalian, domestic, and interdependence sovereignty, but not international legal sovereignty. In Belarus national leaders have even been skeptical about retaining the state's international legal personality. In Hong Kong new institutional arrangements, inconsistent with both international legal and Westphalian sovereignty, were devised to enhance the credibility of China's commitment to maintain a climate that would sustain Hong Kong's attraction for international business.

Sovereignty has been a central concept for all of the major ways of understanding international relations. Sovereignty, however, has never been taken for granted. Entities inconsistent with one or the other of the central attributes associated with sovereignty have always existed. Rulers have been able to imagine alternative institutional forms. In violation of Westphalian sovereignty, the foreign policies of major powers, and sometimes lesser ones as well, have sometimes been designed to change the domestic political structures of other states. It was the fate of minorities, associated with regional stability, that engaged the major powers of Europe in the Balkans from the 1830s through the 1930s and again in the 1990s. Anxious about its own security the Soviet Union imposed communist regimes on its Eastern European satellites after the Second World War. The member states of the European Union, Germany above all, have wanted to constrain their own domestic autonomy, including their basic constitutional independence, by enmeshing themselves in a new kind of transnational authority structure. Decision makers have frequently been concerned not with balancing against rivals, and not with reaching cooperative agreements to overcome market failure, but rather with the nature of the domestic political structures of their own and other polities. For rulers, intervening in the internal affairs of other states, or compromising the domestic autonomy of their own, has often been an attractive, or at least the best available, option.

By so readily accepting the bundled nature of sovereignty, students of international politics have constrained the range of issues they have addressed. Altering the domestic political structures of other states, violating their Westphalian sovereignty, has always been an option for rulers just as invasion has been an option, but much more has been written about war. And even less is understood about the conditions under which alternatives to conventional notions of sovereignty are viable. The cases described in this volume involve situations in which sovereignty in its fully bundled form does not provide an optimal outcome. In some instances, including Hong Kong and Taiwan, decision makers have found a plausible alternative. In others, such as Tibet, they have not.

The concluding essay in this volume discusses the conditions under which departures from conventional sovereignty have taken place. If decision makers are unable to voluntarily construct new rules either unilaterally or multilaterally, or to use coercion to establish such rules, then sovereignty is the default. In the Soviet Union and Yugoslavia the major players could not reach an agreement, and both these countries broke up in ways defined by the rules of international legal sovereignty, although the Westphalian sovereignty of some of the new entities was problematic. The use of coercion is most apparent in Bosnia, where external actors used force to establish arrangements that compromise the autonomy of the new state. In the case of Kosovo, occupying forces have established de facto autonomy for a geographic area that is still formally recognized as part of Yugoslavia. Finally, new institutional arrangements can also be inaugurated through voluntary actions, either unilaterally or through agreements with other states. The establishment of arrangements that provide Taiwan with something very close to international legal sovereignty offers one example. China's acceptance of a different juridical system in Hong Kong, as well as allowing Hong Kong to exercise the rights of an international legal sovereign, such as membership in international organizations and issuing passports, offers another.

In sum, absent voluntary initiatives or coercion, the conventional bundle of sovereignty rules is the default. These rules constrain options in situations in which neither coercion nor cooperation is viable. But rulers can devise innovative solutions, and these solutions can work, especially if they are the result of voluntary agreements that establish equilibrium outcomes.

Notes

1. These distinctions are developed more fully in Krasner 1999, ch. 1.
2. The specific terms of the Peace of Westphalia, most of which have nothing to do with the modern state system and many of which, especially those related to religious toleration in Germany, actually violated Westphalian sovereignty, are discussed at greater length in Krasner 1993.
3. For a discussion of governance costs see Lake 1999.
4. Bull 1977.
5. See, for example, the contributions in Biersteker and Weber 1996.
6. An important exception is Fowler and Bunck 1995.
7. In his discussion of evolutionary game theory Sugden (1989) suggests that a rule that is initially accepted for purely consequential reasons can over time come to be normatively binding and authoritative because it works and is generally accepted.
8. For further discussions of the distinction between authority and control with reference to sovereignty, see Wendt and Friedheim 1996: 246, 251; Onuf 1991: 430; Wendt 1992: 412–13; Shue 1997: 348.
9. An exception is a confederal structure in which the component entities in the federation, as well as its central government, have the legitimate right to engage in contracts with other states. Switzerland is one example. See Oppenheim 1992: 249–53.
10. Thomson 1995: 216.
11. O'Rourke and Williamson 1999; Obstfeld and Taylor 1997; Thomson and Krasner 1989; Eichengreen 1998.
12. Keohane 1984, 1995.

13. Fowler and Bunck 1995, ch. 2; Thomson 1995: 228; Oppenheim 1992: 186–90; Crawford 1996: 500.

14. Oppenheim 1992: 145–46.

15. Oppenheim 1992: 158–73; Peterson 1997: 107–8, 140, 148–52, 197; *Taiwan Relations Act*.

16. Jackson 1990: 6.

17. Oppenheim 1992: 163–64 n. 10.

References

Biersteker, Thomas J. and Cynthia Weber, eds. 1996. *State Sovereignty as a Social Construct*. Cambridge: Cambridge University Press.

Bull, Hedley. 1977. *The Anarchical Society*. New York: Columbia University Press.

Crawford, Beverly. 1996. "Explaining Defection from International Cooperation: Germany's Unilateral Recognition of Croatia." *World Politics* 48, no. 4: 482–521.

Eichengreen, Barry. 1998. *Globalizing Capital: A History of the International Monetary System*. Princeton: Princeton University Press.

Fowler, Michael Ross and Julie Marie Bunck. 1995. *Law, Power, and the Sovereign State: The Evolution and Application of the Concept of Sovereignty*. University Park: Pennsylvania State University Press.

Jackson, Robert H. 1990. *Quasi-States: Sovereignty, International Relations, and the Third World*. Cambridge: Cambridge University Press.

Keohane, Robert O. 1984. *After Hegemony: Cooperation and Discord in the World Political Economy*. Princeton: Princeton University Press.

———. 1995. "Hobbes's Dilemma and Institutional Change in World Politics: Sovereignty in International Society." In Hans-Henrik Holm and Georg Sorensen, eds., *Whose World Order? Uneven Globalization and the End of the Cold War*. Boulder, Colo.: Westview Press.

Krasner, Stephen D. 1993. "Westphalia and All That." In Judith Goldstein and Robert O. Keohane, eds., *Ideas and Foreign Policy*. Ithaca: Cornell University Press.

———. 1999. *Sovereignty: Organized Hypocrisy*. Princeton: Princeton University Press.

Lake, David A. 1999. *Entangling Relations: American Foreign Policy in Its Century*. Princeton: Princeton University Press.

Obstfeld, Maurice and Alan M. Taylor. 1997. *The Great Depression as a Watershed: International Capital Mobility Over the Long Run*. Working paper 5960, National Bureau of Economic Research, Cambridge, Mass.

Onuf, Nicholas Greenwood. 1991. "Sovereignty: Outline of a Conceptual History." *Alternatives* 16:425–46.

Oppenheim, L. 1992. *Oppenheim's International Law*, 9th ed. Edited by Sir Robert Jennings and Sir Arthur Watts. Harlow, Essex, U.K.: Longman.

O'Rourke, Kevin H. and Jeffrey G. Williamson. 1999. *Globalization and History: The Evolution of a Nineteenth-Century Atlantic Economy.* Cambridge: MIT Press.

Peterson, M. J. 1997. *Recognition of Governments: Legal Doctrine and State Practice.* New York: St. Martin's Press.

Shue, Henry. 1997. "Eroding Sovereignty: The Advance of Principle." In Robert McKim and Jeff McMahan, eds., *The Morality of Nationalism.* New York: Oxford University Press.

Sugden, Robert. 1989. "Spontaneous Order." *Journal of Economic Perspectives* 3:85–97.

Taiwan Relations Act. 1979. *U.S. Code.* Title 22, ch. 48, secs. 3301–16.

Thomson, Janice E. 1995. "State Sovereignty in International Relations: Bridging the Gap Between Theory and Empirical Research." *International Studies Quarterly* 39, no. 2: 213–33.

Thomson, Janice E. and Stephen D. Krasner. 1989. "Global Transactions and the Consolidation of Sovereignty." In Ernst-Otto Czempiel and James N. Rosenau, eds., *Global Changes and Theoretical Challenges: Approaches to World Politics for the 1990s.* Lexington, Mass.: D. C. Heath.

Vattel, Emer de. 1758 (1852). The Law of Nations; or, Principles of the Law of Nature, applied to the Conduct and Affairs of Nations and Sovereigns. From the New Edition (translated by) Joseph Chitty. (Philadelphia: T. & J. W. Johnson, Law Booksellers, 1852).

Wendt, Alexander. 1992. "Anarchy Is What States Make of It: The Social Construction of State Politics." *International Organization* 46:391–425.

Wendt, Alexander and Daniel Friedheim. 1996. "Hierarchy Under Anarchy: Informal Empire and the East German State." In Thomas J. Biersteker and Cynthia Weber, eds., *State Sovereignty as a Social Construct,* 240–72. Cambridge: Cambridge University Press.

Wolff, Christian, Freiherr von. 1764 (1964). Jus gentium methodo scientifica pertractatum. New York: Oceana.

2

Sovereignty

The Practitioners' Perspective

THOMAS C. HELLER AND ABRAHAM D. SOFAER

Sovereignty is a powerful and complex idea, serving many useful purposes in international law and diplomacy. It is used to support a variety of positions on international issues and has come to be associated with myopic nationalism and irrational resistance to transnational regulation. It is sometimes described in absolute terms, as reflecting a particular status secured at the Peace of Westphalia in 1648. In reality, it is a vague formula, with shifting components and uses, arrived at over centuries of experience, and reflecting the complex situation in which nations currently function in the world order.[1] Its varied use and abuse has led Stephen Krasner, among others, to conclude that the concept of sovereignty is "mired in hopeless confusion."[2]

Why, despite the confusion, controversy, adulation, and scorn that surrounds it, is the concept of sovereignty used so extensively and casually in international diplomacy and legal practice? For essentially three reasons, in our view.

First, sovereignty signals a status that has many specific, functional purposes in international diplomatic and legal practice, and to that extent it has concrete and useful meaning. The concept is often used improperly or inaccurately, and such notions as sovereign equality, territorial integrity, and political autonomy are far from absolute. But sovereignty remains useful in practice because it functions as a performative that denotes a core of widespread agreement about powers and obligations that attend the status of statehood. The inconsistencies in applying the rules under which sovereignty is accorded and the exaggerated and ambiguous claims that are made as to its meaning interfere with neither its legal value nor its utility.

Second, sovereignty is more than a useful phrase for characterizing diplomatic and legal issues or outcomes. States dominate the transnational arena, although the constitution of this arena is changing. States are increasingly surrendering some of their policy options through international agreements and sharing their authority and functions with international institutions and nongovernmental forces. The potential consequence of this trend is captured in the notion of interdependent sovereignty discussed elsewhere in this volume and widely cited in international relations analysis as evidence of sovereignty's decline.[3] As understood by practitioners, however, the commitments by which states bind themselves in advance to principles or rules, and their delegations to international and nongovernmental entities of the management even of important elements of transnational affairs, do not legally constitute a surrender of sovereign power, but rather its exercise.

The commitments and delegations nations have made over the last fifty years do, however, represent a process that has changed the roles of states. It may eventually alter their powers. States have delegated to international organizations and private entities the power to administer programs, to adjudicate controversies (especially over trade issues), and to propose policies. Sometimes, these delegations are under standards so vague as to confer significant discretion. Such delegations may be so broad that they conflict with national laws or could become so extensive that sovereignty would be surrendered. In general, though, states have retained control over the prescription, application, and enforcement of the law governing transnational issues. Customary law has in certain areas been used in efforts to impose duties on states without their consent; but these efforts rarely succeed, and when they do it is because states acquiesce and passively accept developments that they have the power to reject. States that are members of the European Union (EU) have materially limited aspects of their powers to prescribe and apply rules, particularly in commercial and human rights matters but increasingly in matters of national finance and foreign affairs. Even assuming these developments in Europe represent a course of conduct that will continue—which is by no means clear—the result would nonetheless not alter the fact that, absent more radical change, the EU states have not yet surrendered, nor can they be regarded as irreversibly in the process of surrendering, the powers that qualify them for statehood, or any combined amount of authority that would deprive them of ultimate control over their domestic and transnational affairs. In the final analysis, the EU states may choose to merge their sovereignty into a regional entity, as the states of the Confederation chose to do in 1789. That would reduce the number of states in the world but would not alter the fact that sovereign states control the transnational arena.

Third, the notion of sovereignty has indeed been used for "bad" purposes, as critics contend, and it is subject to result-oriented manipulation. It has been attacked as the rationale for xenophobic nationalism and as an obstacle to universal moral standards in various fields. The concept of sovereignty cannot reasonably be blamed, however, for the world's horrors and imperfections. In fact, the exercise by states of their sovereign powers continues to represent the most important vehicle available to state and nonstate actors for collective action while maintaining the diversity of values and individuality that a sovereign-state system implies. The notion of sovereignty has facilitated, rather than prevented, numerous, significant changes in transnational affairs brought about by the commitments and delegations to which states have consented through explicit agreement, as well as by the gradual development of what can legitimately be regarded as customary law. From the practitioners' perspective, therefore, proposals to "deconstruct" or abandon sovereignty are misdirected and impractical, since constructive change will far more likely be facilitated through the continued transformation of sovereignty than through its abandonment.

The Utility of Sovereignty in Transnational Affairs

The concept of sovereignty serves many useful and some indispensable functions in transnational affairs, on which practicing lawyers and diplomats heavily rely. It reflects an understanding within the international community to establish a system through which particular groupings of peoples are recognized and function as states, with important consequences.

To qualify as a state (possessing sovereignty), an entity must have a defined territory and population under the control of its own government, which has the capacity to engage in relations with other states.[4] If an entity qualifies as a state, it is eligible for acceptance as a state, and with acceptance comes certain rights, capacities, and obligations, including the following:

- The right to its territorial integrity
- The right to use necessary and proportionate force in individual or collective self-defense

- The right to govern its population by prescribing, applying, and enforcing law within its jurisdictional competence
- Eligibility to become a member and fully participate in the United Nations and other international bodies, to seek loans and other financial assistance from international institutions, such as the International Monetary Fund and World Bank, and to join in litigation in the International Court of Justice (ICJ) as a party
- The capacities of a legal person, such as to own, purchase, or transfer property, to enter into contracts, and to seek and be subject to legal remedies
- Immunities from the application of national law for its noncommercial activities, its diplomats and diplomatic property, and its head of state
- The capacity to join with other states in making international and transnational law through international treaties, agreements, and conduct
- The duty to respect the territorial integrity, political independence, and rights of other sovereign nations
- The duty to abide by international norms of conduct agreed to by treaty or considered universal and part of customary law

Some of these rights, capacities, and obligations are possessed by or may apply to entities other than states. Many of these attributes relate exclusively to sovereign nations, however, including the right to membership in the United Nations and the capacity to make international law through agreements and conduct.[5] Furthermore, a particular capacity—such as to make binding agreements—may have a very different meaning when exercised by a nonsovereign rather than a state. Only a sovereign, for example, can negotiate on behalf of and bind all its citizens or make agreements respecting its public territory and resources. Sovereigns alone, moreover, have broad power to establish the extent to which contractual undertakings are binding and enforceable, as well as to declare that certain rules or interests are not subject to consensual modification by private parties.[6]

For most legal purposes, the concept of sovereignty should be understood as more performative than normative. It denotes a roster of legal capabilities, privileges, and obligations that attend the recognition of a political entity as a state more than it authorizes a principled account of the criteria by which polities may claim and merit statehood. International legal sovereignty describes aspects of what states, constituted as such, may do and expect with regard to both the domestic societies they govern and other external, often competitive, political organizations. The normative principles of state establishment (and, more infrequently, of state termination) garner less agreement and have been subject to changing political norms over the modern period in which the vast majority of new claimants have presented themselves as candidates for admission to the state-centered system of international law. Recently, cultural norms, especially ethnicity and religion, have increasingly influenced the process by which states are recognized, with ethnic or religious self-governance depicted as the most perfect protection of minorities.[7]

Given this background, it is not surprising that the process for securing acceptance as a state (not to be confused with being recognized as the government of a state) is conceptually imperfect and subject to political influence. Entities that would seem to qualify for statehood in terms of the governing principles of an era are not entitled to, and are sometimes denied, acceptance as states. Entities unqualified under such principles, on the other hand, are sometimes accepted as states or accorded forms of recognition associated with statehood. The Republic of China (Taiwan) arguably meets the requirements of statehood in that it controls a population on the physical territory of the island of Taiwan and conducts its own foreign affairs. Yet after the People's Republic of China became recognized as the proper representative of all China in the United Nations, Taiwan lost its acceptance as a state, even with respect to the people and territory it actually controls.[8] Other examples include North Korea, which the United States refused to accept as a state, and Rhodesia, whose recognition was forbidden by the Security Council due to its racist policies. On the other hand, Ukraine and Belarus were accepted as member states by the United Nations even though they had no foreign relations authority and lacked important domestic powers, independent of the Soviet Union.[9] Some groups having no territory under their control are recognized as representatives of peoples entitled to statehood, such as the Palestine Liberation Organization (PLO), which is accorded observer status in the UN General Assembly.[10]

Some determinations apparently inconsistent with the principles that are said to govern eligibility for statehood are based on other, established principles. For example, that an entity formed in violation of the UN Charter may not be accepted as a state accounts for the nonacceptance of North Korea, Rhodesia, and Transkei, as well as for the General Assembly's rejection of South Africa's control over Namibia and the U.S. rejection of the Soviet Union's incorporation of Estonia, Latvia, and Lithuania. Furthermore, while political considerations undoubtedly have a significant impact on the way in which the eligibility rules are applied, their effects are mitigated by the fact that where acceptance is warranted objectively, but denied politically, it has generally been a matter of time before acceptance is secured. During such delays, states are required to treat as states those entities that qualify as states, even if they have not yet been accepted as such.[11]

The refusal strictly to apply statehood eligibility rules sometimes occurs because making a political statement is more important to a state than consistency. The Western powers accepted an increase of Soviet-bloc voting strength in the General Assembly by agreeing to UN membership for Ukraine and Belarus but preserved in principle the right of those states to independence. With regard to Taiwan, its nonacceptance as a state is the result of both principled and practical considerations. China's claim that Taiwan is part of China has been widely acknowledged, and only recently has Taiwan suggested that it will pursue statehood.[12] Grants of immunity or other privileges to international and nongovernmental organizations unqualified for statehood reflect the increasing recognition by states that nonstate actors should be given capacities necessary or useful in conducting their assigned responsibilities. This process could theoretically extend to granting "nations"—ethnic groups sharing strong cultural bonds—special powers or privileges irrespective of territorial lines, as Gidon Gottlieb has suggested.[13] Only states are able to grant such powers, however, and they are likely to do so only insofar as the grants serve useful purposes and pose no threat to the capacity of states to exercise sovereign authority. In short, inconsistencies in the application or conceptual integrity of the rules concerning eligibility for sovereignty do not undermine the concept's utility; and they rarely create controversy or uncertainty. In fact, these inconsistencies reflect a valuable flexibility, enabling states to avoid difficulties, accommodate conflicting agendas, and respond to ethnic and religious differences.

Sovereignty is also imperfect in that some of its supposedly fundamental characteristics are inaccurate descriptions of reality or are regularly disregarded in practice. States are far from "perfect equals." Their autonomy has always been subject to conflicting obligations, and their territorial integrity has never been guaranteed. In this regard, Krasner distinguishes between "international legal sovereignty" (encompassing the recognition of states and their rights in the international system), which is "almost always honored" because of its advantages to states and rulers, and "Westphalian sovereignty" (encompassing the alleged attributes of sovereignty), which is and always has been "myth."[14]

Exaggerated claims, inaccurate generalizations, or extralegal idealizations about the characteristics of sovereignty have not diminished the concept's utility. Practitioners (lawyers and diplomats) ascribe as much meaning to the "perfect equality of nations" as they do to the Declaration of Independence's "all men are created equal." They see the notion of equality as a device for enhancing the efficiency of the conduct of international diplomacy. They know, and have always known, that "sovereign equality" guarantees states nothing, not even their continuity, let alone their protection or influence. The autonomy of states is similarly an important value in international law, but for practitioners it has always coexisted with other, sometimes conflicting values, such as the protection of alien and minority rights and the requirement to refrain from committing internationally recognized crimes. Similarly, the territorial integrity of states is guaranteed only in principle and is subject to the obligation to refrain from acts of aggression against other states. In Serbia, this obligation has been extended even against an ethnic group within a single sovereign entity. Heightened dangers from nuclear accidents or biological and chemical weapons, for example, could well lead in time to further qualifications of territorial sovereignty.

Westphalian ideals of sovereignty have always been a description of norms of control and standards of conduct that states aspire, or are expected, to meet. They do not guarantee results. These standards are understood, moreover, as being qualified by their inherent inconsistency. No state is absolutely sovereign, because it must exercise its powers without infringing upon the rights of other sovereign states. States must also abide by obligations arising from customary law and treaties, among which is the UN Charter.

To say, therefore, that aspects of certain definitions of sovereignty are "myths" is correct but not determinative of the concept's utility. Sovereignty has been and remains the cornerstone of an entire, evolving system of diplomatic practice, conferring international status and enabling states to interact and cooperate on the basis of agreed methods and common understandings.

The Reality of Sovereign Power

Sovereignty is much more than a useful means for facilitating international exchange and characterizing international law or diplomatic outcomes. It is a powerful reality. True, states are increasingly led or driven to make international commitments and to delegate authority to international agencies and nongovernmental bodies that participate in making, applying, and enforcing the rules of transnational life.[15] Moreover, current trends and the complexities of modern society may further transform the meaning of sovereignty, lessening its significance. These developments have led many commentators to pronounce that sovereignty is in crisis. For us, this thickening net of treaties, regional associations, and international agencies is more an expression of the value of sovereignty than a threat to its continuing importance. But these developments do raise interesting problems about both the formal legal meaning and effective power of sovereignty. In our view, delegations to international or private entities are consistent with the legal conception of sovereignty. The sense of crisis of sovereignty is better attributed to the decline in effective power over internal governance that many states now experience, causing increased reliance on international agreements to deal with problems beyond the unilateral reach of many states. States still determine the course of events on virtually all issues of transnational concern, however, and will do so for many years to come.

States have long made commitments to one another (and to other entities and individuals), but the number and significance of these have increased greatly since the United Nations was created. More than 1,500 multilateral treaties have been made in the last fifty years, many of which concern fundamental functions of government. The UN Charter includes commitments concerning international security, human rights, economic cooperation, and international relations. The treaties of the EU commit adherents to abide by specific rules and decisions in major aspects of economic activity and in the protection of human rights.

It is possible, under international law, for a state to commit itself so absolutely on issues that it loses its sovereignty by agreement. That is what must have happened when the original states of the United States, after securing their independence from Britain, agreed to the Constitution. It is settled law, however, that a state's commitment to act in a particular manner with respect to some aspect of its sovereign power or to abide by certain principles is not a surrender of sovereignty but an aspect of its exercise. The power of states to exercise their sovereign discretion in a binding manner was recognized in the very first decision of the Permanent Court of International Justice (PCIJ), in dealing with the assertion that a treaty negotiated after the First World War that required Germany to give access to all vessels through an internal waterway could not be valid because it constituted a surrender of sovereignty, in particular the right of a state to maintain its neutrality. The PCIJ recognized that "any convention creating an obligation . . . [to perform or refrain from performing a particular act] places a restriction upon the exercise of the sovereign rights of the State, in the sense that it requires them to be exercised in a certain way. But the right to enter into international engagements is an attribute of State sovereignty."[16] In principle, therefore, such commitments are an aspect of sovereign power and are not inconsistent with its existence or proper exercise.

The recognition in international law of the capacities of sovereign states to pursue national goals through binding treaties and other agreements mirrors the basic liberal tenet that autonomous individuals may seek self-realization through contracts that limit their future liberties. The vast array of delegations by nations to international and nongovernmental entities has materially changed the way in which the world is governed. States have long engaged in such delegations, however, beginning in the modern era with river management in seventeenth-century Europe and continuing with the development of postal and other services some two hundred years ago.[17] Assigning responsibilities for aspects of transnational governance is consistent with this established practice, as well as with the propriety of similar delegations in national law systems, both public and private.[18]

Whether delegations of authority by a state are inconsistent with or erode the state's sovereignty therefore requires an appraisal that goes beyond reciting their number and importance. One measure of significance is whether the delegations surrender some aspect of sovereignty required to qualify for acceptance as a state. To remain eligible for sovereign treatment under international law a state must retain control over its territory, its population, its foreign affairs, and its power to make international law through agreements. It surrenders none of these attributes of sovereignty by establishing a given policy and delegating the administration of that policy to international agencies or other entities. The overwhelming majority of all functions of international or nongovernmental entities stem from such delegations, through which states are able to enlist the assistance of international agencies, while retaining ultimate control over what law will govern their actions and over the enforcement of that law.[19]

Rather than reflecting a diminution in the sovereign authority or actual power of states, these delegations enhance the capacity of states (and the international system) to cope with complex problems requiring transnational or private-sector management or expertise. Delegations made to private entities in particular provide no evidence of sovereign decline; their authority depends entirely upon state power.

The voluntary character of commitments in international law, and the corresponding limited cession of national authority, is underscored by the virtually universal recognition of the right of individual states to refuse to accept nonconsensual modifications of their international obligations; unilaterally withdraw from treaty regimes; maintain the supremacy of domestic law; and, absent agreement, be sanctioned for violating or withdrawing from a treaty by only the loss of reciprocal advantage.

The great bulk of international activity within the United Nations occurs in the General Assembly, in the specialized agencies, and at conferences under their auspices. The General Assembly has acquired more lawmaking influence than was initially anticipated. Through declarations and resolutions that gain consensus, or virtual unanimity, it has promulgated documents that are referred to as legal guides, and it has set out policies to which all or virtually all states have agreed. But the General Assembly has not thereby acquired any part of the sovereignty of states or caused national sovereignty to be diminished. The influence of its declarations or policies depends entirely on their acceptance by all or virtually all states. In a few cases, most notably that of Rhodesia, the General Assembly may be said to have applied law to nonmembers. In principle, however, it has no capacity either to apply or to enforce law. The only enforcement powers it possesses are to expel a member of the United Nations, on recommendation of the Security Council, and to suspend the privileges of a member state for failing to pay its dues.[20] No member has ever been expelled, although some states have been temporarily deprived of their voting authority.

UN agencies have a substantial role in the lawmaking process. Two of them—the International Law Commission (ILC) and the United Nations Commission on International Trade Law (UNCITRAL)—were created for the purpose of drafting treaties. When the ILC purports to describe what the law is on a given subject it usually does so by consensus, so it cannot be far off the mark. The ILC or UNCITRAL may also be correct when proposing what the law is without securing prior agreement from the states, in which case their drafts are influential. When they (or any other group, public or private) propose what the law *should be* they may also be influential, but not as lawmakers. The states that follow the recommended rules make law by that fact. UN-sponsored conferences, and the nongovernmental organizations that increasingly influence their output, do have a substantial impact in some cases on the lawmaking process. These efforts are viewed by many with suspicion, since the groups involved are accountable to no public authority and are focused exclusively on the attainment of narrow objectives rather than the overall public good.[21] But the influence of UN-sponsored conferences and the groups who seek to affect their outcomes depends entirely on their ability to convince states (or the UN Security Council) to adopt particular standards or practices. States make the law that emerges from these exercises.

International agencies operate under multilateral treaties, fashioning regulations, administering rules, issuing decisions, and enforcing at least their membership requirements. The tasks performed by these agencies—many technical and apolitical—include important lawmaking components. For example, agencies often have the power to recommend regulations or supplementary details to implement the general rules or purposes of a treaty. Sometimes these recommendations become law by the mere fact that states do not object to them. International agencies often also apply the rules in treaties, or those created pursuant to treaties. They investigate, decide, mediate, facilitate, and in some instances, are empowered to recommend enforcement measures. All these powers derive from treaties agreed to by states, which heavily influence their administration, sometimes as members on the governing bodies of agencies, as well as in many other ways.

The most significant delegation of authority in the UN system is the charter's grant to the Security Council of authority over international peace and security.[22] The Security Council is empowered to investigate security problems, attempt to resolve them through persuasion, impose sanctions, and if necessary, authorize the use of force.[23] The council acts by a vote of any nine of its fifteen members, but each of the five permanent members may veto any substantive measure.[24] In agreeing to this delegation of power, the states other than the permanent members gave unprecedented authority to the council over their economies, policies, and territories. Each permanent member, on the other hand, became something of a "supersovereign," empowered to vote to authorize the use of coercive measures against all states and to prevent such collective measures from being taken.

The UN Charter thus makes nations unequal with regard to the powers of the Security Council. This altered but did not cause the loss of national sovereignty, even that of the nonpermanent members. The council is not an international agency, but a structural grouping of states through which all UN member states have agreed to act collectively. It has a staff, and the UN secretary-general has authority to propose matters for it to consider. But the measures authorized by the charter can be taken only by the states that are members of the council, ten of whom rotate, and any seven of whom can outvote the five permanent members. The fact that a single permanent member is able to veto any substantive measure enhances that member's power but also significantly diminishes the power of all permanent members and of the council as a whole. The charter also contains provisions that limit the exercise of the council's powers. While the limit on matters of domestic concern in Article 2(7) may be overridden by measures taken under Chapter VII "with respect to threats of peace, breaches of the peace, and acts of aggression," it and the "inherent" right of self-defense in Article 51 remain grounds upon which states can resist council initiatives they consider improper.

The council has in recent years taken some controversial actions, but only one appears genuinely debatable as a constitutional matter—the sanctions imposed during the conflict in the former Yugoslavia, which had the effect of depriving Bosnia of the right to receive arms. The Somalia intervention involved a state that had no functioning government. Haiti had signed an agreement with the United Nations committing itself to take the measures that later were imposed through the threat of force. The authorization concerning Kuwait was based on an armed attack on Kuwait by Iraq, and the actions in the former Yugoslavia on the breakdown of peace and a perceived threat to international security. These measures are extraordinary when compared with the situation that existed prior to the charter. But the sovereignty of states is assumed to encompass obligations concerning international security and human rights. The principal difference today, as compared with the past, is that these obligations are now more broadly perceived and are occasionally enforced.

The most significant delegations of power by states to international bodies are those conferred on the European Community (EC) and other European institutions by the Treaty of Rome and the subsequent development of the treaties of the EU. A process is underway in Europe that can already be characterized as one in which certain aspects of sovereign power are shared or relocated. The process is continuing and may result in even greater sharing and shifts in authority. The treaties among the states of Europe have resulted in a set of institutions with significant powers and with an underlying methodology of administration fundamentally different from the methodology applied in other international regimes. The first of the "three pillars" of EU governance is the EC, which has a preponderance of powers in the area of economic activity, exercisable in most cases by decision processes requiring less than unanimous assent, and the governmental machinery—including the European Court of Justice (ECJ)—to review and apply its laws. The second pillar enables intergovernmental bodies, composed of representatives of the member state executive branches, to determine common positions on foreign affairs issues and recommend joint security policies. The third pillar, justice and home affairs, in an increasingly complex mosaic of voting rules and judicial capacities established by the Maastricht and Amsterdam treaties, now reaches deep into issues of frontier control, asylum and immigration, and policing long imagined to be at the very core of sovereign territorial control.[25] In addition, all EU member states subscribe to the extensive jurisdiction of the European Court of Human Rights at Strasbourg.

In several important ways, this system differs from international law systems under UN-sponsored treaties or other regional arrangements. EU law, for example, is supreme within its areas of authority,[26] whereas national law is recognized by many states as capable of overriding international commitments. Majority voting is increasingly being used to decide EC issues, whereas in most other international bodies important decisions require consensus or supermajorities.[27] The EC is also deemed to have implied powers, including the power to make treaties on certain subjects, whereas grants to international agencies are usually strictly construed and do not extend to powers such as treaty making. EC law directly affects individuals and gives them duties and rights against states and other individuals; international law, by contrast, generally makes states the exclusive mediators of duties and rights created by international regimes. The EC determined that it could protect fundamental human rights; no other international entity has the power to hear and determine such claims.[28] Enforcement of EC rules is less comprehensive than state law but far more meaningful than the orthodox international law sanction of loss of reciprocal advantage. Recent treaty commitments and ECJ rulings have elaborated new financial remedies to penalize member states that are delinquent in enacting EU law domestically or in enforcing directly applicable EU obligations through their national institutions.[29]

Significant limitations still exist in the EU's powers, however, particularly the scope of its authority. Even in some first-pillar economic issues where integration has gone furthest, individual states may veto proposed policies or rules.[30] New treaties or amended treaty provisions apply only to member states that consent, including common frontier controls, participation in the European Monetary Union, and most social legislation. The emergence of a variable geometry of transnational EU institutions, with member states participating in some and remaining outside of others, has been recognized and accepted as inevitable by the Amsterdam treaty.[31] Moreover, the Constitutional Court of Germany has warned that EC law must be understood to incorporate the fundamental human rights rules of national constitutions and has suggested that the entire EC structure is a federation of states, rather than a separate entity. Concurrently, the incorporation in EU treaties of the principle of subsidiarity, or the priority, whenever practical, of national rather than supranational management of law and policy, testifies to the ongoing problem of democratic legitimacy in the acquisition of more authority by central EU institutions.[32] Viewed in terms of the recognized prerequisites for eligibility for statehood, it is clear that the EU member states remain in control, even in relations with other EU members, of their territories, their populations, and the conduct of their foreign policies. Nonetheless, it is clear also that what has happened in Europe with regard to the sharing of sovereignty is far more thoroughgoing than anything else in the international arena, resulting in what may properly be characterized as multilevel governance, albeit subject to state concurrence, compliance, and enforcement.[33]

In weighing the effect of the UN Charter or the EU treaties and activities on the sovereignty of member states, an important consideration is whether they retain the power to withdraw. Many international treaties expressly provide for the withdrawal of adherents; in others such authority may be implied. Some types of treaties cannot be terminated, because of the implication that the parties contemplated no termination would ever occur, as in the case of a treaty that settles a border dispute between two states.[34] But such situations are special and rare.

Some authority exists for the proposition that, once having agreed to be bound by the UN Charter, a state has no option but to continue as a member. In 1965, Indonesia purported to withdraw from the United Nations.[35] The secretary-general expressed his regret at Indonesia's decision, but without accepting that it was effective.[36] When, in 1966, Indonesia announced that it had "decided to resume full cooperation with the United Nations,"[37] the UN Office of Legal Affairs took the position that Indonesia had not withdrawn and therefore did not need to be readmitted.[38] This delicately handled set of events hardly establishes the proposition that states may not withdraw from the United Nations. The charter contemplates that states may be expelled or that the exercise of their rights may be suspended. It seems unlikely that a party to an agreement could be denied its benefits but could not decide to forego them. Furthermore, a state determined to withdraw from UN membership would presumably resort to claims of invalidity or material breach, arguments available under international law to terminate any treaty.[39] Some of the obligations that states are believed to accept under the UN Charter may be unavoidable, but because of their nature as customary law, not their association with membership in the United Nations.

On the other hand, many European legal theorists argue that withdrawal from the EU is impermissible. This reflects yet another difference between the EU and international law agencies or private entities. It seems unlikely, however, that a European state could as a practical matter be prevented from withdrawing from the EU or any other EC institution or activity. As J. H. H. Weiler notes, the position of lawyers on the withdrawal issue is based on "precisely the type of legal analysis that gives lawyers a bad name in other disciplines."[40] The fact that states are unlikely to withdraw from the EU rests, properly, on their sovereign appraisal of the value and advantages of EU membership.

An aspect of international law and practice that creates a serious conceptual challenge to the concept of the sovereign power of states is the notion of customary law, especially as it is currently being construed by some human rights groups and international law scholars. How can a state be sovereign in establishing law for its territory or in the conduct of its domestic and foreign policy if it can be deemed to have violated a norm to which it has not explicitly consented in a treaty or other enforceable agreement?[41]

For theoreticians of sovereignty, the notion of peremptory principles of law that bind states regardless of their explicit consent is indeed confusing. The confusion is exacerbated, moreover, by deliberate use of this concept to force standards of conduct and obligations upon states without their approval and sometimes despite their opposition. Properly applied, however, the concept of customary law is consistent with the sovereign power of states to control their obligations. Customary law, properly defined, "results from a general and consistent practice of states followed by them from a sense of legal obligation."[42] This definition makes clear that while law can be inferred from custom, that process is permissible only in circumstances consistent with consent. Not only must states act generally and consistently in a certain manner for such law to arise, but they must do so out of a sense of legal obligation and not merely for convenience or advantage.[43] A single state is able to exempt itself from a rule of customary law by objecting to it prior to its becoming universally accepted.[44] Any principled application of this doctrine would require clear evidence, moreover, that the particular form of enforcement of a rule has become customary law, not only some general principle upon which the rule is based. Thus, for example, while the general principle that states not engage in torture may be customary law, it does not follow that all states are obliged or even allowed to use force to stop all torture in the world, or even to provide fora for suits to recover damages for such conduct.[45]

Judged by these standards, aspects of what some advocates claim is customary law represent their aspirations rather than rules of conduct accepted and practiced by states out of a sense of obligation. Indeed, many rules claimed to be customary are often violated with impunity. Exaggerated claims of customary law do pose a threat to state sovereignty insofar as they represent efforts to force rules upon states to which they have not agreed.[46] Such instances are rare, however. More often, states are led by such efforts to accept rules that they might otherwise have avoided; state acceptance of such rules, whether due to passive consent, lack of care, or outright embarrassment, is nonetheless an exercise of sovereignty, and not evidence of its disappearance.

A similar process occurs when international institutions, such as the ICJ, and states, groups, or individuals seeking to establish rules of international law claim such norms exist when they do not.[47] Their efforts in these situations often fail (giving international law an even worse reputation than it deserves).[48] When such efforts succeed, however, they do so not because some supranational power exists that is able to force a state to adhere to a rule that fails the tests for customary or treaty law, but rather because states choose to accept and enforce the norms thus advanced.[49] Debate about what constitutes compulsory international norms can have great value as a medium of political communication about what may constitute an evolving consensus on state obligations and practices. But this process is ultimately controlled by states and reflects the continued, pivotal importance of their acceptance as a prerequisite to effective implementation, particularly of such "soft" or exploratory law.

Beyond these specific issues, scholars widely contend that sovereignty has been and will continue to be changed and shared, if not diminished, by the combined effects of all these activities. Irrespective of legal rationalization, a widespread perception exists that sovereignty, when understood as autonomous and effective control over national territories, is on the wane. The baseline against which this decline should be measured is unclear, since states have long responded to external pressures and internal preferences by adopting transnational solutions.

In the international system the reality of conditionality and regulatory competition is broadly felt. For example, a peripheral nation facing the prospect of being left outside the European trading bloc or a developing state unable to attract capital because its intellectual property laws do not conform to World Trade Organization standards clearly experiences compulsion to reform its institutions that effectively, if not theoretically, compromises its sovereignty. Simultaneously, changing conditions of internal governance have reduced the roles and competences states can continue to exercise. Privatization has reduced the sphere of state production and direct economic control. Deregulation has increased as competition in the provision of energy, transport, and telecommunications infrastructure has displaced earlier public organization of natural monopolies. The growth of autonomous central banks and other independent agencies limits the reach of political authorities. The explosion of information technologies makes borders porous to uncontrollable flows of ideas and capital. States or scholars who understand sovereignty as reflecting unconstrained political control over discrete national markets may properly be disappointed.

The impact of these external and internal forces on effective sovereignty is not felt equally in all states. The United States and China are not subject to conditionality or regulatory competition as are most other nations. Those states that have traditionally relied on markets more heavily than administration may experience less decline of governmental power. These asymmetries have contributed to the proliferation of international agreements and regimes. States increasingly rely on regional institutions and treaties that substitute for reduced domestic governance and offer a more favorable, politically negotiated, common outcome than they are likely to achieve in the market of international competition. The mobility of portfolio capital and the need to attract direct foreign investment has brought about convergence in economic law and created a dynamic that favors explicit harmonization of uniform norms to forestall an alternative-market-induced homogeneity. The threat of reduced effective sovereignty has led toward multilevel governance as a prevailing practice, with an unruly mix of regional and functional organizations of overlapping asserted memberships and jurisdictions.

In turn, as these transnational agreements are institutionalized, they become fertile soil for the proliferation of executive secretariats, permanent bureaucracies, cross-national industry and labor associations, nongovernmental organizations, and quasi-public scientific or expert (epistemic) communities that populate the new ecology of international life. Such organizations express themselves through a legal discourse of universal civil, gender, and environmental claims that can no longer be ignored by nation-states. They demand and receive increasingly direct recognition of derivative legal rights asserted by individuals and collective nonstate actors. Moreover, nonstate, transnational actors engaged in criminal (mafias) or military (terrorist) activities have assumed a stature that makes problematic the classical, international law doctrine that only states must be treated as effective or responsible actors. The international system is in motion, stimulated in part by inadequacies felt by nation-states reacting to limits on their internal autonomy.

To say these events constitute a crisis brought about by sovereignty or that obviates the continuing importance of sovereignty only confuses the issue. Despite a context of reduced or shared authority, states remain the decisive transnational agents in this process. The concept of international legal sovereignty retains its coherence and validity as the vehicle through which changes are agreed upon or rejected. The relative value of these formal capacities may seem less weighty when measured in political terms against the diminished abilities of states unilaterally to implement domestic agendas or to dominate international regimes. But the formal powers and functionality that sovereignty confers remain the fabric even of these profound political changes. Indeed, our point is that the notion of international legal sovereignty accommodates itself to (and even facilitates) shifts in behavior by nation-states, however motivated, and has always done so.

In sum, nation-states remain the dominant power in both theory and practice in transnational affairs. Changes in the distribution of authority have taken place that are profound and that may fairly be claimed to reflect trends that will ultimately lead to increased sharing of authority with international and private entities. This process is consistent, however, with the manner in which states have always acted; it has not deprived states of their predominant authority, and it will continue only with the consent of states as their preferred course for the management of transnational affairs.

Sovereignty as a "Bad Word"

The most fundamental attack on the concept of sovereignty assumes its utility and its continuing accuracy in suggesting that states control the distribution of transnational power. It proposes, however, that sovereignty as a concept and the control that states exercise as sovereign powers cause so much harm that the notion of sovereignty should be reexamined, deconstructed, or even discarded.

The distinguished international law scholar Louis Henkin concludes for example that "sovereignty is a bad word" that has been used for so many improper purposes and so imprecisely that it should be "decomposed." Its "essential characteristics," he proposes, which remain "indicia of Statehood today," should be preserved, but uses of the concept that are unnecessary or inaccurate should be jettisoned along with the word itself.[50] Richard Lillich writes that sovereignty should be made to serve what he regards as its true Westphalian purpose of protecting and developing the human dignity of the individual.[51] Richard Falk finds the world changing in the direction of a "global ethos," in which the state must give way, moving from a "boundary-obsessed territorialism" to a regime that seeks to achieve agreed-upon, transnational ends, with accountability for national leaders that violate established norms. He acknowledges that the state has proved a "resilient" concept in responding to the need for change but wonders: "Is the state flexible enough to preside over its own partial dissolution, circumvention, and reconstruction?"[52] Former UN Secretary-General Boutros Boutros-Ghali has argued that the concept of sovereignty, which was never intended to be "absolute," should not be permitted to prevent changes needed to strengthen the United Nations.[53] Critical legal scholars see sovereignty as hopelessly ambiguous, because it leaves unresolved the ultimate question of whether nation-state sovereignty obtains its legitimacy from the international order and is therefore subservient to it or whether the international order is the product of nation-state consent. Until this fundamental question is resolved, they contend, international legal sovereignty will remain subject to conceptual manipulation and accordingly will be useless as a meaningful predicate for international rules.[54]

Responding comprehensively to this type of critique of sovereignty is beyond the scope of this essay, which is intended to explain why practicing lawyers and diplomats rely upon sovereignty—i.e., because it is useful and an accurate reflection of reality. Most practitioners would likely agree on the need for major transnational reforms to realize widely shared goals in commerce, human rights, environmental protection, and international security. They would insist, however, that sovereignty is not so bad a word that it should be decomposed, reinterpreted, reconstructed, or discarded, and that the interests it serves and its very flexibility make it preferable to alternative vehicles for transnational governance.

To begin with, the decomposition of sovereignty is difficult to articulate, let alone accomplish. The uses of sovereignty that Henkin finds improper include its assertion as a barrier to international cooperation on human rights and what he regards as the excessive deference given to sovereign nations in international fora. Yet the aspects of sovereignty that he finds accurately describe the power of states—"independence, equality, autonomy, 'personhood,' territorial authority, integrity and inviolability, impermeability and 'privacy' "—include some of the very elements invoked to justify unwarranted obstructionism or deference. Similarly, Falk's comments on the future reconstruction of sovereignty do not describe how sovereignty should or will be defined to accommodate the changes he foresees and, at the same time, to serve the purposes it currently serves in international affairs.

Moreover, the concept of sovereignty is not responsible for the world's horrors and imperfections. Alleged violations of sovereignty are always among the arguments made by opponents of proposed changes in international law or practice. These arguments are rarely instrumental, however, in preventing changes.

The many treaties and delegations agreed to by states in recent years demonstrate sovereignty's flexibility. Existing international institutions are already able to regulate most important transnational issues. The UN Security Council is empowered to maintain international security and has gone far beyond peacekeeping in authorizing military interventions to reverse the illegal occupation of Kuwait, to stop gross human rights violations in the former Yugoslavia, to enforce written commitments for democratization in Haiti, and to save humans from starvation in Somalia. The council has also imposed sanctions on Libya for the bombing of Pan Am Flight 103 in 1988, created an international tribunal to determine Iraq's economic liabilities for its invasion of Kuwait, and established tribunals to investigate, try, and punish violators of international conventions, crimes against humanity, and serious breaches of the laws of war in the former Yugoslavia and Rwanda. Much more could have been done in these situations, and much sooner. But these shortcomings stemmed from a lack of effective leadership, political skill, and moral commitment, not from the persuasive power of arguments based on overblown versions of sovereignty.[55]

Proposals that would have the effect of reducing the sovereign powers of states often fail, but not merely because people are irrationally attached to the powers of the states in which they live. They fail because they are undesirable as a policy matter, because they involve increases in authority or resources for what many states regard as an inefficient United Nations, or because they are inconsistent with state constitutions. Some arguments against transnational initiatives based on state sovereignty and constitutions are overblown.[56] But objections to transfers of authority from individual states often reflect legitimate concerns, however frustrating their assertion may be to advocates of reform. Former UN Secretary-General Boutros-Ghali failed in his efforts to convince the United States and other nations to empower the United Nations, not because of conceptual arguments based on sovereignty, but because of the heady agenda he decided simultaneously to pursue—going beyond the Security Council's humanitarian interventions to nation-building exercises, proposing the formation of a military force at the council's disposal, and attempting to create a fiscal base for UN funding independent of member state contributions.[57] Efforts to strengthen the United Nations and to prevent horrendous violations of human rights will be made again in future years, and expansive notions of sovereignty will not prevent their acceptance, if pursued with sufficient political skill and resolve, and when they have widespread support among states. The North Atlantic Treaty Organization's (NATO's) willingness to act against Serbia's treatment of Kosovo Albanians demonstrates, to a discomfiting extent, the readiness of many of the world's greatest powers to disregard arguments based on territorial sovereignty in at least some humanitarian crises.

Finally, while the notion of sovereignty will remain subject to manipulation so long as the status of states within the international system remains ambiguous, this seems preferable to accepting as definitive the notion that the international order is wholly subordinate to state systems. The international order, including its burgeoning nongovernmental sector, depends on its acceptance by states; but from that dependence many important and useful developments are able to emerge. As Wolfgang Friedmann, who narrowly escaped from what was perhaps the world's most evil government, wrote: "The states are the repositories of legitimated authority over peoples and territories. It is only in terms of state powers, prerogatives, jurisdictional limits and lawmaking capabilities that territorial limits and jurisdiction, responsibility for official actions, and a host of other questions of coexistence between nations can be determined. It is by virtue of their law-making power and monopoly that states enter into bilateral and multilateral compacts, that wars can be started or terminated, that individuals can be punished or extradited."[58] Sovereignty is, in other words, the conceptual basis upon which entities achieve legitimization as states. States, in turn, provide the primary vehicle for virtually all international activity, as well as the source of authority for making effective the growing nongovernmental transnational activity in the world today.

Absent agreement on what would replace states as the vehicle for transnational governance, a sudden, significant decline in the sovereign powers of states could dangerously destabilize the very processes that sovereignty is currently blamed for obstructing. For lawyers and diplomats, therefore, sovereignty is a necessity, and despite its ambiguities and changing meaning, it remains the most useful and accurate description available of state authority. Those who seek to modify sovereignty's orthodox import must especially understand the ongoing effective influence of state power in the formation of the multilevel governance (involving both international and nongovernmental entities) that may in part come to supplement or supersede it.

Arguments based on sovereignty's demise generally reflect a fundamental misunderstanding of its nature. The concept of sovereignty is not a set of established rules, to which states must bend their conduct in order to preserve their capacities. It is instead an ever-changing description of the essential authorities of states, intended to serve rather than control them in a world that states dominate. Hence, virtually anything that states choose to do to enhance their capacity to deal with the complicated problems of a changing world is seen by those engaged in the practice of statecraft as perfectly normal—an exercise rather than a diminution of sovereignty. If states lacked the power to commit themselves in advance to specific policies or to delegate authority to international institutions or private entities to implement such policies, they would be weaker—not stronger—entities than the sovereign states of today's complex world. Their continued dominance of international affairs would be less certain, as they would be less capable of responding to and coping with contemporary challenges.

Sovereignty is perceived as a concept in crisis and eventual decline because even the more effective nation-states cannot alone satisfy the aspirations of modern, domestic constituencies and have therefore agreed or been forced to share their juridical powers and governmental functions with other individual and collective actors in an increasing variety of transnational fora. While the future may bring some new concept that replaces sovereignty, that day remains distant, and the concept's continued utility, relevance, and durability is no more tellingly demonstrated than by its indispensable role as the conceptual and functional vehicle by which the future of the nation-state will be determined.

Notes

1. See Krasner 1993.
2. Krasner 1996:1.
3. See, e.g., Chandler 1990.
4. American Law Institute 1987, sec. 201. The modern attributes of sovereignty are the emergent effects of an extended process of war and negotiations, finally settled between the Peace of Westphalia and the Concert of Vienna, in which the territorially based political organizations now recognized as states contested with urban leagues, dynasties, empires, and churches. See Spruyt 1994.
5. Nongovernmental bodies such as the Red Cross, "which has important functions under the Geneva Conventions on the Laws of War . . . in general have not been accorded the status of international legal persons. Their legal capacity and their rights are governed by applicable municipal law." Henkin 1993:346.
6. "A contractual . . . clause should be held unenforceable if enforcement would contravene a strong public policy . . . whether declared by statute or by judicial decision." *M/S Bremen v. Zapata Off-Shore Company*, 407 U.S. 1, 15 (1972).
7. See Weber 1976; Heller 1997.
8. Currently, Taiwan—the Republic of China (ROC)—is recognized by some twenty-seven states. Taiwan's diplomatic relations with these twenty-seven countries do not constitute an international acceptance of Taiwan as a state, but rather represent a recognition of the ROC government as the representative of China. Throughout its long history, China has been represented by distinct state systems and different governments such as the Qing dynasty and the Qing government as well as the People's Republic of China (PRC) and the PRC government. The ROC and its government are among these entities. Many have argued that Taiwan qualifies for statehood, since Taiwan has its own government that controls a population on the territory of the island of Taiwan and conducts its own foreign affairs, and since Taiwan has already been recognized in the past as an independent state. But to make such an argument, one has to reject China's claim of sovereignty over the territory of the Taiwan island, a claim that has been recognized by most states in the world. As to Taiwan's membership in organizations such as the Asian Development Bank (ADB), Hong Kong, now formally a part of China, is also an ADB member. Some intergovernmental organizations (such as the World Trade Organization) do grant membership to nonstate entities.
9. The Soviet Union purported to confer upon the thirty-seven so-called socialist republics powers over their foreign affairs and to establish their own military forces. In reality, they had no "meaningful autonomy . . . in the conduct of their international relations," creating a legal situation that was "intriguing," but unlikely to allow the Ukrainian and Belarusian memberships in the United Nations to serve as a precedent in other contexts. Hannum 1988:273–74.
10. See generally American Law Institute 1987, sec. 202, reporters' notes at 79–84. The PLO's status in the General Assembly was enhanced in July 1998 to allow it to

cosponsor resolutions on Middle East peace and to reply on the record to speeches but still not to vote or put forward candidates for UN committees. While this shift left the PLO short of recognition as a state, it signaled the intention of the General Assembly to accord such recognition in the future. See "How the U.N. Voted," *New York Times*, July 8, 1998, A8.

11. Convention on Rights and Duties of States, 1933, 49 Stat. 3097 (Art. 3). The United States insisted, for example, that North Korea had breached its Charter obligations in launching the Korean War, even though the United States had not accepted North Korea as a member of the United Nations.

12. China has protested strongly against such suggestions by Taiwan and against domestic U.S. legislation—the Taiwan Relations Act, *U.S. Code*, vol. 22, secs. 3301–16—that appears to give Taiwan the ability to do many of the things that a state can do. The Taiwan Relations Act in fact contradicts the official U.S. position that there is only one China and that Taiwan is a part of it. In his official visit to China in June 1998, President Clinton reiterated what has come to be known as "the three no's": "I had a chance to reiterate our Taiwan policy, which is that we don't support independence for Taiwan, or two Chinas, or one Taiwan–one China. And we don't believe that Taiwan should be a member in any organization for which statehood is a requirement." Jonathan Peterson and Tyler Marshall, "Clinton Backs China on Issue of Free Taiwan," *Los Angeles Times*, June 30, 1998, A1.

13. See Gottlieb 1993:35–40.

14. Krasner 1996:12.

15. See, e.g., Mathews 1997.

16. S.S. *Wimbledon Case*, PCIJ, ser. A, no. 1, at 25 (1923).

17. For example, following years of at times arduous negotiations, the first International Telegraph Convention was signed May 17, 1865, by 20 countries, and the International Telegraph Union—later, in 1934, to become known as the International Telecommunication Union—was born. On September 15, 1874, the Postal Congress met in Berne, Switzerland, creating the second oldest international organization, the Universal Postal Union, which transformed the territories of twenty-one nations into a single unit for the exchange of postal correspondence and standardized and simplified postal rates and procedure.

18. Rabkin (1998:16) rests his argument against broad delegations on "analogy with [U.S.] domestic practice," but the Supreme Court long ago ceased relying on the nondelegation doctrine except perhaps where protected interests are at issue. The "doctrine has had very little bite" in the domestic arena, and "is an even more toothless barrier in the context of foreign affairs." Gunther and Sullivan 1997:399, 403.

19. See generally Szasz 1995.

20. UN Charter, Arts. 6, 19.

21. See, e.g., Rabkin 1998:41–42; Mathews 1997:52–56.

22. UN Charter, Art. 24(1).

23. UN Charter, Arts. 33–38, 41, 42.

24. UN Charter, Art. 27(3).

25. See Ehlermann 1998.

26. See *Italian Finance Administration v. Simmental, S.p.A.*, Ct. of Justice Eur. Comm., case no. 106/77, 1978 E.C.R. 629.

27. See generally Weiler 1991.

28. A similar, but less effective, American Convention on Human Rights also exists, as well as an Inter-American Court of Human Rights to decide cases and issue advisory opinions interpreting and applying the convention. See Buergenthal 1982.

29. See Ehlermann 1998.

30. This is particularly true for fiscal measures, although it should be noted that limits imposed on budget deficits and related indexes of tax and expenditure behavior by the conditions for entry and operation of the European Monetary Union may impose serious constraints on member state autonomy in these areas as well.

31. See Ehlermann 1998.

32. Giandomenico Majone 1998.

33. The vote by some 120 states to create an International Criminal Court (ICC) will have a bearing on the power of international institutions if it in fact results in an ICC with the powers contemplated in the treaty. See Rome Statute of the International Criminal Court (adopted July 17, 1998, A/CONF.183/9). The ICC would be empowered to indict and punish individuals from states that are not parties to the treaty, and would not be subject to the control of the Security Council (which could only delay ICC actions, and then only by passing a resolution calling for such a delay). The crimes upon which the ICC would be authorized to act include some that remain controversial; the crime of "aggression" is included but left to be determined by the "Assembly of States," which is nothing more than the state parties to the ICC treaty. The Assembly of States could well be viewed as the General Assembly, freed in the ICC context of the constraints of the UN Charter on its power to legislate. Moreover, the treaty will come into existence once only 60 of some 160 states in the world ratify it, and the Assembly of States will be empowered to define crimes by a two-thirds vote.

34. See generally Ian M. Sinclair 1984:181–97.

35. See letter dated January 20, 1965, from the first deputy prime minister and minister of foreign affairs of Indonesia addressed to the secretary-general, reprinted at 4 *International Legal Materials* 364 (1965).

36. See UN, doc. A/5899, S/6202, February 26, 1965.

37. See telegram from ambassador of Indonesion to the United States addressed to the secretary-general, UN, doc. A/6419, S/6498, September 19, 1966.

38. Schwelb 1967.

39. American Law Institute 1987, sec. 335.

40. Weiler 1991:2412.

41. Perceptive discussion of the relationship between consent and the creation of customary obligations can be found in Malanczuk 1997:46–48. See also American Law Institute 1987, sec. 102, comments b and d (addressing sources of international law, including "practice" as customary law and the effect of dissent from practice).

42. American Law Institute 1987, sec. 102(2).

43. At this point, the list of principles established as customary law is limited, but it is growing and arguably includes piracy, slavery, genocide, and other crimes against humanity (such as torture and rape), apartheid, and some forms of terrorism. The consensus in favor of these principles is universal, even though nations continue to violate them in fact. The source of these rules, therefore, is ultimately the states them-selves, and their acceptance reflects the fact that the meaning of sovereignty has always included the notion that states should abide by universally accepted norms of conduct. Acceptance of a particular norm does not necessarily mean, however, that states have agreed to any particular form of its enforcement. That is a separate issue, on which the same degree of consensus is required before the remedy at issue can be considered a mandatory limit on states. See Scharf 1996.

44. American Law Institute 1987, sec. 102, comment d.

45. See the illuminating treatment of these issues in Scharf 1996.

46. Rabkin (1998:50–56) collects examples of how customary law for many inter-national law scholars has come to have little or nothing to do with actual practice.

47. The ICJ has weakened its authority by in effect prescribing rules, allegedly based on customary law, in the face of contrary, consensual practice. See Sofaer 1989.

48. Consider, most recently, the contentious effort to create the ICC in Rome during the summer of 1998. See note 27. The statute that resulted was actually not based on international consensus. Two permanent Security Council members voted against it, and they and the other states who voted no represent more than half of the world's population.

49. See Victor 1997.

50. Henkin 1989-IV:24–28.

51. Lillich 1984:406–7.

52. Falk 1992:198–213.

53. Boutros-Ghali 1992/93:90, 98–99.

54. See generally Purvis 1991.

55. It was the mishandling by the U.S. government of the intervention in Somalia, not any lack of multilateralist inclination, that led to its humiliation there when it was forced to withdraw a "warrant" issued for the arrest of a local warlord, and that caused thereafter its tragic decision to block the Security Council's effort to save some 500,000 people from a genocidal slaughter in Rwanda. See Reuters, "Ex-US Official, in Paris, Again Assails Washington's Failure to Intervene in Rwanda in '94," *New York Times,* July 8, 1998, A10 (criticism of the Clinton administration by Herman Cohen, former assistant secretary of state for African Affairs, 1989–1993, in testimony before a French parliamentary committee on the Rwandan massacres: "After the earlier killing of Amer-ican soldiers in Somalia, I could understand there was no question of sending Amer-ican troops to Africa, but I could not accept the United States opposing the sending of African troops."). See also Ann Scales, "Clinton Concedes US Erred in Rwanda; Cites Inadequate Response to Killing, Calls it Genocide," *Boston Globe,* March 26,

1998, A1 (apology of President Clinton for lack of action: "We did not immediately call these crimes by their rightful name: genocide."). See generally Carnegie Commission on Preventing Deadly Conflict 1997.

56. Rabkin (1998:69) claims, for example, to "discern at least two firm rules limiting the [constitutional] power to make international agreements: they must be genuinely *international* and must be genuine *agreements* [i.e., exchanges including reciprocity]." He cites little support for proposing these vague standards as constitutional limitations on the treaty power, and the examples he offers demonstrate their lack of meaningful guidance. He argues, for instance, that human rights treaties are neither international nor reciprocal (1998:71), despite the strong interest all states have in protecting their nationals from improper treatment and in accepting limitations on their own powers domestically in order to obtain corresponding commitments from other states concerning the treatment of people.

57. See Boutros-Ghali 1995.

58. Friedmann 1964:213.

References

American Law Institute. 1987. *Restatement (Third) of the Foreign Relations Law of the United States.* St. Paul, Minn.: American Law Institute.

Boutros-Ghali, Boutros. 1992/1993. "Empowering the United Nations." *Foreign Affairs* 71, no. 5: 89.

———. 1995. *An Agenda for Peace.* New York: United Nations.

Buergenthal, Thomas. 1982. "The Inter-American Court of Human Rights." *American Journal of International Law* 76:231.

Carnegie Commission on Preventing Deadly Conflict. 1997. *Preventing Deadly Conflict.* Washington, D.C.: Carnegie Commission on Preventing Deadly Conflict.

Chandler, Alfred D., Jr. 1990. *Scale and Scope: The Dynamics of Industrial Capitalism.* Cambridge, Mass.: Belknap Press.

Ehlermann, Claus Dieter. 1998. "Differentiation, Flexibility and Closer Cooperation: The New Provisions of the Amsterdam Treaty." Unpublished paper, Robert Schuman Centre, European University Institute, Florence, Italy.

Falk, Richard. 1992. *Explorations at the Edge of Time: The Prospects for World Order.* Philadelphia: Temple University Press.

Friedmann, Wolfgang. 1964. *The Changing Structure of International Law.* New York: Columbia University Press.

Gottlieb, Gidon. 1993. *Nation Against State: A New Approach to Ethnic Conflicts and the Decline of Sovereignty.* New York: Council on Foreign Relations Press.

Gunther, Gerald and Kathleen M. Sullivan. 1997. *Constitutional Law,* 13th ed. Westbury, N.Y.: Foundation Press.

Hannum, Hurst. 1988. "The Foreign Affairs Powers of Autonomous Regions." *Nordic Journal of International Law* 57:273.

Heller, Thomas C. 1997. "Modernity, Membership, and Multiculturalism." *Stanford Humanities Review* 5:2.

Henkin, Louis. 1989-IV. "International Law: Politics, Values and Functions." *Recueil des Cours* 216:24.

Henkin, Louis, Richard Crawford Pugh, Oscar Schachter, and Hans Smit. 1993. *International Law: Cases and Materials*, 3d ed. St. Paul: West Publishing.

Krasner, Stephen D. 1993. "Westphalia and All That." In Judith Goldstein and Robert O. Keohane, eds., *Ideas and Foreign Policy: Beliefs, Institutions, and Political Change*, 235–64. Ithaca: Cornell University Press.

———. 1996. "Sovereignty and Its Discontents." Unpublished paper, Stanford University Department of Political Science, Stanford, Calif.

Lillich, Richard B. 1984. "Sovereignty and Humanity: Can They Converge?" In Atle Grahl-Madsen and Jiri Toman, eds., *The Spirit of Uppsala*, 406–12. New York: W. de Gruyter.

Majone, Giandomenico. 1998. "Europe's 'Democracy Deficit': The Questions of Standards." *European Law Journal* 4:5.

Malanczuk, Peter. 1997. *Akehurst's Modern Introduction to International Law*, 7th rev. ed. London and New York: Routledge.

Mathews, Jessica T. 1997. "Power Shift." *Foreign Affairs* 76, no. 1: 50.

Purvis, Nigel. 1991. "Critical Legal Studies in Public International Law." *Harvard International Law Journal* 32:81.

Rabkin, Jeremy. 1998. *Why Sovereignty Matters*. Washington, D.C.: American Enterprise Institute Press.

Scharf, Michael. 1996. "Accountability for International Crime and Serious Violations of Fundamental Human Rights: The Letter of the Law: The Scope of the International Legal Obligation to Prosecute Human Rights Crimes." *Law and Contemporary Problems* 59, no. 4: 41.

Schwelb, Egon. 1967. "Withdrawal from the United Nations: The Indonesian Intermezzo." *American Journal of International Law* 61:661.

Sinclair, Ian M. 1984. *The Vienna Convention on the Law of Treaties*, 2d ed. Manchester: Manchester University Press.

Sofaer, Abraham D. 1989. "Adjudication in the International Court of Justice: Progress Through Realism." *The Record of the Association of the Bar of the City of New York* 44:462.

Spruyt, Hendrik. 1994. *The Sovereign State and its Competitors*. Princeton: Princeton University Press.

Szasz, Paul. 1995. "General Law-Making Processes." In Oscar Schachter and Christopher C. Joyner, eds., *United Nations Legal Order*, 35–108. New York and Melbourne: Press Syndicate of the University of Cambridge.

Victor, David G. 1997. "The Use and Effectiveness of Non-Binding Instruments in the Management of Complex International Environmental Problems." In *Pro-*

ceedings of the American Society of International Law, 91st Annual Meeting, 241–50. Washington, D.C.: American Society of International Law.

Weber, Eugen J. 1976. *Peasants into Frenchmen: The Modernization of Rural France, 1870–1914.* Stanford: Stanford University Press.

Weiler, J. H. H. 1991. "The Transformation of Europe." *Yale Law Journal* 100:2403.

3

Sovereignty from a World Polity Perspective

JOHN BOLI

For several centuries, sovereignty has been considered an attribute of states. The state is the locus of ultimate authority in society, uniquely qualified to represent society as a whole in its relations with the external world. No body, no organization, no power stands higher than the state; the world is a basically feudal structure composed of lordly states all jealously guarding their respective domains.[1] As a result, conflict is structural and endemic; cooperation is strategic and fragile. International interaction and exchange constitute potential challenges to state sovereignty that must be regulated and managed.

This image of sovereignty is not simply that of "realist" or "neorealist" scholarly analysis.[2] It is also the image that has prevailed in the development of international law and in the practice of states with regard to trade, immigration, citizenship, war, and a host of other areas. It is a fundamental assumption about the nature of things in the state-organized world for the great majority of theorists and practitioners of national and world politics. Indeed, it is hardly too much to say that it constitutes a core element in the very definition of the state. If the state is not the ultimate locus of authority, it is not a state.

Oddly, one question that is crucial to the meaningfulness of sovereignty is not often raised in discussions of the concept: With respect to what is the state sovereign? What is the social unit over which the state rules? We tend to take that unit, the "nation" or national polity, very much for granted. The *nation*-state has been such a fundamental part of our conceptual universe for the past two centuries that it seems quite natural, obvious, and inevitable.

Here I want to question this naturalistic assumption.

All social units are based, at the deepest level, on naturalistic assumptions about social reality.[3] In the West we assume, for example, that individuals are "obviously" the basic building blocks of society (rather than various types of family or lineage units, as in most societies historically) and that collectivities, especially organizations, are essentially collections of individuals with a quite limited degree of "thingness" separate from their members. These assumptions are given substance and veracity by the fact that they are "realized" in social structure: we construct organizations, movements, and institutions based on these assumptions and thereby tautologically confirm their empirical validity, turning them into undeniable social facts.

Just so, the reality and significance of the national polity have become obvious in the modern period through the construction of national states, national accounting systems, national markets, national citizenship, and national culture, as well as through structures and events that have been organized and interpreted as inter-national exchange, competition, cooperation, and conflict. The assumption that the national polity is real is now reflected in so much structure, accounting, and interpretation that we can hardly imagine a world constructed any other way. What we habitually forget is that, like any other collectivity, the national polity is an "imagined community,"[4] not an inevitable one.

Sovereignty is normally considered an attribute of the state, but a focus on the national polity suggests otherwise. Terminological casualness leads many analysts virtually to equate the polity and state, in the way that the older term *State* subsumed both the polity (the social unit constituted by a body politic) and the state (the structures by which central authority is organized within that unit). If we take the distinction between polity and state seriously, it makes little sense to speak of sovereign states per se. States are always associated with polities. Where sovereignty is located is then an open question. Various social theories attribute sovereignty to God, a monarch, a social elite, "the people," the law or constitution, and so on.[5] Relatively few theories follow the extreme Hegelian practice of locating it, as von Treitschke did, in the state itself.[6]

Claims of sovereignty are thus claims about the polity as it is organized and represented by the state. The question of whether a state is sovereign or not is predicated on the existence of a polity governed by that state. It is this predication that I will problematize here.

I begin with a brief historical review of the sovereignty issue as a matter of conflict between three types of polities: universalist (European or Christian), national, and local. This review leads to the important conclusion that sovereignty is a theory about the location of ultimate authority, not an empirical description. In the third and fourth sections I discuss the concept of the "world polity" and the dialectical relationship between the world polity and national polities in the modern era. Here I show that the ontological status of the national polity has always been ambiguous; correspondingly, the degree to which the theory of national sovereignty has been "validated" in social structure has always been limited.

The fifth section discusses developments in the twentieth-century world that have specific effects on the theory and practice of sovereignty. I end with a brief analysis of events in the past few years, depicting them as the final outburst of nationalism in a world in which sovereignty is shifting to the global level to a greater extent than ever before.

Sovereignty as a Problem of Polities

The doctrine of sovereignty originated at the intersection of three dialectical tensions. The first was the tension between universalism and segmentation. As Hinsley[7] emphasizes, throughout medieval times universalistic claims to ultimate authority were asserted by the pope as vicar of the Church and the Holy Roman emperor as the divinely anointed secular supremacy. Segmented authority was sought by the kings, princes, and electors who reigned in the various regions of Christendom.[8] At stake was the issue of whether Christendom was to be organized as a single "European" polity or as a conglomerate of separate princely polities constituting distinct units within a diffusely European cultural framework.[9]

The second tension was that between the princes and their respective subordinates—not so much their individual "subjects" as the corporate entities making up medieval society: estates, guilds, towns, villages, monastic orders.[10] Most prominent in the struggle for authority "from below" were, of course, the various nobilities, who used the devices of councils and parliaments to restrict princely authority. Efforts to assert independence by other corporate units produced such phenomena as free towns, peasant revolts, heretical religious movements, and guild monopolies.[11] In a structural sense, then, the emergence of the doctrine of sovereignty involved an extended contest between three polity levels: the European polities of "universal" Christendom and the more limited Empire, the "kingdom" polities of the princes, and a variety of "local" polities. This was the struggle on the secular plane.

The third dialectical tension was a more spiritual wrestling match, the struggle between God and humanity. In the theory of authority that prevailed in Christendom until the modern period, all authority derived ultimately from God.[12] This theory complicated the authority contest at every level. In the universal polity, pope and emperor challenged each other's legitimacy. In the kingdoms, monarchs challenged the Church by seeking control over the clergy, while the Church made claims to the right to appoint or approve successors to the throne. In local polities, nobles claimed authority to appoint priests, bishops ruled over manorial domains, burghers rejected the Church in favor of alternative interpretations of the Word, and so on.[13]

Hinsley agrees with most scholars in identifying the first clear statement of the doctrine of sovereignty as Jean Bodin's *Six livres de la république* of 1576. Hinsley argues that this work could not have appeared earlier because the necessary conditions for a fully developed doctrine had not been met. What was required was a relatively clear separation of the state from society coupled with a relatively high degree of integration of society with the state. For these conditions to be met, in the first place the state must be constituted as such. It must be territorial (even if boundaries were vague); it must exercise legal jurisdiction; it must be capable of enforcing its authority through sanctions. In short, the monarch must rule, not merely reign. In the second place, the authority of the state must extend throughout society. Sovereignty made no sense when the kingdom was divided into many subpolities that could evade the state's jurisdiction, when the king was merely *primus inter pares*. The contest between the kingdom polity and local polities must be resolved in favor of the kingdom.

These conditions had been attained by the sixteenth century, at least in the more developed states. But what prompted Bodin to construct his theory was not the structural conditions making sovereignty an established fact but precisely the opposite, the civil and religious wars in France that called into question the very existence of the polity. Bodin urged that the king be seen as sovereign, that is, as "the final and absolute political authority in the political community,"[14] because this was the only feasible means of putting an end to the slaughter.

Bodin's was not merely a French theory. It was a product of western Christendom, for the French state had emerged in a context of perpetual military competition with other developing states.[15] The segmentation of the universal polity was a multicentric process in which none of the monarchies, in the absence of the others, would have become a modern state. And Bodin's doctrine did not presume the complete demise of the European polity of Christendom. On the contrary, the reality of the European polity was incorporated in those aspects of Bodin's doctrine that limited the absoluteness of the monarch, to wit, divine and natural law. Divine law was the Word, which was seen as applying everywhere. Natural law (the rules inherent in the "nature" of the world itself and discoverable through the exercise of reason) was equally universal. Both these overarching symbolic structures were seen as constraining royal authority; the larger European or Christendom polity remained active as national polities became increasingly important social units.[16]

The other constraint on royal authority came from the local polities. For Bodin held that the monarch was also bound by traditional or customary law. Customary law was those practices that had taken on the nature of binding obligations among the people, not only the nobility but also among the lower estates, both in town and countryside. They could not be set aside by the monarch any more than by the people themselves. Significantly, less than three decades after Bodin's work was published, a German Calvinist came forward with a theory that adopted the same concept of sovereignty but located it in a radically different place. Bodin had argued that sovereignty must be vested in the monarch if authority were to be exercised effectively (a conclusion reiterated by Hobbes seventy-five years later). Althusius argued, on the contrary, that sovereignty could lie only with the people. He gave the strivings from below that had always resisted the construction of states a cogent theoretical justification. The people had the right (in extreme cases, the duty) to resist an abusive ruler, for ultimate authority lay in their hands.

In my view, the conceptual apparatus that had been established by the seventeenth century contained all the issues that have continued to frame the sovereignty problem to our time.[17] In current terminology, the "external" aspect of sovereignty is the problem of whether world polity forces prevent the individual state from wielding ultimate authority over its associated "national" polity. The "internal" aspect is the problem of whether local polity forces have this same inhibitory effect. Exactly where sovereignty resides—in the state itself; in an elite formed by a party, the military, or industrial capitalists; or in the citizens as they are represented by political institutions (parliament, law, the constitution)[18]—remains a disputed question. Even the issue of whether sovereignty lies within society or outside it (with a divine being) persists. In the West the latter dispute has been largely resolved in favor of society, but elsewhere, particularly in Islamic countries, it is far from settled.[19] And as I note below, challenges to state sovereignty based on natural law doctrines have made a comeback in the twentieth century.

Sovereignty as a Theory of Legitimate Authority

As the foregoing review suggests, the sovereignty of the state can best be described as the preeminence of the national polity in relation to both the larger world polity and various local polities.[20] The sovereign state is constitutionally "independent"[21] or "insular";[22] it is "not subject without consent to external . . . control by any like authority";[23] it can "act externally with a freedom that is limited only by voluntarily-accepted constraints."[24] In other words, chains of authority relations do not extend above the state. No external actor can legitimately command the sovereign state and apply sanctions if its commands are not heeded.

With respect to the relationship between the sovereign state and actors within the national polity a less stringent conception applies. Other actors, especially organizations, may exercise authority (that is, give legitimate commands and enforce them), but the sovereign state has ultimate authority. This condition is expressed variously: the courts are the loci of final appeal, no one is above the law, "the buck stops here" (at the Supreme Court, the legislature, the presidency). Any disputes about the exercise of authority, whether between labor and management, feuding religious groups, warring tribes, or grumpy next-door neighbors, can finally be settled under the aegis of the state.

Note that both aspects of sovereignty are essentially theories about the legitimacy of authority. External sovereignty does not imply that the state will be entirely unconstrained in its action. It is, instead, the claim that the state is authorized to reject commands from any outside body. Whether the state can make that rejection stick is another matter; the theory is often violated by the facts. Similarly, with respect to internal sovereignty, the state is certainly constrained in its exercise of authority internally, but sovereignty amounts to the claim that the state is the highest authority. This implies that the state is seen as entitled to apply sanctions to enforce its commands or decisions, but it by no means guarantees that such sanctions will in fact be applied. The state's authority can be subverted by bribery, violence, negligence, and numerous other means.

The essence of sovereignty is thus theoretical, not empirical; it is the theory that the national polity, as organized by the state, is the pinnacle of authority, neither subordinate to the world polity nor defied by local polities or organizations.[25] How much the sovereign state is in fact influenced by external or internal actors is a question of power, status, will, and effectiveness, but not one of authority per se.

How, then, do we determine whether or not a state is sovereign? James promotes Manning's conception of "constitutional independence"[26]—that is, the state's constitution cannot be "part of a larger constitutional arrangement." He argues that this conception identifies those states that are "eligible to participate fully and regularly in international relations," which he sees as the most important operationalization of the concept. Without belaboring the point, in my view James fails in this attempt,[27] but he does show quite successfully that no particular conception of sovereignty is problem-free. The term is used loosely to cover a large number of concepts,[28] not only by scholars but also by spokespersons for states and other bodies. As we shall see, this is a conclusion of substantive interest in its own right.

James's discussion is typical of most contemporary analyses of sovereignty: it places much greater weight on the issue of the autonomous authority of the state vis-à-vis the larger world than on the establishment and maintenance of ultimate internal authority. This too is a substantive observation of interest.

On the Concept of the World Polity

From the perspective of a single national polity, the outside world consists of much more than a "system of states" or "world economy" or "international system." Rather, the global environment is a sea teeming with a great variety of social units—states and their associated polities, military alliances, business enterprises, social movements, terrorists, political activists, nongovernmental organizations—all of which may be involved in relations with the polity.[29] Some of these actors are seen as beneficial, others as antagonistic. In either case, they are all part of the larger world and must be dealt with in some way.

Besides actors, the world polity contains raw materials, labor, manufactured products, scientific knowledge, and other "resources" that can be used for state and national development. It contains structures of rules regarding access to those resources and theories explaining why they are essential to the national polity's existence or success. At a more abstract level, the world polity contains complex sets of rules (that is, models) regarding how the polity can and should structure its relations to the larger world, in both cooperation and conflict. Some rules are formal and explicit, such as rules of positive international law, contracts, and interstate organizations.[30] Others are informal, such as international customary law, state "practice," and generalized expectations regarding what states and other actors may and ought to do.[31]

Finally, the world polity contains a multitude of even more loosely structured "cultural" elements that are seen as both desirable (because they symbolize the so-called leading edge of human development) and sinister (because they undermine local authenticity): rock and classical music, various literary works, film and television programs, world languages (above all, English), magazines and journals. A range of material products are culturally constructed as globally "present": soft drinks, transistor radios, blue jeans, wristwatches, fast foods. Along with these are a variety of cultural prescriptions regarding life's purposes and goals, institutionalized at the world level, that place conflicting demands on the polity: freedom versus equality, individual self-actualization versus national development, national aggrandizement versus the pursuit of peace, and so on.

My point about all these elements of the world polity and world culture is not that they are systematically analyzed for their relevance to a given polity's situation. I claim only that from any national polity's point of view, the external environment constitutes a single worldwide polity full of danger and opportunity.[32] The composition and appearance of the world polity vary in considerable measure; Guatemalans are likely to perceive the United States and Philips Electronics as greater threats than do the French, for example. But a great many of the actors, resources, cultural elements, and ideologies are known throughout the world and perceived in fairly uniform terms, and there is widespread implicit agreement about what is not of world polity significance: purely local customs, languages, and rituals, unrationalized technologies and skills, traditional political structures, and so on.

I hasten to add that no reification of the national polity or state is intended here. Polities are not integrated, homogeneous units. Rather, the "national" character of the polity is also a cultural theory that is more or less supported by observable reality. In some cases the theory is upheld by such a wide array of organizational and cultural structures reifying the polity that the theory has become a "social fact." In most cases the theory is only a prescription that the state attempts, with varying degrees of sincerity, to meet by building a nation out of the heterogeneous units within its territory.[33] The state aims to bound the "nation" from the world polity and reduce the significance of internal local polities so that multifaceted national development will be facilitated.[34]

Similarly, the typical state is not the unitary, rational, coherent organization that common-sense usage assumes.[35] Rather, the state organization consists of an aggregate of disparate individuals in more or less rationalized positions that are structured in a multitude of bureaucratic units. Like all large organizations, in the usual case the state's goals are undefined or vague, its various segments have conflicting goals and policies, and decision making is largely collective and structural (Mann's term is the "cock-up" theory of the state).[36] Such organizational incoherence implies that state agents have complex relationships with and perceptions of the world polity, which in turn implies that an enormous range of social dimensions involving the world polity evoke state concern. This range is continually expanding as the complexity and incoherence of the state increase. This point will be developed further in the next section.

Dialectics of the National Polity and State in the World Polity

The tension between the world polity and national polities is dialectical in that it involves mutually reinforcing contradictions. Modern states and polities originated in a common, competition-oriented cultural framework, and their further development has always involved the dual process of reliance on the external framework and ceaseless efforts to buffer themselves from it.[37]

State and national reliance on the world polity is multidimensional, as the preceding discussion has suggested. As a cultural canopy, the world polity provides legitimacy through participation in the state system[38] and conformity to worldwide standards regarding the proper nature and behavior of states.[39] The world polity provides universalistic knowledge and know-how that can be used to promote both state and societal competitiveness. It further provides such social theories as "dependency" and "cultural imperialism" and "political realism" by which to explain and justify the polity when it fails to meet world standards or violates world polity principles.

At the organizational and material level, the world economy makes it possible to trade for materials, products, and technical assistance that are essential to state power and national development. World communication systems make knowledge and data rapidly available. World political bodies provide fora within which the state can negotiate, evaluate the competition, and reach agreements that it believes to be advantageous. In short, the world polity is constantly used and elaborated by the state and polity in the ongoing pursuit of power and progress.

At the other pole of the dialectic lie world-level processes that constrain national polities and states. Culturally, natural law doctrines of inviolable human rights and the duty of states to ensure the fulfillment of those rights call into question the moral and practical adequacy of the national polity and state.[40] The universalistic laws of the sciences affirm the uniformity and interdependence of the biosphere, strengthening the claim that only world-level programs can successfully preserve nature's health and beauty.[41] Then, too, there is a seemingly inexhaustible world polity spring from which social theories claiming the obsolescence, impropriety, and incapacity of the state bubble forth.[42] National states cannot manage the global economy, financial system, or resources. National states are the cause of war and conflict. National states inhibit efficiency by erecting barriers to market freedom. National states prevent the solidarity of the working classes and the triumph of socialism.

The very interconnections that provide access to coal and computers and consultants also represent threats, however; they indicate that the state is constantly subject to the influence of such external actors as states, corporations, governmental and nongovernmental associations, and individuals.[43] The state is caught between the perceived need to plug into the world polity and the contradictory desire to bound itself from the world polity in the name of independence and self-determination.

But bounding is increasingly difficult. Technical development produces boundary-transcending technologies and side effects: broadcasting devices, long-range weaponry, surveillance satellites, acid rain, radioactivity.[44] Economic development produces aggressive corporations seeking new markets and cheap labor and promising benefits that make their offers hard to refuse.[45] The glamour of popular world culture produces internal demands that boundaries be relatively permeable;[46] everyone wants to tune in to what's hot. The result is a dialectic at the interface: while the volume of flows across national polity boundaries increases, state efforts to regulate those flows intensify. The territorial boundary becomes the scene of incessant accounting and surveillance rituals as the state struggles to maintain the distinction between the world and its national polity.

Another dialectic is at work between the national polity and local polities. The state operates under the theory that relations between the state and citizens should be unaffected by intermediate collective identities; discrimination of any sort is illegitimate.[47] Where the nation has become most "real," as in Scandinavia, intermediate subpolities activating such identities have little social significance. Local polities are reduced to collections of individuals constructed as politically authorized possessors of "rights," and the associations such individuals form to represent their rights are only weakly reified. Where the nation is less developed, more corporate local polities, such as ethnic and religious groups, tribes, villages, and regions, have considerable substance.

In either case, the reification of the national polity entails the subordination of local polities to central authority while also empowering local polities, organizations, and individuals as political participants. As a general rule, authority must be shared if it is not to be resisted. Hence the growing internal authority of the state, which is in large part due to the dialectic between world and national polities, is further stimulated by the dialectic between national and local polities. As the state's claims on society increase, so too do society's claims on the state.[48]

This dialectic has its backside as well. State claims on society are often resisted by local polities and organizations, not least because the state is often seen as unable or unwilling to improve local conditions. The state is centralized, bureaucratic, standardizing, but social problems are local, personal, idiosyncratic. Or the state is run by exploiting elites who sacrifice local welfare to national and self-aggrandizement. Whatever the theory, the legitimacy of the state is thrown into doubt.[49] The situation becomes even more problematic when local polities bypass the state to make direct links to the world polity, especially if they are pressing claims for autonomy.[50]

Hence the national state and polity are caught in the middle, both strengthened by world and local polities and challenged by them.[51] What we should keep in mind is that this has always been the case. Sovereignty is a theory of the state's primacy in relation to local polities and the external world polity, but as an empirical matter these relationships are always problematic and subject to change.

Twentieth-Century World Development and Issues of Sovereignty

The twentieth century featured a number of lines of development impinging on state sovereignty. The most general of these is what I call the intensification of the world polity, aspects of which are commonly described as "interdependence," the development of "international systems," the consolidation of a "world economy" or "world culture," and so on.[52] World polity intensification refers to the reification of the world-as-a-single-unit through interaction among all sorts of units and actors.[53] This interaction takes the form of communication, warfare, economic exchange, ideological conflict, the sharing of knowledge, and much more. It can be said to have world polity character under either of two conditions: (1) the interaction occurs across national polity boundaries, or (2) the units involved activate "protopolities" that are larger than, or not limited to, national polities.

The first condition directly reflects the continuing issue of whether national polities or the world polity constitute the primary, highest-order collectivity. Interaction that crosses national boundaries ipso facto calls into question the primacy of the national polity, for such interaction is not "contained in" or "identified with" any single polity. It instead invokes the more universalistic rules, norms, and cultural understandings that make up the wider world culture.[54]

The second condition refers to a different type of interaction, most often between units characterized as "transnational," "international," "regional," "worldwide," and the like: scientific bodies, treaty organizations, churches, professional associations, human rights groups, etc. Interaction between such units is of world polity character regardless of where it occurs, for the units themselves are constructed on world cultural conceptions and principles.[55] They activate either the world polity as such or various transnational subworld polities that include geographic regions, cultural areas (francophone, Islamic, Slavic), politico-cultural spaces (the British Commonwealth), and so on.

In my view, the social processes yielding world polity intensification of the first type (interaction that is accounted as occurring between national polities) constitute the externally oriented aspect of what is usually called "national development."[56] Several lines of scholarship in historical sociology, world-system studies, and international relations have abundantly demonstrated that neither nations nor development would have emerged without this constant interaction.[57] I therefore see this type of world polity intensification as national development (including the expansion of states and of the state system as a whole) writ large.

The second type of world polity intensification is a bird of another feather. Interaction that activates nation-transcending polities is the primary means whereby explicitly universalistic cultural rules and conceptions develop.[58] For example, universalistic rules and conceptions regarding states are most likely to crystallize and receive formal institutionalization in conferences and associations of states rather than as the result of individual states acting unilaterally or in dyadic arrangements. It was the conference at Westphalia that made state sovereignty an established cultural rule, the conferences at Utrecht and Vienna that made the balance-of-power theory of European politics predominant, the League of Nations that first brought the legitimacy of warfare into serious doubt.[59] Similarly, the conceptions and rules of international law are more the work of the international community of legal scholars than the result of national or international court rulings in particular cases, for it is the scholars who interpret, generalize, and transform into principles the case law that serves as their raw data.

Two important developments have resulted from this second type of world polity interaction. The first is the emergence of a world model of the national polity and state, the second the growing social reality and importance of the construct of world citizenship. Each of these has important implications for state sovereignty.

THE NATIONAL POLITY AND STATE AS A WORLD MODEL

Until the twentieth century many types of political organization existed concurrently: nation-states, empires, colonies, dependencies, stateless societies. As world polity interaction has intensified, the nation-state model of societal organization has gradually taken on the character of a social imperative.[60] Initially, European powers attempted to impose this model on stateless regions.[61] Later, local elites demanded it for themselves, and by the end of World War II the dismantling of colonial empires was at the top of the political agenda.[62] "National self-determination" became an "inalienable right" of all "peoples."[63] This doctrine and the model of national polity and state that underlies it have been expressed in their purest form in UN debates and documents.

Sovereignty is accorded a central role in the world model of the nation-state. Every territorial unit is to be organized by a sovereign state formally equal to all others;[64] no polity is to be formally subordinate to any other.[65] Every state is to build up the internal apparatus necessary to subordinate all local polities to a unitary authority structure and enable the state to speak as the sole representative of the polity in the world forum. Every state is to take measures to bound the polity and control interaction between it and the world polity. The state is to be "responsible" for the national polity in the world arena, and to create it if it does not already exist.[66]

WORLD CITIZENSHIP

The second development is the construct of world citizenship.[67] This conception is reflected in such referents as "humanity," "the human species," and "mankind," and it is elaborated in doctrines of "human rights," "the brotherhood of man," "world peace," and so on. World citizenship is the set of mostly informal rules linking individuals to the world collectivity, just as national citizenship is the set of more formal rules linking individuals to the national collectivity.

The ideology of world citizenship implies that every human being is a member of the world polity, which thereby constitutes a "society,"[68] "community,"[69] or even "village."[70] Every human being is ultimately responsible for everyone else, and the world polity is represented by every human being ("no one is free unless all are free"). Individuals as world citizens are morally obliged to set aside particularistic distinctions in everyday action and discourse. World citizens should act together in solidarity to make the world a better place, overcoming all the destructive antagonisms of nationalism, ethnocentrism, tribalism, casteism, and so on.

Like the world model of the national polity and state, world citizenship doctrine receives its purest expression in nation-transcending arenas and interaction. Its most highly legitimated single expression is the Universal Declaration of Human Rights. Transnational associations (INGOs) codify, promote, and "embody" world citizenship;[71] they also are bold enough to rail at states who fail to abide by the principles implied by the construct.[72] More materially, the worldwide diffusion of education, economic exchange, and technology has made world citizenship an apparent reality in that individuals with a fairly standard set of "modern" capacities and knowledge are increasingly able to flourish anywhere.

IMPLICATIONS

Figure 3.1 presents a schematic representation of arguments I will develop further. The upper segment of the figure has been discussed in the preceding sections. World polity intensification is reciprocally reinforced by national development and state expansion, leading to a world model of the nation-state society and to the construct of world citizenship, both of which are broadly institutionalized.

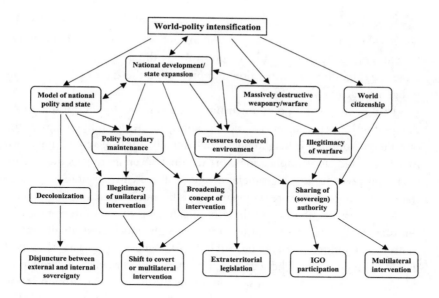

Figure 3.1 World-Polity Effects on National Sovereignty

One undiscussed element in the upper segment of the figure is "massively destructive weaponry/warfare." Weapons of mass destruction are an inherent feature of national development, for national development means that the entire polity's resources can be mobilized for relatively specific purposes. Even without nuclear weaponry, a national polity directed by a bureaucratic state is a massive weapon capable of generating millions of deaths and ravaging huge territories.[73] Continuing development implies continually escalating destructiveness. Throughout most of the history of the world polity, the use of that destructiveness in war has been considered an absolute prerogative of the state.

To the arguments represented by figure 3.1. First, it should be clear that the world model of the national polity and state, combined with ongoing national development and state expansion, produces tremendous pressures on states to maintain polity boundaries and control the world polity environment they face. States are the creatures of the world polity and, therefore, its antagonists. The development of all nation-states means the increasing vulnerability of all;[74] increasing interchange leads to theories seeing "interdependence" as a challenge to the national polity.[75] Sovereignty is "at bay";[76] national sovereignty is "perforated";[77] many states are sovereign "by courtesy only."[78] The perceived need for defensive state action to control penetrative external forces becomes more pressing,[79] while the pressures on the state to preempt external forces by extending its jurisdiction and promoting the external success of its indigenous actors intensify.[80]

Thus, as the world polity intensifies, state concern to delimit the polity, reduce the influence of outside actors, and gain greater influence over the outside environment is heightened. Conceptually this triple concern has two major, contradictory implications: (a) national sovereignty becomes an increasingly powerful ideological claim, and (b) the incapacity of the sovereign state acting alone to ensure national success becomes increasingly apparent.

Put differently, the first of these implications is that **(I) intervention by one state in the polity of another is increasingly considered illegitimate.**[81] States may continue to intervene, but they risk being castigated as violators of darkly venal character. The second implication leads directly to a corollary of central significance. As a means of combining the doctrine of nonintervention (sovereignty) with the need to control the external world environment, **(II) states feel increasingly willing and compelled to share authority** through organizational forms activating protopolities larger than the national polity.[82]

In an intergovernmental organization (IGO), for example, states can maintain the theory that they are merely exercising, not yielding, sovereignty while simultaneously forming protopolities that comprehend the territories of all the member states for coordinated action in selected social domains.[83] If this means that some or even all states in the IGO feel heavily constrained by the views of their fellow members, so be it. They nevertheless gain greater predictability vis-à-vis the world polity and increased security against intervention.

The propensity of states to share authority is further strengthened by the ideology of world citizenship. In combination with the destructiveness of modern weaponry, world citizenship tends to delegitimate warfare.[84] War is predicated on processes incompatible with world citizenship: nationalism, distrust of one's fellow citizens, ethnocentrism. If war is illegitimate, means for its control and eventual elimination must be constructed. The sharing of sovereign authority is a logical means to that end—and in many analysts' view, it is the only such means with any prospect of success.[85]

Second, world citizenship directly legitimates authority sharing through the doctrine of the responsibility of all for everyone. We are all citizens of the planet, the planet depends on healthy rain forests, ergo all states should cooperate to save the Amazon jungle. Or control pollutants. Or prevent nuclear proliferation.

The sharing of (sovereign) authority leads to several further outcomes, some of which remain unstudied (lower row of figure 3.1). First, **(IIa) states are increasingly likely to join IGOs;**[86] second, **(IIb) states are increasingly likely to accept organizational structures that give IGOs increasing autonomy,** that is, the capacity to make decisions opposed by some or many member states.[87] Third, the increasing pressure on states to control the world polity environment leads to the phenomenon of **(IIc) extraterritorial legislation.**[88] States attempt to regulate drug trafficking, the transfer of military technology, terrorism, and other problems through laws that reach beyond the national polity's boundaries. State jurisdictional arenas thus begin to overlap. As an extreme case, international criminal law assumes the complete overlap of national jurisdictions. Not surprisingly, international criminal law is still considered quite controversial.

The lower left side of figure 3.1 presents two additional outcomes. First, the ongoing expansion of the state, in combination with pressures to bound the polity from outside, produces a **(III) general broadening of the concept of intervention.**[89] The state once concerned itself primarily with war, justice, and taxation; now the state is responsible for economic development, social welfare, immigration policy, environmental preservation, and a host of other things. This expansion means that effective state action requires polity bounding across a widening range of activities and with respect to many types of external actors. The result is a tendency on the part of states, and many scholars, to equate sovereignty and independence and condemn any influence by outside actors as intervention.[90] Sovereignty is interpreted to mean absolute state control over the polity, at least with regard to outside actors; authority is mistaken for power.[91] We therefore find new conceptions of intervention emerging in the twentieth century, particularly the concepts of economic and cultural intervention and of "collective" intervention by such bodies as the International Monetary Fund.

The broadening of the concept of intervention and the increasing illegitimacy of interventionary acts do not guarantee that intervention decreases. Pressures to intervene are also growing. The net result appears to be a modest decrease in the rate of intervention and a more marked **(IIIa) shift from overt to covert intervention,** that is, acts that are not officially recognized and that lie in the gray conceptual area between illegitimate intervention and legitimate "influence."[92]

The final outcome I wish to call attention to is a result of the decolonization process generated by the institutionalization of the doctrines of self-determination and sovereign equality. Many new states have not had the organizational capacity to create or maintain unitary authority structures in the territories they oversee.[93] This implies that there is a growing **(IV) disjuncture between the external sovereignty accorded to states by the world polity and the internal sovereignty they are presumed to have.** This conclusion is reflected in the international relations literature itself, as we have seen. Discussions of sovereignty often neglect the issue of internal state authority, taking it more or less for granted that "a state is a state" and therefore problematizing only the freedom of action of states in external relations.

The widespread claim that state sovereignty is in decline reflects an inadequate understanding of the concept of sovereignty. Sovereignty is a political theory about the locus of authority in the national polity, and the principle that the state constitutes this locus is deeply institutionalized in world and national structures. In the globally dominant theory, the state derives its sovereignty from the ultimate source of authority, "the people," and it exercises that sovereignty on the people's behalf. Loss of sovereignty would therefore imply the assumption of authority and jurisdiction in the national territory by some body or organization other than the state. Such cases are not unknown; in recent years, we have seen the United Nations establish authoritative control of a number of national polities in which the state has collapsed, and in some cases (e.g., the United States in Haiti, NATO in Kosovo) the United Nations has authorized other actors to assume authority in disorderly countries. In all such cases, however, the primary goal has been the reestablishment of a functioning sovereign state exercising jurisdiction over a reconstituted national polity under democratic political structures, in line with the doctrine of state sovereignty derived from the citizenry. In no case in recent decades have we observed the formal incorporation of a national polity under the jurisdiction of an external state or IGO, or the concession of sovereignty to a tyrant or oligarchy, as the generally desired resolution of a state crisis.

While the principle of state sovereignty stands firm, the array of external actors and forces that impinge on the state and influence state policy and behavior has expanded rapidly. States must manage an increasingly intrusive and powerful external environment, and to succeed as states (that is, to actualize the general model of the properly constituted and functioning state) they must enmesh themselves ever more thoroughly in international and global structures and flows. By and large, however, despite the numerous instances of state breakdown or collapse, states' capacity to manage their national polities has increased in tandem with the increasing complexity and integration of the world polity. States must deal with ever more problems, and they have ever greater resources and organizational muscle to do so. States may have to run just to keep in place, but they keep on running rather steadily even though they often seem to be struggling.

What has changed in the postwar period, above all, is the perception of the inadequacy of the state to cope with the globalizing world. Problems are increasingly likely to be conceived in global or regional terms; likewise for proposed solutions. States therefore turn increasingly to IGOs as collective actors exercising shared state sovereignty, the better to coordinate action and enhance each state's capacity to manage its respective polity. The prevailing theory about IGOs continues to hold that such arrangements are voluntary and revocable; the ideology of state sovereignty shines through. Formally the ideology is not belied; even in the European Union, which stands at the pinnacle of shared-sovereignty organization, every state retains the option of withdrawing from membership if EU authority begins to seem excessive. In practice, participation in shared-sovereignty arrangements is often deemed not only desirable but absolutely necessary by states, even though they continually worry about loss of control and influence ("sovereignty" in its distorted usage) with respect to the IGOs they constitute.

What has also changed in recent decades is the spread of the nation-state to all corners of the world and the emergence of the broadly based expectation that all states are to live up to the general model of the state. Where world cultural expectations far exceed state capacity and competence, as is often the case with respect to young states that preside over poor, marginal, fragmented national polities, observers are especially likely to espy declining state sovereignty and effectiveness—even when the states at issue are growing or extending their regulatory apparatus at a modest pace. This mismatch between externally anchored expectations and what can reasonably be achieved by newer states in peripheral countries, overwhelmed as they are by the task of dealing with the enormous power and influence of innumerable external actors, will only get worse. The expectations and demands on modern states are growing too fast for even the most developed states to keep up.

Barring major catastrophe or war, world polity integration and interconnectedness will continue increasing into the foreseeable future. The external pressures on states will expand, even as states are routinely challenged from within by groups seeking autonomy or the establishment of independent states. Ever more problems will be defined as global or regional in scope and therefore requiring transnational responses; ever more responsibilities will be placed on the shoulders of states by domestic and international interest groups, nongovernmental organizations, and IGOs. But global cultural and organizational support for the doctrine of state sovereignty is not likely to diminish. *Au contraire*, the role of the state as a crucial actor in world development is central to the structure and operations of the contemporary world polity. The political theory of state sovereignty derived from the ultimate authority of "the people" is likely to remain well entrenched for many decades to come, though it will also remain disputed, questioned, and, no doubt, much misunderstood.

Notes

This work was supported in part by a grant from the Swedish National Research Board. The comments and suggestions of George Thomas, Tom Burns, and John Meyer, as well as those of many participants in two conferences where earlier versions were presented, are gratefully acknowledged.
1. Meyer 1987.
2. Aron 1984 [1962]; Morgenthau 1960; Keohane 1986.
3. Meyer, Boli, and Thomas 1987; Meyer et al. 1997.
4. Anderson 1983.
5. Nettl 1968.
6. See Aron 1984.
7. Hinsley 1986.
8. Cf. Aron 1984; Laski 1917.
9. Watson 1992; Holsti 1985.
10. Bloch 1961.
11. Mann 1986; Anderson 1974.
12. Ullmann 1966.
13. Tierney 1964; Southern 1970.
14. Hinsley 1986:26.
15. Anderson 1974; Tilly 1975; Giddens 1985; Elias 1982; Evans, Rueschemeyer, and Skocpol 1985.
16. Gierke 1950.
17. On the elaboration of this apparatus by Grotius, see Asser Instituut 1985; by Vattel and Wolff, see Bull 1984a.
18. See Nettl 1968.
19. Cf. Thomas 1985; Jansen 1979; Naff 1984.

20. Local polities are not always contained within the would-be national polity. The Kurds, for example, champion a national polity construct that includes territory under the jurisdiction of three established states.

21. James 1986.

22. Manning 1962.

23. Fawcett 1971.

24. Reynolds 1975.

25. Cf. Thomas 1985.

26. James 1986:25.

27. James's own analysis reveals that some states that are constitutionally independent, like Taiwan after the 1960s and the Bantustans created by South Africa, have not been able to participate in international relations at all. Further, he ignores the many ambiguities in the concept of constitutional independence itself.

28. Kavanaugh 1974; Goodwin 1974.

29. Mansbach, Ferguson, and Lampert 1976; Mitchell 1984; Burton 1972.

30. Weston, Falk, and D'Amato 1980; Falk, Kratochwil, and Mendlovitz 1985; McDougal and Riesman 1981; Friedmann 1964.

31. Luard 1977; Miller 1985; Beitz 1979; Paenson 1983.

32. Krasner 1985; Robertson 1987; Meyer 1987; Boli 1987.

33. Bendix 1964; Tilly 1975; Anderson 1983.

34. Of course, nation building is also a "grass-roots" enterprise conducted by social movements, voluntary organizations, business groups, and so on. Yet the state is always crucial for nation building because it maintains and reifies the territorial boundaries that are activated by movements and organizations within the emerging national polity.

35. Meyer 1987.

36. Meyer and Scott 1983; Brunsson 1982; Wildavsky 1979; Mann 1993.

37. Meyer 1987; Meyer et al. 1997; Boli 1987.

38. Jackson and Rosberg 1982; Farley 1986.

39. Gong 1984; Boli and Thomas 1999.

40. Beitz 1979; Burton 1984; Friedmann 1964.

41. Brown 1972.

42. See Holsti 1985; Stone 1984; Landheer, Loenen, and Polak 1971.

43. Mansbach, Ferguson, and Lampert 1976; Mansbach and Vasquez 1981; Pettman 1979; Hollist and Rosenau 1981.

44. Smith 1980; Nordenstreng and Schiller 1979; Galtung 1980.

45. Vernon 1971; United Nations 1973, 1983.

46. Smith 1980.

47. See Boli 1989; Grimm 1986.

48. Cf. Giddens 1985; Kaufmann 1986; Schmitter and Lehmbruch 1979; Katzenstein 1978.

49. See Migdal 1988.

50. Cf. the articles in Duchacek, Latouche, and Stevenson 1988.

51. Luard 1977; Banks 1984; Friedmann 1964.

52. Boulding 1985; Wallerstein 1974, 1980; Keohane and Nye 1977; Nettl and Robertson 1968; Robertson 1987.

53. Boli 1993.

54. Interaction across boundaries also has the effect of reifying the boundaries insofar as states maintain such rituals as stamping passports, conducting customs inspections, examining auto insurance papers, and so on. The relationship between the world polity and national polities is always double-edged.

55. Note that it is not the units themselves that must be "larger than" the national polity, but rather the polity that is activated in interaction among the units. When individuals interact under the assumptions of world citizenship, whether as members of international nongovernmental organizations (INGOs) or simply as "human beings," they are engaged in world polity activity even though individuals are evidently smaller than national polities. Of course, individuals usually give little thought to the type of polity activated by their interaction. Unfortunately, the same can be said of most scholars studying that interaction.

56. Some analysts dispute that world polity intensity is in fact increasing, since such indicators of interchange as the mean level of trade/GNP and labor mobility have been fairly constant in the twentieth century or have even declined (see Deutsch 1974; Goodwin 1974). What one cannot deny, however, is that absolute levels of interchange have increased exponentially in virtually every measurable dimension (Inkeles 1975) and that perceptions of interdependence are rising fast. On the other hand, much of the apparent increase in interchange is a result of the reification of the national polity itself. Exchanges and flows are increasingly likely to be accounted as occurring either between national polities or within them, to the exclusion of all alternative accounting schemes. Hence the perpetual problem of finding data that do not take national polities as the units of analysis.

57. Giddens 1985; Mann 1986; Elias 1982; Wallerstein 1974, 1980; Bull and Watson 1984; Aron 1984.

58. Boli and Thomas 1999; Meyer et al. 1997.

59. Luard 1976; Friedmann 1964.

60. Strang 1988; Meyer et al. 1997.

61. Bull and Watson 1984.

62. Klein 1974.

63. See McDougal and Riesman 1981; Paenson 1983.

64. Klein 1974.

65. James 1986; Goodwin 1974.

66. For simplicity I speak of "a" world model, but competing variants posit different relationships between state and citizen and varying degrees of state penetration of society. The so-called liberal, socialist, welfare, and related models are, however, quite uniform in most fundamental respects. Only a few world models (Islamic models, above all) depart significantly from the dominant variants, but to this point such

models have not made much headway in replacing the basic democratic/rational bureaucratic/secular state model.

67. Boli 1998, 1989; Barkun 1968; Jenks 1958.
68. Burton 1972; Landheer, Loenen, and Polak 1971.
69. Cobb and Elder 1970.
70. McLuhan and Powers 1989.
71. Boli and Thomas 1997, 1999.
72. Boli and Thomas 1999; Willets 1982.
73. Giddens 1985.
74. Kissinger 1961; Aron 1984.
75. Smith 1980; Keohane and Nye 1977; Falk 1969.
76. Vernon 1971.
77. Duchacek, Latouche, and Stevenson 1988.
78. Klein 1974.
79. See Fatouros 1969.
80. Krasner 1985; Olmstead 1984.
81. Bull 1984b; Thomas 1985; Goodwin 1974; Weston, Falk, and D'Amato 1980; Henkin 1985.
82. Jacobson, Reisinger, and Mathers 1986; Jacobson 1979; Skjelsbaek 1971; Demmitt and Thomas 1987; Archer 1983; Armstrong 1982.
83. Cf. Hill 1984; Goodwin 1974.
84. Aron 1984; Lauterpacht 1985; Mayall 1978.
85. Clark and Sohn 1966; Landheer, Loenen, and Polak 1971; Miller 1985; Speer 1985.
86. Jacobson, Reisinger, and Mathers 1986.
87. See Detter 1964; Luard 1977; Willets 1988.
88. Kavanaugh 1974; Kratochwil 1985; Paenson 1983.
89. Thomas 1985; Bull 1984b.
90. See Kavanaugh 1974; Goodwin 1974.
91. James 1986; Hinsley 1986; Barkun 1968.
92. Henkin 1985; Bull 1984a.
93. Jackson and Rosberg 1982; Migdal 1988; Klein 1974; McKinlay and Little 1986.

References

Anderson, Benedict. 1983. *Imagined Communities: Reflections on the Origin and Spread of Nationalism.* New York: Verso.

Anderson, Perry. 1974. *Lineages of the Absolutist State.* London: New Left Books.

Archer, Clive. 1983. *International Organizations.* London: Allen and Unwin.

Armstrong, David. 1982. *The Rise of the International Organisation: A Short History.* London: Macmillan.

Aron, Raymond. 1984. *Paix et guerre entre les nations.* 8th ed., orig. 1962. Paris: Calmann-Lévy.

Asser Instituut. 1985. *International Law and the Grotian Heritage.* The Hague: T. M. C. Asser Instituut.

Banks, Michael, ed. 1984. *Conflict in World Society: A New Perspective on International Relations.* Brighton, England: Wheatsheaf Books.

Barkun, Michael. 1968. *Law Without Sanctions: Order in Primitive Societies and the World Community.* New Haven: Yale University Press.

Bassiouni, M. Cherif. 1974. *International Extradition and World Public Order.* Leyden, Netherlands: A. W. Sijthoff; and Dobbs Ferry, N.Y.: Oceana.

Beitz, Charles R. 1979. *Political Theory and International Relations.* Princeton: Princeton University Press.

Bendix, Reinhard. 1964. *Nation-Building and Citizenship.* New York: Wiley.

Bloch, Marc. 1961. *Feudal Society.* 2 vols. Chicago: University of Chicago Press.

Boli, John. 1987. "World-Polity Sources of Expanding State Authority and Organization, 1870–1970." In George M. Thomas, John W. Meyer, Francisco O. Ramirez, and John Boli, *Institutional Structure: Constituting State, Society, and the Individual,* 71–91. Beverly Hills: Sage.

———. 1989. *New Citizens for a New Society: The Institutional Origins of Mass Schooling in Sweden.* Oxford: Pergamon Press.

———. 1993. "World Polity Dramatization Via Global Events." In Roland Robertson and William Garrett, eds., *Religion and Global Order: The Contemporary Circumstance,* forthcoming.

———. 1998. "Rights and Rules: Constituting World Citizens." In Connie L. McNeely, ed., *Public Rights, Public Rules: Constituting Citizens in the World Polity and National Policy,* 271–93. New York: Garland.

Boli, John and George M. Thomas. 1997. "World Culture in the World Polity: A Century of International Non-Governmental Organization." *American Sociological Review* 62, no. 2: 171–90.

———, eds. 1999. *Constructing World Culture: International Nongovernmental Organizations since 1875.* Stanford: Stanford University Press.

Boulding, Kenneth E. 1985. *The World as a Total System.* Beverly Hills: Sage.

Brown, Lester R. 1972. *World Without Borders.* New York: Random House.

Brunsson, Nils. 1982. "The Irrationality of Action and Action Rationality: Decisions, Ideologies, and Organizational Actions." *Journal of Management Studies* 19 (January): 29–43.

Bull, Hedley. 1984a. Introduction to Hedley Bull, ed., *Intervention in World Politics,* 1–6. Oxford: Oxford University Press.

———, ed. 1984b. *Intervention in World Politics.* Oxford: Oxford University Press.

Bull, Hedley and Adam Watson, eds. 1984. *The Expansion of International Society.* Oxford: Oxford University Press.

Burton, John W. 1972. *World Society*. Cambridge: Cambridge University Press.

———. 1984. *Global Conflict: The Domestic Sources of International Crisis*. Brighton, England: Wheatsheaf Books.

Clark, Grenville and Louis Sohn. 1966. *World Peace Through World Law*. Cambridge: Harvard University Press.

Cobb, Roger W. and Charles Elder. 1970. *International Community: A Regional and Global Study*. New York: Holt, Rinehart and Winston.

Demmitt, Kevin and George M. Thomas. 1987. "State Formation and Global Involvement: An Analysis of Inter-Governmental Organizations." Paper presented at the annual meeting of the American Sociological Association, August, Chicago. Arizona State University, Department of Sociology.

Detter, Ingrid. 1965. "Law Making by International Organizations." Ph.D. diss., Faculty of Law, University of Stockholm.

Deutsch, Karl. "Between Sovereignty and Integration: Conclusion." In Ghita Ionescu, ed., *Between Sovereignty and Integration*, 181–87. London: Croom Helm.

Duchacek, Ivo D., Daniel Latouche, and Garth Stevenson, eds. 1988. *Perforated Sovereignties and International Relations: Trans-Sovereign Contacts of Subnational Governments*. New York: Greenwood.

Elias, Norbert. 1982 (1939). *The Civilizing Process*. Vol. 2, *State Formation and Civilization*. Trans. Edmund Jephcott. Oxford: Basil Blackwell.

Evans, Peter B., Dietrich Rueschemeyer, and Theda Skocpol, eds. 1985. *Bringing the State Back In*. Cambridge: Cambridge University Press.

Falk, Richard A. 1969. "The Interplay of Westphalia and Charter Conceptions of the International Legal Order." In Richard A. Falk and Cyril E. Black, eds., *The Future of the International Legal Order*. Vol. 1, *Trends and Patterns*, 32–72. Princeton: Princeton University Press.

Falk, Richard A. and Cyril E. Black, eds. 1969. *The Future of the International Legal Order*. Vol. 1, *Trends and Patterns*. Princeton: Princeton University Press.

Falk, Richard A., Friedrich Kratochwil, and Saul H. Mendlovitz, eds. 1985. *International Law: A Contemporary Perspective*. Boulder, Colo.: Westview Press.

Farley, Lawrence T. 1986. *Plebiscites and Sovereignty: The Crisis of Political Legitimacy*. Boulder, Colo.: Westview Press.

Fatouros, A. A. 1969. "The Participation of the 'New' States in the International Legal Order." In Richard A. Falk and Cyril E. Black, eds., *The Future of the International Legal Order*. Vol. 1, *Trends and Patterns*, 317–71. Princeton: Princeton University Press.

Fawcett, James. 1971. "General Course on Public International Law." In *Académie de droit international, recueil des cours 1971*, Vol. 1, 363 ff. Leyden, Netherlands: Sijthoff.

Ferguson, Yale H. and Richard W. Mansbach. 1989. *The State, Conceptual Chaos, and the Future of International Relations Theory*. Boulder, Colo.: Rienner.

Friedmann, Wolfgang. 1964. *The Changing Structure of International Law*. London: Stevens and Sons.

Galtung, Johan. 1980. *The True Worlds: A Transnational Perspective.* New York: Free Press.

Giddens, Anthony. 1985. *A Contemporary Critique of Historical Materialism.* Vol. 2, *The Nation-State and Violence.* Cambridge, England: Polity Press.

Gierke, Otto. 1950. *Natural Law and the Theory of Society, 1500 to 1800.* Cambridge: Cambridge University Press.

Gong, Gerrit W. 1984. "China's Entry into International Society." In Hedley Bull and Adam Watson, eds., *The Expansion of International Society,* 171–84. Oxford: Oxford University Press.

Goodwin, Geoffrey L. 1974. "The Erosion of External Sovereignty." In Ghita Ionescu, ed., *Between Sovereignty and Integration,* 100–17. London: Croom Helm.

Grimm, Dieter. 1986. "The Modern State: Continental Traditions." In Franz-Xaver Kaufmann, Giandomenico Majone, and Vincent Ostrom, eds., *Guidance, Control, and Evaluation in the Public Sector: The Bielefeld Interdisciplinary Project,* 89–109. Berlin: Walter de Gruyter.

Henkin, Louis. 1985. "The Reports of the Death of Article 2(4) Are Greatly Exaggerated." In Richard A. Falk, Friedrich Kratochwil, and Saul H. Mendlovitz, eds., *International Law: A Contemporary Perspective,* 389–93. Boulder, Colo.: Westview Press.

Hill, Christopher. 1984. "Implications of the World Society Perspective for National Policies." In Michael Banks, ed., *Conflict in World Society: A New Perspective on International Relations,* 174–91. Brighton, England: Wheatsheaf Books.

Hinsley, F. H. 1986. *Sovereignty.* 2d ed. Cambridge: Cambridge University Press.

Hollist, W. Ladd and James N. Rosenau, eds. 1981. *World System Structure: Continuity and Change.* Beverly Hills: Sage.

Holsti, Kalevi Jaakko. 1985. *The Dividing Discipline: Hegemony and Diversity in International Theory.* Winchester, Mass.: Allen and Unwin.

Huntington, Samuel P. 1993. "The Clash of Civilizations?" *Foreign Affairs* 72, no. 3: 22–49.

Inkeles, Alex. 1975. "The Emerging Social Structure of the World." *World Politics* 27:467–95.

Ionescu, Ghita, ed. 1974. *Between Sovereignty and Integration.* London: Croom Helm.

Jackson, Robert H. and Carl G. Rosberg. 1982. "Why Africa's Weak States Persist: The Empirical and the Juridical in Statehood." *World Politics* 35 (Oct) 1: 1–24.

Jacobson, Harold K. 1979. *Networks of Interdependence: International Organizations and the Global Political System.* New York: Knopf. 2d ed., 1984.

Jacobson, Harold K., William M. Reisinger, and Todd Mathers. 1986. "National Entanglements in International Governmental Organizations." *American Political Science Review* 80 (March): 141–59.

James, Alan. 1986. *Sovereign Statehood: The Basis of International Society.* London: Allen and Unwin.

Jansen, G. H. 1979. *Militant Islam.* London: Pan Books.

Jenks, C. Wilfred. 1958. *The Common Law of Mankind.* New York: Praeger.

Katzenstein, Peter J., ed. 1978. *Between Power and Plenty: Foreign Economic Policies of Advanced Industrial States*. Madison: University of Wisconsin Press.

Kaufmann, Franz-Xaver. 1986. "The Blurring of the Distinction 'State Versus Society.' " In Franz-Xaver Kaufmann, Giandomenico Majone, and Vincent Ostrom, eds., *Guidance, Control, and Evaluation in the Public Sector: The Bielefeld Interdisciplinary Project*, 128–38 Berlin: Walter de Gruyter.

Kaufmann, Franz-Xaver, Giandomenico Majone, and Vincent Ostrom, eds. 1986. *Guidance, Control, and Evaluation in the Public Sector: The Bielefeld Interdisciplinary Project*. Berlin: Walter de Gruyter.

Kavanaugh, Dennis. 1974. "Beyond Autonomy? The Politics of Corporations." In Ghita Ionescu, ed., *Between Sovereignty and Integration*, 46–64. London: Croom Helm.

Keohane, Robert O. 1986. *Neorealism and Its Critics*. New York: Columbia University Press.

Keohane, Robert O. and Joseph S. Nye. 1977. *Power and Interdependence: World Politics in Transition*. Boston: Little, Brown.

Kissinger, Henry A. 1961. *The Necessity of Choice*. New York: Harper and Row.

Klein, Robert A. 1974. *Sovereign Equality Among States: The History of an Idea*. Toronto: University of Toronto Press.

Krasner, Stephen D. 1985. *Structural Conflict: The Third World Against Global Liberalism*. Berkeley: University of California Press.

———. 1988. "Sovereignty: An Institutional Perspective." *Comparative Political Studies* 21, no. 1: 66–94.

Kratochwil, Friedrich. 1985. "The Role of Domestic Courts as Agencies of the International Legal Order." In Richard A. Falk, Friedrich Kratochwil, and Saul H. Mendlovitz, eds., *International Law: A Contemporary Perspective*, 236–63. Boulder, Colo.: Westview Press.

Landheer, B., J. H. M. M. Loenen, and Fred L. Polak, eds. 1971. *World Society: How Is an Effective and Desirable World Order Possible? A Symposium*. The Hague: Martinus Nijhoff.

Laski, Harold J. 1917. *Studies in the Problem of Sovereignty*. New Haven: Yale University Press.

Lauterpacht, H. 1985. "The Grotian Tradition in International Law." In Richard A. Falk, Friedrich Kratochwil, and Saul H. Mendlovitz, eds., *International Law: A Contemporary Perspective*, 10–35. Boulder, Colo.: Westview Press.

Lindberg, Leon N. 1970. "Political Integration as a Multi-Dimensional Phenomenon Requiring Multivariate Measurement." *International Organization* 24 (Autumn): 649–731.

Luard, Evan. 1976. *Types of International Society*. New York: Free Press.

———. 1977. *International Agencies: The Emerging Framework of Interdependence*. London: Macmillan.

Mann, Michael. 1986. *The Sources of Social Power*. Vol. 1, *A History of Power from the Beginning to A.D. 1760*. Cambridge: Cambridge University Press.

———. 1993. *The Sources of Social Power.* Vol. 2, *The Rise of Classes and Nation-States, 1760–1914.* Cambridge: Cambridge University Press.

Manning, C. A. W. 1962. *The Nature of International Society.* London: Bell.

Mansbach, Richard W., Yale H. Ferguson, and Donald E. Lampert. 1976. *The Web of World Politics: Nonstate Actors in the Global System.* Englewood Cliffs, N.J.: Prentice Hall.

Mansbach, Richard W. and John A. Vasquez. 1981. *In Search of Theory: A New Paradigm for Global Politics.* New York: Columbia University Press.

Mayall, James. 1978. "International Society and International Theory." In Michael Donelan, ed., *The Reason of States: A Study in International Political Theory,* 122–41. London: Allen and Unwin.

McDougal, Myres S. and W. Michael Riesman. 1981. *International Law in Contemporary Perspective: The Public Order of the World Community.* Mineola, N.Y.: Foundation Press.

McKinlay, R. D. and R. Little. 1986. *Global Problems and World Order.* London: Frances Pinter.

McLuhan, Marshall and Bruce R. Powers. 1989. *The Global Village: Transformations in World Life and Media in the 21st Century.* New York: Oxford University Press.

Meyer, John W. 1987. "The World Polity and the Authority of the Nation-State." In George M. Thomas, John W. Meyer, Francisco O. Ramirez, and John Boli, *Institutional Structure: Constituting State, Society, and the Individual,* 41–70. Beverly Hills: Sage.

Meyer, John W., John Boli, and George M. Thomas. 1987. "Ontology and Rationalization in the Western Cultural Account." In George M. Thomas, John W. Meyer, Francisco O. Ramirez, and John Boli, *Institutional Structure: Constituting State, Society and the Individual,* 12–37. Beverly Hills: Sage.

Meyer, John W., John Boli, George M. Thomas, and Francisco O. Ramirez. 1997. "World Society and the Nation-State." *American Journal of Sociology* 103, no. 1: 144–81.

Meyer, John W., and Michael T. Hannan, eds. 1979. *National Development in the World System: Educational, Economic, and Political Change, 1950–1970.* Chicago: University of Chicago Press.

Meyer, John W. and W. Richard Scott. 1983. *Organizational Environments: Ritual and Rationality.* Beverly Hills: Sage.

Migdal, Joel S. 1988. *Strong Societies and Weak States: State-Society Relations and State Capabilities in the Third World.* Princeton: Princeton University Press.

Miller, Lynn H. 1985. *Global Order: Values and Power in International Politics.* Boulder, Colo.: Westview Press.

Mitchell, C. R. 1984. "World Society as Cobweb: States, Actors, and Systemic Processes." In Michael Banks, ed., *Conflict in World Society: A New Perspective on International Relations,* 59–77. Brighton, England: Wheatsheaf Books.

Morgenthau, Hans. 1960. *Politics Among Nations: The Struggle for Power and Peace.* New York: Knopf.

Naff, Thomas. 1984. "The Ottoman Empire and the European States System." In Hedley Bull and Adam Watson, ed., *The Expansion of International Society*, 143–70. Oxford: Oxford University Press.

Neale, A. D. and M. L. Stephens. 1988. *International Business and National Jurisdiction*. Oxford: Clarendon.

Nettl, J. P. 1968. "The State as a Conceptual Variable." *World Politics* 20, no. 4: 559–92.

Nettl, J. P. and Roland Robertson. 1968. *International Systems and the Modernization of Societies. The Formation of National Goals and Attitudes*. London: Faber and Faber.

Nordenstreng, Kaarle and Herbert I. Schiller, eds. 1979. *National Sovereignty and International Communication*. Norwood, N.J.: Ablex.

Olmstead, Cecil J., ed. 1984. *Extra-Territorial Application of Laws and Responses Thereto*. Oxford: International Law Association and ESC Publishing.

Paenson, Isaac. 1983. *English-French-Spanish-Russian Manual of the Terminology of Public International Law (Law and Peace) and International Organizations*. Brussels: Bruylant.

Pettman, Ralph. 1979. *State and Class: A Sociology of International Affairs*. London: Croom Helm.

Reynolds, P. A. 1975. "International Studies: Retrospect and Prospect." *British Journal of International Studies* 1 (April): 1–19.

Robertson, Roland. 1987. "Church-State Relations and the World System." In Thomas Robbins and Roland Robertson, eds., *Church-State Relations: Tensions and Transitions*, 39–51. New Brunswick, N.J.: Transaction Books.

Rohn, Peter H. 1974. *World Treaty Index*. 5 vols. Santa Barbara, Calif.: ABC-CLIO Press.

Schmitter, Philippe C. and Gerhard Lehmbruch, eds. 1979. *Trends Toward Corporatist Intermediation*. Beverly Hills: Sage.

Skjelsbaek, Kjell. 1971. "The Growth of International Nongovernmental Organization in the Twentieth Century." *International Organization* 25 (Summer): 420–45.

Smith, Anthony. 1980. *The Geopolitics of Information: How Western Culture Dominates the World*. London: Faber and Faber.

Southern, R. W. 1970. *Western Society and the Church in the Middle Ages*. Harmondsworth, England: Penguin.

Speer, James P. 1985. *World Polity. Conflict and War: History, Causes, Consequences, Cures*. Fort Bragg, Calif.: Q.E.D. Press.

Stone, Julius. 1984. *Visions of World Order: Between State Power and Human Justice*. Baltimore: Johns Hopkins University Press.

Strang, David. 1988. "The Grammar of Sovereignty." Ph.D. diss., Stanford University, Department of Sociology.

Thomas, Caroline. 1985. *New States, Sovereignty, and Intervention*. Aldershot, Hants, England: Gower.

Thomas, George M., John W. Meyer, Francisco O. Ramirez, and John Boli. 1987. *Institutional Structure: Constituting State, Society and the Individual*. Beverly Hills: Sage.

Tierney, Brian. 1964. *The Crisis of Church and State, 1050–1300*. Englewood Cliffs, N.J.: Prentice Hall.

Tilly, Charles, ed. 1975. *The Formation of National States in Western Europe*. Princeton: Princeton University Press.

Ullmann, Walter. 1966. *The Individual and Society in the Middle Ages*. Baltimore: Johns Hopkins University Press.

United Nations. 1973. *Multinational Corporations in World Development*. New York: Department of Economic and Social Affairs, United Nations.

———. 1983. *Multinational Corporations in World Development: Third Survey*. New York: Department of Economic and Social Affairs, United Nations.

Vernon, Raymond. 1971. *Sovereignty at Bay: The Multinational Spread of US Enterprises*. Harmondsworth, England: Penguin.

Wallerstein, Immanuel. 1974. *The Modern World-System: Capitalist Agriculture and the Origins of the European World-Economy in the Sixteenth Century*. New York: Academic Press.

———. 1980. *The Modern World-System II: Mercantilism and the Consolidation of the European World-Economy*. New York: Academic Press.

Watson, Adam. 1992. *The Evolution of International Society*. London: Routledge.

Weston, Burns H., Richard A. Falk, and Anthony A. D'Amato. 1980. *International Law and World Order: A Problem-Oriented Coursebook*. St. Paul, Minn.: West.

Wildavsky, Aaron. 1979. *Speaking Truth to Power: The Art and Craft of Policy Analysis*. Boston: Little, Brown.

Willets, Peter. 1988. "The United Nations as a Political System." In Paul Taylor and A. J. R. Groom, eds., *International Institutions at Work*, 21–38. London: Pinter.

———, ed. 1982. *Pressure Groups in the Global System: The Transnational Relations of Issue-Orientated Non-Governmental Organizations*. London: Pinter.

4

The Issue of Sovereignty
in the Asian Historical Context

MICHEL OKSENBERG

Stephen Krasner poses an interesting and important question: does the concept of sovereignty and its associated ideas, on which so much of international relations appears to be based, preclude solutions to a number of the world's pressing contemporary problems?

In a series of studies, through careful analyses of four analytically distinct meanings of "sovereignty" and a demonstration of the many and varied departures in behavior from each of these meanings, Krasner has illuminated the fluidity of the concept.[1] Krasner considers the discrepancy between the professed ideals embodied in the notion and the actual behavior of its adherents to be "organized hypocrisy." He amasses impressive evidence to document the extraordinary flexibility of contemporary international arrangements, and concludes that sovereignty—so central to notions in Western political theory about interstate relations and the nature of the state—is not a confining or constraining concept. It appears to be infinitely malleable in the hands of leaders who are willing to interpret or ignore it in ways that suit their immediate needs and interests.

To quote from the conclusion of Krasner's *Sovereignty: Organized Hypocrisy:* "Domestic political institutions . . . can be set in a hierarchical structure of authority and underpinned by widely shared values. International institutions operate in a more fluid environment. There are no constitutive rules that preclude rulers from contracting to establish whatever kind of institutional form might serve their needs."[2]

In fact, Krasner's argument is subtle. He does not say that norms, concepts, or ideas of rulers are irrelevant in explaining their behavior. Rather, he asserts, "Norms in the international system will be *less constraining* than would be the case in other political settings because of conflicting logics of appropriateness, the absence of mechanisms for deciding among competing rules, and power asymmetries among states."[3] Elsewhere, he describes the Westphalian model of sovereignty as a "well understood cognitive script, one that is sometimes honored and sometimes not."[4] Krasner explains that scripts are classificatory schemes—cognitive models that filter perceptions and suggest behavior.

Elsewhere, to be sure, Krasner appears to embrace the notion that rulers in the anarchic international system are totally unbound by norms and rules. "Rulers, not states—and not the international system—make choices about policies, rules, and institutions."[5] And they choose what they wish on the basis of their interests. However, in an important qualification, Krasner then acknowledges that whether rulers violate or adhere to international principles or rules is based on calculations of material *and ideational* interest.[6] Phrasing the same argument differently, he notes, "The international system is an environment in which the logics of consequences *dominate* the logics of appropriateness."[7] In short, leaders tend to be more concerned with outcomes than rules. However, values and concepts do affect behavior, although less so if they are murky and unenforceable. Ideas matter but do not dictate behavior.

This article elaborates upon the opening that Krasner has provided. More specifically, it seeks to develop and defend this position: the organizing concepts that leaders and led throughout today's world believe should undergird the international system structure their range of choice and tilt them toward some solutions over others. These concepts, of which sovereignty is central, permit a wide range of choice. They are not very constraining. But adherence to them creates certain tendencies, propensities, or predispositions to accept some solutions more readily than others. They render some solutions of the past less viable today and enable solutions today that were inconceivable in the past. They weight choice in certain directions, still permitting choice in many different directions but making some choices more difficult than others.

From this point of view, the wide range of practices that can be observed within a world that professes adherence to the concept of sovereignty need not suggest the concept poses no constraints. It may be a sufficiently loose concept—as Krasner amply demonstrates—that leaders who profess adherence to it can engage in a wide range of practices and obtain peaceful remedies to most of the world's seemingly intractable interstate and intrastate disputes. Yet it may be a sufficiently compelling or disciplining concept that leaders imbued with it will be more inclined to prefer some solutions than others and hence be reluctant to embrace some of the available remedies. Thus, such current arrangements as those involving Taiwan, Andorra, the European Union, and General Noriega point to the flexibility of the international system and the norms that justify it, as Krasner stresses, but as he also notes, such arrangements are unusual. And the paucity of such arrangements suggests that sovereignty and its associated ideas discourage or discipline leaders from readily, widely, and regularly accepting them.

Further, the concept of sovereignty is not static or uniform. Its meanings have changed over time and assume different guises in different locales. In particular, its associated concepts have undergone continual evolution. At one point, as the word suggests, sovereignty was linked to the notion of monarchy—*the* sovereign—and even to coinage. The self-determination of a government that was to be respected was the right of a ruler to order his realm as he chose, not the self-determination of a people to be ruled as they chose. Hence, sensitivity to time and place is required. Sovereignty may not be confining in some places or during one time span, but it may be quite confining in another context. Diverse behavior among nations in the international arena may not demonstrate the fluidity of the concept in a ruler's mind. It may mean different rulers are constrained by the concept in different ways.

Central to the question Krasner poses, in short, is the issue of evidence. Without denying the critical importance and relevance of the evidence that Krasner employs—the wide range of practices both in the past and present within interstate systems that accept sovereignty as a guiding norm—another dimension merits exploration: what do specific political leaders believe sovereignty to entail? Ascertaining the beliefs of political leaders, to state the obvious, is tricky business. But one observation is certain: few political leaders have as sophisticated and nuanced an understanding of the concept as Krasner does. Most probably operate under a more simplistic and blunt appreciation of the concept. And at this individual level, the concept could frequently be confining. The implications of this observation are discussed in the conclusion.

It is worth noting too that the meanings of sovereignty, as Krasner's writings recognize, grow out of Western theories of interstate relations. They are embedded in the interstate system that the Western powers extended to the rest of the world. And with the notion of sovereignty in its full richness of meanings comes other, closely associated concepts: national identity and nationalism; the concept of the nation-state; the right of nations to self-determination; the regulation of interstate relations through international law; national independence and the need for well-delineated boundaries separating nation-states. While sovereignty does not include all these concepts within its broad definition, many of these ancillary notions either are implicit in or follow logically from the concept of sovereignty. In short, to ask whether sovereignty is a constraining concept is almost like asking whether the entire conceptual basis of the current system of interstate relations is constraining.

Other interstate systems such as city leagues, protectorates, satrapies, tributary states, and empires did not enshrine sovereignty. Through a comparison of various types of interstate systems, one can identify the effect of the notion of sovereignty and its associated concepts. That is, many non-Western interstate systems did not have sovereignty in all four of Krasner's meanings as an organizing concept before the coming of the West. Sovereignty entered the lexicon of these cultures and polities with the arrival of the West. In many parts of the globe before the nineteenth century, states, kingdoms, tribes, and empires interacted untutored or undisciplined by the concept of sovereignty in the full, four meanings that Krasner elaborates in his introductory essay to this volume. Western expansion imposed the concept upon the world.

Analogous or similar indigenous concepts, to be sure, may have existed, such as the notion of one final source of authority within the state (for example, in China, the monopoly of authority vested in the imperial institution) or the right of rulers to regulate the movements of people into and out of their domain (a right asserted by the Chinese, Korean, and Japanese rulers before the word *sovereignty* was imported into their languages). But the concept in its full and rich meanings was not present in much of the globe until fairly recently.

Thus, students of international relations enjoy an interesting opportunity. They can attempt to assess whether solutions to certain types of interstate problems that vex the contemporary world were perhaps more or less easily reached within systems where the notion of sovereignty in its full array of meanings was absent. That is to say, if the viability of institutional arrangements in today's global system depends solely on the power and interests of actors and is not significantly constrained by the international institutional environment, then we should expect interstate behavior in the contemporary world to exhibit greater or at least the same latitude of choice as in systems that did not harbor the notion of sovereignty.

But the comparison of different interstate systems is fraught with methodological difficulties. Today's interstate system is global and exists in a demographically and technologically transformed world, with rulers commanding modern weaponry, while the interstate systems of earlier eras were regional and linked preindustrial societies that did not have access to weapons of mass destruction. One cannot ascertain conclusively whether differences among distinctive interstate systems in their preference for certain kinds of interstate arrangements over others are attributable, on the one hand, to differences in their organizing concepts, or on the other hand, to differences in their scope, technologies, and destructive capabilities.

Despite these methodological difficulties, this essay engages in such a "macrocomparison." It explores how the introduction of the concept of sovereignty to East Asia has affected the way in which the rulers of China approach their policies toward Taiwan, Tibet, and Hong Kong. It compares policies of the deep past with those of the present. It first sketches the nature of the East Asian system in the early 1800s, both in terms of the myths or ideals about the system and in terms of its actual operation. It examines the Taiwan, Hong Kong, and Tibet "solutions" prior to the Western penetration and compares them with China's current posture toward its peripheral areas. This prompts speculation about how the changes in conceptualization of interstate relations have altered the goals, calculus, and practice of leaders and led alike.

The paper concludes that the importation of sovereignty in its full meanings — especially the Westphalian notions of territoriality and autonomy and the notion of international recognition as a defining characteristic of nationhood — has had a profound impact on the aspirations of all the actors involved. Because the concept of sovereignty and its associated notions now structure the East Asian regional system, solutions available in the early 1800s are now much more difficult to achieve, while other solutions, inconceivable in the 1800s, have become possible. The arrival of sovereignty in its full meaning still leaves the actors with a wide range of choice, with many solutions more optimal than current tension-producing arrangements. In this regard, this essay supports Krasner's observations about the flexibility of the current international system. But it also concludes that the notion of sovereignty makes certain ambiguous solutions of the past concerning the status of Taiwan, Tibet, and Hong Kong more difficult, and in this sense the concept constrains practitioners of the statecraft practiced under its banner. Further, the increasing association of sovereignty with self-determination and democracy offers new solutions and poses additional difficulties to prior arrangements. To return to Krasner's terminology, sovereignty provides a "script" with which to analyze issues and prescribe remedies. And the script presents a different analytical framework than an interstate system that operates without it.

The East Asian Regional System in the Early 1800s

The imperial Manchu court—the Qing dynasty—in Beijing propagated an elaborate myth about how the emperor and the bureaucracy under his alleged command conducted the empire's affairs with its neighboring kingdoms, nomadic groups, and religious orders. The myth helped sustain the alien Manchu regime (1644–1912) within the domain controlled directly by the emperor's civilian bureaucracy. Kingdoms, nomadic groups, and religious orders outside this domain were reluctant to challenge this construct about how the emperor's rule brought order and morality to the larger region. Moreover, many of the rulers outside the emperor's immediate bureaucratic domain accepted the myth as legitimate; they apparently believed that the principles embodied in the myth were the proper way to organize relations between them and the imperial court in Beijing as well as between them and their own neighbors.

The complex Chinese myth about the East Asian system included these four central features:[8]

• The participating states or protostates dealt with one another at the symbolic level in hierarchical fashion, acknowledging the superiority of the Qing emperor, to whom they paid periodic obeisance through elaborate rituals.

• The authority of the imperial institution, both within and outside its immediate domain, rested upon its moral and cultural superiority. The superior virtue of the emperor enabled him to bring order and prosperity to the realm.

• The authority of the emperor did not end precisely at a boundary. He had the right and obligation to become involved in the affairs of kingdoms, tribes, and religious orders beyond his own domain in order to bring peace and harmony to this larger realm.

• Many rulers on the Chinese periphery—especially in Japan, Korea, and Vietnam—to varying degrees emulated the Chinese system in their internal rule and patterned their relations with their neighbors in ways similar to Chinese rituals.

In many ways, this system at the level of myth or stated ideal stood in stark contrast to the Westphalian ideal. The participants were not equal. Boundaries were not well demarcated. The purpose of the system was to foster virtuous rule; facilitation of commerce was incidental to the system. Personal relations and ritual rather than international law regulated relations among the participants.

The myth about how the East Asian interstate system worked did not coincide with the operational code. Just as Krasner identifies the discrepancies between stated norm and practice in the contemporary world, organized hypocrisy flourished in East Asia:

• Examples exist of agreements between the Chinese government and other governments, with the two interacting as equals, as in the arrangements with Russia in the Treaty of Nerchinsk and the agreement over Nepal in the 1790s. And as Morris Rossabi has argued in his *China Among Equals,* the Chinese imperial institution had a long tradition of interaction with Inner Asian states on equal footing in pre-Qing times.[9]

• Although the Qing court asserted the unquestioned supremacy of its authority within China, it also had a tradition of benevolently allowing aliens to govern themselves when residing within the realm, on the grounds that such people did not have a sufficient degree of cultural attainment and virtue to meet the higher Confucian standards. As John Fairbank noted, herein were the origins of the "treaty port" arrangements with the West that allowed the foreigners to rule themselves within territories assigned to them by the Qing court.[10]

• Although interstate relations ostensibly were not primarily for the purpose of commerce, in fact the kingdoms, tribes, and religious orders that paid obeisance to the Qing court benefited financially from the transaction. The act enabled them to engage in trade, and they received gifts for their recognition of Qing suzerainty.

The imperially propagated ideal about how the imperial institution conducted its external relations was part of a much larger set of myths about the nature of China itself. First, the widely accepted official historiography asserted that each dynasty replicated the previous one. Chinese history was cyclical, characterized by the rise and fall of dynasties following a similar dynamic. As Evelyn Rawski and Pamela Crossley have stressed, this myth was particularly useful to the alien Manchu rulers, who portrayed themselves as keeping within the Chinese tradition and who masked the distinctive aspects of their rule.[11] In fact, each dynasty differed from its predecessor, and each rose and fell for somewhat distinctive reasons. Chinese history more accurately had both developmental and cyclical aspects to it.[12] Second, the origins of Chinese civilization supposedly were in the Wei River valley, near today's Xian, and the Han people then gradually carried their civilization to the lower Yangtze and then to south China. This construction of history neglected the contributions to the Chinese cultural amalgam made by the earlier settlers of the regions near today's Shanghai and Guangzhou and by the people of Inner Asia, the South Asian subcontinent, and Southeast Asia. Chinese culture by the early 1800s was the product of diverse sources absorbed from abroad and within, as the dominant culture gradually incorporated other peoples in its spread over the subcontinent.[13] Third, Chinese statecraft supposedly relied on men of letters—the literati—and the persuasiveness of Confucian moralism, much more than on men of arms and the use of military force, to unify and pacify the realm. As more recent Western writings have noted, this view woefully neglected the role of force in Chinese statecraft.[14] Fourth, the commercial world was supposedly subordinate to the scholar-bureaucrats, an interpretation that understated the political power of merchants and artisans, at least at the lower levels of the bureaucratic hierarchy.[15] Finally, the official ideology attributed its origins to Confucius and his disciples, as well as to the Neo-Confucians who helped to revive Confucianism in Song times. It did not acknowledge its intellectual debts to other strands of thought, such as Chinese Legalism, Daoism, and Buddhism, that had been woven into the fabric of thought. It portrayed a Han people unified by a common culture while neglecting the diversity that existed within Confucian practice at the local levels.[16]

By stressing the continuities of the Chinese system, its indigenous roots, and its uniformity, the myths—which also bore an imperfect relationship to reality—helped to sustain China's fragile unity. China's political integration was always problematic, and inculcation of the myth as the reality and preservation of an illusion that it was being observed by both the imperial court and its subjects, by both those within and outside the realm, were part of the glue keeping the Manchu empire together. The ability of the emperor to exercise his power was intimately related to his ability to maintain the facade of adherence to the ideal. The system demanded opaqueness—in Krasner's terms, required organized hypocrisy—concerning the extent to which the ideal was discarded in practice.

Not surprisingly, therefore, a more pragmatic and realistic operational code guided actual behavior. This operational code owed much to the practices of interstate relations within China during its periods of disunity.[17] The strategies it recommended had many practices in common with Western theories of realpolitik: an appreciation of the use of force, a recognition of balance-of-power politics, an emphasis on intelligence and deception, and the need for flexibility and the burden of alliances in interstate relations. As Alistair Johnston has demonstrated, the Chinese strategic culture—its "operational code"—did not differ significantly from that in the West when it came to such crucial matters as use of force.[18] And in the commercial domain, as the recent and influential writings of William Rowe and Susan Mann have stressed,[19] the operational code acknowledged the value of merchants and trade to the state, as long as their activities did not challenge the prevailing myth of imperial and bureaucratic supremacy and did not cause social disorder. Yet the organized hypocrisy of the traditional East Asian interstate system differed from the West's system of organized hypocrisy. Its "ideal," unlike the Western ideal, lacked the concept of sovereignty; the deviations from the ideal took somewhat different forms of opportunistic behavior than in the West.

Against this background, it becomes possible to understand the traditional approach that the emperor and his institution adopted toward Taiwan, Hong Kong, and Tibet. And we can understand why Western military might and Western organizing concepts destroyed that system of organized hypocrisy and undermined the ideological basis of Manchu rule. Even though some of the concepts of the traditional system remain in the minds of some Chinese leaders, they cannot resurrect the previous system or recreate previous solutions in the new international environment. Many Taiwanese and Tibetans, whose forefathers were content with an ambiguous national identity—indeed were blissfully unaware that they needed to have one—now seek recognition on the world stage as rulers and citizens of a full-fledged nation-state. Rulers who, had they lived in the prior era, would have been comfortable conducting relations with one another under an ambiguous formal status now seek precision and transparency. Today, they demand to be treated as equals. If not, their stature and dignity are adversely affected, and their political standing among their constituencies suffers. Turning specifically to Taiwan, Hong Kong, and Tibet, we can see how the introduction of the Western concept of sovereignty to the equation has altered the structure of choice for both those in Beijing and those in Taipei, Hong Kong, Lhasa, and Dharamsala (the home of the Tibetan government-in-exile). A wide range of possibilities other than the current arrangement still exists in all three cases, but the range is different. In some respects, the latitude of change is more constrained than under a system without the notion of sovereignty, and in other respects, the concept facilitates new arrangements. But the script has been altered in significant ways.

The Solution for Taiwan, Hong Kong, and the China Coast before the Western Arrival

In the early 1800s, the islands along the southeast China coast were only loosely under imperial control. Nominally, they fell within the imperial domain, ruled by civil servants who were part of the Qing bureaucracy. Taiwan was part of Fujian province, the province across the Taiwan strait. Hong Kong was part of Baoan county. Trade supposedly was regulated and channeled through designated ports. The reality was more complex.

As John Fairbank, Paul Cohen, and Mark Mancall have all stressed, from the Tang dynasty, two Chinas existed in uneasy tension: maritime China and bureaucratic China.[20] Maritime China refers to the entrepreneurial and commercial Chinese along the southeast coast who conducted trade and in Ming and Qing times settled in enclaves such as Penang, Malacca, Kuching, today's Bangkok, Manila, and small ports in today's Indonesian archipelago. Bureaucratic China refers to the bearers of the Confucian tradition, suspicious of merchants and the outside world. The two existed in an uneasy symbiotic relationship, each needing the other, yet each perceiving the other as a threat. The bearers of the bureaucratic traditions feared that maritime China threatened China's unity, while the traders devised strategies to minimize the rapaciousness and constraints of bureaucratic China. However, maritime China brought wealth to the relationship while bureaucratic China brought a modicum of order. When the two achieved a balance, the realm flourished. When one or the other totally dominated the relationship, the realm suffered.

Until the early 1800s, Taiwan was at the periphery of maritime China.[21] The island was part of Fujian province. An influx of Han immigrants from Fujian were pushing the earlier settlers into the mountain regions. These indigenous people traced their origins primarily to Southeast Asia and Oceania. The new Han settlers turned the island's marshlands and sparsely populated regions into productive agricultural land. The Qing bureaucracy was not well represented in this marginal part of the empire, and order was largely provided through the rule of several large, wealthy, and powerful clans. Traders used the few small, natural harbors as bases for commerce to the Ryukyus, Korea, and Kyushu to the north and the Philippine and Indonesian islands to the south, as well as with such mainland ports as Xiamen, Fuzhou, Wenzhou, and Ningbo. Much of this trade fell outside the officially sanctioned commerce; local officials were willing to cooperate with the nominally illegal trade—which might be dubbed "piracy" in official reports if it got out of hand—since the fees the bureaucrats charged and the bribes they received helped finance underfunded local government. The prosperity that the tea trade brought to Fujian helped sustain a high-quality educational system in the province that prepared candidates well for the national civil service examination system, thereby feeding bright Fujianese into the civil service system.[22]

Beginning in the 1500s, Portuguese, Dutch, and Spanish traders inserted themselves into this indigenous coastal trading system, plying the waters from today's Nagasaki to the Philippines, the Indonesian archipelago, and then onward to Europe and the New World. Taiwan played a central role in this trade, especially in the 1600s.[23] Real pirates also flourished out of Taiwan harbors, seizing ships also engaged in extralegal trade from Korea, Japan, and the Ryukyus to harbors further south, but as long as their activities were not too disruptive, local officials had minimal incentive to crack down. Crackdowns would signal that not all was well on the China coast; the myth would be called into question. From the vantage of local officials, it was better to preserve the myth and report that all was well than to report that the system was eroding. Local officials would bear the brunt of imperial displeasure over lapses in the system.

More extensive trade centered further south, at Guangzhou in the Pearl River delta. Here, at appointed times in accord with the imperial system, a thriving trade flowed to Southeast Asian ports and even South Asia. Portugal had acquired Macao in 1557 to facilitate its participation in trade flowing to and from the delta. John Fairbank's classic *Trade and Diplomacy Along the China Coast* and Michael Greenberg's study of the arrival of British traders recount how the British in the late 1700s at first fit in, then built upon, and by the mid-1800s outgrew this trading system and supplied Chinese appetites for new products—especially opium.[24] Stimulated by their greater naval power and commercial interests as well as their different concepts of how an interstate system should be organized, the British sought unfettered access to Chinese markets and treatment as equals by the Chinese government.

The clash of interests and ideologies from 1839 to 1901 resulted in three major military engagements between the British and Chinese, the dispatch of British forces to occupy Beijing on two occasions, and the subversion of the Qing system of rule. Concepts of sovereignty, modern nation-states, nationalism, and national autonomy penetrated China and altered views of how China should conduct its interstate relations. New institutions were developed in order to enable the Qing to conduct a foreign policy along Western lines. But these efforts proved inadequate to the challenge, especially because the external crisis coincided with severe domestic problems.

Foreign powers saw in the decline of the Qing state opportunities for themselves. Britain gained Hong Kong in 1842, adding to its territory too in 1861 and 1898. Japan embarked on its own pattern of imperialism, obtaining Taiwan as a colony through the Treaty of Shimoneseki following the Sino-Japanese War of 1894–95. Other powers gained spheres of influence. The traditional Chinese system of organized hypocrisy along the China coast proved unable to withstand a militarily and conceptually more powerful way of organizing the region.

The Chinese-Tibetan Relationship before the Western Arrival

Modern Tibet dates to the seventeenth century.[25] Throughout the Ming dynasty (1368–1644), Tibet was plagued by clashing sects of Tibetan Buddhism and rivalries among different tribes. Ming influence in the region was minimal. Rather, the Mongols projected military force even to Lhasa. And a portion of the Mongols, who themselves were deeply divided, assisted in the ascent of the Dalai Lama and his sect. In 1642, backed by Mongol military force, the Fifth Dalai Lama unified Tibet, basing his fusion of religious and spiritual authority in Lhasa. The extent of his authority waxed and waned in subsequent decades depending on the moral authority each Dalai Lama was able to gather and the political cunningness of his regents and advisers. The Qing became deeply immersed in Tibetan politics in the 1600s and 1700s, stationing a small garrison and appointing a permanent representative in Lhasa in 1720.

Politically, from the 1600s on, several Dalai Lamas entered into un-ambiguously tributary relations with the imperial court, and on several oc-casions, a Dalai Lama sought political and military intervention by Qing authorities. The imperial court also involved itself in age-old rivalries among the Tibetan monasteries, cultivating some and thereby alienating others. Bei-jing frequently had a closer relationship with the Panchen Lama and mon-asteries near Shigatse than it did with the Dalai Lama in Lhasa. During the Qing dynasty, emissaries from Tibet were invited to join leaders of other Inner Asian kingdoms, tribes, and other types of political entities who gath-ered at Chengde, several hundred kilometers north of Beijing, to pay obei-sance to the emperor. The Qing court retreated to Chengde in the summer and held court for those Inner Asian leaders who looked upon the emperor as their protector and patron. To make the Tibetans feel at home at Chengde, the Qing constructed a replica of the Potala in Lhasa. All these dimensions of the imperial-Tibet relationship might suggest Chinese suze-rainty.

In reality, however, Qing political involvement in Tibet was superficial, sporadic, and often by invitation, while the influence of Tibet on China was slight. As Warren Smith notes in his summary, the Qing regarded Tibet as a "dependent ally."[26] It was neither part of the "interior empire," which the Qing ruled directly, nor outside the imperial realm. It was treated as part of the "exterior empire," within the realm but not part of the interior realm. As the Qing emperor Qianlong claimed in 1787, when referring to an envoy of the Dalai Lama: "The Interior and Exterior of our Empire are only family. Moreover, Tibet has long been incorporated into our territory, and should not be compared with Russia, which is still savage." Smith labels Tibet as a "pro-tectorate," with the extent of Qing intervention and rule varying both geo-graphically and temporally. Smith concludes that the Qing regarded all three portions of the area that most Tibetans consider to be their territory—central Tibet, Kham to its east, and Amdo to its northeast—to have been in the process of full assimilation into its direct political administration, a process beginning in the most accessible areas of Amdo and proceeding south and westward toward the central region.

Qing administrative control over Tibet reached its apogee in the 1700s and then gradually declined in the 1800s. The ebbing Chinese influence coincided with increased British activity in the Himalayan states of Nepal, Bhutan, and Sikkim, which had paid obeisance to the Dalai Lama, and as the nineteenth century wore on, the British became more interested in Tibet itself, particularly the western region where mountain passes granted access to India from Central Asia. The British feared that Russia might seek to extend its influence from Central Asia to Tibet and then to India itself. In response to the increasing British presence, the Dalai Lama sought to keep the Qing involved in Tibet, and he and his advisers inflated Chinese strength to deter British penetration.

Today, proponents of an independent Tibet assert that Tibet was never under the extensive control of a Han Chinese government, that the two periods of maximum imperial control occurred in the alien Yuan and Qing dynasties, when China was under Mongol and Manchu rule, and that the Thirteenth Dalai Lama declared independence in 1913 when Tibetans expelled remnant Qing forces garrisoned in Tibet. However, Beijing claims that for centuries, Tibet has been a part of China except during those periods when China lacked a central government. Neither the Qing nor its successor governments ever acknowledged the Dalai Lama's claim of independence. And throughout the twentieth century all the major powers accepted Chinese claims of sovereignty over Tibet. In fact, as a cursory reading of modern Tibetan history reveals, relations between the imperial government in Beijing and the leading Buddhist lamas of the Tibetan theocracy were sufficiently ambiguous and varied over time and place to make both claims credible. The situation was multilayered.

In the religious domain, although both Tibetan Buddhism and Chinese Buddhism fall within the Mahayana school or sect of Buddhism, significant differences separate the two. Tibetan Buddhism is an amalgam of Buddhist influences from India and China as well as original Tibetan Bon animistic traditions. In both the Yuan and Qing dynasties, the imperial court patronized Tibetan Buddhism (such as building and supporting the Yong-he gong, the ornate Tibetan Buddhist temple in the northeast quarter of Beijing) less out of religious conviction than as a technique for asserting imperial influence over Tibet. Nonetheless, Tibetans could interpret the patronage as an acknowledgment of the spiritual authority of the incarnate lamas.

According to Joseph Fletcher, "From the Qing point of view, the Dalai Lama was a mighty ecclesiastic and a holy being, but nonetheless the emperor's protégé. From the Tibetan point of view, the emperor was merely the Lama's secular patron. This meant that in Tibetans' eyes the Dalai Lama's position was superior to that of the Qing emperor, because in Tibet . . . the monastic community was the ruling body, and lay persons, no matter how rich or powerful, were thus in a subordinate position. The Tibetan government was well aware of the Qing view of the matter, but it was impolite for the Tibetans to question the Qing interpretation."[27]

The complexity of Qing-Tibetan relations was evident from the outset.[28] In late 1652, just eight years after the founding of the new dynasty, the Fifth Dalai Lama journeyed to meet the Shunzhi emperor. Overlapping interests drove the two together. The Qing wished to prevent Mongol-Tibetan cooperation against the Qing; the Dalai Lama sought enhanced stature against rival Tibetan lamas and their external supporters. The Dalai Lama suggested a locale outside the Great Wall. The emperor consulted his advisers before responding to a request that apparently would have been unprecedented in Chinese protocol. According to Warren Smith, "To journey outside the wall would have symbolized an alliance between two Inner Asian — Tibetan and Manchu — powers and implied less than submission of the Dalai Lama to the Manchu."[29] Smith also notes, "A visit to Beijing signified submission, at least in a nominal sense, within the protocol of China and Inner Asia."[30]

In the end, the Dalai Lama proceeded to Beijing. On January 15, 1653, the Dalai Lama had an audience with the emperor, but he stopped thirty feet short of the throne. He did not perform the ritual *koutou* (three kneelings and nine head knockings), and the emperor descended from his usual throne. The emperor assumed the superior position, facing south as demanded by Chinese cosmology, and his temporary throne was higher than the seat of the Dalai Lama. Concerning this delicate exchange, Smith concludes that although Tibetan Buddhist historians interpreted the historic journey as the beginning of independent rule of the Dalai Lamas, the same event may be seen as the beginning of Tibet's subservience to China. For independent leaders of state did not travel to meet each other in those days. Only vassals and envoys entered the Forbidden City.

Also emblematic of the deliberately fostered ambiguity was the method of selecting the high-level incarnated lamas: the Dalai Lama, the Panchen Lama, and so on. Again to quote from Fletcher:

> The traditional method had been based on a series of tests (administered by Buddhist clerics), such as the ability of the infant candidate to distinguish objects that had belonged to his previous incarnation. The winning candidate had customarily been a nobleman on whom the chief Tibetan officials agreed. In 1793 the Qing Emperor had sent a golden urn to Lhasa, ordering that thenceforth the names of the leading candidates should be written on

slips of paper and placed in the urn, then drawn by lot. The Qing court decreed that the candidates should be commoners, and had sent the urn to prevent Tibetan officials from choosing the Dalai Lama in accordance with the interests of the dominant political group among the nobility. From the Qing point of view, it was also unthinkable that an important dignitary like the Dalai Lama should be chosen by any system that excluded the emperor's authority . . . . Upon the death of the Dalai Lama, therefore, the Lhasa government was obliged both to lead the Tibetan public to suppose that the traditional method of selection had been used and at the same time to reassure the Qing authorities that the Dalai Lama had in fact been selected by lot from the urn.[31]

Fletcher states that the extent to which the lottery-run urn was actually used remains a mystery, though it probably was used in 1841 and 1858. Fletcher concludes, "The Tibetans were willing to use the urn to keep up the semblance of Qing protection when the imperial power was weak, but when the Qing was strong, the Tibetans left some doubt about the urn's use so as to emphasize Tibetan autonomy."[32]

Using another script that lacked the concept of sovereignty, the Qing and the Dalai Lama and his supporters created a complex and changing relationship. Today, with a different script in a different technological era, neither the rulers in Beijing nor the Dalai Lama and his supporters are prepared to tolerate the ambiguity that their predecessors embraced for nearly three centuries.

The Current Situation

This article does not need to recount the course of events along the China coast and in Tibet in the twentieth century. Rather, it seeks to demonstrate that a set of arrangements that were viable in the past, rooted in another system of interstate relations, cannot be recreated in today's interstate system. In that sense, the concept of sovereignty and its associated ideas are confining. The rulers in Beijing, Taipei, Lhasa, and Dharamsala have a different set of aspirations and understandings about how the interstate system should work than their predecessors. They have been influenced by Western notions, and they also labor under imperfect understandings of their own past and of the meanings of sovereignty. Imbued with a sense of nationalism and suffering from the scars of China's encounter with the outside world, China's elderly leaders feel obligated to assert their right to rule over all territory they believe their imperial predecessors controlled. (Mongolia is an important exception, and when this exception is raised in discussion with Chinese strategic thinkers and foreign policy analysts, it raises clear discomfort. Down deep, many Chinese probably believe Mongolia should be within their domain.) The rulers in Beijing believe that the concept of sovereignty, as they understand its meaning, strengthens their historical claim to both Taiwan and Tibet.

Meanwhile, in Taiwan, self-identities are changing. A populace once content to conceive of itself as Chinese is beginning to think of itself as a Taiwanese nation. Many on the island aspire to the designation of a nation-state equal in status, dignity, and international recognition to that of the People's Republic. They seek sovereignty in all of its meanings.

Taiwanese President Lee Teng-hui gave expression to this yearning in his controversial May 1999 formulation that the People's Republic and Taiwan were two equal states. Lee stated that the PRC must acknowledge this situation before discussions between the two sides can take place. While insisting Taiwan was a province of the PRC, the Beijing precondition for negotiations was a Taiwan acknowledgment that there is "one China" and Taiwan is a part of it. The two sides could discuss what "one China" meant. Hence, Beijing's position left open the possibility that negotiations could proceed with the two sides differing on the respective status: Beijing claiming the meeting was between center and province; Taipei asserting the meeting was between equals. The Lee Teng-hui insistence on Beijing's recognition of equality precludes such ambiguity. Each side, committed to the concept of sovereignty, interprets its meaning to its liking.

While the majority on the island is not yet prepared to carry this claim to its logical conclusion and formally proclaim independence, enough voters in a now democratic polity are of this persuasion to be a major constraining force on the leaders. In no small measure, the power of a powerful and attractive set of ideas—of which sovereignty is central—threatens the continued viability of a "solution" that has existed for forty years: the People's Republic of China and the Republic of China, each claiming to be the legitimate government of one China, coexisting in an uneasy, tension-ridden truce. The damage that would be wrought by military conflict and the economic benefits that would be derived from accommodation impel both sides to reach a new "solution." But deep distrust and animosity between the two and their different understandings of the meaning of sovereignty—an ideal both cherish—constrain reaching a new solution.

Hong Kong demonstrates the validity of the Krasner point. There, a solution of "one country, two systems" has been accepted by the international system. Hong Kong is part of the World Trade Organization; China is not. The court of final jurisdiction must have foreign representation. The Chinese People's Liberation Army is based in Hong Kong, but the Hong Kong government controls the movement of goods and people across its border and manages its own currency. The ingenious set of arrangements and the rest of the world's embrace of it underscores the flexibility inherent in the international system. Few other than Hong Kong democratic forces and their supporters claim that the solution does injustice to the concept of sovereignty in its full meaning.

But one must also ask why this Rube Goldberg arrangement, so susceptible to breakdown, was necessary in the first place and why Deng Xiaoping demonstrated such ingenuity in conceiving of it. All the authoritative accounts by Percy Craddock, Michael Yahuda, Stephen Chang, and Jonathan Dimbleby trace the origins to the 1979 approach of Governor Murray MacLehose and then the disastrous Prime Minister Thatcher 1982 visit, when Deng emphatically rejected British offers to return the sovereignty of Hong Kong to China while Britain remained on as administrator of the Chinese territory. Deng's posture can be explained in this fashion, though no citation can be offered to prove it: Deng's pragmatism required a solution that would continue the economic benefits that China derived from Hong Kong, while his nationalism and his interpretation of sovereignty impelled him to terminate the British presence and assert PRC authority over the territory. The defining moment came with his almost off-the-cuff remark that, of course, the PLA would be stationed in Hong Kong after reversion. (Neither Deng nor Jiang Zemin has insisted that the PLA should be based in Taiwan, but that in my opinion is due to the Chineseness of the ROC military.) In short, the concept of sovereignty proved flexible enough to permit a creative solution to a difficult problem but was sufficiently constraining in the way Deng interpreted it to preclude Hong Kong's enjoyment of self-determination and an independent status in world affairs.

The Tibet issue is perhaps the clearest case where the repertoire of solutions drawn from the sovereignty medicinal kit seems inadequate to the challenge at hand; indeed by introducing concepts of independence and autonomy, the kit has probably compounded the problems. Let us be clear.

The underlying problem is not conceptual in nature. Rather, as elsewhere in the world, practitioners of lowland sedentary agriculture and bearers of industrial civilization—the Han—are pressing upon a largely nomadic and upland people. The clash has been tragic wherever it has occurred. National security concerns and long-term economic interests also spur the Chinese central government to assert greater control over the region than it had in the past.

But ideas imported from the West also intrude. The brutal Han suppression of the traditional Buddhist religious system since the mid-1950s has been the primary factor generating resentment of Han rule among the Tibetan populace. But that resentment can be more easily conceived and articulated now that the ideas of independence, autonomy, self-rule, democracy, and freedom are part of the intellectual milieu, especially among the exile Tibetan community. External support has been available in fluctuating amounts since the mid-1950s, giving encouragement to those who might otherwise have been quiescent or suppressed. Demands are being made for delineated boundaries and cultural exclusivity that surely would not have been made in the past. For example, the exile community is becoming more insistent of the reunification of all territory previously inhabited by Tibetans, and some Tibetans speak of removing the Han who have settled in these areas over the past fifty years and more. Younger Tibetans residing abroad are showing signs of disenchantment with the Dalai Lama's commitment to nonviolence and his willingness to accept a solution of less than independence. Those most familiar with the situation in Tibet have a sense of foreboding about the future of its culture and its people.

This is not to say that the international system offers no better remedies for Taiwan, Hong Kong, and Tibet. The concept of sovereignty, as Krasner argues so well, has ample room for a rich range of solutions. A China explicitly organized along confederal lines would seem to be in the interests of all concerned, including Beijing. But in Taiwan, Hong Kong, and Tibet, significant portions of the populace want more. They seek well-defined boundaries, leaders that they can choose, symbols that signify the equality of the international status of their leaders with the leaders of other entities—especially those residing in Beijing—and the right to conduct their own foreign policy. All these notions, as this article has stressed, have come to the region with the notion of sovereignty. And in this sense, the concept constrains the range of viable choice available to the leaders in Taipei, Beijing, Lhasa, and Dharamsala.

Notes

1. Krasner 1999a, 1999b; Krasner, "Problematic Sovereignty," in this volume.
2. Krasner 1999b:238.
3. Krasner 1999b:6 (emphasis added).
4. Krasner 1999b:69.
5. Krasner 1999b:7.
6. Krasner 1999b:9.
7. Krasner 1999b:6 (emphasis added).
8. Fairbank 1968.
9. Rossabi 1975, 1983.
10. Fairbank 1964.
11. Crossley 1997.
12. Hucker 1975.
13. No single source has fully developed this view. It arises from recent archaeological findings that reveal an earlier and wider existence of pottery and bronzes that previously were attributed to the inhabitants of the Wei River valley. Moreover, evidence is accumulating of greater contact between early Chinese and other civilizations.
14. Waldron 1990; Johnston 1995.
15. Rowe 1984, 1989; Mann 1987.
16. De Bary 1960, 1983; Schwartz 1964, 1985; Elman 1984.
17. Johnston 1995; Walker 1953; Wang 1963.
18. Johnston 1995.
19. Rowe 1984, 1989; Mann 1987.
20. Cohen 1984; Fairbank and Goldman 1998; Mancall 1984; Cohen 1997.
21. For the history of Taiwan, see Wills 1974; Myers 1972a, 1972b, 1973; Gold 1986.
22. Gardella 1994, ch. 1.
23. Wills 1974.
24. Fairbank 1964; Greenberg 1951.
25. Beckwith 1989; Fletcher 1978; Goldstein 1989, 1997; Grunfeld 1987; Richardson 184; Crossley 1997; Smith 1996; Stein 1972.
26. Smith 1996:145–49.
27. Fletcher 1978:101.
28. Smith 1996:108–13.
29. Smith 1996:111.
30. Smith 1996:111.
31. Fletcher 1978:101–2.
32. Fletcher 1978:102.

References

Barfield, Thomas J. 1989. *The Perilous Frontier: Nomadic Empires and China, 221 B.C. to A.D. 1757.* Cambridge, Mass.: Blackwell.

Beckwith, Christopher I. 1987. *The Tibetan Empire in Central Asia*. Princeton: Princeton University Press.

Boorman, Scott A. 1969. *The Protracted Game: A Wei-ch'i Interpretation of Maoist Revolutionary Strategy*. New York: Oxford University Press.

Cheong Weng Eang. 1997. *Hong Merchants of Canton: Chinese Merchants in Sino-Western Trade, 1684–1798*. Richmond, Surrey, United Kingdom: Curzon Press.

Cohen, Paul. 1984. *Discovering History in China: American Historical Writing on the Recent Chinese Past*. New York: Columbia University Press.

Crossley, Pamela 1997. *The Manchus*. London and New York: Blackwell.

De Bary, William Theodore, ed. 1960. *Introduction to Oriental Civilizations: Sources of Chinese Tradition*. New York: Columbia University Press.

———. 1983. *The Liberal Tradition in China*. New York: Columbia University Press.

Elman, Benjamin A. 1984. *From Philosophy to Philology: Intellectual and Social Aspects of Change in Late Imperial China*. Cambridge: Harvard University Press.

Fairbank, John. 1961. "The Ch'ing Tributary System." In *Ch'ing Administration*, 107–60. Cambridge: Harvard University Press.

———. 1964. *Trade and Diplomacy on the China Coast: The Opening of the Treaty Ports, 1842–1854*. Cambridge: Harvard University Press.

———, ed. 1968. *The Chinese World Order: Traditional China's Foreign Relations*. Cambridge: Harvard University Press.

Fairbank, John and Merle Goldman. 1998. *China: A New History*. Cambridge: Belknap Press of Harvard University Press.

Fletcher, J. 1978. "Ch'ing Inner Asia and the Heyday of the Ch'ing Order in Mongolia, Sinkiang and Tibet." In *The Cambridge History of China*, vol. 10, 35–38, 351–95.

Gardella, Robert 1994. *Harvesting Mountains: Fujian and the China Tea Trade, 1757–1937*. Berkeley and Los Angeles: University of California Press.

Gold, Thomas B. 1986. *State and Society in the Taiwan Miracle*. Armonk, N.Y.: M. E. Sharpe.

Goldstein, Melvyn C. 1989. *A History of Modern Tibet, 1913–1951*. Berkeley: University of California Press.

———. 1997. *The Snow Lion and the Dragon: China, Tibet, and the Dalai Lama*. Berkeley: University of California Press.

Greenberg, Michael. 1951. *British Trade and the Opening of China, 1800–42*. Cambridge: Cambridge University Press.

Grunfield, A. T. 1987. *The Making of Modern Tibet*. Armonk, N.Y.: M. E. Sharpe.

Hucker, Charles O. 1975. *China's Imperial Past: An Introduction to Chinese History and Culture*. Stanford: Stanford University Press.

Johnston, Alastair Iain 1995. *Cultural Realism: Strategic Culture and Grand Strategy in Chinese History*. Princeton: Princeton University Press.

Krasner, Stephen D. 1999a. "Globalization and Sovereignty." In David A. Smith, Dorothy J. Solinger, and Steven C. Topik, eds., *States and Sovereignty in the Global Economy*, 34–52. London and New York: Routledge.

————. 1999b. *Sovereignty: Organized Hypocrisy*. Princeton: Princeton University Press.

Mancall, Mark. 1984. *China at the Center: 300 Years of Foreign Policy*. New York: Free Press.

Mann, Susan. 1987. *Local Merchants and the Chinese Bureaucracy, 1750–1950*. Stanford: Stanford University Press.

Myers, Ramon. 1972a. "Taiwan Under Ch'ing Imperial Rule, 1684–1895: The Traditional Economy." *Journal of the Institute of Chinese Studies of the Chinese University of Hong Kong* 5, no. 2: 373–409.

————. 1972b. "Taiwan Under Ch'ing Imperial Rule, 1684–1895: The Traditional Society." *Journal of the Institute of Chinese Studies of the Chinese University of Hong Kong* 5, no. 2: 413–51.

————. 1973. "Taiwan as an Imperial Colony of Japan: 1895–1945." *Journal of the Institute of Chinese Studies of the Chinese University of Hong Kong* 6, no. 2: 425–51.

Richardson, Hugh E. 1984. *Tibet and Its History*. Boulder, Colo.: Shambala Books.

Rossabi, Morris. 1975. *China and Inner Asia: From 1368 to the Present Day*. New York: PICA Press.

————, ed. 1983. *China Among Equals: The Middle Kingdom and Its Neighbors, 10th–14th Centuries*. Berkeley and Los Angeles: University of California Press.

Rowe, William T. 1984. *Hankow: Commerce and Society in a Chinese City, 1796–1889*. Stanford: Stanford University Press.

————. 1989. *Hankow: Conflict and Community in a Chinese City, 1796–1895*. Stanford: Stanford University Press.

Schwartz, Benjamin I. 1964. *In Search of Wealth and Power*. Cambridge: Belknap Press of Harvard University Press.

————. 1985. *The World of Thought in Ancient China*. Cambridge: Belknap Press of Harvard University Press.

Smith, Warren W., Jr. 1996. *Tibetan Nation: A History of Tibetan Nationalism and Sino-Tibetan Relations*. Boulder, Colo.: Westview Press.

Stein, R. A. 1972. *Tibetan Civilization*. London: Faber and Faber.

Vogel, Ezra F., ed. 1997. *Living with China: U.S.-China Relations in the Twenty-First Century*. New York and London: Norton.

Waldron, Andrew. 1990. *The Great Wall of China: From History to Myth*. New York: Cambridge University Press.

Walker, Richard Louis. 1953. *The Multi-State System of Ancient China*. New Haven, Conn.: Shoe String Press.

Wang Gungwu. 1963. *The Structure of Power in North China During the Five Dynasties*. Kuala Lumpur: University of Malaysia Press.

————. 1991. *China and the Chinese Overseas*. Singapore: Times Academic Press.

Wills, Jack. 1974. *Pepper, Guns, and Parleys: The Dutch East India Company and China*. Cambridge: Harvard University Press.

5

One Sovereign, Two Legal Systems:
China and the Problem of Commitment
in Hong Kong

JAMES McCALL SMITH

Sovereignty and Commitment in Hong Kong

The historic transfer of sovereignty over Hong Kong from the United Kingdom to the People's Republic of China (PRC) on July 1, 1997, marked a watershed moment in the annals of China's relations with the West. As the last pocket of officially alien territory on the China coast, Hong Kong had been a prominent and enduring reminder of the system of colonial treaty ports established during the late Qing dynasty, a time of internal division and external weakness on the mainland.[1] During the decades of civil conflict that followed the collapse of imperial rule in 1912, Chinese government officials, both Nationalist and Communist, laid consistent claim to sovereignty over Hong Kong and other treaty ports, which they viewed as a standing affront to China's territorial integrity.[2] Chinese officials thus greeted the territory's long-awaited "return to the motherland" in 1997 by staging celebrations in city squares and stadiums across the mainland and by showering the new Hong Kong Special Administrative Region (HKSAR) with lavish commemorative gifts.[3] In his inaugural speech Hong Kong Chief Executive Tung Chee-hwa described July 1 as "a joyous day for all Chinese people," who in his words had "finally" become "masters of our own house."[4]

The emotional 1997 transition converted China's long-asserted claim to sovereign control of Hong Kong from rhetorical construct to political reality. Official Beijing policy since at least 1972—when as a new member of the United Nations the PRC successfully requested that Hong Kong be removed from the list of colonial territories slated for eventual independence—had been that the settlement of the question of Hong Kong was "entirely within China's sovereign right."[5] During the postwar era, the Chinese Communist Party (CCP) saw Hong Kong as Chinese territory temporarily administered by Great Britain. The only outstanding issue in Beijing's view was when conditions would become "ripe" for resolving the final status of Hong Kong, which in the official PRC phrase was "a question left over from history" to be dealt with at some unspecified point in the future.[6] For more than three decades after 1949 a fragile but mutually beneficial status quo held.[7] With Hong Kong serving as a valuable window for China to the international economy,[8] the leadership in Beijing was extremely reluctant to raise the issue for fear of destabilizing the territory and also perhaps jeopardizing the PRC's aspirations to become a full member of the international community.[9]

British officials first broached the question of Hong Kong's future indirectly—through a discussion of commercial leases in the New Territories—during a visit to Beijing by the governor of Hong Kong, Lord MacLehose, in March 1979.[10] By that point the PRC had begun to solidify its status as China's sole representative in the international arena, to repudiate the political instability of the Cultural Revolution, and to initiate a series of market-oriented economic reforms in which Hong Kong, as a regional center of international trade and finance, was expected to play a pivotal role.[11] Although critics accuse the British of forcing the issue prematurely, conditions for resolving the Hong Kong question had begun to ripen in China; moreover, the expiration of Britain's lease to the New Territories loomed on the horizon. The response of paramount leader Deng Xiaoping to MacLehose's discreet inquiry captured the intrinsic ambivalence of the Chinese position. Deng pronounced that the PRC would not in any way compromise its claim to sovereignty over Hong Kong or endorse the prospect of continued British administration after 1997, a statement that surprised and unnerved MacLehose, but the paramount leader added that China "will have to adopt special policies to look after the very special conditions of Hong Kong so that investors can put their hearts at ease."[12] At that point, officials in Beijing had yet to determine a detailed strategy for dealing with Hong Kong.[13] Nevertheless, their preoccupation with the maintenance of stability was evident in the vague assurances Deng offered to the business community even before negotiations with Britain over the final status of the territory had begun. The crux of China's dilemma was how to reconcile its long-standing assertion of the right to exercise sovereign control over Hong Kong with its desire to maintain the confidence of local Chinese and foreign residents, thereby ensuring the territory's continued stability and prosperity.

The innovative solution later proposed by the Chinese and endorsed by the British was an elaboration of the well-known concept of "one country, two systems," a formula first introduced during the late 1970s for Taiwan, not Hong Kong.[14] After two years of contentious talks behind closed doors, Chinese and British negotiators invested that concept with substance in the "Twelve Points" of the 1984 Sino-British Joint Declaration.[15] On the question of sovereignty, the Joint Declaration is unambiguous. Consistent with CCP doctrine, Article 1 carefully notes that the PRC "has decided to resume the exercise of sovereignty over Hong Kong with effect from 1 July 1997." Similarly, Article 1 of the Basic Law—the miniconstitution for Hong Kong adopted by China in 1990—declares the HKSAR to be "an inalienable part" of the PRC.[16] While resuming its right to exercise complete and exclusive sovereignty over Hong Kong after 1997, the PRC pledged in the Joint Declaration to grant the new HKSAR a high degree of political autonomy and to maintain its social and economic systems for fifty years after the transition. The scope and specificity of Chinese commitments to Hong Kong's autonomy in 1984 were striking and well received in the territory. The Twelve Points address issues ranging from freedom of academic research to the convertibility of the Hong Kong dollar. The treaty's annex elaborates on these policies at length, as does the Basic Law.

The numerous commitments to Hong Kong's autonomy enshrined in the Joint Declaration and Basic Law resemble federalism, but the arrangement is not a simple division of authority between the central government and a political subunit. Hong Kong's founding documents represent limited violations of the principle of sovereignty. In the terminology of Krasner, the Joint Declaration and Basic Law contravene both international legal and Westphalian notions of sovereignty.[17] Under international law, the HKSAR enjoys a personality or identity that is distinct from that of the PRC. This personality, moreover, exceeds in scope that of any nonsovereign territory in the international system.[18] Although China retains control over foreign and defense affairs, the Joint Declaration and Basic Law provide Hong Kong the specific authority to forge international agreements; to participate independently in international organizations and conferences under the name "Hong Kong, China"; to maintain its own currency; to enforce its own customs regulations as a free port; to establish trade or economic missions abroad; and to issue its own passports. All these activities are traditionally the sole province of sovereign states. Moreover, in partial violation of the Westphalian concept of the exclusion of external authority, the Joint Declaration and Basic Law provide that the common law of the United Kingdom, as applied in Hong Kong, remain in force after 1997, along with all other forms of Hong Kong law (subject to amendments by the HKSAR legislature) except those that violate the Basic Law.[19] Finally, Hong Kong's independent Court of Final Appeal may as required invite foreign judges from other common law jurisdictions to sit on the court and may refer to precedents from other common law systems in justifying its rulings.[20]

As Krasner has demonstrated, violations of sovereignty such as these provisions for the HKSAR have been a recurrent feature of international politics since the inception of the modern state system in the seventeenth century.[21] In this essay, however, I contend that Hong Kong is an unusual case of problematic sovereignty. Unlike Krasner's paradigmatic examples of sovereign lending or minority rights, the limited violations of PRC sovereignty over Hong Kong were for the most part self-imposed. As in other cases, the power and interests of state actors determined the inventive institutional features of the HKSAR. Yet in Hong Kong, the predominant state actor—the PRC—sought credibly to constrain *its own* sovereign prerogatives in an attempt to bolster the confidence of local residents and foreign investors in the territory's economic viability and political stability. The institutional blueprint for the HKSAR was not the product of imposition by foreign powers. Nor was it the result of contracting with foreign powers, despite contentious Sino-British diplomatic exchanges. Instead it was Beijing's unilateral solution to a basic trade-off between sovereignty and commitment in Hong Kong.

Throughout more than fifteen years of bilateral negotiations over Hong Kong's future, PRC officials maintained a controlling position at the table. Britain's convergence strategy of the mid-1980s, whereby London in effect gave Beijing a veto over significant issues of political reform and constitutional design, reflected a Whitehall consensus that China had both local capabilities and time on its side.[22] Early in the negotiations in 1982, the British had proposed an arrangement for Hong Kong that might satisfy the PRC's nationalist claim to sovereignty while preserving the status quo. The model was Macao, a neighboring enclave recognized by both the PRC and Portugal as sovereign Chinese territory administered by Portugal. On the basic issue of control in Hong Kong, however, PRC officials proved unyielding. They rejected as colonial connivance all British attempts to adopt the Macao model by conceding

to China the legal question of sovereignty while retaining de facto administrative control of the territory.[23] To Beijing officials, sovereignty and administration in Hong Kong could not be severed. They insisted that Britain concede the issue of sovereignty as a precondition for any detailed talks on the
territory's future status. For more than six months British Prime Minister Margaret Thatcher maintained that the treaties ceding Hong Kong and Kowloon
to the United Kingdom remained legally binding, but by May 1983 she quietly
relented, conceding the sovereignty issue in the expectation that arrangements
to safeguard the territory's stability and prosperity could be agreed upon.[24]
From that point forward, in negotiating the Joint Declaration and later in the
regular bilateral sessions of the Joint Liaison Group (JLG), British officials
lobbied for a high degree of autonomy, but it seems unlikely that they extracted significant commitments that the PRC had not planned to make in
some form.[25] The main provisions of the Joint Declaration, for example, were
anticipated in previous statements from Beijing.[26] When the two sides later
parted ways, most notoriously regarding Governor Chris Patten's 1992 electoral
reforms, Chinese officials simply announced their intent to dismantle any
unilateral British actions upon resuming sovereignty in July 1997. In the case
of Patten's elected Legislative Council, which was disbanded at midnight on
June 30, the threat did not prove idle.[27]

The principal audience to which authorities in Beijing were playing during negotiations in the early 1980s was the Hong Kong public, in particular
the Chinese and foreign business communities. In relations with Britain, the
outgoing colonial power, the PRC arguably had little to lose: the Foreign
Office in London largely shared Beijing's ambitions for a smooth transition.
Were China to lose the confidence of foreign investors and local Hong Kong
residents, by contrast, disaster scenarios of emigration and capital flight were
not difficult to conjure. The potential consequences—economic and political, domestic and international—for the PRC if the Hong Kong transition
soured were far-reaching.[28] Among the relevant considerations was how the
resumption of sovereignty over Hong Kong would affect relations with Taiwan,
for which an adapted version of "one country, two systems" remained Beijing's
model solution. As evidence of Hong Kong's volatility, the region's stock,
currency, and real estate markets all plunged after Beijing's September 1982
announcement that it intended to resume the exercise of sovereignty over all
of Hong Kong by 1997.[29] The Joint Declaration, which was signed in December 1984, reassured local residents to some extent, but doubts lingered through
the 1980s and then intensified sharply after Tiananmen in 1989—prompting

an exodus of registered companies and an increase in the number of Hong Kong residents emigrating or seeking foreign passports.[30]

To curb the threat posed by its resumption of sovereignty in Hong Kong, the PRC by design compromised that sovereignty. Under international law, as Heller and Sofaer (in this volume) note, states have long enjoyed the legal authority to cede, waive, or restrict their sovereign rights.[31] Unilateral decisions to do so by powerful states remain rare events, but the Joint Declaration and Basic Law represent just such an attempt on the part of China. The mechanisms relied upon by PRC officials to bolster the credibility of their commitments in the eyes of Hong Kong residents were two legal systems. Institutional provisions in both international and local law are designed to signal Beijing's commitment to the substantive provisions of the Joint Declaration and Basic Law. In the international sphere, Hong Kong's continuing participation as a distinct entity in a range of international agreements and organizations potentially reinforces the autonomy of its economic and social systems. The most prominent example is the way in which Hong Kong's membership in the World Trade Organization (WTO) underscores China's pledge to maintain Hong Kong as a free port and separate customs territory.[32] In the local legal system, the preservation of Hong Kong's reputation in Asia as a model of judicial independence and efficient administration of the common law may help guarantee China's commitments to both property and human rights in the territory.

Qualifiers such as "potentially" and "may" are required at this stage because it remains unclear whether China will respect in practice the delegations of authority it initially made in principle. The PRC compromised its sovereign prerogatives in the Joint Declaration and Basic Law, but Beijing was careful to do so in a revocable manner. In the Basic Law and during the last few years leading up to the transition, Chinese officials took several steps back from their initial promises, drawing intense criticism from democracy activists in Hong Kong and abroad. Among the actions with relevance to Hong Kong's international status and judiciary, the PRC moved to ensure its supreme position on questions of the HKSAR's participation in international treaties and organizations, restricted the number of foreign judges on the Court of Final Appeal, and imposed new procedural safeguards through which Beijing might deny the Court of Final Appeal jurisdiction or influence its rulings on sensitive issues.

The motivation behind these late maneuvers lies in the fact that the legal arrangements that most enhance China's credibility also pose the most acute political risks to the CCP regime. Hong Kong's external autonomy, for example, could be used to legitimate local or foreign support for the territory's independence, any hint of which Beijing strenuously opposed from the start of negotiations with Britain.[33] In terms of the judiciary, the political risks are more direct and compelling. Judges with the authority to enforce contracts impartially might also be able to empower and protect "subversive" democrats and former mainland dissidents residing in Hong Kong. This threat became more pronounced in the wake of the 1989 Tiananmen protests, when thousands of Hong Kong residents marched in solidarity with the students in Beijing, to whom they donated millions of dollars in financial and material support.[34] In the sensitive months after June 4, 1989, PRC officials started to reassess their commitments to Hong Kong's autonomy. Among other sources of concern, Beijing had no experience with the workings of an independent judiciary, prompting one senior mainland official to ask a foreign scholar in the summer of 1990: "What happens if the judges get it wrong?"[35]

Aware of these risks to some degree from the start, the PRC did not fully lash itself to the mast of Hong Kong's autonomy in the Joint Declaration. Its motives were mixed. Chinese officials renounced more binding institutional options, like the continuation of British administration, as incompatible with the resumption of Chinese sovereignty. On similar grounds, Beijing rejected any supranational enforcement mechanism or dispute settlement process for the Joint Declaration.[36] Still, the pledges China made to Hong Kong's external autonomy and independent judiciary represent remarkable departures from traditional notions of sovereignty. In the years leading up to the transition, PRC officials worked to ensure that those pledges, in the context of Chinese constitutional law, might be lawfully revoked in the event that the economic benefits of Hong Kong's autonomy diminish or the associated political risks multiply.

Since the transition, Beijing has largely made good on its commitment to noninterference, despite a storm of controversy over the response of PRC officials to judicial rulings on the right of abode.[37] Hong Kong's autonomy is by no means secure, but neither has it been surrendered. Instead it remains contingent on actions taken by government officials in Beijing, Hong Kong, and abroad—and, of course, on the response of local residents and foreign investors. Given China's ongoing trade-off between sovereignty and commitment, between political control and economic advantage, the outcome at this stage is indeterminate by design. The next sections of the essay examine two realms where Beijing imposed limits on its sovereign prerogatives in Hong Kong: the region's international status and local judicial system.

The International Legal Personality of the HKSAR

Hong Kong is an extremely international place. Though small in geographic size and population, it plays host to a disproportionately large number of international financial and commercial transactions. Its stock and foreign exchange markets are consistently among the world's ten largest. Hong Kong ranks as the seventh largest trading economy in the world, and its shipping container port is the world's busiest.[38] There is considerable migration to and from the territory, and a significant Hong Kong Chinese diaspora resides in Australasia and the West. In several respects, Hong Kong even meets basic criteria applied to identify states in the international system (permanent population, well-defined territory, effective rule by local government), which prompted James Tang to conclude that it should be termed a "quasi-state."[39] For these reasons and others, in the words of legal scholar Yash Ghai, "No constitutional arrangements for the autonomy of Hong Kong would have been effective without a significant devolution of external affairs to the HKSAR."[40]

Although it explicitly reserved responsibility for foreign and defense affairs to the central government, the Joint Declaration in 1984 promised Hong Kong exactly the type of external autonomy that Britain and many local residents sought, especially in the economic sphere. It provides that Hong Kong "will retain the status of a free port and a separate customs territory" as well as the "status of an international financial centre," with its markets for foreign exchange, gold, securities, and futures intact.[41] "There will be the free flow of capital," the treaty declares, and the Hong Kong dollar will circulate freely and "remain freely convertible."[42] More significant, in terms of sovereignty, the Joint Declaration stipulates that the HKSAR "may establish mutually beneficial economic relations with the United Kingdom and other countries" and that under the name of "Hong Kong, China" it may "on its own maintain and develop economic and cultural relations and conclude relevant agreements with states, regions and relevant international organizations."[43]

The annex of the treaty elaborates that the HKSAR has the authority to issue passports in its name, apply immigration controls, and conclude visa abolition agreements with foreign states or regions. It also provides that the HKSAR "may, as necessary, establish official and semi-official economic and trade missions in foreign countries" and may, with the approval of Beijing, serve as host to foreign consular missions. With regard to existing international agreements, the annex provides that treaties to which the PRC is not a party "may remain implemented" in Hong Kong. The PRC pledges to assist in the application of "relevant" pacts of this type and to facilitate the continued participation of the HKSAR "in an appropriate capacity" in international organizations of which the PRC is not a member. Finally, with regard to basic rights, the annex stipulates that the provisions of the International Covenants on Civil and Political Rights and on Economic, Social, and Cultural Rights shall remain in force "as applied to Hong Kong."[44]

The Basic Law of 1990 specifies the scope of these provisions in greater detail than the Joint Declaration, but for the most part mirrors the treaty's terms word for word. Article 13 introduces a distinction between "foreign affairs," for which the PRC is responsible, and the "relevant external affairs" that the HKSAR is to conduct "on its own" in accordance with the Basic Law. The contrast appears to be between matters of state and diplomacy, which the PRC alone directs, and the economic and cultural matters expressly within the control of the HKSAR. In another key phrase, Article 151 gives Hong Kong broad treaty-making powers within "the appropriate fields." The exact scope of these fields where Hong Kong may act "on its own" is not clear, but the same article provides an illustrative list: "the economic, trade, financial and monetary, shipping, communications, tourism, cultural and sports fields." There are also provisions regarding civil aviation and shipping agreements, where Hong Kong is to retain its separate status.[45] Beyond these specific areas, Hong Kong may remain part of "relevant" agreements and organizations that exclude the PRC, but only with the PRC's authorization and assistance.[46]

Discussions regarding the status of the HKSAR in various international agreements and organizations occupied British and Chinese negotiators in the JLG, where China's position on specific issues emerged. Beijing cooperated in clarifying Hong Kong's formal status relatively early. By 1996, PRC approval of Hong Kong's continuing participation remained pending for only three relatively obscure organizations. The final decision was to grant Hong Kong independent standing as a full member only in certain cases. The HKSAR retains a secondary status as part of the PRC delegation in a majority of the organizations for which China's approval was required.[47] To be specific, there are eight organizations—including the WTO, Asian Development Bank, and World Health Organization—in which Hong Kong is a full member. In another six, such as the International Maritime Organization, Hong

Kong is an associate member. And in nineteen organizations—including a number of high-profile entities such as the International Monetary Fund, the World Bank, the International Labor Organization, the International Atomic Energy Agency, Interpol, the International Telecommunications Satellite Organization, and the World Intellectual Property Organization—Hong Kong participates as part of the PRC delegation.[48] In practice, this arrangement has led to rather peculiar and unprecedented situations. The inclusion of expatriate civil servants from Hong Kong—as a number of HKSAR officials are not Chinese nationals—in official PRC delegations reportedly caused momentary confusion at international conferences in the first year after the transition.[49]

With regard to treaties, the situation in the JLG was more complex than for international organizations. By the end of 1995, China had endorsed Hong Kong's participation in no fewer than 173 multilateral agreements.[50] Once consensus was reached in the JLG on each pact, Britain and China sent notes to the UN secretary-general and the depository of the treaty recording their intent to continue its application in Hong Kong after July 1, 1997. Unless objections were received from other signatories, the treaties were assumed to remain in force for the HKSAR. For bilateral treaties, which cover such areas as extradition, air services, investment promotion, and mutual legal assistance, the JLG system operated differently. A model agreement was first prepared and endorsed by Britain and China in the JLG, then Hong Kong was authorized by the PRC to negotiate separate treaties with individual states. This two-stage process resulted in a number of delays: as late as June 1996, Hong Kong had reached bilateral agreements with less than a third of its approved negotiating partners.[51] At the first stage, Britain and China had difficulty drafting a model agreement on the reciprocal enforcement of judgments in civil and commercial matters, which prompted criticism from leading Hong Kong barristers and solicitors. Obstacles also arose at the second stage because of the sensitive nature of the issues involved. Regarding treaties on the surrender of fugitive offenders, for example, a number of countries were concerned that returnees might be handed to the Chinese legal system or that Hong Kong's judiciary might not remain as competent and independent as in the past.[52]

The initial delays experienced by Hong Kong in negotiating sensitive bilateral agreements underscore a crucial fact about Hong Kong's position in the international system: the HKSAR's autonomy in international law depends heavily on its recognition by foreign states. Even if declared autonomous by the PRC, Hong Kong cannot participate in international treaties and organizations without the consent of other member states. If they so desire, such states can simply refuse to be bound by earlier treaties involving Hong Kong on the grounds that the change in sovereignty constituted a fundamental change in circumstances or that the territory could no longer fulfill its obligations.[53] In this respect, the international community has the power to exercise a constitutive effect on Hong Kong, helping establish it as an autonomous nonsovereign actor—or to deny recognition and thereby undermine Hong Kong's external autonomy. The reluctance of numerous states to enter mutual legal assistance, extradition, and visa abolition agreements with the HKSAR well in advance of the transition reflected genuine uncertainty about the extent to which Hong Kong's legal and immigration systems would remain sufficiently independent of PRC control.

This apparent uncertainty on the part of the international community seems appropriate. The texts of the Joint Declaration and Basic Law leave a number of issues regarding the scope of Hong Kong's external autonomy unresolved. For example, analysts have aired concerns about the interpretation in practice of several basic legal principles. Beijing, as noted, retains residual control of foreign and defense affairs while Hong Kong may act "on its own" only in "relevant external affairs" and "appropriate fields" where the PRC has made express delegations of authority—primarily in the economic and cultural spheres. The distinction between foreign and external affairs, however, blurs upon close examination, and it seems that the definitions of "relevant" and "appropriate" will be left to the central government to determine on a case-by-case basis, not unlike the process in the JLG. Even for fields the Joint Declaration unambiguously identifies as appropriate, such as civil aviation, the HKSAR has been required to seek explicit approval from the PRC for various transactions.[54] These requirements seem to diminish the value of provisions authorizing Hong Kong to act "on its own" in such areas. In international organizations, it remains unclear whether Hong Kong delegations will be allowed to take policy positions contrary to those of the PRC. In the context of the General Agreement on Tariffs and Trade after 1986, Britain and Hong Kong clashed publicly on questions of barriers to trade in textiles and apparel. When China gains entry to the WTO, analysts cannot predict whether the HKSAR might be allowed to take an independent line on issues where the interests of Hong Kong and the PRC diverge. Open differences of opinion would provide a signal of autonomy to the international community, but Beijing may regard that signal as bearing too high of a domestic political price. In another scenario, were Beijing to engage in a retaliatory trade war with the

United States, it is not clear if the HKSAR would be exempt from imposing sanctions. If it were not exempt, the international response to Hong Kong's resultant breach of WTO obligations could have a defining impact on the region's status.

In this uncharted territory, states have hesitated to commit to treat Hong Kong as autonomous until they have time to assess the working relationship and division of authority between diplomats from the central government and HKSAR civil servants. This hesitation is sensible, but if foreign skepticism of Hong Kong's autonomy is carried to an extreme it could have self-fulfilling features. By treating Hong Kong *as if it were* autonomous in relevant external affairs, states increase the probability that the PRC will allow Hong Kong *actually to be* autonomous. If the international community were to treat the HKSAR as if it were directly controlled by mainland authorities, officials in Beijing would have less to lose by asserting direct control. This logic is grounded in the fact that in the international system Hong Kong enjoys special privileges denied to China that are of benefit to both the HKSAR and China itself. Again, an obvious trade example is permanent most-favored-nation access to foreign markets under the WTO. Hong Kong retains comparable advantages over the PRC in the areas of immigration, investment, law enforcement, textile quotas, and high-technology or dual use export controls.

The constitutive power of international recognition plays an explicit role in official U.S. policy toward Hong Kong. Under the terms of the 1992 United States–Hong Kong Policy Act, which Congress drafted with assistance from prominent Hong Kong democrats, the United States expresses its support for democratization and human rights in the territory after 1997 and explicitly recognizes in U.S. law the special autonomous status of Hong Kong.[55] This recognition, however, is made conditional on the HKSAR remaining "sufficiently autonomous" under the terms of the Joint Declaration. The statute requires the secretary of state to issue annual reports to Congress through the year 2000 summarizing conditions in Hong Kong. On the basis of these reports or other factors, the act authorizes the president at any time after July 1, 1997, to issue a determination that Hong Kong is "not sufficiently autonomous" and by executive order to suspend the application of any U.S. laws that accord Hong Kong treatment preferable to that of the PRC.[56] The relevant areas of U.S. law include trade, export controls, and immigration, among others. The Bush administration was reportedly ambivalent about the legislation, especially insofar as the proposed sanctions—suspending U.S. law vis-à-vis the HKSAR—could do more harm to Hong Kong, the beneficiary of the act, than to the PRC, which the statute was designed to put on notice.[57] Within the Clinton administration and in Congress, there have been similar debates between officials eager to give Hong Kong's civil servants the benefit of the doubt—and thereby a shot at autonomy—and those who prefer to take a hard line with both Hong Kong and the PRC on issues of intellectual property protection, textile transshipment, and high-technology exports.[58]

In addition to the United States, other countries and the Vatican have taken strong stances with Beijing, sometimes privately, on the question of Hong Kong's autonomy. Chinese officials tend to resent and openly denounce any such statements or conditions as illegitimate interference in the PRC's domestic affairs, emphasizing their exclusive sovereign rights in the territory. Nevertheless, the diplomatic practices of foreign states will play a meaningful role in determining the level of autonomy to be enjoyed by the HKSAR. Despite its explicitly nonsovereign status, Hong Kong's political fate—like that of Taiwan, as discussed by Madsen in this volume—will hinge in part on the reaction of the international community, which has thus far welcomed the PRC's departure from the traditional sovereignty script in Hong Kong.

The Rule of Law and the Court of Final Appeal

The remarkable economic success of Hong Kong in recent decades as a regional center of international finance and trade has long been attributed in large part to the rule of law in the territory.[59] The phrase, of course, has many connotations. In the context of Hong Kong, the rule of law has been identified at times with laissez-faire, market-oriented policies or the absence of widespread government corruption, both of which have traditionally distinguished Hong Kong from some of its neighbors in Southeast Asia. In this section, I focus on the rule of law as it relates to the local judicial system—and in particular to the political independence, final adjudicatory authority, and broad jurisdiction of Hong Kong's judicial institutions.

During the early 1980s, as the PRC began to craft its approach to the Hong Kong question, a number of alternative institutional designs were available for the territory's judiciary after the resumption of Chinese sovereignty. One option, advocated by the British during the negotiations, was the status quo: an independent judiciary enforcing British and local common and statutory law with the power of final adjudication residing in the Judicial Committee of the Privy Council in London, a colonial institution whose law lords reviewed from five to twenty appeals each year from Hong Kong. At the other extreme on the spectrum of options, as defined by Bueno de Mesquita, Newman, and Rabushka, was a Chinese supreme court applying mainland Chinese law.[60] Between these poles were two options in which local Hong Kong law would be maintained: in one case by courts directly accountable to Beijing, in the other by an independent local court staffed by Western-trained judges. Chinese officials decided that promising, as they did in the Joint Declaration, to allow the laws in force in Hong Kong to remain "basically unchanged" was a prerequisite for confidence in the territory's autonomy. The question, then, was what type of judicial system would apply these laws.

British officials, the Hong Kong government elite, and the local business community all lobbied for an independent supreme court staffed by British judges. In other words, they sought to keep the Privy Council in London as the highest court of appeal. Their contention was that anything short of the status quo would compromise the reputation of the territory's legal system, given the shortage of appellate expertise in the Hong Kong legal community. The coalition could also point to the fact that in a number of former British colonies and Commonwealth members, fully independent governments still maintained the avenue of appeal to the Privy Council for the sake of continuity and professionalism in the local legal system.[61] Even Singapore, an authoritarian city-state envied by Beijing for its combination of economic dynamism and political stability, allowed appeals to the Privy Council into the 1990s. That right was withdrawn in 1997, however, after a panel of law lords in London sharply criticized as unjust the Singaporean government's use of criminal statutes to harass, unseat, and disbar a prominent opposition legislator.[62]

The PRC, as noted, had already rejected out of hand the extension of British colonial administration after 1997 in any form. In the judicial system, an area they considered sensitive, mainland officials were never willing even to contemplate it.[63] The maintenance of appeals to the Privy Council was thus a dead letter from the start, despite considerable support for such an option in Hong Kong. Reports suggest that Beijing's initial preference was instead to establish a judiciary that would be accountable to mainland authorities, perhaps not unlike the Joint Declaration's provisions for an appointed chief executive.[64] In addition to objections from Britain, this plan generated sharp opposition within Hong Kong from local and international business associations, whose members wanted guarantees on the impartial enforcement and procurement of contracts.[65] Deng and the PRC elite, recognizing the salience of the issue to the business community, reportedly compromised by agreeing to the principle of an independent local judiciary with the power of final adjudication.[66]

Annex I of the Joint Declaration spelled out the terms of the judicial deal, which were generally praised both in Hong Kong and abroad. It endorsed the principle of judicial independence, noting that the courts "shall exercise judicial power independently and free from any interference" and that judges "shall be immune from legal action in respect of their judicial functions." The annex also provided that the existing judicial system would be maintained except for the addition of a new Court of Final Appeal (CFA) with the "power of final judgment." The CFA itself, moreover, "may as required invite judges from other common law jurisdictions" to join. And judges at all levels in the HKSAR, who are to decide cases in accordance with local laws, also "may refer to precedents in other common law jurisdictions." With regard to the selection of judges, the annex calls for an "independent" commission of "local judges, persons from the legal profession, and other eminent persons" to recommend candidates to the chief executive, who is to act on the basis of their recommendations. Judges may be removed from office only if a tribunal of no fewer than three local judges considers them unable to fulfill their duties or finds them guilty of misbehavior.[67]

Although the basic principles were in place, the substantive and procedural details of the CFA's operations had yet to be determined. As it happened, these details eventually became the source of tremendous contention both within Hong Kong's nascent body politic, the Legislative Council (Legco), and at the international level between Britain and China in the JLG. The basic delegations of local judicial independence and the power of final adjudication were made by the PRC, perhaps reluctantly, with the interests of the business community in mind. After the tragic events of Tiananmen in 1989, however, the protection of human rights suddenly claimed center stage in Hong Kong. This dramatic shift prompted Beijing to reconsider its position on the CFA and to reassess the domestic political risks of an independent judiciary, staffed in part by foreign judges, with the power of final judgment on issues closely related to China's pledge in the Joint Declaration to honor freedoms of person, speech, press, assembly, association, travel, and demonstration, among others, in the HKSAR.[68]

The initial signs of a reconsideration on the part of the PRC came in the Basic Law, the second draft of which was released after Tiananmen and then adopted by the National People's Congress (NPC) in Beijing on April 4, 1990.

For the most part, its language faithfully implemented the terms of the Joint Declaration with regard to the territory's judicial system. But the Basic Law included two controversial clauses that were not part of the earlier Sino-British accord. Both provisions, in the eyes of critics, threaten to undercut the authority and jurisdiction of the CFA.

The first clause is Article 158, which introduces a distinction between the power of adjudication and the power of interpretation. Such a distinction is rarely made in common law systems, where judges adjudicate by interpreting statutes, judicial precedents, and other forms of legal authority. Under Article 19 the Hong Kong judicial system retains the power of final adjudication, but Article 158 assigns the power to interpret the Basic Law to the Standing Committee of the NPC in Beijing, a powerful entity within China's constitutional framework. In its different functions, the NPC Standing Committee combines executive, legislative, and judicial responsibilities, including powers of interpretation over mainland laws. Article 158 stipulates that the NPC Standing Committee "shall authorize" the courts of the HKSAR to interpret, in adjudicating cases, the provisions of the Basic Law that are "within the limits of the autonomy" of the region. When HKSAR courts interpret provisions of the Basic Law concerning affairs outside the region's realm of competence—such as issues within the responsibility of the central government or regarding the relationship between Beijing and the HKSAR—they are required to seek a binding interpretation from the NPC Standing Committee through the CFA. Before issuing its interpretation, the NPC Standing Committee must first consult with the Committee for the Basic Law, an appointed body of twelve experts—six from Hong Kong and six from the mainland—to which Beijing turns for advice on legal issues concerning the HKSAR.[69] Using its powers of interpretation, the NPC Standing Committee also has authority to invalidate or propose amendments to any Hong Kong laws, new or old, that it believes do not conform with the Basic Law.[70] Critics fear that the NPC Standing Committee's broad powers of interpretation will enable mainland officials to influence or effectively reverse specific CFA rulings. The controversial right of abode case, where this authority was first exercised, is the example to which they point in alarm.[71]

The second controversial clause in the Basic Law is Article 19. Although it mirrors the Joint Declaration in granting Hong Kong courts the power of final adjudication, Article 19 introduces new limitations on the jurisdiction of HKSAR courts. Specifically, it provides that local courts "shall have no jurisdiction over acts of state such as defense and foreign affairs." Instead of relying implicitly on the definition of acts of state in common law jurisdictions, where the doctrine developed and is narrowly construed,[72] Article 19 establishes a process by which HKSAR courts must first obtain a certificate from the chief executive on any questions of fact relevant to acts of state. The findings in this certificate, for which the chief executive in turn must first gain approval from the central government in Beijing, are then binding on the courts. This process of review by political authorities has troubled human rights monitors as a potential threat to the CFA's jurisdiction, given the tremendous uncertainty regarding how broadly "acts of state" will be defined. The Basic Law's use of the expansive phrase "such as" with defense and foreign affairs has not reassured observers who are prone to pessimism.

Together, these two features of the Basic Law give political authorities in Beijing and Hong Kong potential means of constraining the interpretive powers of HKSAR courts and limiting their jurisdiction, especially in regard to sensitive political issues. The Basic Law drew some criticism on this score in 1990, but it was not until the JLG reached a secret agreement on the composition of the CFA in late September 1991 that political anxieties regarding the judiciary's future reached a critical mass. The Sino-British agreement, reached only after three years of negotiations, specified that the CFA would be composed of five judges: the chief justice must be a Chinese citizen and permanent Hong Kong resident without the right of abode in any foreign country; three judges may be either Chinese or expatriate residents of Hong Kong; and the fifth member would be invited on a rotating basis from one of two panels, the first a list of retired Hong Kong judges and the second a list of prominent retired judges from Commonwealth countries and Ireland.[73] The implication was that instead of having the right to invite "judges" from common law jurisdictions, as provided in the Joint Declaration and Basic Law, the CFA would at any time include a maximum of one foreign judge — and perhaps none at all.

British officials sought to portray the agreement as a victory for Hong Kong's legal system, in that China agreed in principle to the importance of establishing the CFA before July 1997 so that its judges could gain experience and earn the confidence of the local community prior to the transition. Nevertheless, the composition of the court as defined in the 1991 agreement was different from that proposed by the Hong Kong government before Tiananmen. In 1988 Hong Kong's Executive Council, the highest policymaking body in the colony, proposed that the CFA include two judges from a rotating panel of active jurists from England, Australia, New Zealand, and Canada. The remaining three members would be Hong Kong judges, one of whom would serve as chief justice.[74] In the JLG the Chinese rejected this formula, preferring a maximum of one foreign judge—with a chance of zero—to the certainty of two. Three years later the British capitulated.

This restriction on the number of foreign judges eligible to sit on the CFA shocked many segments of the Hong Kong community and brought together an unusual coalition of representatives in Legco to rally behind the rule of law. The Hong Kong Bar Association and Law Society were joined by seven other professional groups in a statement condemning any limitations on the number of foreign judges. In October 1991 Legco held an in-house debate on the JLG agreement at which representatives' concerns were aired at length. Two months later, on December 4, 1991, the members of Legco took the historic step of voting 34-11 against the Sino-British accord. The motion proposed by the legal community's representative, Simon Ip, merely stated that there should be "more flexibility to invite overseas judges to sit on [the CFA] than has been agreed by the British and Chinese governments."[75] Though mild in its wording, the motion was still an unprecedented rebuke to the British administration: never before in the history of Legco had its representatives rejected a government initiative.[76]

The 1991 Legco motion on the CFA had multiple consequences. Thanks in part to this setback, Governor David Wilson announced his retirement within a month of the vote. Although Britain and China had agreed on the importance of establishing the court well in advance of the transition, no further action was taken for several years. The original goal was to set up the CFA by 1993, but in a political environment poisoned by Tiananmen in 1989, the Legco vote in 1991, and finally the unilateral electoral reforms of Governor Chris Patten in 1992, British and Chinese officials alike preferred to postpone the issue. In public Governor Patten's administration continued to promise that a bill codifying the 1991 agreement was forthcoming, but Britain did not submit a draft version to the PRC until May 1994. The Chinese did not respond in the JLG for more than four months. When they finally did so, Beijing's anxieties about an independent judiciary were laid bare.

In the spring of 1995, the PRC set forth three proposals to amend the draft bill, each of which would have undermined the rule of law in Hong Kong. First, it contended that the CFA should not be able to rule on the "constitutionality of laws"—for example, in cases arising out of the controversial 1991 Bill of Rights or the Basic Law. Second, it sought to establish a mechanism that would allow the NPC in Beijing to issue a "post-remedial verdict" overturning CFA rulings to which China objected. Finally, it sought to define "acts of state" to include "other things" in addition to foreign affairs and defense and insisted that any issues certified to be "acts of state" would be beyond the jurisdiction of the court.[77] Patten's team and British representatives on the JLG took these objections to mean that China evidently preferred not to reach an agreement, for they went far beyond what had been discussed in 1991. Agreement in the JLG, in the recollection of one British team member, seemed "completely unattainable and politically impossible."[78]

The British at this point were in a difficult situation. The administration's draft bill had been repudiated not only by Beijing but also by the legal profession in Hong Kong. Patten circulated the draft to local barristers and solicitors on October 30, 1994. In early December the Bar Association voted overwhelmingly (247-15) to reject the CFA statute.[79] The 1991 JLG pact, which the British aimed to honor, thus failed to win endorsement from either the PRC or the local community. The PRC wanted to place additional restrictions on the CFA's jurisdiction and to secure a veto over its rulings, while legislators in Hong Kong sought to abolish the limit on the number of foreign judges and to entrench a narrow common law definition of acts of state. Patten's team debated whether to submit the draft bill to Legco for a vote. It seemed likely that a bill based on the 1991 pact might very well be rejected, given opposition from both pro-Beijing representatives and local civil libertarians. If the bill managed to pass, however, Chinese officials proclaimed that they were ready to derail any judicial "through train" and establish the CFA on their own terms in 1997.[80] Either outcome would constitute a blow to confidence in the rule of law. Still, little time was left if the CFA were to be established before the transition, and concern was mounting in the business community about the potential economic impact of a vacuum at the apex of the Hong Kong judiciary.[81] Patten thus sought approval from London to table a draft bill in Legco with or without China's endorsement. Despite opposition from cabinet colleagues desperate to avoid another falling out with Beijing, Patten won a green light from Prime Minister John Major to proceed.[82]

This green light—a credible commitment by Britain to force the issue—brought China back to the table, and a second CFA agreement was finally struck in the JLG on June 7, 1995. The 1995 pact reflected the terms of the 1991 agreement regarding the composition of the court, maintaining the same formula for the participation of no more than one foreign judge. To reach agreement, however, Britain surrendered its insistence that the CFA be established before the transition; Beijing was adamant that the court not begin its operations until 1997. British officials also yielded for the first time on the question of acts of state, incorporating the ambiguous language of the Basic Law. To defend these decisions, Patten noted that China had relinquished its positions on the creation of a postverdict remedial mechanism and the non-justiciability of constitutional issues. Critics of Britain, however, asserted that these were never serious proposals on the part of the Chinese—instead they were trivial concessions to provide cover for what civil libertarians regarded as treacherous capitulations by the British side.[83] Again the response in Legco was one of intense criticism, at least among Democratic Party members and independent legislators anxious about civil liberties. In the business community, however, there was considerable relief that at last a deal had been reached, averting a legal vacuum, with China fully on board.[84] When the CFA agreement came to Legco for a vote, this latter sentiment prevailed. The CFA Ordinance became law in July 1995 by a vote of 38-17. Repeated attempts by the Democratic Party to amend key provisions in the bill, such as by deleting references to acts of state or moving up the court's start date, were rejected by a margin of two to one.[85]

In the year and a half following ratification of the CFA Ordinance, attention focused on who would serve on Hong Kong's highest court. There was anxiety in the legal community that Hong Kong simply did not have legal experts of the caliber required for a court of final appellate review.[86] Others worried that even if there were qualified candidates in the Hong Kong bar, the most talented might balk at the prospect of serving on a judiciary whose jurisdiction and interpretive powers might at any time be curtailed from above by Beijing. Finally, the business community expressed concern about the prospect of mainland officials awarding seats on the CFA as consolation prizes to candidates who were not selected as chief executive-designate.[87]

These fears were put to rest at the end of 1996 when Chief Executive-designate Tung Chee-hwa named a highly respected barrister, Andrew Li Kwok-nang, to serve as the first chief justice of the CFA.[88] Li's selection gave the CFA's reputation a much-needed boost in Hong Kong and abroad. His subsequent moves to build the court's roster in collaboration with the Judicial Officers Recommendation Commission were also welcomed, especially the naming of six prominent Commonwealth jurists to serve on the roster of nonpermanent judges available to fill the CFA's fifth slot by invitation.[89] Many permanent Hong Kong judges at all levels, moreover, remain expatriates.[90] The Basic Law provided for substantial continuity on the bench, explicitly allowing all members of the judiciary to remain in office.[91] It imposes a nationality test on only two positions, requiring that the CFA chief justice and the chief judge of the High Court be Chinese nationals and permanent residents of Hong Kong with no foreign right of abode.[92]

The CFA held its first hearing in September 1997 and, like the judicial system overall, initially won significant praise.[93] Several positive developments bolstered the judiciary's reputation. Voting procedures in the Judicial Officers Recommendation Commission were defined to ensure that the representatives of the government, the secretary for justice and the chief justice, do not enjoy a veto over nominees to the bench, enhancing the impartiality of the selection process.[94] As provided for in the Basic Law, the recommendations of that body are binding on the chief executive, which is an improvement over the British system.[95] Also significant was a less formal move by the CFA to establish the position of foreign judges on the bench. In addition to the six Commonwealth jurists, eleven Hong Kong judges are eligible for service on the CFA as nonpermanent members. Any judges on the nonpermanent roster can be chosen to fill the fifth seat in a given case. The consistent practice under Chief Justice Li, however, has been to draw exclusively from the list of foreign judges for the fifth slot. In the first two years after the transition, one Commonwealth judge participated in every single CFA judgment, presumably to bolster the court's reputation.[96] This custom may not endure, but it helped allay fears that foreign judges would have a limited role, if any, to play under the disputed terms of the CFA Ordinance.

By far the most controversial judgment in the early months of the CFA was its January 1999 ruling in the right of abode case, in which migrants from the mainland tested the Basic Law's definition of who has the right to permanent residency in the HKSAR. In a unanimous decision drafted by Chief Justice Li, the CFA overturned a lower court ruling and invalidated aspects of Hong Kong's Immigration Ordinance, substantially expanding the pool of potential migrants.[97] The resultant political controversy stemmed from logistical and legal considerations. In practical terms, the HKSAR government claimed that the ruling would confer permanent residency on some 1.6 million mainland Chinese. Even if inflated, such estimates helped make the ruling unpopular with the general public, which feared that a flood of migrants could overwhelm the territory's infrastructure and social service systems.[98] In legal terms, both Hong Kong and mainland officials were taken aback by the CFA's refusal to submit the case for interpretation and by its assertion of authority to review acts of the NPC and the Standing Committee. The initial response of the Hong Kong government was to request a "clarification" of the ruling, an unprecedented move. The CFA obliged with a carefully phrased statement, acknowledging the full authority of the NPC and the Standing Committee to do any act that is consistent with the Basic Law—including the issuance of a binding interpretation under Article 158.[99]

The legal community urged the Hong Kong government to defuse the crisis by amending the Basic Law, believing that response would do the least damage to the territory's autonomy. Averse to delay, HKSAR officials chose instead to request an interpretation from the NPC Standing Committee. In June 1999 the Standing Committee held that the CFA had improperly decided not to refer the case for interpretation and had misinterpreted the relevant provisions of the Basic Law. This reinterpretation does not reverse existing CFA decisions regarding specific plaintiffs, but it does bind the Hong Kong judiciary regarding all future claims, significantly curtailing the impact of—and in effect reversing—the CFA's original ruling. The impact of this legal battle in the long term will depend on whether the abode case proves to be a rarity driven by exceptional circumstances, as the Hong Kong government contends.[100] Critics claim it may encourage future interventions by mainland authorities in local judicial proceedings, which would constitute a death knell for the rule of law in Hong Kong.[101]

Hong Kong's Court of Final Appeal is in place, but questions regarding its political independence and powers of judicial review remain unresolved. Some analysts expect it to construe acts of state narrowly, protecting its jurisdiction, and when possible to avoid preliminary referrals to the NPC Standing Committee for interpretation, as it sought to do—albeit unsuccessfully—in the right of abode case.[102] Others assert that the Basic Law's provisions on acts of state and the NPC Standing Committee's powers of interpretation represent crucial institutional weaknesses that China is certain to use to constrain the CFA's authority.[103] Conclusions of either type, positive or negative, at this point are premature. It remains unclear whether and if so to what extent the PRC will make use of its recently devised constitutional procedures to undercut the power of final appellate review promised to the CFA in the Joint Declaration. The institutional design of Hong Kong's legal system does not determine the level of autonomy the HKSAR's courts will enjoy in the future. Judicial independence, Hong Kong style, is an ongoing strategic game with multiple potential outcomes. The judges of the CFA, aware of Beijing's sovereign prerogatives, are likely to tread lightly in areas of extreme political sensitivity to the mainland, especially after the right of abode controversy. Beijing, aware of potential protests both in Hong Kong and by the international community, is likely to respect the HKSAR's judicial autonomy—especially in matters of commercial law—and perhaps even to back down if challenged by a broad coalition of opponents.[104]

The institutional blueprint for Hong Kong's future in the Joint Declaration and Basic Law included limited violations of China's international legal and Westphalian sovereignty, as defined by Krasner in this volume. These violations were not the product of foreign state imposition, as in cases of minority rights; nor were they the outcome of negotiations with powerful state actors or international organizations, as in cases of sovereign lending. Instead they were entirely a Chinese invention. Although Britain clearly advocated for the highest level of autonomy possible on behalf of its former colony, British authorities did not have the power to impose enduring political arrangements in Hong Kong. On every issue of significance, China's resumption of sovereignty gave the PRC an effective post-1997 veto, which it exercised in the case of Governor Chris Patten's controversial electoral reforms. The principal threat to Chinese interests in Hong Kong was not the potential response of Britain or other state actors—although reputation in the international community may well have been a second-order concern. Instead, the leadership in Beijing responded to the potential flight of capital and individuals from Hong Kong, a very international and highly mobile Chinese society composed primarily of refugees from the mainland and their descendants.[105] It is interesting to note that China's anxiety on this issue, which was shared by British officials eager to avoid an exodus of refugees or massive market instability,[106] may also reflect an erosion in Hong Kong of another aspect of sovereignty: the ability of public authorities to control transborder flows of goods, capital, persons, etc.

Against the economic risks of emigration and capital flight, which were especially acute during the 1980s, Chinese officials weighed the domestic political risks of an independent judiciary and external autonomy for Hong Kong. In 1984 mainland authorities, then eager to sustain Hong Kong's prosperity and stability, opted to limit their own sovereign prerogatives in the Joint Declaration. After witnessing the territory's response to Tiananmen in 1989, however, Beijing perceived the domestic political risks of autonomy to have multiplied. The PRC thus ensured during the 1990s that the Basic Law and later the CFA Ordinance gave Beijing a veto over its previous delegations of sovereign responsibilities. It crafted these vetoes with care so as not to destroy confidence in the HKSAR's autonomy outright—but very nearly overstepped in the contentious talks with Britain regarding the Court of Final Appeal. Instruments far more blunt were available to the PRC. Amendments to the Basic Law, for example, have been within China's sovereign prerogative.[107] But mainland officials have proven too sensitive to the negative ramifications, international and domestic, of a Hong Kong transition gone awry to minimize their domestic political exposure altogether. Instead they strategically inserted flexibility into the HKSAR's constitutional system, allowing Chinese authorities lawfully to revoke their commitments in the Joint Declaration if and when circumstances require. If the economic benefits of Hong Kong's autonomy diminish (say, in a market collapse or gradual deterioration of the HKSAR's importance to southern China) or the political costs of that autonomy increase (say, in widespread public protests against repressive actions on the mainland), Beijing may very well revoke its self-imposed sovereign limitations and assume direct political control of the region.

In broader comparative perspective, the HKSAR is by no means unique as an example of limited sovereignty. There have been analogous schemes in the international system. China's blueprint for the HKSAR resembles institutional arrangements for associated states within the British empire after 1967 or between New Zealand and the Cook Islands since 1964. Like the PRC in the case of Hong Kong, both the United Kingdom and New Zealand granted internal autonomy and limited international legal personality to those territories while retaining responsibility for foreign and defense affairs. Those arrangements, however, were contractual in a way that China's hierarchical relations with the HKSAR are not. Britain and New Zealand did not impose external dependence; rather, they proposed it. Moreover, their dependent territories maintained the right to opt out of the arrangement and become fully independent. This exit option was de facto in the Caribbean, where all but one of Britain's associated states terminated the relationship, and de jure for the Cook Islands and New Zealand.[108]

In the case of China and Hong Kong, by contrast, the obvious reversion point if the Joint Declaration is breached or the Basic Law amended is direct PRC control, not Hong Kong independence. Critics contend that the Basic Law itself constituted a partial breach of the Joint Declaration and that subsequent PRC actions reveal that China's tactical commitment to "two systems" has already been abolished. Such pessimism at this point is overstated. With the high-stakes game of sovereignty and commitment having just begun, it remains too soon to reach conclusions about the viability of Hong Kong's novel exercise in local autonomy. "One country, two systems" has not yet become a clear manifestation of "organized hypocrisy," the term Krasner applies to the concept of sovereignty itself.[109]

Notes

Generous support for this research came from the Henry R. Luce Foundation, the David C. Lam Institute for East-West Studies, and the Hong Kong Transition Project. For helpful comments I would like to thank Richard Baum, Bruce Dickson, Stephen Krasner, Michel Oksenberg, and Derek Scissors.

1.   Although the Portuguese enclave of Macao returned to Chinese administration two years after Hong Kong, in December 1999, both Portugal and the PRC regarded it as sovereign Chinese territory since an agreement in the late 1970s. See Pereira 1991. For accounts of Chinese foreign relations and the establishment of treaty ports during the late Qing era, see Fairbank 1953, 1968.

2.   For an account that emphasizes the historical parallels between Communist and Nationalist approaches to the Hong Kong question, see Lane 1990.

3.   Some "100,000 carefully chosen" residents filled Tiananmen Square in Beijing, the largest crowds allowed since the pro-democracy protests of 1989. See Jasper Becker, "Celebrating Masses Throng Tiananmen," *South China Morning Post*, July 1, 1997, 12. The HKSAR government placed gifts from Beijing and from all thirty-one Chinese provinces or regions on display at Government House, the former residence of British governors. See Alex Lo, "Mainland's Handover Gifts an Embarrassment of Riches," *South China Morning Post*, July 17, 1997, 8.

4.   "A Future of Excellence and Prosperity for All," Hong Kong Information Services Department, July 1, 1997, 11; "Tung Leads the Way," *South China Morning Post*, December 12, 1996, 1.

5.   Ghai 1997:38.

6.   Lane 1990:3.

7.   The informal "conditions" required by the PRC in the late 1950s for the maintenance of the status quo were that the British maintain order and not allow Hong Kong either to become self-governing or to serve as a base for Nationalist agitators. See Wilson 1990:196–99.

8.   Hong Kong served as the principal gateway for remittances from overseas Chinese to the mainland, which as early as the 1960s were estimated to run at $500–600 million per year. Added to the charges for provision of water and food to Hong Kong, this cash flow represented nearly half of China's entire hard currency income. Hong Kong was also the locus of grain deals struck with Canada, Australia, and Argentina in 1961 after the disastrous harvests of the Great Leap Forward. Finally, with the opening of the Chinese market from the late 1970s, Hong Kong firms quickly became one of the principal sources of investment and employment on the mainland. See Yahuda 1996:23–26.

9. Moreover, the Taiwan situation was deemed a higher priority than either Hong Kong or Macao by some Beijing officials. See Lane 1990:67–81.

10. Under the 1898 Treaty of Peking, the United Kingdom acquired a ninety-nine-year lease to the New Territories, more than 300 square miles of sparsely populated territory to the north of the Kowloon peninsula and on outlying islands. With that lease set to expire in June 1997, investors from Hong Kong and abroad had begun to encourage British officials to seek approval for extensions of individual commercial leases in the New Territories beyond the treaty deadline, eliding the issue of sovereignty. MacLehose made the request, but Deng flatly rejected the proposal and reasserted China's intent to resume sovereignty over Hong Kong. For accounts of the meeting from the British perspective, see Cottrell 1993; Roberti 1994; Cradock 1994; Dimbleby 1997:38–43.

11. Spence 1990, ch. 23. For accounts of Chinese reforms, see Baum 1980 and Harding 1987.

12. This quotation was translated from a speech given in May 1997 by Wong Man Fong, a former deputy secretary-general of the Xinhua News Agency, who was involved in the formulation of Chinese policy toward Hong Kong. See Wong 1997:4.

13. For a firsthand account of Chinese policymaking on Hong Kong, see Wong 1997, ch. 1, who describes the decision to resume sovereignty in principle as a "painful process" on which no resolution was reached until December 1981, after which a task force was assigned to consider alternative approaches. Similarly, Lane (1990:88) reports that no plan had been drafted by mid-1981.

14. Wang 1995:42–44; Roberti 1994:42.

15. See Joint Declaration of the Government of the United Kingdom of Great Britain and Northern Ireland and the Government of the People's Republic of China on the Question of Hong Kong, December 19, 1984. The treaty, hereinafter referred to as Joint Declaration, appears at *International Legal Materials* 23 (1984): 1371.

16. See The Basic Law of the Hong Kong Special Administrative Region of the People's Republic of China, April 4, 1990, which is hereinafter referred to as Basic Law. It is reprinted in *International Legal Materials* 29 (1990): 1519.

17. Krasner, "Problematic Sovereignty," in this volume.

18. For a discussion of Hong Kong's novel international status, see Mushkat (1997:pp. ix, 1–41), who describes the HKSAR arrangements as "without direct parallel in international law" and notes that its external autonomy is "said to be matched by no other non-sovereign government in the contemporary international system." Wang (1995:110) draws a similar conclusion after comparing the HKSAR to a historical study of twenty-five nonsovereign autonomous regions, noting that "with regard to foreign affairs and the economy, the SAR will enjoy much more power than other autonomous regions."

19. For analysis of the common law's application in Hong Kong, see Wesley-Smith 1993. For analysis of stress within Hong Kong's constitutional system under the Basic Law, see Davis 1990.

20. Joint Declaration, Annex I, sec. 13; Basic Law, Arts. 82, 84.

21. Krasner, "Problematic Sovereignty," in this volume.

22. Throughout the postwar era Hong Kong imported much of its food and nearly all of its drinking water from the mainland, leaving the territory in precarious straits in the event of a full-scale crisis with China. See Wilson 1990:196–97. During the negotiations with Britain, Deng at one point threatened to recover Hong Kong by force if necessary. Fresh from victory in the Falklands, Prime Minister Margaret Thatcher reportedly had to be persuaded by her defense secretary, Michael Heseltine, that Hong Kong was indefensible. See Dimbleby 1997:44–46.

23. The Macao model itself was an ad hoc solution driven by PRC concerns regarding Hong Kong—and, as such, was never considered an option for the British colony. When Portugal initially expressed interest in returning Macao to Chinese rule, Beijing at first balked because of the anxiety such a precedent might cause in Hong Kong, whose future status then remained uncertain. PRC officials preferred to deal with Hong Kong—and the final status of Macao, which reverted to Chinese administration in 1999—only when conditions became ripe. See Wong 1997.

24. Lane 1990:93–98. Recalling the decision to relinquish Britain's claim to Hong Kong island, Thatcher noted: "Hong Kong island is less than 8 per cent of the territory. All the rest is China mainland. There is no way we could say, 'We're going to keep the sovereignty of Hong Kong.' There was no way in which we could defend it. More than that: they didn't need to march in. The Chinese could have just turned off the supply of water and food which came from the mainland. So I had very few cards in my hand." As quoted in Dimbleby 1997:44.

25. Summarizing the negotiations for the Joint Declaration, Ghai (1997:54) contends that "a balance sheet of the results of this protracted process shows that China got substantially all it wanted."

26. Even before Thatcher's visit to Beijing in September 1982, the core principles of Beijing's approach had been enunciated in a sixteen-character formula: "Recover sovereignty. No change in social systems. Hong Kong people rule Hong Kong. Preserve stability." See Roberti 1994:41–42. Moreover, a group of Hong Kong students returned from a trip to Beijing in July 1983 with news of a ten-point plan almost identical to the Twelve Points of the Joint Declaration. See Wang 1995:48.

27. For an account of Patten's reforms and China's response, see Dimbleby 1997, chs. 6–14.

28. For a summary of the political, economic, and international significance of Hong Kong to the mainland, see Yahuda 1996, ch. 1. According to Wong (1997:19), the former Xinhua official, Deng was well aware of the risks of chaos in Hong Kong and offered his cadres the following edict in early 1982: "A small confusion is unavoidable, a medium-scale confusion is possible, but you must try your best to avoid a major confusion in Hong Kong."

29. Within a few months asset values on the stock exchange fell by one-third. Land values in choice segments of Hong Kong island and Kowloon fell to as low as one-fifth of their pre-September 1982 prices. Finally, the Hong Kong dollar exchange

rate fell from HK$6.20 per US$ in mid-1982 to HK$9.55 per US$ by September 1983. See Bueno de Mesquita, Newman, and Rabushka 1985:65–67.

30.   In terms of business behavior, the proportion of firms listed in Hong Kong that were also incorporated in the territory hovered above 90 percent from 1984 to early 1989. By the end of 1989, however, that figure had fallen to 76 percent and by 1994 to less than 40 percent. Of firms listed continuously during that decade, more than 30 percent changed their domicile from Hong Kong to another location. See Newman and Weimer 1997. With regard to emigration, the Hong Kong government estimates that from 1980 to 1986 roughly 20,000 residents emigrated annually. The figure rose to 30,000 in 1987 and then climbed sharply to 60,000 in 1990 and 66,000 in 1992. See Skeldon 1994:30. Finally, surveys suggest that the proportion of Hong Kong residents willing to admit in anonymous telephone interviews that they had obtained a foreign passport rose from three-tenths of 1 percent in 1984 to approximately 10 percent in 1994. See Hong Kong Transition Project 1997:29.

31.   Lawful arrangements under which states forgo the territorial exclusion of external authority include servitudes and leases. See Shaw 1997:366–68.

32.   Hong Kong became a member of the General Agreement on Tariffs and Trade in 1986 with the approval of Britain and China, not long after the Joint Declaration came into force. See Mushkat 1997:29. Negotiations for China's accession to the WTO repeatedly stalled during the 1990s due to objections by the United States and other members that Beijing's liberalization commitments were inadequate.

33.   The mere suggestion that Hong Kong itself had some autonomous standing during negotiations of the Joint Declaration prompted strident protests from Beijing. The PRC considered itself the only legitimate representative of Hong Kong people and viewed the talks as strictly bilateral, condemning any and all comparisons of the process to a "three-legged stool" that balanced the interests of China, Britain, and Hong Kong. See Roberti 1994. The extreme sensitivity of PRC officials on this issue reflects in part the problems China, as an extensive territorial unit, has experienced with separatist movements in Tibet, Xinjiang, and other remote or semiautonomous regions.

34.   Wilson 1990:220–6.

35.   As quoted in Yahuda 1996:9.

36.   From Beijing's perspective, Britain's responsibilities in Hong Kong ended completely and irreversibly on June 30, 1997, such that British officials have no formal role to play in overseeing or monitoring implementation of the Joint Declaration. The two countries sparred on this issue in discussions of what if any role the JLG would play after the transition, since it is to remain in existence until the year 2000. Chinese JLG team leader Zhao Jihua, for example, asserted: "We disagree when the British side says the JLG should play a monitoring role." His British counterpart Huge Davies admitted: "There is a limit to the influence and power that Britain can bring about if there are actions taken by the Chinese which are inconsistent with the Joint Declaration." See Linda Choy and No Kwai-Yan, " 'Limited' British Influence After Handover," *South China Morning Post*, May 31, 1997, 6.

37. In an April 1999 report on Hong Kong, the U.S. Department of State (1999:1) concluded, "There has been no evidence of interference from the Chinese central government in local affairs, with one possible exception." That exception is the right of abode crisis, sparked by a January 1999 Court of Final Appeal ruling that would increase migration from the mainland to Hong Kong. In response, the HKSAR government invited the Standing Committee of the National People's Congress in Beijing to reinterpret specific provisions of the Basic Law on which the Court of Final Appeal relied. Democratic Party chairman Martin Lee condemned this move as "a dagger striking at the heart of the rule of law" and in symbolic protest walked out of the Legislative Council with eighteen other representatives, all dressed in black. See Chris Yeung, "Beijing Abode Plea Endorsed," *South China Morning Post*, May 20, 1999.

38. U.S. Department of State 1999.

39. Tang 1993.

40. Ghai 1997:429.

41. Joint Declaration, Art. 3(6) and (7).

42. Joint Declaration, Art. 3(7).

43. Joint Declaration, Art. 3(10).

44. Joint Declaration, Annex I, sec. XIII. The phrase "as applied to Hong Kong" reflects the fact that Britain applied the UN covenants to Hong Kong only with reservations. For a discussion of the implications, see Ghai 1997:376–82.

45. Basic Law, Arts. 124–35.

46. Basic Law, Arts. 152–53.

47. There were ten organizations—including APEC—for which China's endorsement was not required. See Mushkat 1997, app. A.

48. For a full list, see U.S. Department of State 1999.

49. According to the representative of the PRC Foreign Ministry responsible in part for Hong Kong's external affairs, "Such unique arrangements found many foreign delegates amazed, and some delegates even felt the arrangements unbelievable." See Ma Yuzhen, " 'One Country, Two Systems' Principle and Commissioner's Office of the Foreign Ministry in Hong Kong," translation of speech given in Hong Kong, April 28, 1998.

50. Ghai 1997:455–57.

51. See Lee 1996, app. I.

52. Ghai 1997:457 n. 15.

53. Ghai 1997:455 n. 14.

54. Ghai 1997:434.

55. See United States–Hong Kong Policy Act, U.S. *Code*, vol. 22, sec. 5731 (1992), signed by President George Bush on October 5, 1992, secs. 2(2) to (6) and 201. Hereinafter U.S.–Hong Kong Policy Act.

56. U.S.–Hong Kong Policy Act, secs. 202, 301.

57. Ghai (1997:460–1) reports that the Bush administration managed to water down several provisions during the legislative process.

58. Driven by allegations of espionage, recent tensions in U.S.-China relations prompted the Senate in June 1999 to pass legislation imposing additional controls on high-technology exports to Hong Kong. The bill's sponsor, Sen. John Ashcroft, stated, "Prudence demands that if China diverts sensitive U.S. technology, we impose on Hong Kong and Macao the same export controls that govern sales to China itself." See Mark Landler, "U.S. Move Has Hong Kong Worried It Will Lose Trade," *New York Times*, June 25, 1999.

59. For recent scholarly invocations of the phrase, see Yahuda 1996:9, 139–40; Bueno de Mesquita, Newman, and Rabushka 1996:21–24.

60. Bueno de Mesquita, Newman, and Rabushka 1985:127–29.

61. As of February 1997, no fewer than eleven former British colonies in the Caribbean retained the right of appeal to the Privy Council, as do Mauritius and New Zealand. See "The Caribbean: A Relic of Empire," *The Economist*, February 8, 1997, 43.

62. The politician was J. B. Jeyaretnam, secretary-general of the Worker's Party and in 1981 the first opposition figure to win election to parliament since the 1960s. He was convicted in 1986 on criminal charges. In 1988 the Privy Council found him innocent of the charges but did not have the jurisdiction to reverse his conviction. By 1997, after a new rash of politically motivated libel suits, Singapore had abolished the right of appeal to the Privy Council. See a series of articles and letters in *The Economist*, February 8, 1997, 38; October 27, 1990, 21; December 2, 1989, 8.

63. In a minor historical irony, the British initially decided in the 1840s to allow Chinese residents of Hong Kong to remain subject to Chinese laws as administered by Chinese imperial officials. Although Chinese laws did remain in force for personal, family, and property matters into the 1970s, they were administered by British and Hong Kong judges. The British reneged on their initial plan to provide Chinese officials a role in the territory, writes Ghai (1997:23), because they were "anxious that these might provide the Chinese with an argument that they exercised some sovereignty in Hong Kong." It was exactly on this basis, of course, that the PRC rejected a role for the Privy Council in 1984.

64. Annex I, sec. I, of the Joint Declaration stipulates that the HKSAR chief executive "shall be selected by election or through consultations held locally and be appointed by the Central People's Government." Interviews in March 1997 with pro-democracy activists in Hong Kong suggest that Martin Lee, who later became leader of the Democratic Party, used his influence with PRC officials—which was still intact during the early 1980s, though he has since been banned from visiting the mainland—to lobby aggressively against the establishment of a court in Beijing, which was apparently the preference of some Chinese authorities.

65. Bueno de Mesquita, Newman, and Rabushka (1985:127–29) portray the issue as a source of contention between Deng and local business interests, both Chinese and foreign, who strongly preferred an independent judiciary.

66. This preference configuration and "compromise" are reported in Bueno de Mesquita, Newman, and Rabushka 1985:128–29.

67. Joint Declaration, Annex I, sec. III.

68. Joint Declaration, Annex I, sec. XIII. The Joint Declaration, as an international treaty, is not directly enforceable in Hong Kong courts. The Basic Law is the instrument through which the Joint Declaration is given effect in Hong Kong's legal system. It too, however, enumerates a similar list of basic rights and freedoms; see Basic Law, Arts. 27–41.

69. Basic Law, Art. 158. For a discussion of the Committee for the Basic Law, see Ghai (1997:191–93), who generally characterizes it as a useful concession to the concept of "one country, two systems" at the intersection of two very different legal traditions.

70. Basic Law, Arts. 17, 160.

71. In the right of abode case, the Hong Kong government requested a reinterpretation of two Basic Law provisions on which the CFA relied. See Chris Yeung, "NPC Lays Down the Law," *South China Morning Post*, June 27, 1999.

72. The act of state doctrine in the common law excludes from the jurisdiction of courts sovereign actions taken by the executive in the field of foreign affairs, such as declarations of war. As an aspect of sovereign immunity, it also is applied in U.S. law to exclude from the jurisdiction of U.S. courts actions taken by foreign sovereigns within their own territory. See Shaw 1997:132–34, 492–94.

73. See *South China Morning Post*, September 28, 1991, 1; Lo 1993:108–9.

74. Lo 1993:109.

75. Lo 1993:117.

76. See Cheek-Milby 1995.

77. Dimbleby 1997:275–76.

78. The assessment was from Alan Paul, who later became head of the British team. See Chris Yeung, "The Challenges Ahead," *South China Morning Post*, December 14, 1997, 11.

79. Connie Law, "Barristers Reject Court Bill," *South China Morning Post*, December 9, 1994, 3. The governing council of the Law Society, a much larger association of solicitors, reversed its initial stance against the CFA bill but by doing so prompted an uprising among the rank and file membership. See Quinton Chan, "Solicitors Go All Out for Revenge: Rebels Plot Revolution in Law Society After Switch on Court of Final Appeal," *South China Morning Post*, January 22, 1995, 1.

80. This announcement was made by Lu Ping, senior PRC official for Hong Kong and Macao affairs. See So Lai-fun and Linda Choy, "Appeal Court Judges at Risk," *South China Morning Post*, December 11, 1994, 1.

81. Reports suggested that by 1995 large firms had begun to have "arbitration clauses drafted into contracts to have disputes heard outside Hong Kong" in the event that the CFA was not in place. See article by Scott McKenzie in *South China Morning Post*, May 9, 1995, 1, Business section. From 1991 onward, the business community lobbied Britain and China to reach some consensus on the CFA and thereby resolve a major source of uncertainty about the territory's future. Local business leaders cared less than civil libertarians about the details of the CFA's jurisdiction over sensitive

political issues. Instead they wanted Sino-British consensus on a court that would command respect internationally as an impartial enforcer of contract law. See Lo 1993:118–19; "Appeal Court a Necessity Before 1997: Legal Expert," *South China Morning Post*, September 22, 1993, 2.

82. For a discussion of debates within the Major administration on the CFA, see Dimbleby 1997:275–84.

83. See Jonathan Mirsky, "Patten Yields to China on Appeal Court Delay," *The Times*, June 10, 1995, 14; Martin Lee, "Colonial Cop-Out," *Economist*, July 15, 1995, 6.

84. Chris Yeung and No Kwai-yan, "Business Groups Lobby for Court Bill," *South China Morning Post*, July 12, 1995, 2.

85. See *South China Morning Post*, July 27, 1995.

86. According to one report, "When the Sunday Morning Post asked barristers and solicitors which judges they would most like to see sitting in the new court, the answer in an alarming number of cases was 'none.' " See Emma Batha, "Court Short at the Top," *South China Morning Post*, July 9, 1995, 11.

87. The chairman of the Hong Kong General Chamber of Commerce expressed his concerns to Lu Ping, director of the Hong Kong and Macao Affairs Office, in Beijing. See Angela Li, "Fears Raised on Filling Top Posts," *South China Morning Post*, May 7, 1996, 3.

88. See *South China Morning Post*, December 31, 1996, 1. For a flattering profile of Li, see Robin Fitzsimons, "Hong Kong's Mr Justice," *The Times*, January 13, 1998.

89. The appointment of two British judges from the House of Lords Appellate Committee—Lord Nicholls of Birkenhead and Lord Hoffmann—was made official by the Provisional Legislative Council on January 8, 1998. There are two judges from New Zealand, Lord Cooke of Thorndon and Sir Edward Somers, both of whom served on the Privy Council. Finally, the two Australian judges on the roster are Sir Anthony Mason, a former chief justice, and Sir Daryl Dawson, a former high court judge. See Fung 1998 and U.S. Department of State 1998:21.

90. According to Fung 1998, the majority of Hong Kong judges are non-Chinese, with none from mainland China.

91. See Basic Law, Art. 93.

92. See Basic Law, Art. 90.

93. For a laudatory editorial, see "Court on Course," *South China Morning Post*, September 10, 1997, 18. Also see Fung 1998 for a favorable analysis of initial rulings by the Court of Appeal on constitutional issues.

94. Under British rule, such decisions were unanimous and thus subject to veto by the government, then in the person of the attorney general. The current system requires a supermajority, such that judicial appointments can be made with the approval of seven of the nine commission members. In theory, this rule implies that the government representatives could be outvoted. Other members of the commission include two judges, one barrister, one solicitor, and three persons with no connection to the practice of law, all of whom are appointed by the chief executive to renewable

two-year terms. See section 3 of the Judicial Officers Recommendation Commission Ordinance, available online at <http://www.justice.gov.hk>.

95. See Basic Law, Art. 88. Under British rule, the advice of the Judicial Service Commission was not legally binding on the governor, although the tradition was to accept such recommendations. See Fung 1996–97, 298.

96. This statistic holds only for substantive judgments on appeals, for which five judges are required. Only three judges—none of whom come from the roster of non-permanent judges—are required for determinations, which cover applications for leaves to appeal and interlocutory matters. CFA judgments and determinations are available online at <http://www.info.gov.hk/jud/guide2cs/html/cfa/index.htm>.

97. The ruling, which consolidated three causes of action, appears at *International Legal Materials* 38 (1999): 551.

98. See Erik Guyot, "Hong Kong's Plan to Limit Immigration Spurs Protests but Finds Crucial Support," *Asian Wall Street Journal*, May 20, 1999.

99. The crucial passage of the February 1999 clarification read: "The Court's judgment on 29 January 1999 did not question the authority of the Standing Committee to make an interpretation under Article 158 which would have to be followed by the courts of the Region. The Court accepts that it cannot question that authority. Nor did the Court's judgment question, and the Court accepts that it cannot question, the authority of the National People's Congress or the Standing Committee to do any act which is in accordance with the provisions of the Basic Law and the procedure therein." The text is online at <http://www.info.gov.hk/jud/guide2cs/html/cfa/judmt/facv_14_16_98a.htm>.

100. Chief Secretary Anson Chan, for example, termed the reinterpretation "an exceptional decision made in exceptional circumstances" that she hoped would not recur. See Chris Yeung and No Kwai-yan, "Anson Pushes Two Systems," *South China Morning Post*, June 30, 1999.

101. See Margaret Ng, "Death Knell for the SAR's Rule of Law," *South China Morning Post*, May 21, 1999.

102. In that ruling, the CFA specified two conditions under which requests for interpretation should be made. More controversially, it also claimed that it is for the CFA "alone to decide, in adjudicating a case, whether both conditions are satisfied." For the full text, see *International Legal Materials* 38 (1999): 551.

103. See, for example, the critical conclusions of Lee 1997 and cautious optimism of Tan 1997.

104. Interestingly, Bueno de Mesquita, Newman, and Rabushka (1996:105–9) portray Hong Kong's judicial freedom as one of very few issues on which protests by the international community may be capable of forcing Beijing to back down from violations of the Joint Declaration. The reasons are as follows: (1) opinion on the mainland regarding judicial independence is increasingly divided; (2) the potential political and economic costs of intransigence are high, given the importance of the rule of law in Hong Kong; and (3) Hong Kong's judicial autonomy is the subject of

international agreements that give foreign powers a legitimate basis on which to protest.

105. For survey data documenting the "self-internationalization" and mobility of Hong Kong society, see DeGolyer 1997.

106. Britain's passage of the Nationality Act in 1981, which denied residents of Hong Kong and other dependent territories the right of abode in the United Kingdom, came after Governor MacLehose—but before the Hong Kong public—was aware of China's resolve to resume sovereignty. See Roberti 1994:29–31.

107. For analysis of the amendment process, see Ghai 1997:176–79.

108. See Krasner 1998:24.

109. Krasner, "Problematic Sovereignty," in this volume.

References

Allen, Jamie. 1997. *Seeing Red: China's Uncompromising Takeover of Hong Kong.* Singapore: Butterworth-Heinemann Asia.

Baum, Richard, ed. 1980. *China's Four Modernizations: The New Technological Revolution.* Boulder, Colo.: Westview Press.

Bueno de Mesquita, Bruce, David Newman, and Alvin Rabushka. 1985. *Forecasting Political Events: The Future of Hong Kong.* New Haven: Yale University Press.

———. 1996. *Red Flag Over Hong Kong.* Chatham, N.J.: Chatham House.

Cheek-Milby, Kathleen. 1995. *A Legislature Comes of Age: Hong Kong's Search for Influence and Identity.* New York: Oxford University Press.

Cottrell, Robert. 1993. *The End of Hong Kong: The Secret Diplomacy of Imperial Retreat.* London: John Murray.

Cradock, Percy. 1994. *Experiences of China.* London: John Murray.

Davis, Michael C. 1990. *Constitutional Confrontation in Hong Kong: Issues and Implications of the Basic Law.* New York: St. Martin's Press.

DeGolyer, Michael. 1997. "The Self-Internationalization of Hong Kong." Unpublished paper.

Dimbleby, Jonathan. 1997. *The Last Governor: Chris Patten and the Handover of Hong Kong.* London: Little, Brown.

Fairbank, John K. 1953. *Trade and Diplomacy on the China Coast.* Cambridge: Harvard University Press.

———, ed. 1968. *The Chinese World Order: Traditional China's Foreign Relations.* Cambridge: Harvard University Press.

Fung, Daniel. 1996–97. "Foundation for the Survival of the Rule of Law in Hong Kong: The Resumption of Chinese Sovereignty." *UCLA Journal of International Law and Foreign Affairs* 1, no. 2: 283–319.

———. 1998. "In Hong Kong, the 'Rule of Law' Reigns Supreme." *National Law Journal* 14 (September): C2.

Ghai, Yash. 1997. *Hong Kong's New Constitutional Order: The Resumption of Chinese Sovereignty and the Basic Law*. Hong Kong: Hong Kong University Press.

Harding, Harry. 1987. *China's Second Revolution: Reform After Mao*. Washington, D.C.: Brookings Institution.

Hong Kong Transition Project. 1997. "Hong Kong: Bridge to the Future." David C. Lam Institute for East-West Studies, Hong Kong, June.

Lane, Kevin P. 1990. *Sovereignty and the Status Quo: The Historical Roots of China's Hong Kong Policy*. Boulder, Colo.: Westview Press.

Lee, Donna. 1997. "Discrepancy Between Theory and Reality: Hong Kong's Court of Final Appeal and the Acts of State Doctrine." *Columbia Journal of Transnational Law* 35:175–211.

Lee, Jane C. Y. 1996. "China's Influence and Hong Kong's Changing International Relations Strategy." Paper prepared for International Conference on Hong Kong in Transition, September, Lingnan College, Hong Kong.

Lo Shiu-hing. 1993. "The Politics of the Court of Final Appeal Debate in Hong Kong." *Issues and Studies* (February): 105–31.

Mushkat, Roda. 1997. *One Country, Two International Legal Personalities*. Hong Kong: Hong Kong University Press.

Newman, David and David L. Weimer. 1997. "The Credibility of the PRC Commitment to a Market Economy in Hong Kong: Hypotheses and Evidence." *Economics and Politics* (November) vol. 9, no. 3, pp. 251–80.

Pereira, F. G. 1991. "Towards 1999: The Political Status of Macao in the Nineteenth and Twentieth Centuries." In R. D. Cremer, ed., *Macao: City of Commerce and Culture*. 2d ed. Hong Kong: API Press.

Rafferty, Kevin. 1991. *City on the Rocks: Hong Kong's Uncertain Future*. 2d ed. London: Penguin Books.

Roberti, Mark. 1994. *The Fall of Hong Kong: China's Triumph, Britain's Betrayal*. New York: Wiley.

Shaw, Malcolm N. 1997. *International Law*. 4th ed. Cambridge: Cambridge University Press.

Skeldon, Ronald. 1994. "Hong Kong in an International Migration System." In Ronald Skeldon, ed., *Reluctant Exiles? Migration from Hong Kong and the New Overseas Chinese*. Armonk, N.Y.: M. E. Sharp.

Tan, M. Lucy. 1997. "From the Privy Council to the Court of Final Appeal: Will the Area of Non-Justiciability be the Same in Hong Kong After July 1, 1997?" *Loyola of Los Angeles International and Comparative Law Journal* 19:413–30.

Tang, James T. H. 1993. "Hong Kong's International Status." *Pacific Review* 6:205.

U.S. Department of State. 1998. *United States Hong Kong Policy Act Report, as of April 1, 1998*. Washington, D.C.: Bureau of East Asian and Pacific Affairs.

———. 1999. *United States Hong Kong Policy Act Report, as of April 1, 1999*. Washington, D.C.: Bureau of East Asian and Pacific Affairs.

Wang Enbao. 1995. *Hong Kong, 1997: The Politics of Transition*. Boulder, Colo.: Lynne Rienner.

Wesley-Smith, Peter. 1993. "The Common Law of England in the Special Administrative Region." In Raymond Wacks, ed., *Hong Kong, China, and 1997: Essays in Legal Theory*. Hong Kong: Hong Kong University Press.

Wilson, Dick. 1990. *Hong Kong, Hong Kong*. London: Unwin Hyman.

Wong Man Fong. 1997. *China's Resumption of Sovereignty Over Hong Kong*. Hong Kong: David C. Lam Institute for East-West Studies.

6

The Struggle for Sovereignty Between China and Taiwan

ROBERT A. MADSEN

The Communist Party that rules the Chinese mainland and the Nationalist Party that dominated Taiwan through early 2000 have quarreled with one another for the better part of a century. Initially their conflict assumed the form of a civil war whose purpose was to decide which of the two states would unite all of China's territories under its aegis. After the founding of the People's Republic of China (PRC) in October 1949, however, the dispute entered a new and theoretically more interesting phase. In this period the struggle occasionally became violent but was generally waged diplomatically. Its objective, for each of the contenders, was to garner exclusive recognition from the international community that it was the sovereign government of China. Beijing and Taipei fought over this status for many reasons, including the tangible benefits it would bring, the greater domestic legitimacy it would confer, and a visceral desire to eliminate the indignities that lingered from the imperialist era of the nineteenth and early twentieth centuries. But more important in the present context, the two states wanted international recognition because they believed that it would help determine which of them achieved its original goal of asserting control over China's many regions. They realized that geopolitical and diplomatic factors would ultimately decide the issue of this contest, but each reckoned that attaining formal sovereignty would contribute marginally to the outcome it desired.

This essay examines the dispute between the People's Republic of China and the authorities who govern Taiwan—the Republic of China (ROC), as they prefer it to be called—over the principle of national sovereignty. More precisely, it shows how that concept interacted with more tangible forces in guiding the evolution of relations between the two governments. It does this chronologically, by reviewing the role that sovereignty played in modern Chinese history before 1949, describing the rivalry between the PRC and the ROC after 1949, and then showing how Beijing used her expanding system of ambassadorial relationships in the late 1960s and 1970s to increase the pressure on Taiwan to accept political subordination as part of the PRC. The analysis finally explains how Taipei responded to this pressure in the 1980s and 1990s by developing a different mode of existence that was based on economic liberalism, gradual democratization, and international responsibility. The paper thus argues that formal legal sovereignty is not essential to a state's survival. To safeguard its interests, a government must communicate frequently and dependably with other international actors. Sovereign status is helpful because it entails diplomatic mechanisms that fulfil this requirement in a simple and straightforward manner, thereby obviating the need to expend time and resources devising unique institutions. If deprived of these standard mechanisms, however, an isolated polity can still accomplish its most pressing objectives. Taiwan's experience illustrates one means through which this can be accomplished: to anticipate the argument, a "pariah state" can design its domestic policies to engender goodwill abroad and, upon this foundation, construct an informal diplomatic structure that suffices to protect its most vital foreign interests. Over the latter half of the twentieth century this sort of "alternative legitimacy" may in fact have become more feasible than it was in the past.

Before proceeding, it is helpful to recall the exact meaning of the term *sovereignty*. Using Stephen Krasner's tripartite definition, a government enjoys international legal sovereignty if it is widely recognized by other states and routinely participates in treaties and multilateral conventions. Membership in the United Nations would be apposite evidence in this regard. Second, a government possesses the attribute of domestic sovereignty if it effectively controls events within its own borders. Thus crime and radical political groups, for example, must not rise to the level where they challenge the established order. International capital flows, information exchanges, and other forms of "interdependence" are similarly controlled or regulated so as to prevent them from threatening the state's viability. Third, a government is sovereign in a Westphalian sense if its institutions are "autonomous" and not subject to significant interference from outside powers. In practice, this external sovereignty is frequently compromised. This can happen voluntarily, as when the states of Western Europe acceded to the European Union, or coercively, as in the case of the Soviet Union's influence over the lesser members of Comecon and the Warsaw Pact. Combining these three characteristics, a thoroughly sovereign country would determine its own internal organization, prohibit other countries from intervening in its domestic affairs, and maintain strong and regular contacts with the rest of the world.

The Historical Context

The theory of national sovereignty was not indigenous to China: like many other modern ideas, it was of Western provenance and clashed fundamentally with the empire's traditional political philosophy. Yet once the Chinese state and its universal pretensions had collapsed, the concept became germane because succeeding political parties saw it as offering a more modern legitimacy and a more compelling basis for their intercourse with other countries. As John Boli has observed, sovereignty is a matter of authority: the right of a state to use power within its borders and that state's acceptance by foreign actors.[1] Hence the doctrine's tenets tend to converge, explicitly or implicitly, with the ambitions of political leaders who are seeking to justify the ascendancy they have achieved through more mundane means. This was certainly the case in China, where in the closing years of the nineteenth century and the early decades of the twentieth century a variety of parties emerged that were committed to establishing their country's juridical equality with, and territorial independence from, the great Western nations and Japan. Because of this coincidence of theory and practice, the aforementioned definition of national sovereignty provides a useful framework in which to analyze China's recent history. That history, in turn, shows why the principle remains at the heart of the dispute between the PRC on the mainland and the ROC on Taiwan.

Unfamiliar with the forces that were shaping a new and stronger Europe, in the seventeenth and eighteenth centuries the Ch'ing dynasty saw no reason to adopt the institution of sovereignty. The Manchurian rulers of China had rituals and ceremonies that they used to impress their subjects and emissaries from other governments, but they did not associate these customs with a legal concept shared by a broader community of states. Instead of recognizing other countries as legitimate polities and exchanging ambassadors with them, the

Ch'ing insisted on treating them as "tributaries."[2] The small colonies of Portuguese, Spanish, and Dutch traders that were appearing along the south China seaboard were assimilated into this system and forced, formally at least, to assume inferior rank for themselves and for the governments that they represented. The only European state that the Ch'ing dynasty deigned worthy of sustained communications was Russia, whose cooperation was necessary to ensure the stability of Central Asia, but even here the language of the tributary system was normally employed.[3] Beijing likewise neglected to post a network of diplomatic envoys in foreign capitals, where they might have gathered information about economic and political developments that would eventually affect China quite dramatically. The imperial court simply had no understanding of, or interest in, the procedures through which Western states interacted with one another.

This situation changed somewhat during the nineteenth century, as the European powers became more insistent in their dealings with China. One after another, these countries cajoled the Ch'ing dynasty into letting them open legations on Chinese soil and, in subsequent exchanges, demanded and were given a wide range of "extraterritorial" privileges and immunities as well.[4] Such arrangements enabled the foreigners to carve out spheres of influence within China and to form friendly relationships with local rulers whom Beijing viewed as hostile. By the end of the century Russia was politically involved in Chinese Turkestan, Mongolia, and Manchuria; as was Britain in Tibet, Sichuan, Hunan, and, of course, Hong Kong; France in Yunnan and Guangxi; and Japan in Taiwan. Thus the formation of regular intergovernmental relations between China and the rest of the world coincided with a diminution in her Westphalian prerogatives and—inasmuch as the Ch'ing were simultaneously losing control of trade, capital flows, and information exchanges—in her domestic sovereignty. Even now, however, China's leaders refrained from dispatching embassies to learn about, and from, the Europeans. In contrast to Japan, whose missions to the West contributed significantly to her emergence as a regional force in the decades after the Meiji Restoration, China underestimated the utility of international legal sovereignty and therefore failed to use it to protect herself against the threats that were mounting overseas.[5]

Nor was the Manchu regime immune from serious internal challenges in the nineteenth century. In the peripheral regions of Tibet and Turkestan, for instance, Beijing ruled only indirectly, through satraps that occasionally declared their independence and sometimes launched raids on other parts of China. These were distant reaches, and here the Ch'ing court attempted only to collect taxes and to enforce a basic quiescence even at the best of times. Meanwhile, there were also strict limits to Beijing's authority in the Chinese heartland, where decades of rapid economic growth, a burgeoning population, and progressively greater exposure to the outside world had severely strained the capacities of the imperial state. Indicative of this problem was a series of popular rebellions, partly xenophobic in nature, that claimed the lives of some 60 million people between 1850 and the early 1870s and provided an excuse for the West to prize further concessions from the embattled government.[6] This pattern repeated itself in the Boxer Rebellion of 1899–1900, when contingents of European and American troops were brought in to quell an insurrection and then demanded money and additional extraterritorial privileges as indemnification for their losses.[7] Clearly, the Ch'ing dynasty was caught in a vicious cycle: foreign meddling stimulated internal unrest, which in turn angered the great powers and led to further encroachment from abroad. Westphalian and domestic weakness were intimately connected.

Though China had formed normal ambassadorial ties to many other countries by the Republican period, which lasted from 1912 to 1949, she was still unable to exert complete control over her domestic affairs or to exclude foreign governments from acting within her borders. The most conspicuous manifestation of this dual inadequacy came in April 1919, when the Versailles Conference awarded Germany's Pacific colonies to Japan rather than restoring them to China.[8] When word of this decision reached the ROC, popular unrest swept through the country's major cities and produced the May Fourth Movement, a disorganized civil and cultural campaign that sought largely to define China's place in the modern world. Though not expressly political, this campaign damaged the prestige of the nascent ROC by highlighting her impotence vis-à-vis the Europeans and the Japanese, and intensified public support for the country's reunification so that it could resist further foreign impositions. In this sense the movement's goals were quite similar to Krasner's categories of domestic and Westphalian sovereignty.

Yet China's nationalistic yearnings would go unsatisfied for a very long time to come. While Chiang Kai-shek and his colleagues in the Kuomintang (KMT) leadership had adopted many of the rituals of Western states—celebrating an annual National Day on October 10, for example, and wearing uniforms and conducting martial parades—their actual powers were quite narrowly circumscribed. During the 1920s and 1930s large swathes of Chinese territory were ruled by warlords who, though ostensibly dedicated to the cause of national unity, operated with effective autonomy in the territories they dominated. From a fairly early date the ROC endeavored to subjugate these rival centers of influence. In 1926 Chiang Kai-shek launched his "Northern Expedition" against some of the warlords; and in 1927 the KMT turned on its erstwhile allies, the Chinese Communist Party (CCP), slaughtering many of its members and driving others into hiding.[9] The motive behind these exercises was to consolidate the Nationalist Party's power, but their effect, if successful, would have been to establish China's domestic sovereignty and to augment the resources available for use against her external enemies.

For precisely this reason the countries that were most active in violating China's Westphalian sovereignty opposed the KMT's pursuit of domestic supremacy. In 1931, for instance, militarists in Tokyo and the Kwantung Army in Mukden made the fateful decision to transform Manchuria into the puppet state of Manchukuo, which they felt would serve as a bulwark against Chinese nationalism and as a more dependable base for Japanese activity in Northeast Asia.[10] The interrelationship between domestic fractiousness and international aggression was evinced again in 1936. At this point Tokyo was expanding her involvement along China's eastern seaboard, and indigenous resentment against the Japanese was deepening. Chiang Kai-shek registered this sentiment, but he was preoccupied with the danger to his regime posed by Mao Zedong's armies and chose to focus his energies on their deracination. He wanted, in other words, to acquire uncontested domestic sovereignty before trying to assert China's external prerogatives. Chiang's agenda was not widely shared among the ROC leadership, however, and in December several Nationalist generals and a patriotically inclined warlord kidnapped him and forced him to reverse his priorities by agreeing to form an anti-Japanese United Front with the Communists.[11] Sadly for the Chinese, the formation of this bipartisan coalition soon provoked additional intrusions from abroad: in July 1937 the Japanese army precipitated the Marco Polo Bridge incident, thereby inaugurating World War II in the Pacific.[12] As these events indicate, the men who oversaw the Japanese presence on the Asian mainland were determined to stop China from attaining internal unity lest that accomplishment pave the way for her achievement of Westphalian autonomy.

Still, the Japanese may have overestimated the extent to which the ROC would succeed in evolving a single political organization that could eventually reintegrate the country's various regions. After all, the KMT and the CCP had built their United Front for the sole purpose of combating Japan's forces and did not expect it to last far beyond the end of the War of Resistance. Ideologically and personally, the leaders of the two parties remained deeply and bitterly antagonistic; and throughout the Japanese conflict they worked almost constantly to undermine each other's power and to amass weaponry and other matériel for use in the civil conflagration that they thought would soon ensue.[13] Thus the image of Chinese unity that the Japanese found so disquieting was actually illusory, a facade to which neither the Communists nor the Nationalists were wholly dedicated.

During the struggle against Japan, incidentally, both parties believed that China's future civil war would be waged on the mainland. All of their earlier battles had taken place on the continent, and in the early 1940s there was little reason to believe that the focus of the conflict would eventually shift to Taiwan and the Strait. Indeed, the relationship between the island territory and the rest of China was rather tenuous.[14] It is true that the vast majority of Taiwan's inhabitants were ethnically Chinese, but most of these people had migrated there hundreds of years before; and during the eighteenth and nineteenth centuries the island had enjoyed de facto independence or answered to a Japanese colonial administration for vastly more years than it had been subject to active Ch'ing rule. In addition, the Taiwanese claimed some distinct cultural and linguistic traits and hence could perhaps be regarded as a separate nation. In the 1930s even Mao Zedong opined that the island was not part of China and would remain separate from the Communist state that he and his partisans intended to found.[15] Taiwan's disposition accordingly seemed a trivial matter, far removed from the internecine strife that had consumed China for so long.

This changed during World War II, when Washington, and to a lesser extent London, decided to treat the ROC as a great power.[16] There were several reasons behind this policy, including agitation from the China lobby in the United States, wishful thinking that Nationalist China might soon become a force for regional stability, and a shared desire to steel Chiang's sometimes questionable resolve to fight against the Japanese. All of these factors militated in favor of support for the Kuomintang. In the Cairo Declaration of 1943, therefore, Franklin D. Roosevelt, Winston Churchill, and Chiang Kai-shek declared that "the territories Japan has stolen from the Chinese, such as Manchuria, Formosa and the Pescadores" should be returned to the ROC at the war's end.[17] Joseph Stalin endorsed this proposition at the Tehran Conference, and the Big Three confirmed it again during the

Potsdam discussions of July 1945. Tokyo likewise acquiesced when, upon her capitulation to the Allies a month later, her armed forces surrendered the lands they had occupied to the Nationalists rather than the Communists or the people of Taiwan.[18] These events largely clarified the island's status: Now that the major international powers had acknowledged that it was part of China, neither the KMT nor the CCP could renounce it without jeopardizing their nationalistic credentials. The bonds between Taiwan and the mainland grew tighter still in the late 1940s, when the ROC repaired to the island and began preparing to attack the PRC. Once that had happened, the fledgling Communist state in Beijing came to see conquering Taiwan as a defensive imperative as well as a matter of national dignity.[19] In this way a series of decisions by outside powers and the retreat of the Kuomintang transformed Taiwan from a peripheral and irrelevant region into an essential component of China's domestic sovereignty.

There were of course other parts of China in which Beijing's writ did not run. Foreigners held sway over Hong Kong and Macao; the Soviet Union still possessed some of the privileges that the czars had exacted from the old Ch'ing dynasty; and Tibet retained a high degree of autonomy.[20] Mao Zedong and his partisans took these infringements on China's territorial integrity very seriously and would turn their attention to their elimination beginning in the early 1950s. But Taiwan was more urgent, so in late 1949 and early 1950 the PRC started assembling an amphibious force with which to cross the Strait and conquer the ROC.[21]

These plans were interrupted, however, by events to the north. For some time the Truman administration had been hoping to distance itself from the rump state on Taiwan and to establish at least a minimal relationship with the newly founded PRC.[22] Then came North Korea's invasion of the Republic of Korea on June 25, 1950, an event that played into the hands of the McCarthy faction and the China lobby, which now exhorted the White House to resume its assistance to Chiang Kai-shek and the KMT.[23] In the meantime some American officials were independently concluding from the PRC's behavior on the mainland that she might not be an appropriate diplomatic partner for the United States. On June 27, therefore, the administration decided to interpose the Seventh Fleet between the Chinese mainland and Taiwan and to initiate a program of economic and defensive aid to Taipei that would expand considerably in subsequent years and ultimately enable the ROC to sustain herself in her insular redoubt indefinitely.[24] The Chinese Civil War was effectively suspended, with mutually repugnant governments ensconced in Beijing and Taipei and precluded by Washington from attacking each other.

Besides saving the KMT from an eventual defeat, this American intervention also bolstered the ROC's domestic status; for with the constitution suspended for the duration of "the Communist rebellion," the Nationalists had no electoral mandate to justify their control of Taiwan.[25] Instead, their rule was founded on brute force, the party's mainland ambitions, and apparent prominence in the "free world." Washington's commitment underscored these ideological forms of legitimacy and thereby improved the ROC's domestic position. The PRC, on the other hand, saw the U.S. actions as yet another example of imperialist interference in China's internal affairs. This impression gained further credence in 1952 when, after more agitation from the China lobby, Washington encouraged Tokyo to sign a peace treaty with Taipei; again in 1954, when the United States and the ROC concluded a bilateral defense treaty; and yet again during the Strait crises of 1954–1955 and 1958, in which Washington appeared to support Taipei's military policies and even threatened to use nuclear force against the PRC.[26] The Truman, Eisenhower, and Kennedy administrations were never comfortable working this closely with Taipei, but Beijing was generally unaware of their reservations. To her these more conspicuous instances of U.S. cooperation with Taiwan indicated that the ROC's existence represented a breach not merely of China's domestic integrity but also of her Westphalian rights.

In summary, China's modern history illuminates several facets of the principle of sovereignty. First, the concept implied very different things in Asia and the West. The Europe of the seventeenth through nineteenth centuries, where the doctrine reached its most extensive articulation, had endured centuries of sanguinary wars as one country after another sought to secure continental predominance as Rome had once done. Here sovereignty meant a renunciation of the imperial precedent, a lowering of national aspirations, and a theoretical recognition that Europe's most prominent polities had a right to coexist with equal privileges. In China, on the other hand, the principle required greater assertiveness, as her successive governments sought to compel other powers to treat her as a fully qualified member of the international community. In both cases it was the countries' initial circumstances—strength or impotence—that dictated the direction in which the concept would impel them. China's experience secondly demonstrates that the elements of sovereignty are often identical to the natural objectives of politics. Thus the Chinese governments of the early twentieth century intended to crush their domestic rivals, expel the foreign forces operating within China's territories, and obtain legal parity with the European powers—goals that correspond quite closely to Krasner's definition of that institution. A third salient point is the relation between the internal and external attributes of sovereignty: the fact that acquiring one of these characteristics enables a government to concentrate more effectively on achieving the other. Imperial Japan understood this reality and hence could not look with equanimity upon the Nationalists' and Communists' attempts to unify China. It is finally worth noting that the conduct of a state's enemies can sometimes alter its perception of its own sovereignty. To adduce the obvious example, the PRC does not see Taiwan as Chinese territory because the island always was such but rather, at least in part, because of decisions made in the 1940s and early 1950s by the Allies, Japan, and the Kuomintang.

Round One: The UN Battle

As explained above, the newly founded PRC was determined to assert control over all of China's territories and to eradicate the influence of the foreign entities that were operating there without her approval.[27] She pursued these concrete aspects of national sovereignty not because of any abiding commitment to the institutions of international law but because they happened to accord with her foremost political goals. It is true that some in the Communist leadership, apparently including Zhou Enlai, thought that regular interaction with the West would yield substantial diplomatic benefits, but many others disdained the legal conventions of the imperialist powers and hoped to cooperate primarily with revolutionary regimes. Representing a third pole in this debate, Mao Zedong was reportedly a realist who saw little value in normal diplomatic mechanisms unless they brought tangible advantages like greater trade or more influence in other countries. The main point on which these various factions did agree was that the Communist Party would not renounce its fundamental policies: socialism, political and economic independence, and the war against the Nationalist government immured on Taiwan.[28] Short of violating these priorities, there was an additional consensus in the Chinese capital in the summer and autumn of 1949 that the PRC should seek membership in the United Nations as well as diplomatic relations with any foreign government that promised to sever its ties to the ROC.[29] Later, when a large number of countries rebuffed these entreaties, Beijing would become relatively skeptical, withdrawing her ambassadors and concentrating her attention more exclusively on the communist world. It would take the events of the next two decades to convince the leaders of the PRC that such a narrow diplomatic focus was inimical to China's fundamental interests.

Putting that point aside momentarily, the most successful of the PRC's early diplomatic initiatives was her entrance into the USSR's system of alliances. The new Chinese government and most of the states of the Eastern bloc exchanged ambassadors in October 1949 or soon thereafter.[30] Then, in April 1950, Moscow acceded to a thirty-year defensive treaty that would afford Beijing $300 million in economic aid and transfer to her a variety of industrial and military technologies.[31] But China paid a very high price for this assistance; she was obligated to support the Kremlin's foreign policies, for instance, and granted the Soviet Union the right to continue using railways and port facilities in northeast China for several more years. Ending these infringements on China's Westphalian rights would have to be postponed until Beijing could satisfy her more urgent need for greater domestic authority, economic prosperity, and security. So the PRC proceeded to secure her position in the communist camp; and when the United States, Western Europe, and the United Nations hesitated to accept her as an equal diplomatic partner, she became more obdurate in her dealings with them. In late 1949 and early 1950 the PRC and her agents accordingly requisitioned a number of foreign properties in violation of international law, rejected friendly overtures from several capitalist countries, and adopted a broadly distrustful posture regarding the United Nations and other intergovernmental organizations.[32] At this juncture China was not prepared to engage in what the West considered proper diplomacy.

Beijing's attitude underwent a partial change beginning in late June 1950, when Washington persuaded the United Nations to authorize a multilateral intervention against the North Korean armies that had just crossed into South Korea. In fact, the Truman administration had reached the decision to enter the war many hours before bringing the matter to the Security Council's attention and would have proceeded even in the absence of that body's approval.[33] The record is clear on that score. But obtaining the Council's endorsement was nonetheless critical, since it brought a number of other countries to Seoul's aid and thereby lent an air of global legitimacy to what was largely an American enterprise. Moreover, given the United Nations' internal dynamics, the chances of repealing the endorsement before the United States was ready for a ceasefire were exiguous. For the duration of the conflict, therefore, the allied effort would bear the imprimatur of the international community, and Pyongyang and her allies, Moscow and Beijing, would occasionally seem to be fighting unjustly. The PRC foresaw this development as soon as the council announced its adoption of the U.S. resolution on June 27 and immediately set about trying to have it overturned. It was at this point that Beijing's absence from the United Nations first seriously impinged upon her interests, for she could not lodge a protest in the General Assembly or appeal to the Security Council for redress. Nor could Moscow veto the UN decision, since her ambassador was still boycotting that organization in protest against its refusal to recognize the new Chinese state the previous autumn and winter.[34] Thus the PRC's relative isolation complicated her national defense in a palpable and very significant manner.

If the short-term effect of the Korean War was to drive Beijing and Moscow closer together, over the next several years this episode went some way toward reminding the Chinese leaders that they needed to earn the goodwill of a wider range of foreign governments—including neutral and even anticommunist states—in order to render it more difficult for Beijing's enemies to combine against her.[35] This heightened interest in diplomacy collaterally opened new vistas for the PRC's competition with the ROC, in which Beijing tried intermittently to persuade the world to acknowledge her supremacy over China and to derecognize the Nationalist state. The KMT resisted this fiercely, for Taipei depended on the "free world's" recognition to preserve her seat in the United Nations and to help justify her authoritarian rule at home on Taiwan. If international legal sovereignty was important to Beijing as a means of fending off external threats, in other words, Taipei valued that trait largely because it reinforced her domestic integrity.

Progress in this diplomatic competition came very slowly for Beijing. During the middle and late 1950s the Eisenhower administration sporadically hoped for an accommodation with the PRC, but due partly to the machinations of Taipei's friends and agents in North America, this desideratum was never publicly espoused.[36] Instead, Washington consistently called upon the other members of the "free world" and many sympathetic third-world countries to stand fast in support of the ROC, and as a result the General Assembly annually adopted Washington's moratorium against discussion of the China question. This widespread recalcitrance rankled, of course, but it did not initially cause Beijing any insuperable difficulties. After all, China was still fairly close to the USSR, which had returned to the Security Council in the autumn of 1950 and hence could preclude the United Nations from reaching unfriendly decisions. In the latter half of the decade, however, Beijing's situation became progressively more precarious. By 1959 and 1960 Sino-Soviet relations had deteriorated to the point where Beijing believed that the Kremlin might acquiesce in, or even sponsor, international actions that contravened her interests.[37] In these circumstances the PRC had, of necessity, to construct her own network of international connections in order to compensate for the attenuation of her alliance with Moscow.

China had in fact already built some bridges to noncommunist countries—witness Zhou Enlai's performance at the Bandung Conference of 1955, the PRC's subsequent encouragement of the Nonaligned Movement, and her more conciliatory approach to the West during the middle 1950s.[38] But this effort accelerated markedly at the beginning of the next decade, when Beijing tried to establish her credentials as a rival to Moscow for leadership in the international communist movement and as a patron of independence movements in the developing world.[39] The timing of this démarche was propitious for the PRC, since the wave of decolonization that swept across the globe in the early 1960s was producing a host of new states— many of which were flattered to receive attention from Beijing and quickly agreed to recognize her as China's sovereign government and to vote for her in the annual UN debates. Taipei naturally fought a rearguard action against this trend. In 1961 she availed herself of the assistance of the U.S. Agency for International Development and inaugurated Operation Vanguard, a program of economic and financial aid for poor countries that was designed largely to guarantee their loyalty to the ROC in the United Nations.[40] This magnanimity slowed the erosion of Taiwan's status somewhat. More determinative of her fate, however, was the fact that despite some profound misgivings about the ROC government, the Kennedy and Johnson administrations continued to champion Taipei's cause and thereby stopped Beijing from achieving international legal sovereignty for several more years.

By 1965, however, the tide had clearly turned in Beijing's favor. The PRC had now acquired fifty ambassadorial relations to Taiwan's sixty; and in that year's UN contest the General Assembly spit evenly—forty-seven ballots cast for each side—on the question of which state should be regarded as representing China.[41] This tally was far short of the two-thirds vote required under the "important question" procedure that Washington was now employing, but it was still a disturbing omen for the ROC since it implied that Beijing would gain a sufficient majority within the next few years. Clearly the anticommunist coalition that had assisted the Kuomintang regime for the previous fifteen years was on the verge of disintegration.

Viewed with this fact in mind, the Cultural Revolution that ensued in the summer of 1966 was a tremendous boon for Taiwan. This tragedy began when Mao Zedong decided that perpetuating his own preeminence and ensuring the survival of his political philosophy were more important than either China's domestic stability or the progress that the PRC had made toward international legal sovereignty.[42] He therefore unleashed forces that did immense damage to the country and coincidentally managed to offend most of the world's governments. In the incipient stages of the revolution, for example, agents of the PRC fomented antigovernment demonstrations in Hong Kong and riots in Burma; and over the next two years Beijing recalled all but one of her ambassadors from their posts abroad so that they might undergo "reeducation."[43] Needless to say, these events had a negative impact on thinking in the United States, where some officials surmised that the PRC, rather than the USSR, was now the foremost threat to global peace.[44] In normal circumstances this alienation from the international community might not have entailed excessive risks, since China was fairly close to autarky and did not require much help from multilateral organizations and foreign countries. Yet if a diplomatic or military crisis did occur, Beijing's isolation would become considerably more risky; for reestablishing cordial relations with other states would require some time, and in the interim she would not have recourse to the assistance those governments might afford. As during the Korean War, Beijing's refusal to engage in normal diplomatic processes would constrain her diplomatic freedom and jeopardize her security.

Mao Zedong and the other Chinese leaders awoke to this danger in 1968, when Leonid Brezhnev sent troops into Czechoslovakia and asserted, in his eponymous doctrine, that the USSR sometimes had the right to use force against other socialist countries.[45] This dictum induced great concern in Beijing; for rather than limiting Moscow's interests to the Eastern European lands that she had dominated since the late 1940s, Brezhnev spoke in universal terms that at least potentially included China. This admitted the possibility that the Kremlin might try to exploit the PRC's isolation by launching a preemptive strike against her garrisons before Beijing could enlist the assistance of other governments. Chinese alarm on this point received another fillip in March 1969, when violent clashes occurred along the Sino-Soviet border and Moscow began hinting that she might attempt to destroy the PRC's nuclear facilities.[46] The Ninth Congress of the Chinese Communist

Party reacted to this in April by proclaiming an end to the most disruptive "mass action stage" of the Cultural Revolution and then hastily started cultivating friendlier ties to other governments.[47] Ambassadors were accordingly sent out first to Albania; then to France, North Vietnam, and Cambodia; and later to fourteen other states, including Pakistan. Even more significant, the PRC now concluded that limited cooperation with Washington might be useful as a counterpoise to Moscow's power. Once again, military concerns were dictating that Beijing adhere more closely to the norms of international law even if doing so constrained Chairman Mao in his quest for uncontested domestic authority.

Predictably, given this perceived need for better communications with other governments, between 1969 and 1971 Beijing reinvigorated her quest for membership in the United Nations and a permanent seat on the Security Council. The greatest factor behind this decision was assuredly the threat posed by the USSR, but the continuing rivalry with the Kuomintang regime on Taiwan also entered into the PRC's calculations. So, while negotiating ambassadorial exchanges with the governments of Britain (whose legation had been withdrawn during the Cultural Revolution), Italy, Canada, and several other countries, the PRC quietly let it be known that she would expect those states to vote for her in the annual General Assembly polls.[48] Some sources claim that Beijing even requested that the Nixon administration provide tacit support for her UN campaign.[49] This argument seems reasonable, for opinion regarding Taiwan was so intense in the Chinese capital that the pro-Western faction could not have prevailed in pursuing a rapprochement with the United States if it had not sought substantial concessions on the Taiwan issue. For many in Beijing, this was the sine qua non of normal relations with the capitalist superpower.

The PRC's bid for international acceptance presented a real dilemma for the Nixon administration, since Washington's long friendship with Taipei and the residual influence of the China lobby rendered a hasty retreat from Taiwan impolitic. Still, the White House shared the increasingly prevalent view that by drawing Beijing into a nexus of diplomatic relationships the world could give her a stake in the status quo and thereby persuade her to moderate her domestic and foreign policies.[50] While the primary area in which they hoped that this effect would manifest was East Asia's geopolitics, Nixon and Kissinger also felt that a more engaged China would be less likely to act aggressively toward Taiwan because such behavior would imperil her recent economic and political gains. In other words, Washington believed that Beijing would sacrifice some of her domestic autonomy in exchange for greater legal sovereignty and the concomitant enhancement of her Westphalian stature. To this end, in 1971 the administration adopted a dual strategy, ordering the State Department to work with the ROC's diplomats in anticipation of that year's UN election—thus appeasing Taiwan's allies in the United States—while the president and Kissinger proceeded more quietly to develop their détente with China.[51]

Until his death two decades later Nixon would maintain that in 1971 he thought he could implement this complicated strategy without affecting Taiwan's situation in the United Nations. Some scholars, however, think this improbable in light of the many signs, already evident at the time, that Washington's actions were causing other governments to distance themselves from Taipei. Indeed, in his memoirs Henry Kissinger retrospectively admits that the American "opening to Peking effectively determined the outcome of the UN debate."[52] Thus the General Assembly decided, on October 25, 1971, to oust the ROC and welcome the PRC by a vote of 75–35, with 17 abstentions. For Beijing, this was a seminal victory. Henceforth she would possess her own veto power and could independently block hostile actions by the USSR, the United States, or any other country that attempted to turn the United Nations against her. In addition, the PRC could now use that body's facilities to gather information on other countries, lobby for her own causes, and negotiate quiet bilateral deals when public diplomacy proved inconvenient. Beijing's new prominence likewise translated into a broader range of diplomatic relationships: by the end of 1972 an additional nineteen states had switched their recognition from the ROC to the PRC, and over the next six years another score of countries would do so.[53] This achievement significantly reduced the likelihood that China would ever again be as isolated as she had been during the Cultural Revolution.[54]

If the General Assembly decision of 1971 marked a triumph for the PRC, it conversely represented a defeat for the ROC. Strictly speaking, Taipei was never expelled from the United Nations.[55] Sensing the impending decision, on the morning of October 25 her diplomats walked out of the assembly several hours before the vote was actually conducted. This gambit enabled the Nationalist government to salvage a bit of pride: thereafter the ROC would insist that she had quit the organization in disgust rather than participate in an immoral act. Yet Taipei had in effect been discomfited, and no degree of press censorship could prevent the people of Taiwan from realizing that their government's claims to leadership in the global community had been roundly rejected. This was not only embarrassing to the Kuomintang but positively harmful; for even those citizens of Taiwan who had long since concluded that the ROC would never return to the mainland had been impressed by Taipei's ability to command other countries' respect. Now, by contrast, the KMT had only her ambassadorial relationship with the United States as evidence of international influence and was consequently reduced to relying more heavily on the threat of force to discourage violent challenges from opposition groups. Though hard to quantify objectively, this diminution of the ROC's domestic sovereignty was an injury that the ROC leaders considered quite grave. In addition, the General Assembly vote meant that Taipei would lose the freedom to discuss her concerns with other states in the United Nations' New York headquarters; and that her participatory rights in such affiliated organizations as the World Bank, the International Monetary Fund, and the Asian Development Bank—which had been helping to finance Taiwan's economic development—would soon be questioned.[56]

Overall, therefore, Beijing and Taipei's competition in the United Nations was a matter not only of honor but also of practical advantage. In the first place, whichever state occupied the China seat in that body and was recognized by most of the world and consequently faced a relatively benign security outlook. That this consideration was meaningful to the CCP was demonstrated by the speed with which Beijing curtailed the excesses of the Cultural Revolution and reengaged in conventional diplomacy after the USSR's invasion of Czechoslovakia. Clearly the PRC felt that international legal sovereignty would confer on her a useful degree of political and military flexibility and that these gains were more important than unfettered domestic autonomy. Another, and more subtle, function of legal sovereignty was the greater opportunity it afforded diplomats to monitor the thinking of leaders in other countries and to negotiate public and confidential understandings. These requirements can be fulfilled without regular diplomatic tools, to be sure, but doing so on an ad hoc basis is difficult and slow, and therefore problematic. Finally, and most crucially, the ROC's defeats in the early 1970s undermined her legitimizing ideology and thereby impaired her internal sovereignty. Taiwan thus became a pariah state, unable to derive significant domestic prestige from her relations with foreign actors—other than the United States—and unsure how to conduct her intergovernmental affairs prospectively.[57] In the event Taiwan would succeed admirably in coping with these problems, but her accomplishments in this regard should not obscure the very real concern that the KMT rulers felt immediately after their departure from the United

Nations. After all, China's experience in the nineteenth and early twentieth centuries offered little reason for a weak and isolated state to feel optimistic about its relations with the West, Japan, and the proximate Soviet giant.

Round Two: The "Peace Offensive"

If Chinese history through 1971 demonstrated that international legal sovereignty was highly desirable, whether a state could exist indefinitely without that attribute was still an open question. Fortunately for the historian, Beijing's policy toward the ROC in the 1970s and early 1980s provides an empirical case with which to test this proposition. During this period Beijing could not act militarily against Taiwan lest she anger the rest of the world and put her recent economic and political gains at risk, so she resorted instead to diplomacy as a means of completing Taipei's isolation and then forcing her to accept subordination within the PRC.[58] Yet implicit in Beijing's strategy was an assumption that the ROC had once possessed full legal sovereignty and was now losing it. Insofar as they considered and accepted this premise, Mao Zedong, Zhou Enlai, and their colleagues were overlooking two crucial points. First, Taipei's authority over China had never been as absolute as the term *sovereignty* implies, so depriving her of that characteristic would not necessarily increase her vulnerability very much. Second—and even worse from the PRC's perspective—was the possibility that by discrediting Taiwan's "national mission" of returning to the mainland Beijing might force her to articulate an alternative legitimacy that would prove more persuasive both at home and internationally. In this way the Chinese political campaign might paradoxically enhance the ROC's stature.

To clarify these points a brief historical digression is in order. The ROC's status as the government of China had in fact long been dubious. When the Kuomintang retreated across the strait in the late 1940s, Chiang Kai-shek and his partisans lost the ability to enforce the domestic and Westphalian rights that they claimed over the mainland. The ROC's position with regard to international legal regimes was initially somewhat more solid; but by late 1949 Great Britain, the United States, and many other states wanted soon to shift their ambassadorial relations from Taipei to Beijing, which ruled the vast majority of China's people and territory and hence could more reasonably be treated as her government. Movement toward the PRC ceased temporarily with the onset of the Korean War, but resumed in the middle 1950s. Taiwan reacted to this by redoubling her efforts, and those of her friends abroad, to discourage the United States, Japan, South Korea, and other signally important countries from abandoning her.[59] Though this agitation retarded the pace of change, it failed to obviate the fundamental illogicality that underlay the ROC's international legitimacy: for even at the height of the Cold War, Taipei's commitment to continental China was widely regarded as implausible.

In view of this fact, the ROC seems to have made a serious mistake when, in the middle 1950s, she forfeited a chance to establish herself as the sovereign government of Taiwan. This possibility arose after the strait crisis of 1954–1955, when Beijing sought an accommodation with the West and embarked on a series of negotiations with Washington, initially in Geneva and then in Warsaw.[60] There is no way to know how much ground the PRC was prepared to concede in these talks, but she hinted that she might attenuate her claims to Taiwan in order to form an independent relationship with the United States. Washington would almost certainly have agreed to such a settlement, inasmuch as it would have permitted her to maintain parallel communications with both Chinese polities. The situation on the island was likewise auspicious. The KMT government had by now consolidated its power and enjoyed ambassadorial relations with a wide variety of other states. If at this point Taipei had abjured her ties to the mainland and sought recognition as the government of Taiwan, or as the "Republic of China on Taiwan," she may well have been embraced as such by those "free world" countries that felt a residual loyalty to her and yet wanted to adopt a more pragmatic attitude toward the PRC. The Nationalists could then have set about forming military alliances with regional powers so as to sustain Taiwan's Westphalian independence. The external elements of sovereignty would thus be combined in support of a new and smaller, but considerably more credible, Nationalist state. This transition would doubtless have been difficult to manage—the ROC would need to reformulate her domestic legitimacy, for instance, and relations with the PRC would remain complex—but the benefits of more secure diplomatic status were so compelling that Taiwan should at least have explored this option.

In the early 1960s there were some signs that Taipei was contemplating a change of this sort; but then Chiang Kai-shek and the other Kuomintang leaders reverted to their customary adamance, alleging that the ROC was China's rightful government and that the PRC should be overthrown.[61] The resulting situation was far from ideal. On the one hand there was a profound, albeit latent, defect in the ROC's moral foundation because so few countries sincerely believed her propaganda about the mainland. Most of Taiwan's treaties, executive agreements, and ambassadorial relationships were thus based on a territorial and ideological claim that the world acknowledged only with great reluctance. On the other hand the ROC's contention—shared, incidentally, by Beijing—that the international community could recognize but one of the rival states ensured that when other countries eventually bowed to reality and exchanged ambassadors with Beijing, they must simultaneously sever their official connections to Taipei.[62] This is precisely what happened in the early 1970s, when the General Assembly endorsed the PRC's membership in the United Nations and scores of countries promptly removed their embassies to Beijing. No one can deny that this was a serious reversal for the ROC, since it deprived her of valuable diplomatic organs and further eroded her domestic legitimacy; but the damage was not as severe as if Taipei had simultaneously lost a universally accepted raison d'être.

Beijing, however, believed that Taiwan was considerably weaker in the 1970s than before and accordingly tried to perfect the island's isolation so as to render the KMT government more compliant. This "peace offensive" comprised several different endeavors: trying to destroy the rest of the ROC's international relationships, further weakening her popular legitimacy, and trying to entice her into talks aimed at Taiwan's eventual reintegration into the mainland Chinese state.[63] Once these discussions had started, the PRC reckoned, foreign and domestic pressure on the Nationalist regime would mount and Taipei would have no choice but to accept Beijing's terms. This approach to the Taiwan problem was implemented throughout the 1970s and 1980s, but there were three periods in which the Communists worked particularly assiduously to aggravate the Nationalists' plight.

The earliest of these began in late 1971, when Beijing told those governments and international agencies that desired relations with her that they must first conform their policies to the United Nations' judgment by ceasing to interact with Taipei. Besides persuading many individual states to do this, by the end of 1974 the PRC had engineered Taiwan's expulsion from UNESCO, the World Health Organization, the Universal Postal Union, the International Telecommunication Union, the World Meteorological Organization, the International Atomic Energy Agency, the International Telecommunication Satellite Organization, the International Air Transport Association, and many other multilateral bodies.[64] During these years Beijing also discouraged countries from cooperating informally with Taiwan's citizens and their associations. In 1975 and 1976, for example, she prevailed upon the governments of West Germany, New Zealand, Canada, and several other nations to prohibit visits by certain civic groups from Taiwan because those groups claimed to represent the "Republic of China."[65] On some occasions the PRC even tried to dissuade private companies such as American Express and Union Carbide from doing business with, or making investments on, Taiwan. This commercial prohibition was not applied consistently, but it did cause some foreign enterprises to reconsider their contacts with the ROC, and it further tarnished the KMT's reputation on Taiwan.

This blow to Taipei's authority was of course intentional. In early 1972 Beijing started broadcasting messages to the people of the ROC in Mandarin Chinese and in the Hakka and Minnan dialects spoken by the ethnic Taiwanese.[66] These messages warned that the reunification of the island and the mainland under the PRC's auspices would occur one way or another and called upon the ROC citizenry to press its leaders to join in voluntary talks so that this could be accomplished without bloodshed.

It was the PRC's expectation that these assaults on Taiwan's domestic and international character would deprive the Nationalists of the support they needed to survive as an effectively independent state and that Taipei would thereupon start searching for a way out of her predicament. This Beijing offered in the form of a personal appeal to Chiang Kai-shek and his colleagues in the autumn of 1973.[67] In an adumbration of the "one nation, two systems" formula that would later be applied to Hong Kong, Beijing pledged that if the KMT facilitated China's unification, Taiwan would be given unique privileges as an autonomous region. The island could then manage its own internal affairs; maintain distinct economic, legal, and military systems; and continue using the ROC's national flag and other indicia of sovereignty. Thus the Nationalists could protect their subjects' way of life while exchanging their delicate international circumstances for the safer, if humbler, position of a provincial government.

The second stage in the PRC's peace offensive started in early 1979, a time when the ROC's international environment was especially inclement. On the first of January, Washington had switched her diplomatic recognition from Taipei to Beijing and formally given notice that the 1954 Mutual Defense Treaty would be terminated in a year's time. This was an event whose approach the senior Nationalists had long dreaded, both because it would strip away the last of their international prestige, thereby vitiating their control over the people of Taiwan, and because it would undermine the island's security from Chinese attack.[68] For while Deng Xiaoping and other PRC leaders had privately assured the Carter administration that they did not intend to use military force against the "renegade province," Beijing's public stance was that she would never forswear the right to suppress insurgencies within her borders violently: such, after all, was the essence of domestic sovereignty.[69] Washington responded to these statements by declaring that she would not let Taiwan's fate be determined coercively; but this pledge was not entirely persuasive, for there was no basis for such a commitment to an unrecognized territory in U.S. or international law. Furthermore, American attorneys retained by Taipei counseled that the ROC's derecognition had invalidated many of the statutes on which her commercial, financial, cultural, and juridical communications with the United States were predicated.[70] All these problems could be addressed if the White House and Congress dedicated several weeks to revising the U.S. legal code, but Taipei was not confident that this task would be performed quickly and thoroughly enough to reassure the people of Taiwan and the international business community.

To capitalize on these anxieties, at the beginning of January 1979 the PRC issued a Message to Compatriots in Taiwan that urged the people of that island to return quickly to "the embrace of the motherland."[71] This document added to Beijing's earlier overtures a suggestion that Taiwan and the mainland initiate trade, postal, academic, cultural, athletic, and tourist exchanges without delay. Deng Xiaoping expanded on this proposal in subsequent weeks, reiterating that if the Nationalists accepted Beijing's sovereignty they could stay on as the government of Taiwan for a very long time to come.[72] In the event the ROC denounced these offers as tendentious, but at least Beijing had established a record of forbearance that might be useful in future talks with the Americans. Such, after all, was presumably one of the main motives behind the message. In the meantime, Chinese officials continued their campaign to isolate the ROC; and in April and May 1980 the World Bank and the International Monetary Fund respectively heeded the PRC's wishes by admitting her and ousting Taiwan.[73]

The third phase of Beijing's peace offensive was launched in the autumn of 1981, and it, too, was influenced by pending negotiations between Washington and Beijing. In April 1979 Congress had passed the Taiwan Relations Act, a public law stipulating that the United States would continue supplying armaments to the ROC to ensure that she was not subject to military intimidation.[74] The PRC disliked this measure because it perpetuated the American involvement in territory that Washington had recognized as subject to Chinese rule. Beijing tolerated this violation of her Westphalian prerogatives, however, because she required Western economic and diplomatic support and because the Carter administration implemented the law with circumspection. The Reagan administration, by contrast, was much more assertive in assisting Taiwan; and by late 1981 the PRC was actively trying to persuade Washington to desist from this encroachment upon her sovereign rights—or at least gradually to reduce the volume of U.S. weapons sales to Taiwan and to set a date for their total cessation.[75] If the White House did not relent on this score, Chinese diplomats warned, Beijing would sever the recently formed bilateral relationship. But the PRC sincerely wanted a reconciliation with the United States, so she complemented her threat with a promise that Washington could trust her to act with great restraint in her dealings with Taiwan. This assurance took the form of a Nine Point Proposal, issued on September 30, that Beijing said would guide her future relations with Taipei.[76] In this document the PRC clarified her previous proposals by pledging that if Taiwan accepted autonomous status as a subordinate part of China, she would receive preferential access to the PRC's financial reserves and benefit from the protection of the People's Liberation Army.

Soon after the promulgation of the Nine Point Proposal, Beijing shifted her attention to other matters. In August 1982 Washington agreed that the supply of American military equipment to Taipei would diminish over time, but then the Reagan administration signaled that the United States would make no more compromises at Taiwan's expense.[77] By 1983 or 1984 the PRC had grudgingly accepted that fact and was no longer insinuating that she might recall her ambassador from Washington in protest.[78] Better, the Chinese rulers calculated, to content themselves with the progress that had been made and to await a more suitable time to press Washington for additional concessions. Meanwhile Beijing's diplomats were busy persuading London to adopt the "one nation, two systems" concept as a framework for Hong Kong's retrocession to Chinese control. This work was important in its own right, for it would eliminate Britain's historical infringement upon China's Westphalian sovereignty, but it was also very significant for Taiwan. For if Hong Kong were successfully incorporated into the PRC, the international community would presumably demand that Taiwan bow to the same fate.

The Nationalists understood this perfectly well, but they were gratified to see the PRC's focus diverted so that they could concentrate on the Sisyphean task of reinforcing what remained of Taiwan's international stature. Most obviously, by 1983 Taipei had lost her affiliations with all but one consequential multinational organization—the Asian Development Bank—and her ambassadorial connections to every major country but South Africa, South Korea, and Saudi Arabia.[79] These setbacks were not fatal, but they complicated a vast array of Taiwan's overseas activities. To take one example, the ROC had been forced to curtail her security and intelligence cooperation first with Japan, Thailand, and the Philippines; then with the United States; and now, in the middle 1980s, with Singapore and Indonesia.[80] Largely as a result of these developments, Taipei felt compelled to spend progressively larger amounts of time and energy persuading small, often insular, countries to establish diplomatic relations with her.[81] This was not a new effort—the ROC had been using foreign aid to "buy" the friendship of poor countries since 1961—but now the results expected of this program were more modest; and some of Taiwan's newly acquired friends felt free to shift their embassies to the PRC if she offered better terms.

Besides impeding her military and political initiatives, the diminution in the ROC's international legal sovereignty also adversely affected her economy. This can most easily be seen in the flow of foreign direct investment into Taiwan in the early 1970s, which was on a pronounced upward trajectory until international opinion turned in Beijing's favor and companies started to doubt Taiwan's political stability and commercial viability. Private capital flows from the United States stayed fairly constant during the pivotal years of 1971 and 1972, for the Nixon administration was quietly telling American executives and fund managers that Washington would not let her rapprochement with Beijing imperil Taiwan. Companies from other countries, however, received no such intimations and hence felt it judicious to reduce their spending on plant and equipment much more sharply. Thus, the volume of new Japanese investment in the ROC fell from $29 million in 1970 to $12 million in 1971 and then to $8 million in 1972, while the corresponding flow of capital from Europe slowed from $66 million in 1971 to $7 million in 1972.[82] This trend reversed toward the end of the latter year because the Nixon administration continued to issue statements of sympathy for Taipei and, perhaps more important, because Zhou Enlai publicly declared that the PRC would not obstruct Taiwan's trade relations.[83] As would later be the case with Hong Kong, Beijing's intention was to restrict the ROC's formal activities and not necessarily to harm her economy. Still, the ROC and her private corporations had suffered a tremendous shock—one that, if measured in terms of foreign direct investment, was comparable to the disruption caused by the oil crisis of 1973 and 1974. It was therefore very fortunate for the Nationalist state that the United States and the PRC intervened to stop its loss of international legal sovereignty from causing deeper and more lasting damage to Taiwan's financial infrastructure.

A less obvious way in which Taiwan's legal discomfiture hampered her economic development was by depriving the ROC of the tools that most governments routinely use to protect their industries and businesses. In the spring of 1979, for instance, Congress authorized the Carter administration to bestow the standard ambassadorial "privileges and immunities" upon the ROC's now "unofficial" representatives. The White House, however, was annoyed at how Taipei had reacted to the normalization of Sino-American relations and consequently delayed that bestowed for about a year.[84] Even after Taipei was given her privileges and immunities, Washington continued to restrict the ROC's use of diplomatic license plates and several of the other customary governmental perquisites. Nor could Taiwan's emissaries interact with senior officials in the United States as often as they wanted. In other capitals, where there were no legislative acts in her favor, Taipei's situation was even more difficult: here she could no longer arrange private interviews to gauge the sentiments of ranking leaders, negotiate bilateral agreements with them, or complain when they mistreated her citizens. These constraints on their diplomatic maneuverability put Taipei's envoys at a real disadvantage relative to other states' ambassadors and consuls.

This was certainly true of the ROC's communications with the European Economic Community, which in the 1980s, frequently discriminated against Taiwan by imposing unilateral restrictions, with little or no advance notice, on her exports of foodstuffs, textiles, and inexpensive manufactured products.[85] The logic behind this discrimination was simple and powerful. When confronted with protectionist demands from local interests, either the EEC and its individual members could reopen negotiations with recognized exporting nations—which might retaliate or seek redress from transnational organizations—and then try to force the resulting treaties and agreements through their parliaments, or they could forbid the importation of whole categories of goods from Taiwan without any procedural difficulties at all. The latter expedient was understandably employed in many cases. Taipei was also peculiarly vulnerable to legal action: on some occasions foreign governments enforced sanctions against her for transgressing multilateral covenants, such as those governing the harvesting of tuna in international waters, that other states breached with comparative impunity.[86] This pattern of sporadic discrimination also extended to specific businesses and trade associations, for countries sometimes refused to accept ROC passports or to grant normal visa privileges to Taiwan's citizens, thereby forcing them to use circuitous and time-consuming methods to obtain permission to travel abroad.[87]

Moreover, in a few rare and especially egregious instances Taipei's inability to lodge diplomatic protests left her overseas companies uniquely exposed to intimidation and extortion by criminal gangs.[88]

Stepping back from these particular facts, several aspects of the peace offensive and its impact on the ROC are theoretically noteworthy. In the first place, Beijing's protracted campaign to eviscerate Taipei's international powers indicates that she had registered the utility of conventional diplomatic institutions. Whereas the PRC had put her own interests at risk by disregarding formal sovereignty in the early 1950s and during the Cultural Revolution, now she fought to deprive the ROC of that attribute so as to increase her susceptibility to political and military influence. Nor was Beijing incorrect in this expectation, for Taiwan's derecognition led directly to significant defensive and diplomatic problems and, in the absence of American intervention, might possibly have caused real damage to her economy. The ROC's experience further suggests that international legal sovereignty can be subdivided into a moral and a mechanical component. Although the West and Japan did not admit Taipei's claims to China during the 1950s and 1960s, she nevertheless benefited from a network of ambassadorial relationships, participatory rights in multilateral organizations, normal trading status, and many of the other privileges associated with sovereignty until she was deprived of that status in the 1970s. The institutions of diplomacy, in short, functioned effectively in the absence of a persuasive underlying rationale.

If the mechanical aspect of legal sovereignty has some pragmatic value, the corresponding moral justification can be vital. As alluded to above, the three pillars of the ROC's power on Taiwan after 1949 were the Nationalists' continental pretensions, the affinity of the "free world," and brute force. The aspiration to control the mainland lost its credibility in the 1950s and 1960s, but Taipei's formal relations with the noncommunist powers remained intact through the early 1970s. The implications of this should not be underestimated; for the press on Taiwan was tightly censored during these decades and the island's citizens were never informed of the doubts that the outside world felt about their government. To the contrary, visits to the island by foreign dignitaries were trumpeted as evidence of Taiwan's prestige around the globe. This meant that when scores of countries and dozens of multilateral organizations derecognized the Nationalist state within the space of a decade, its standing on Taiwan was severely undermined. It was thus no accident that in late 1980, soon after the termination of the 1954 Mutual Defence Treaty, the Kuomintang's domestic critics started citing the ROC's diplomatic ineptitude as a reason why it must be replaced by a different regime.[89] Unless Taipei found another means of endearing herself to the people of Taiwan, she would soon find herself facing serious threats with only military and police forces to preserve her dominance.

The Changing International Environment

Several different factors may, separately or collectively, explain why the ROC did not succumb to the PRC's peace offensive. One possibility is that however useful the diplomatic institutions and greater legitimacy implied by sovereignty are on the margin, ultimately they are not essential to a state's existence. If this is true, then polities that have lately become isolated have presumably concluded from Taiwan's experience that their situation is not dire and that opening new channels of communications to other countries will be a fairly straightforward matter. Another potential explanation is that the ROC possessed unusual resources that enabled her to weather political and economic storms that might have caused lesser polities to founder. The proposition that Taipei's relationship with Washington was such an asset will be investigated shortly. Finally, it could be the case that the international environment has changed in a manner conducive to the creation of alternative diplomatic systems and that this evolution eased the ROC's transition from the formal legal sovereignty of the 1950s and 1960s to her current ambiguous, but apparently sustainable, condition.

Evidence that this sort of evolution has occurred is in fact abundant. Krasner has shown in a different context that national sovereignty was never as pure in practice as in theory.[90] From the seventeenth through the beginning of the twentieth centuries the great powers of Europe often intruded in the internal affairs of lesser countries, attempting to dictate how they treated ethnic and religious minorities and sometimes taking over management of their finances. A quick perusal of the classic *Dollar Diplomacy* reveals that the United States likewise routinely contravened other countries' Westphalian sovereignty during this period.[91] In this sense there was nothing unusual about the "unfair treaties" and "extraterritoriality" that the imperialists imposed on Ch'ing China. Moreover, such contraventions continued through the present. In the 1990s, for example, Bosnia's acceptance as a full member of the international community was predicated on her agreeing to honor the civil rights of minorities within her borders; and NATO intervened in Yugoslavia's domestic politics to prevent the "ethnic cleansing" of Kosovo.[92] The record is thus one of fairly continuous breaches of countries' external sovereignty.

Yet the nature of these breaches has undergone several qualitative changes over the course of the twentieth century. One such trend is the increasing importance of the individual human being as opposed to the larger group.[93] In part this reflects the greater influence of the United States in global politics and the concomitant ascendance of American social values. Another change from the historical pattern—whereby powerful states usually infringed upon small countries' sovereignty for geopolitical reasons and in an ad hoc manner—is that since World War II the community of nations has increasingly sought to define specific civil rights and to enact these as global rules of conduct. This tendency is embodied in such documents as the Universal Declaration of Human Rights of 1948; the International Covenant on Economic, Social, and Cultural Rights and the International Convention on Civil and Political Rights of 1966; the human rights provisions of the Helsinki Accords of 1975; and the Vienna World Conference on Human Rights.[94] It is true that states often ignore these undertakings, but they have nonetheless introduced new notions of what constitutes legitimacy into the dialogue between governments. Furthermore, to the chagrin of the PRC, Russia, and other countries whose domestic sovereignty is challenged by regional separatism, these new codes of conduct have engendered a presumption that in some circumstances the outside world may rightfully use force to prevent a government from dealing harshly with its internal enemies.[95] Thus the new agreements have altered the traditional notion of sovereignty, with its focus on authority and strength, and created an atmosphere in which adherence to liberal principles is considered relevant to a state's diplomatic stature.

The effect of this evolution has been amplified by another change in world politics: namely, the greater involvement of democratically responsive branches of government and of nongovernmental actors in what was once almost exclusively an executive bailiwick. There were numerous times in the past when popular pressure motivated rulers to interfere in other countries' internal arrangements; in the nineteenth century, to adduce one such case, public agitation played a major role in Europe's gradual dismantling of the Ottoman Empire.[96] But in recent decades this pressure has become somewhat more constant, and independent agencies claiming a right to pass judgment on states' domestic institutions and policies have proliferated. Among these are various branches of the UN bureaucracy, several organs of the Organisation for Economic Co-operation and Development (OECD) and the European Union, and such private entities as Asia Watch and Amnesty International.[97] This phenomenon has had an economic facet as well, with the General Agreement of Tariffs and Trade (GATT), the EU, the World Trade Organization (WTO), and many other bodies all compiling commercial and financial codes that are enforced either through moral suasion or, less frequently, through formal adjudicatory agencies. Legislative bodies in the industrialized nations have likewise evinced a greater assertiveness: these parliaments now regularly examine the behavior of other countries and occasionally apply sanctions against them as punishment for transgressing what have ostensibly become transcendent moral principles.[98] Thus the channels through which private citizens and civic groups can seek to alter governments' behavior have multiplied even as liberal norms have become more firmly entrenched.

The argument here is not that national sovereignty was once a fundamental feature of world politics and has subsequently receded, but rather that a different range of actors now violate that principle and that these violations are justified by reference to putatively catholic ideals. This development is exceedingly important for Taiwan and other isolated states. It implies that they can earn a measure of foreign respect through progressive social policies, and that this moral legitimacy can provide a basis for intercourse with sub- and supranational organizations even in the absence of formal legal sovereignty. These connections, in turn, enable the isolated polity to exert some influence over governments and agencies that would otherwise prefer to ignore its existence completely. Unconsciously at first, but much more sedulously in the 1970s and 1980s, this was precisely what the ROC did. The Nationalists had always tried to affect public opinion in the United States, Japan, South Korea, and a few other critical countries, but now they appealed to a much more diverse audience in a more coherent and strategic fashion. That Taipei largely succeeded in this endeavor, which is examined below, demonstrates that the emergence of new political mores in the second half of the twentieth century has significantly improved the outlook for states that are not widely regarded as sovereign.

Taiwan's Alternative Sovereignty

In the early 1970s there were two ways in which sympathetic parties portrayed the ROC. On the one hand the Nationalists contended that they remained the proper government of China but were temporarily unable to exercise domestic and Westphalian sovereignty over the mainland and had lately suffered the additional indignity of international derecognition. The notion that the KMT might one day reestablish control over China's continental provinces was of course risible; and insofar as Taipei continued to promote it, the likelihood of regaining other countries' formal approval was scant. On the other hand, some observers described the ROC as Taiwan's de facto government, possessed of the internal and Westphalian attributes of normal statehood but lacking the sanction of the world community. This scenario was much more consistent with geopolitical realities. Inherent in it, moreover, was the possibility that Taipei might eventually garner the respect of other countries as the de jure government of Taiwan, thereby uniting in herself all the elements of sovereignty and regaining both the legitimacy and the diplomatic tools commonly associated with that status. This feat would definitely be more difficult to achieve now than during the late 1950s, when Beijing had seemed amenable to looser ties across the strait, but it offered the most logical way out of the ROC's current dilemma.

In the decade after Taipei's ouster from the United Nations, however, overt discussion of independence was inhibited by Chiang Kai-shek's reluctance to concede final victory to the Communists and by a more practical concern that the Kuomintang had not struck deep roots in Taiwanese society. The ROC National Assembly was typical of this problem. It consisted almost entirely of senescent mainlanders who had been elected before the constitution's suspension in 1948 and who, after moving to Taiwan, had never bothered to learn the local dialects. With its commitment to the island this tenuous, there would remain no ideological or emotional rationale for maintaining the polity's integrity if the KMT surrendered its claims to continental China. Hence it made sense for Taipei to persist in arguing domestically that the ROC was China's legitimate government; to continue censoring the press so that the people of Taiwan did not learn the facts to the contrary; and, in the meantime, quietly to implement policies that broadened the state's base of support among its citizenry. The senior Nationalists did not necessarily see this strategy as leading to overt independence, nor did they understand that it might confer on them a new international legitimacy: in their minds, encouraging more loyalty from their subjects was simply a matter of safeguarding Taiwan's stability. It was accordingly fortuitous that the steps they took in pursuit of this end coincided quite closely with the increasingly liberal values of global society. To put the point more provocatively, the ROC may well have grown stronger in the 1980s and 1990s because derecognition forced her to behave in a manner that pleased important interest groups abroad. Thus economic and political reforms, along with some innovative diplomacy and Taipei's crucial defensive relationship with Washington, would combine to form an "alternative sovereignty" that improved Taiwan's situation relative to the PRC considerably.

In part this favorable outcome resulted from initiatives that the KMT had espoused soon after its retreat to Taiwan in the late 1940s. During those gloomy months the foremost objectives of Chiang Kai-shek and his colleagues were fending off attack from Mao Zedong's armies, amassing sufficient military power to launch an eventual counterattack against the PRC, and securing the diplomatic assistance of the United States, Japan, and other powerful countries. But as one author has noted, the Nationalists were also "chastened and purged" by their failure to enact sound economic policies on the mainland and by the consequent loss of public support in the wars against the Japanese, the warlords, and most spectacularly, the Communists.[100] Desiring both to forestall a recurrence of this debacle and to keep their American advisers happy, in 1949 and the early 1950s the party realized that it must neutralize the hostility of the island's eight million ethnic Taiwanese. This would be no easy task, for after years of maltreatment by avaricious agents of the ROC central government, the Taiwanese deeply resented the 1.5 million mainlanders who had crossed the strait in the Kuomintang's train.[101] Nonetheless Chiang Kai-shek, and especially some of his more perspicacious aides, understood that reaching a limited accommodation with the local people was an essential precondition to the successful achievement of the party's most cherished goals.

In the decades after relocating to its island fortress, therefore, the ROC government worked diligently to promote economic development and a more equitable distribution of Taiwan's resources. In the 1950s, for example, Taipei enacted a comprehensive program of land redistribution that weakened the landlord class and helped the island's poor, followed by various measures designed to foster rapid industrialization. As a result the ROC's GDP expanded at a nominal pace of almost 20 percent a year; and the ratio of wealth owned by the richest quintile of the population compared to the poorest improved from 21:1, or about the level of Mexico, to 12:1, which was somewhat better than the corresponding figure for the United States.[102] The next decades brought further sagacious policies; and as a result Taiwan's domestic output rose from $1.6 billion in 1960 to just under $5.6 billion in

1970, and then to some $37 billion in 1980. These statistics implied a nominal growth rate of almost 10 percent per annum, a remarkable performance by any standard. During this period the ROC also made further progress in sharing Taiwan's wealth with the general populace: by the late 1980s the aforementioned measurement of equity had fallen to almost 4.5 to 1—better than any of the European countries and even Japan. Evaluated in terms of life expectancy, infant mortality, the availability of health care services, and purchasing power, Taiwan's standard of living was now approaching OECD levels. In the early 1990s the ROC would in fact become the world's thirteenth largest trading power and have a national income of more than $10,000 per capita.[103]

The social and diplomatic consequences of this economic expansion were subtle but profound. Domestically, the ROC's middle class grew from essentially nothing to a point where it comprised over 30 percent of her population; and although many of the people who formed this class wanted to participate more fully in the island's governance, their highest priority was commercial stability.[104] Indeed, in the 1970s and 1980s the Kuomintang quietly encouraged the Taiwanese to concentrate on making money rather than seeking greater political power.[105] Many citizens grudgingly heeded this advice, and popular support for noncapitalist forms of social organization accordingly waned. There were still malcontents in the ROC, to be sure, but very few of them were willing to jeopardize Taiwan's material accomplishments in order to topple the Kuomintang state. Nor, for that matter, did the PRC's peace offensive hold much appeal for the KMT's domestic opponents, who reasonably doubted that Beijing could match Taipei's economic record. Much had changed since the ROC's misfeasance on the mainland had facilitated the communists' seizure of power in 1949.

The international implications of Taiwan's economic modernization became evident more slowly. But once the Soviet Union had collapsed, thereby alleviating the West's immediate need for China's geopolitical cooperation, many governments started responding to the ROC's accomplishments in a more positive fashion. In order to protect the United States' trade relations, for example, in July 1991 Congress prevailed upon President George Bush to propose that Taiwan be admitted to GATT; and in subsequent years the U.S. legislature considered several resolutions supporting the ROC's application to the WTO.[106] Meanwhile, in 1994 Japan ended a twenty-two year embargo against the Nationalist state by inviting its delegates to the annual meetings of the Asia-Pacific Economic Conference and by hosting a visit to Tokyo by an ROC minister.[107] Three years later the European Parliament passed a motion endorsing Taiwan's entry into several multilateral economic bodies, including the WTO.[108] Then came the financial crises of 1997, which afforded Taipei a valuable new opportunity to earn the friendship of East Asian countries by sending officials on widely publicized trips to offer economic assistance.[109] Despite complaints from Beijing, this itinerant diplomacy continued into 1998 and 1999. In this way the ROC's economic expansion gave other countries an incentive to interact with her more intimately than the PRC had ever agreed to permit.

Gradual—even glacial—political reform likewise offered some compensation for the ROC's loss of international law sovereignty. When the Nationalists first repaired to Taiwan there were few signs that they would eventually become advocates of democratic rule. It is true that at the behest of their American allies, Chiang Kai-shek and his colleagues agreed to conduct elections for local and county offices in the 1950s; but no real opposition to the KMT was allowed to compete in these polls and, more generally, press censorship and political repression remained hallmarks of public life.[110] During these years the national government never sought any sort of democratic mandate: Chiang Kai-shek and his colleagues were an aloof and sometimes minatory presence, controlling the ROC's policies in more or less the same autocratic manner they had exhibited on the mainland. In 1969, however, Taipei started urging more Taiwanese to join the ruling party and began organizing votes for a small number of seats in the three elective chambers of the central government.[111] The scale and frequency of these parliamentary contests increased after Chiang Kai-shek's death in 1975, since his son and successor as Taiwan's preeminent leader, Chiang Ching-kuo, was better attuned to the ROC's domestic and diplomatic needs.[112] Still, the ensuing elections were restricted to so few positions that the Kuomintang's power was never really threatened; and Taipei's record continued to be marred by the occasional mistreatment of KMT critics at home and overseas. Through the early 1980s, therefore, skeptics had reasonable grounds to question Taiwan's democratic credentials.

Yet soon the pace of reform accelerated. In the 1970s the United States and other Western countries had become more vocal in their promotion of human rights; and while Singapore, Hong Kong, South Korea, and other newly industrialized countries ignored much of this pressure, the ROC took it quite seriously. For she was now bereft of normal diplomatic connections to most of the world and therefore relied heavily on other countries' willingness voluntarily to communicate with her. Taipei accordingly felt that she must project at least the appearance of liberal intent.[113] Then came the U.S. derecognition of 1979, which removed the last fig leaf from the ROC's official ideology and left her searching for new ways to justify her rule to the people of Taiwan. This was a crucially important matter, for if the ROC failed to evolve a new legitimacy her political institutions would ossify further and she would become excessively dependent on the KMT's armed forces to sustain her power. In those circumstances the likelihood of internal disorder would rise dramatically. As one analyst later wrote, perhaps with some exaggeration, "democratization was the [Kuomintang's] only hope" to engender a popular basis for its control of Taiwan.[114]

So, the ROC's national elections slowly became more regular and more extensive. In 1986 and 1987 the government finally permitted opposition groups to form political parties, abolished the martial law regime that had been in place for almost forty years, and lifted most of the restrictions governing the press.[115] The pace of this liberalization accelerated again after Chiang Ching-kuo's death in 1988 because his successor as president, the Taiwanese Lee Teng-hui, had fewer allies in the upper reaches of the KMT and hence needed to establish an independent relationship with the ROC citizenry. Under his direction, in the early 1990s Taipei conducted large-scale elections to all of the central government's legislative bodies, renounced the Kuomintang's goal of destroying the PRC, and offered a state apology to the Taiwanese for the ROC's misrule in the years after World War II.[116] Next the Nationalist Party initiated discussions with the opposition over amendments to the constitution that would permit the election of a chief executive by the people of Taiwan. These negotiators considered both parliamentary and presidential schemes; and in the end they opted for a system like that of France, in which the president is chosen independently of the parliament. Among the reasons behind this decision was recognition that a directly elected president would bring Taiwan more sympathy from Japan, the United States, and the European Union.[117] In other words, the KMT and its opposition intentionally altered the ROC constitution so as to harmonize that system with the liberal principles that the West and much of the developing world now considered relevant to a nation's moral status. Having made this alteration, in March 1996 Taiwan conducted the first democratic contest for the office of chief executive that any Chinese state had ever held.[118]

As was the case with Taiwan's economic modernization, the ROC's evolution from an authoritarian and intolerant government into a democratic regime with a fair degree of civil liberty produced a dramatic change in the world's attitude toward her. As late as the middle 1980s, American politicians such as Stephen Solarz, Claiborne Pell, Ted Kennedy, and Jim Leach had routinely declaimed against the ROC as a state that cavalierly ignored the wishes of the Taiwanese majority.[119] A decade later, however, some members of Congress would describe the insular state as a model that the People's Republic of China should emulate. In the autumn of 1997, for example, Representative Tom Lantos exclaimed that "the people of [mainland] China are as entitled to live in a free and open and democratically elected society [sic] as . . . the people of Taiwan."[120] Even scholars such as Harry Harding sometimes opined that "we can only hope that China will move in the same direction as Taiwan."[121] These comments were most welcome in Taipei, for the ROC had not experienced such uniformly hearty acclaim since the 1930s. Even more helpfully, this new respectability facilitated Taiwan's quest for admission to the main global economic fora and enhanced her stature relative to the PRC. In early 1997, for example, several members of Congress simultaneously demanded that Taipei be admitted to the WTO before Beijing and that sanctions be enforced against the PRC for alleged human rights violations.[122] Similar sentiments also issued that year from the European Parliament.[123] There were many different motivations behind this new support for Taiwan, but one of them was the affinity that Taiwan's political liberalization had engendered overseas.

If this new democratic and economic legitimacy partially replaced the moral element of international legal sovereignty that the ROC forfeited in the 1970s, an opportunistic approach to intergovernmental communications enabled her to devise important new diplomatic mechanisms. More precisely, Taipei learned to rely on what might be termed unofficial embassies and on a wide variety of semiofficial and private institutions that could in extreme conditions be pressed into service as informal agents of the Nationalist State. The PRC had in fact been a pioneer in this field. In 1949 and 1950 Beijing refused to exchange fully accredited emissaries with London because she did not want to be seen as accepting British dominance in Hong Kong even though, for practical reasons, she needed to communicate frequently with the colony. Instead, Beijing opted to conduct her business there indirectly, through the local branches of her Xinhua News Agency.[124] For the next five decades this entity managed the PRC's affairs in Hong Kong and acted as an intermediary with the British. In 1952 Beijing developed a similarly unpretentious arrangement to oversee her relations with Tokyo, thereby circumventing the U.S. demand that Japan not recognize the PRC.[125] This system functioned adequately for the next several years, but by the decade's end Tokyo and Beijing were both convinced that they needed a more sophisticated means of managing their interaction. So in 1962 they concluded the Liao-Takasaki Agreement, which stipulated that each country would open an office in the other's capital and use it to supervise her affairs there. In theory, these organs were private, but they were given the standard diplomatic privileges and immunities and they performed many of the duties usually discharged by embassies.

When the ROC became isolated in the early 1970s, she proved equally adept at devising purportedly "nongovernmental" institutions. The earliest example of this occurred after Japan's recognition of China in September 1972, when Tokyo and Taipei reached an understanding that they would replace their embassies with the Interchange Association and the East Asia Relations Association, respectively.[126] These bodies supposedly had no official affiliation, but they processed visa applications, conveyed messages back and forth, supervised commercial and cultural exchanges, and otherwise functioned like governmental agencies. Thus they represented a reversal of the previous pattern whereby the ROC had enjoyed direct ties to Japan, and the PRC was forced to make do with an informal relationship. Later in the decade Taipei replaced her embassies in the Philippines, Spain, and other countries with more modest trade or cultural centers, some of which operated under the purview of the ROC Foreign Ministry and occasionally discussed political matters with representatives of their host governments.[127] In Malaysia and Thailand, on the other hand, it was China Airlines that inherited a limited portfolio of responsibilities from the ROC's now defunct embassies—much as Xinhua News Agency had done for the PRC in the 1950s and 1960s. But by far the most extensive of these unconventional diplomatic connections was created in the spring of 1979, when the Carter administration and Congress spent three months drafting a law that authorized the American Institute in Taiwan (AIT) to manage most aspects of U.S.-ROC intercourse.[128] This apparatus, whose details need not be described here, was highly advantageous to Taiwan because it perpetuated a relationship upon which her security and prosperity were uniquely dependent.

In most cases, however, Taipei could not employ this sort of pseudo-diplomatic expedient because her counterpart governments refused to risk offending Beijing. In these cases the ROC resorted to what she termed "substantive diplomacy," or the use of economic and other indirect means to affect

foreign governments.[129] The passive form of this influence developed spon-
taneously in the early 1970s. By now the volume of the ROC's trade was
expanding with celerity, and this inexorably gave other countries a stake in
her prosperity. At the very least these nations preferred to avoid actions that
might adversely affect Taiwan's economy lest that damage ramify back through
commercial and financial channels to harm their own industries and work-
forces. But soon Taipei was also applying her substantive power in a more
positive way. With the passage of time, some countries decided that they
needed to exchange liaisons with the ROC in order to manage the burgeoning
flow of bilateral trade. In these instances the Nationalists agreed to the maximum possible institutional ties—having Taipei's new trade office report to
the Ministry of Foreign Affairs or perhaps the Ministry of Economics.[130] When
countries hesitated to go this far, Taipei alternatively encouraged industrial
groups and individual corporations from Taiwan to request permission to post
representatives there.

A good example of this partnership between the Nationalist government
and Taiwan's industrial associations was the China External Trade Development Council (CETDC), founded in July 1970.[131] The CETDC was a private
body operated and funded by Taiwan's exporting firms, but ROC officials were
involved in many of its activities. At first its purposes were wholly economic:
the council was chartered to study market conditions in other countries and
to relay this information to Taiwan's manufacturers, who would use it to improve their competitiveness in export markets. But the council gradually assumed additional responsibilities, including the financing of international ad-
vertising efforts, management of permanent trade exhibitions, building a
massive database to help foreign enterprises penetrate Taiwan's market, and
dispatching trade missions to other countries. As the CETDC's duties increased, so too did the number of branches it operated overseas—from the
original five to forty-eight in 1980 and many more thereafter. These agencies
never attained the political significance of the unofficial embassies that Taipei
operated in Tokyo, Washington, and some other capitals, but they were nevertheless very valuable. When the members of the European Community discriminated against Taiwan's exports, for instance, it was the CETDC and a
similar body, the Euro-Asia Trade Organization (EATO), that publicized her
situation and demanded more equitable treatment.[132] On occasion, EATO
likewise asked European companies to pressure their governments to expedite
the issuance of visas to ROC businessmen and to clarify the legal status of
ROC citizens in their courts.

As Taipei learned to work through these various informal mechanisms, she lowered her expectations for how other countries should behave toward her. This was what the Nationalists described in the early 1990s as "pragmatic diplomacy," or a willingness to cooperate closely with foreign governments even if they treated the ROC as less than a sovereign state.[133] Thus, in June 1995 President Lee Teng-hui went to the United States as a private citizen so that he could receive an honorary degree from his alma mater, Cornell University.[134] Beijing was deeply angered that the Clinton administration would allow this, and the resulting rancor caused Sino-American relations to deteriorate in anticipation of the PRC's military exercises near Taiwan a year later. But the episode helped the Kuomintang, both by bolstering Lee's standing in the 1996 presidential election and by enabling Taiwan to break free from some of the diplomatic constraints that Beijing had imposed on her in the 1970s. Equally beneficial was Taipei's practice, beginning in the early 1990s, of sending envoys overseas under assumed names and with false passports so that they could hold clandestine discussions with other governments. The ROC's Vice President Lien Chan surreptitiously traveled to Mexico and Malaysia for that purpose in 1994, as well as to the Czech Republic in 1995 and the Ukraine in 1996.[135] For his part Foreign Minister Chang Hsiao-yen met officials for quiet talks in Indonesia, Malaysia, the United Arab Emirates, and Jordan in 1996 before proceeding to Belgium and other European countries for what soon became a very public "private vacation."[136] In 1997 these men conducted their peripatetic diplomacy even more openly; and by the year's end, such dignitaries as Singapore's Prime Minister Goh Chok Tong and Malaysia's Prime Minister Mahathir Mohammed were making reciprocal visits to Taipei.[137] The ROC's pragmatic diplomacy—something the more intransigent Chiang Kai-shek would never have countenanced—had given her greater visibility than at any point in the two previous decades.

While these informal diplomatic mechanisms and Taipei's new liberalism comprised the superstructure of the ROC's alternative sovereignty, the very foundation of that edifice was her continuing relationship with Washington.[138] After all, foreign approval and intermittent communications with other governments would have been useless without military security. The U.S.-ROC Mutual Defense Treaty, which had safeguarded Taiwan during the tumultuous 1950s and 1960s, terminated in accordance with Jimmy Carter's promises to Deng Xiaoping on January 1, 1980. This event superficially suggested that Washington's commitment to the ROC was faltering and hence that she was becoming more susceptible to pressure from Beijing. Yet in truth the island's defensive position may not have deteriorated very much in those years. The 1954 treaty had actually lost much of its deterrent power when the Nixon administration began negotiating with the PRC in the early 1970s, and even more when the United States withdrew from the Vietnam War, an action that portended a lower American profile throughout Asia and a weakening of Washington's resolve to protect small and beleaguered allies in distant regions of the world.[139] It was therefore highly probable that Beijing and other potential aggressors were discounting the U.S.-ROC alliance long before its formal abrogation.

Fortunately for Taipei, even as the treaty lost its efficacy a new dynamic was developing that was more dependable as a means of preserving Taiwan's safety. As Richard Nixon and Henry Kissinger had expected, drawing the PRC into a web of diplomatic and commercial ties gave her a compelling interest in East Asia's peace and security. The evolution of Beijing's Taiwan policy from military cajolery to the more moderate overtures of the peace offensive reflected that fact. Moreover, this pacific effect was underscored by Washington's remaining obligations to Taipei. For when the Carter administration finalized its normalization pact with China, it insisted that the United States had an "interest" and an "expectation" that Taiwan's future would be determined peacefully and that in the meantime Washington would continue purveying "carefully selected defensive weapons" to the Nationalist government.[140] The Taiwan Relations Act (TRA), adopted by Congress in April 1979, expanded the American duty to protect the ROC still further. This law stated that Washington should decide what defensive armaments to provide to Taipei without taking the PRC's opinions into account, that the White House should maintain the military capacity to repel assaults upon the island, and that the United States would react firmly to any attempt to coerce the people of Taiwan into reaching an accommodation with Beijing.[141] Furthermore, since the law defined "coercion" to include embargoes, boycotts, and other forms of economic pressure, it arguably represented a broader guarantee of the ROC's safety than the alliance had done. Thus the TRA may have erected new obstacles to the PRC's assertion of sovereignty over Taiwan.

It is true that in August 1982 Washington modified the TRA by promising to restrict the volume of arms transfers to the ROC and eventually to end them altogether. But these changes were in fact quite minimal. Judging from the trend subsequently established by the Reagan administration, the United

States would still be supplying weaponry to the ROC in the year 2020; and the unilateral statement of an American interest in Taiwan's future would stay efficacious indefinitely thereafter.[142] Needless to say, this constant support from the United States was extremely helpful to Taipei. In the final analysis the PRC's desire for better relations with the international community was probably the more substantial bulwark of the ROC's security, but Washington's public assurances strengthened the Nationalists' self-confidence significantly and reduced the chances that Beijing might launch an attack against Taiwan in miscalculation. To this extent, Taiwan's relationship with the United States provided the time and stability that the ROC required to build her new diplomatic institutions.[143]

Extrapolating from Taiwan's experience, it is clear that a state can do many things to mitigate the negative effects of losing formal legal sovereignty. By enacting sound domestic policies, for example, a government can develop a popular legitimacy that is largely independent of its stature among other countries. If those internal policies accord with the moral principles currently favored by the international community, they can also inspire a degree of foreign esteem and sympathy that exercises a restraining influence over possible enemies. In the ROC's case this meant that politically sensitive groups in the European Union, the United States, Japan, and other parts of the world became more inclined to react harshly if Beijing attempted to achieve China's reunification through violence or intimidation, since such an action would now be perceived not only as dangerous but also as morally reprobate. Another way in which an isolated state can lessen the impact of derecognition is by creating semiofficial and unofficial presences in other countries, both as a means of monitoring events therein and in order to gain some economic and political leverage. Finally—and most important in the present context—a pariah state's outlook is vastly improved if it retains security relations with at least one great power. This requirement varies, of course, with the magnitude of the threats confronting the vulnerable polity, but in theory any isolated government would be better off if other countries were obligated to protect it. If these various assets are marshaled with sufficient dispatch, a country can survive the loss of formal legal sovereignty. That, at least, is the proposition for which Taiwan's recent history stands.

In conclusion, the conflict between the PRC and the ROC demonstrates that international legal sovereignty is not essential to a state's existence although it is of considerable pragmatic value. In the 1950s and 1960s the PRC's strained relations with the Western world circumscribed her diplomatic freedom and left her somewhat less secure when confronting first a coalition of unfriendly nations operating on the Korean Peninsula under American leadership and then an antagonistic USSR. When Beijing finally embraced the international community in the opening years of the following decade, she obtained a variety of economic opportunities as well as additional resources with which to augment her military and diplomatic powers. These were significant advantages. Conversely, Taiwan's derecognition cost her direct contact with many states, access to some forms of financial and technical assistance, and a degree of domestic legitimacy. There were several points in time—the weeks after the ROC's ouster from the United Nations, for instance; all of 1972, when foreign investors lost confidence in Taiwan's economic viability; and the weeks after Jimmy Carter announced his intention to exchange ambassadors with Beijing—when the Nationalist leaders believed that their future was quite bleak. At these junctures Chiang Kai-shek, Chiang Ching-kuo, and their colleagues were not sure that they would be able to devise a new system for conducting their intergovernmental affairs. In the event Taipei overcame this challenge, but this fact should not overshadow either the profound uncertainty that she initially felt or the concrete problems that her diplomatic defeats really did entail.

Taiwan's experience also offers some indication of how a government can enhance its chances of survival in the absence of formal legal sovereignty. International recognition provides a state with three distinct advantages: embassies and the customary diplomatic privileges, a measure of political acceptance by other governments, and somewhat greater domestic authority. If deprived of the publicity that derives from regular communications with other countries, however, a government can still secure its citizens' allegiance by working more diligently to meet their needs in its domestic policies. In Taipei's case, democratization and economic modernization combined to inform a potent new legitimacy that eviscerated both radical Taiwanese dissentience and the PRC's reunification campaigns, thereby strengthening the ROC during a period when she might conceivably have succumbed to such challenges. Fortuitously, the values of international society have changed over the last several decades such that this economic and political liberalization collaterally engendered more goodwill abroad, especially in the parliaments of Western countries. This foreign approbation, in turn, facilitated the formation of "unofficial" institutional connections that prevented Taipei from becoming totally isolated. This suggests, more generally, that the moral and mechanical com-

ponents of formal legal sovereignty can all be replicated artificially, particularly if a government is willing to respect the moral notions that have gained
such currency since World War II.

It should be borne in mind, however, that Taipei may have been atypi-
cally fortunate in assembling these several characteristics. In the first place,
each of a derecognized state's unofficial relationships must be created de
novo and occasionally at prodigious expense, and some countries are likely
to balk at such difficulties. It is improbable, for example, that the U.S. government would devote so many months of concerted effort to designing a
new diplomatic structure for a state with less historical claim to American
loyalty than the ROC. Similarly, the security relationship with the United
States that underlies Taiwan's network of foreign relations may be, for other
isolated polities, inimitable. It would therefore be premature to conclude
that Taiwan represents an easily replicable model for pariah states or that
the traditional principle of international legal sovereignty will soon become
obsolete. To the contrary, attaining that status is still the easiest and most
reliable way for a polity to acquire the standard package of diplomatic tools
and political prestige.

Finally, if Taiwan's recent history answers some theoretical questions
about sovereignty, it simultaneously poses a range of practical problems. Krasner contends that aberrations in international law become established features of global politics if they endure long enough and if interested parties
are sufficiently committed to them. This is relevant to Taiwan because her
de facto autonomy represents such an aberration; her separation from the
mainland is an infringement on China's domestic rights that Beijing has
tolerated because she does not want to alienate the global community or risk
war with the United States. Taipei, however, is not content to persist in her
current situation in the hope that it will ultimately gain the support of other
countries and thereby become a permanent reality. Rather, since the 1970s
she has edged gradually closer to seeking de jure independence from the
Chinese mainland so that she, too, can share the benefits of international
legal sovereignty. Such, after all, is the hope and ambition of a sizable portion of the ROC electorate. Thus in 1991 Taipei redefined "China" as a
cultural area controlled by two distinct governments; and in July 1999 she
declared that the ROC and the PRC are both legitimate "states" and can
negotiate only on the basis of juridical parity.[144] Neither of these assertions
actually described Taiwan as a sovereign country; but the latter came very
close to doing so, and Beijing reacted with commensurate alarm. In essence,

the ROC is attempting to transform the alternative diplomatic network that she has developed in the last few decades into a more conventional system. Whether this will actually happen depends in large measure on the attitude of the United States and Beijing's willingness, if necessary, to use force to establish her authority over Taiwan. So far this tension between the ROC's aspirations and the PRC's sovereign rights has been managed fairly adroitly, but the likelihood of a clash between these contradictory forces is increasing as Taipei tries to expand the magnitude of the legal aberration that she wants the world eventually to accept.

Notes

The author would like to thank John Meyer and Michel Oksenberg for their comments on preliminary drafts of this paper.

1. Boli, "Sovereignty from a World Polity Perspective," in this volume.
2. Fairbank 1969:3, 7, 9, 11, 14, 17–18, 23, 47–48, 50; Spence 1990:118–20.
3. Fairbank 1969:14, 43; 1986:86.
4. Fairbank 1969:20, 57, 114; e.g., Spence 1990:161–62; Hopkirk 1990:298–300, 502–12; Storry 1982:138–43.
5. Cf. Storry 1982:100, 103, 107, 115–16, with Fairbank 1986:22, 23. and Howe 1996:6.
6. Howe 1996:74–81, 88–91; Fairbank 1969:21; Spence 1990:170–78.
7. Fairbank 1986:47, 115, 136–38; Nish 1996:24. Also, Hopkirk 1990:506–12; Nish 1996:31–32; Snow 1968:73, 153; Sun 1989.
8. Nish 1996:31–32; Snow 1968:73, 153; Sun 1989.
9. Spence 1990:346–54; Snow 1968:36; Nish 1996:33–35.
10. Storry 1982, 186; Howe 1996:8–9; Nish 1996:36–37; Schaller 1979:40–41.
11. Schaller 1979:45–46; Snow 1968:24; Spence 1990:422–24.
12. Storry 1982:202–3; Schaller 1979:48.
13. Schaller 1979:57; Spence 1990:464–65, 478–80, 488–89; Fairbank 1986:244.
14. Oksenberg 1997:54, 62–63. Also, Copper 1986:23–26, 146.
15. Snow 1968:110; Oksenberg 1997:56; Copper 1986:37.
16. Koen 1960:10–15; Spence 1990:468–70.
17. U.S. Department of State 1949:519; Ulam 1974:350–51, 386–87; Schaller 1979:103; Tucker 1990:27.
18. Mendl 1978:3; Clough 1978:6.
19. Kalicki 1975:17; Copper 1986:35–36; Oksenberg 1997:55–56.
20. Ulam 1974:371; Schaller 1979:104; Teiwes 1993:18, 32; Oksenberg 1997:55, 58, 80–81.

21. Clough 1978:96–98; Copper 1986:37.

22. Chang 1990:12–21, 32–37, 47–52, 57–59, 65–68, 78–79; Tucker 1994:30, 33; Kusnitz 1984:26–35.

23. Bachrach 1976:43–45; Koen 1960:232–34; Kusnitz 1984:54, 63; Chang 1990:47–52, 57–59, 65–68, 78–80.

24. Acheson 1969:310, 69; Truman 1955:337–39. This aid was initially seen as an interim measure until an accommodation with Beijing could be arranged. Kusnitz 1984:48; Tucker 1994:30–31, 33–34.

25. Tien 1989:64–65, 91–92, 100, 106, 108; Clough 1978:35, 38–39; Copper 1986:43, 107, 149.

26. Tucker 1994:35, 38, 40–43; Chang 1990:121, 126–28, 132, 165, 188; Kalicki 1975:181–99; Kusnitz 1984:51; Hsieh 1985:86, 93; Clough 1978:98–99.

27. Mao 1977:17; Yahuda 1983:27, 49, 52, 54, 59, 62; Chang 1990:27–29, 32–35, 40; Koen 1960:232.

28. Chang 1990:27.

29. Foot 1995:24; Clough 1978:125.

30. Han 1990:10–12.

31. Chang 1990:32–36; Ulam 1974:492–95; Yahuda 1983:29–30; Chang 1990:64.

32. Kalicki 1975:15–17; Truman 1955:407; Chang 1990:32–35, 68; Koen 1960:232.

33. Truman 1955:338–39, 346–52; Acheson 1969:310, 369.

34. Ulam 1974:517; Wei 1982:378; Clough 1978:150; Chang 1990:66; Tucker 1994:33–34, 48.

35. Chang 1990:77–80.

36. Tucker 1990:254–56; 1994:35–37, 46, 48–9; Chang 1990:102, 146–47; Kissinger 1979:784; Hsieh 1985:174–75; He 1990:226, 231; Kusnitz 1984:64–67.

37. Fairbank 1986:611–21, 625; Ulam 1974:312, 623–24, 628–29, 638, 659; Lieberthal 1989:47, 55, 102, 156, 158.

38. Yahuda 1983:30–31; Spence 1990:553–55; Chang 1990:102; Kusnitz 1984:69, 71, 73–75, 80.

39. Wei 1982:15–17, 19, 21–22, 39–40, 70–72, 289; Porter 1984:64–65; Hsieh 1985:175–76.

40. *International Herald Tribune*, November 10, 1975; Hsieh 1985:184, 186–88; Tucker 1994:61.

41. Clough 1978:151–53; Tucker 1994:48–50, 101–2; Kusnitz 1984:96–101; Hsieh 1985:180–83.

42. Harding 1993:151–52; Spence 1990:440–41, 603–16.

43. Welsh 1993:467–69; Wang 1977:116–17, 156. The number of votes cast against the PRC in the annual UN debate rose from forty-seven in 1966 to fifty-seven in 1967. Foot 1995:216–17.

44. Newhouse 1973:68, 128; Ambrose 1985:214; Kusnitz 1984:117; Tucker 1994:122.

45. Yahuda 1983:193; Spence 1990:615–16.

46. Han 1990:153–56; Kissinger 1979:166–67.

47. Lieberthal 1989:210–12; Wang 1977:120; Harding 1993:156; Kusnitz 1984:118, 131.

48. E.g., Kissinger 1979:708.

49. Han 1990:272; Choudhury 1988.

50. Lord 1990. Also, Kusnitz 1984:131–33, 137.

51. Kusnitz 1984:137–38; Tucker 1994:104–5; Foot 1995:47.

52. Kissinger 1979:772, 784–86; Bush 1987:116; Foot 1995:47; Clough 1978:153.

53. Hsieh 1985, app. 4.

54. The value of this can be seen in the PRC's use of international legal sovereignty in early 1979, when Deng Xiaoping made it appear that China's invasion of Vietnam was tacitly supported by Washington. This reportedly inhibited Moscow from helping Hanoi with military force. *Washington Post*, February 1, 1979; Vance 1983:121; *BBC Summary of World Broadcasts*, February 23, 1979.

55. Shen 1983:62; Bachrach 1976:273; *China Yearbook* 1972–1973:61.

56. On the financial aid, see *New York Times*, January 17, 1969; *United Nations Yearbook* 1969:887; 1970:937; and 1971:715–16; *China Yearbook* 1969–1970:363.

57. Taiwan was one of the states for which this phrase was coined. E.g., Vale 1997:101–2.

58. Generally, Hsu 1980 and Chen 1977.

59. Schaller 1979:44, 55–56, 117–19; Oksenberg 1997:64; Mendl 1978:5, 15–16; Barnett 1960:273, 275; Iriye 1996:48, 57–58.

60. Han 1990:121–30; He 1990:229–30; Chang 1990:161–63, 183, 207–8; Schaller 1979:54–57; Spence 1990:556; Oksenberg 1997:65–66.

61. Copper 1986:148.

62. Wei 1982:23; Kalicki 1975:17; *International Herald Tribune*, July 27, 1971.

63. Hsu 1980; Chen 1977.

64. Hsieh 1985, app. 5; Clough 1978:160; Yim 1991:51.

65. *Japan Times*, November 12, 1975; *Xinhua News Agency*, April 6, 1975; *Financial Times*, April 18, 1973; and *Straits Times*, May 7, 1975; Clough 1978:159, 167; *Washington Post*, November 21, 1976.

66. *China News Analyst*, April 12, 1974, 4–7; Chen 1977:905; *Christian Science Monitor*, May 21, 1973; Hsu 1980:97, 99. Also, *Washington Post*, June 26, 1977.

67. *New York Times*, March 2, 1973; *China News Analyst*, April 12, 1974, 4–7; *The Observer*, April 18, 1975; *Washington Post*, June 26, 1977; Chen 1977:905, 908–9, 912.

68. Sun Yun-hsuan 1989; Chiang 1987; *Newsweek*, January 8, 1979, 29.

69. Beijing threatened to use force against Taiwan if she declared independence, established a military relationship with the USSR, developed nuclear weapons, or refused to discuss reunification for too long. *New York Times*, January 10 and 31, 1979; Shaw 1985:1056, 1062–63.

70. Shen 1983:248–49; Li 1977.

71. *People's Daily*, January 1, 1979; *Beijing Review*, January 5, 1979, 16–17; Shaw 1987:125–26.

72. Quoted in *US News and World Report*, February 12, 1979, 26. Also, Yim 1980:22.

73. Yim 1980:51; *Wall Street Journal*, October 3, 1994; Chiu 1988:212.

74. *Taiwan Relations Act* 1979; *Washington Post*, March 14, 1979; *China Yearbook* 1979:3–4.

75. For example, *Xinhua News Agency*, June 10, 1981; Weinberger 1990:254; Haig 1984:215.

76. *Beijing Review*, October 5, 1981, 10–11; *Reuters*, October 2, 1981.

77. Holdridge 1982:13–14; Haig 1984:215; Weinberger 1990:254.

78. Weinberger 1990:280; *New York Times*, September 30, 1983; *Washington Post*, April 25, 1984; Reagan 1990:370.

79. Ching 1979:131; *Wall Street Journal*, October 3, 1994.

80. *New York Times*, June 11, 1975; *Japan Times*, June 12 and 21, 1975; *Far Eastern Economic Review*, May 8, 1986, 30.

81. Hsieh 1985:263 and app. 4; *Far Eastern Economic Review*, March 3, 1983:32–34.

82. Council for Economic Planning and Development 1987:270; Meyer 1974:127; Clough 1978:185.

83. For example, *Japan Times*, October 26, 1972.

84. Carter 1982:200–201; Sullivan 1983:104; Feldman 1988:30, 32, 35, 36–37; Chien 1984.

85. Euro-Asian Trade Organization (EATO) 1979a, 1979b; Clough 1978:165; Werner 1985:1099.

86. For example, *Asia Intelligence Newswire*, October 26, 1997.

87. Hsieh 1985:271; *The Economist*, January 24, 1998, 35. In 1998, for example, ROC residents wanting to travel to Japan had to apply for "voyage certificates" through that country's embassy in Bangkok. *Kyodo News Agency*, April 29, 1998.

88. For example, *The Economist*, August 8, 1998, 53.

89. Chiang 1987; Parris Chang, testimony, in U.S. Senate Committee on Foreign Affairs 1980:13.

90. Krasner 1999:73–104.

91. Nearing and Freeman 1969.

92. *The Economist*, June 12, 1999, 45–51.

93. Krasner 1999:73–104.

94. For a list of such conventions, all dating from after 1944, see *The Economist*, December 5, 1998, 4. Also, Nathan and Ross 1996:178, 183, 185, 190; Nathan 1997:248.

95. The Kosovo war was an example of this. *The Economist*, June 12, 1999, 45–51.

96. Kinross 1997:510, 518, 526–27, 554–63, 568, 569–70.

97. *The Economist*, December 5, 1998, 6–7, 13–15; Nathan 1996:185, 187.

98. For examples of such critical analysis of Chinese policies, see *Financial Times*, July 10 and 22, 1998; Nathan 1997:255; and Shambaugh 1996:84, 93.

99. Tien 1989:106, 108–12, 146, 155–56.

100. Clough 1978:33; Ho 1978:162

101. Clough 1978:34, 38–39; Tucker 1994:27–29, 50. The worst instance of abuse by the KMT occurred in early 1947, when government agents beat a huckster who was illegally selling cigarettes. Popular anger over this incident exploded into riots on February 28, and these were put down harshly, with an estimated loss of more than ten thousand Taiwanese lives. Gold 1986:50–52.

102. Ho 1978:287–88; Wu 1985:162; Ministry of Economic Affairs 1986:26; Council for Economic Planning and Development 1987:23–25, 210; Tien 1989:26, 27–30.

103. Tucker 1994:167; Thurston 1996:66.

104. Thurston 1996:64; Tien 1989:33, 38, 68.

105. Oksenberg 1997:66; Chiang 1987.

106. Tucker 1994:168–69, 177; Shambaugh 1996:92; Oksenberg 1997:77.

107. Oksenberg 1997:77; *Japan Economic Newswire*, November 6, 1997.

108. *Beijing Review*, June 30, 1997.

109. *The Economist*, December 6, 1997, 44; January 24, 1998, 35; February 21, 1998, 39. *Nikkei Weekly*, January 26, 1998; *Far Eastern Economic Review*, April 2, 1998, 49; *Financial Times*, March 18, 1998; *Beijing Review*, June 30, 1997; *FT Asia Intelligence Wire*, June 16, 1997.

110. Clough 1978:35–37, 55; Thurston 1996:67; Tucker 1994:72.

111. Tucker 1994:150–51; Tien 1989:36–37, 69–70, 72, 77, 85, 184–86; Tien 1991:4.

112. Copper 1986:41. This was an improbable transformation: in previous decades Chiang Ching-kuo had run the ROC's often ruthless security forces. Tucker 1994:72, 149; Tien 1989:74, 94–97.

113. E.g., *Zhongyang Ribao*, December 10 and 11, 1976. Generally, Ching 1979:128.

114. Thurston 1996:67. See also Oksenberg 1997:69.

115. Tien 1991:3; Thurston 1996:63–64; Tien 1989:64–65, 91–92, 100, 110–12; Copper 1986:43, 107.

116. Copper 1986:108; Thurston 1996:54, 59–60; Oksenberg 1997:70.

117. Another factor was the parties' realization that the presidency would need a popular mandate to legitimize its future negotiations with the PRC. Tien 1998; Copper 1986:46; Tien 1991:7.

118. Oksenberg 1997:72; Thurston 1996:52.

119. For instance, Tucker 1994:182–83.

120. Harding 1997. For other examples, see *Federal News Service*, November 13, 1997; *Japan Economic Newswire*, November 6, 1997. Generally, Copper 1986:44.

121. *M2 Presswire*, October 30, 1997.

122. *The Record*, November 2, 1997; *Asian Political News*, November 10, 1997.

123. *Beijing Review*, June 30, 1997.

124. Yahuda 1996:46–47, 89.

125.   Mendl 1978:17–19, 42; Clough 1978:178–82; Ogata 1988:9, 12.

126.   Clough 1978:189–194, 200.

127.   Generally, *Washington Post*, December 26, 1978; Clough 1978:163, 190.

128.   Tien 1989:225; Tucker 1994:135–37.

129.   *China Yearbook* 1975:712; Hsieh 1985:248. See also *The Guardian*, December 5, 1975.

130.   E.g., Clough 1978:166; EATO, *European Trade/Cultural Representatives and Banks*; Ministry of Economic Affairs 1986:26; EATO 1985:7, 14.

131.   China External Trade Development Council n.d.:5, 13, 23, 38, 52, 66, 75. Also, Hsieh 1985: 263; Clough 1978: 162.

132.   For example, EATO 1979a, 1979b, and *Memorandum on Individual Restrictions*; Chang 1987; also, EATO 1985:25.

133.   For example, Siew 1998:36. *Financial Times*, May 5, 1998.

134.   *Deutsche Press-Agentur*, August 19, 1996; *Facts on File World News Digest*, November 6, 1997; *Business Week*, November 3, 1997, 20.

135.   *Deutsche Press-Agentur*, August 19, 23, 1996. Generally, *BBC Summary of World Broadcasts*, August 21, 1996.

136.   *BBC Summary of World Broadcasts*, January 9, 1997; *Deutsche Press-Agentur*, May 19, 1997.

137.   *Deutsche Presse-Agentur*, May 21 and 29, 1997; *The Economist*, January 24, 1998, 35; *BBC Summary of World Broadcasts*, October 15, 1997; *Kyodo News Service*, December 8, 1997; *Financial Times*, January 21 and February 12, 1998.

138.   Oksenberg 1997:73; *Washington Post*, March 14, 1979; Unger 1979:134; Chang King-yuh 1981:609, 615.

139.   For example, Tucker 1994:126.

140.   Carter 1982:197; Brzezinski 1986:231–32.

141.   *Taiwan Relations Act* 1979; Unger 1979:134; *Beijing Review*, September 7, 1981.

142.   *Far Eastern Economic Review*, May 8, 1986, 26; *International Herald Tribune*, April 27, 1987.

143.   Oksenberg 1997:73–74.

144.   *Financial Times*, July 15, 1999; *Reuters*, July 18, 1999.

References

Acheson, Dean. 1969. *Present at the Creation*. New York: Norton.
Ambrose, Stephen. 1985. *Rise to Globalism*. 4th rev. ed. New York: Penguin.
Barnett, A. Doak. 1960. *Communist China and Asia*. New York: Vintage.
Bush, George with Victor Gold. 1987. *Looking Forward*. New York: Doubleday.
Carter, Jimmy. 1982. *Keeping Faith*. New York: Bantam Books.

Chang, C. P. (Congressional Affairs Division, ROC Embassy in Washington, 1974–1978; deputy secretary-general of EATO in the middle 1980s). 1987. Interview by author, Taipei, September 24, 29.

Chang King-yuh. 1981. "Partnership in Transition: A Review of Recent Taipei, Taiwan–Washington Relations." *Asian Survey* (June) Vol. 21(1).

Chen, King C. 1977. "Peking's Attitude Toward Taiwan." *Asian Survey* (October) Vol. 17(2).

Chiang Chun-nan (founder and editor of *Xin Xinwen* [The Journalist] and a spokesman for the opposition movement on Taiwan in the 1980s). 1987. Interview by author, September 28.

Chien, Fredrick. 1984. "The Role of the Coordination Council for North American Affairs in the Context of the US-ROC Relationship." Coordinating Council for North American Affairs, Bethesda, Md., November 1.

———— (section chief, deputy director, and director, Department of North American Affairs, 1962–1972; vice minister, Ministry of Foreign Affairs, 1975–1982; representative, CCNAA, 1983–1988; subsequently, minister of Foreign Affairs). 1986. Interview by author, Bethesda, Md., September 23.

China External Trade Development Council. n.d. *CETDC in Retrospect, 1970–1980.* Taipei: China External Trade Development Council.

China Yearbook. 1967–1970, 1972–1973, 1975, 1979. Taipei: China Publishing Co.

Ching, Frank. 1979. "A Most Envied Province." *Foreign Policy* (Autumn) Vol. 36.

Chiu Hongdah. 1988. "The International Law of Recognition and Multi-System Nations." In Harvey Feldman, Michael Y. M. Kau, and Ilipyong J. Kim, *Taiwan in a Time of Transition.* New York: Paragon House.

Choudhury, Golam. 1982. *China in World Affairs.* Boulder, Colo.: Westview Press.

———— (an official in the Pakistani Foreign Ministry familiar with the secret messages exchanged between Washington and Beijing in 1970 and 1971). 1988. Letter to the author, June 15.

Clough, Ralph N. 1978. *Island China.* Cambridge: Harvard University Press.

Copper, John F. 1986. *Taiwan.* 2d ed. Boulder, Colo.: Westview Press, 1986.

Council for Economic Planning and Development. 1987. *Taiwan Statistical Data Book, 1987.* Taipei: Council for Economic Planning and Development.

Euro-Asian Trade Organization. 1979a. *Memorandum on Lack of Advance Consultation by EEC with the Republic of China on Controls and Quotas.* Taipei: EATO.

————. 1979b. *Memorandum on Unfair Treatment of Textile Exports from the Republic of China to the EEC.* Taipei: EATO.

————. 1985. *A Report on the Euro-Asia Trade Organization on Its 10th Anniversary.* Taipei: EATO.

————. n.d. *European Trade/Cultural Representatives and Banks in the Republic of China.* Taipei: EATO.

————. n.d. *Memorandum on Individual Restrictions.* Taipei: EATO.

Fairbank, John King. 1969. *Trade and Diplomacy on the China Coast.* Stanford: Stanford University Press.

———. 1986. *The Great Chinese Revolution, 1800–1985.* New York: Harper and Row.

Feldman, Harvey. 1988. "A New Kind of Relationship." In Harvey Feldman, Michael Y. M. Kau, and Ilipyong J. Kim, *Taiwan in a Time of Transition.* New York: Paragon House.

Foot, Rosemary. 1995. *The Practice of Power.* New York: Oxford University Press.

Gold, Thomas B. 1986. *State and Society in the Taiwan Miracle.* Armonk, N.Y.: M. E. Sharpe.

Haig, Alexander M. 1984. *Caveat.* London: Weidenfeld and Nicolson.

Han Nianlong. 1990. *Diplomacy of Contemporary China.* Hong Kong: New Horizon Press.

Harding, Harry. 1993. "The Chinese State in Crisis, 1966–1969." In Roderick MacFarquhar, ed., *The Politics of China, 1949–1989.* Cambridge: Cambridge University Press.

———. 1997. Speech of October 28, 1997, in hearings of House International Relations Committee, Subcommittee on International Operations and Human Rights. *M2 Presswire,* October 28, 1997.

He Di. 1990. "The Evolution of the People's Republic of China's Policy Toward the Offshore Islands." In Warren I. Cohen and Akira Iriye, eds., *The Great Powers in East Asia.* New York: Columbia University Press.

Ho, Samuel P. S. 1978. *Economic Development of Taiwan, 1860–1970.* London: Yale University Press.

Holdridge, John. 1982. Testimony Before Senate Committee on Foreign Relations. *U.S. Policy Toward China and Taiwan.* Washington, D.C.: Government Printing Office.

Hopkirk, Peter. 1990. *The Great Game.* New York: Kodansha International.

Howe, Christopher. 1996. "Introduction: The Changing Political Economy of Sino-Japanese Relations." In Christopher Howe, ed., *China and Japan.* Oxford: Clarendon.

Hsieh Chiao Chiao. 1985. *Strategy for Survival.* London: Sherwood Press.

Hsu King-yi. 1980. "Taiwan's Response to Peking's United Front Tactics." *Asian Affairs* (November-December) Vol. 8.

Iriye, Akira. 1996. "Chinese-Japanese Relations, 1945–1990." In Christopher Howe, ed., *China and Japan.* Oxford: Clarendon.

Kalicki, J. H. 1975. *The Pattern of Sino-American Crises.* Binghamton, N.Y.: Cambridge University Press.

Kinross, John Patrick and Douglass Balfour. 1997. *The Ottoman Centuries.* New York: Morrow Quill.

Kissinger, Henry A. 1979. *The White House Years.* London: George Weidenfeld and Nicolson.

Koen, Ross Y. 1960. *The China Lobby in American Politics.* New York: Macmillan.

Krasner, Stephen D. 1999. *Sovereignty: Organized Hypocrisy.* Princeton: Princeton University Press.

Kusnitz, Leonard A. 1984. *Public Opinion and Foreign Policy: America's China Policy, 1949–1979.* London: Greenwood Press.

Li, Victor H. 1997. *De-Recognizing Taiwan: The Legal Problems.* Washington, D.C.: Carnegie Endowment for Institutional Peace.

Lieberthal, Kenneth G. and Bruce Dickson. 1989. *A Research Guide to Central Party and Government Meetings in China, 1949–1986.* Armonk, N.Y.: M. E. Sharpe.

Lord, Winston (member, National Security Council, 1969–1973; special assistant to the president, 1970–1973). 1990. Interview by author, New York City, November 1.

Mao Zedong. 1977. *Selected Works of Mao Zedong.* Vol. 5. Beijing: Foreign Language Press.

Meyer, Armin. 1974. *Assignment: Tokyo.* New York: Bobbs-Merrill.

Ministry of Economic Affairs. 1986. *Economic Development, Taiwan, Republic of China.* Taipei: Ministry of Economic Affairs.

Nathan, Andrew J. and Robert S. Ross. 1996. *The Great Wall and the Empty Fortress.* New York: Norton.

———. 1997. *China's Transition.* New York: Columbia University Press.

Nearing, Scott and Joseph Freeman. 1969. *Dollar Diplomacy.* New York: Modern Reader Paperbacks.

Newhouse, John. 1973. *Cold Dawn, The Story of SALT.* New York: Holt, Rinehart and Winston.

Nish, Ian. 1996. "An Overview of Relations Between China and Japan, 1895–1945." In Christopher Howe, ed., *China and Japan.* Oxford: Clarendon.

Ogata Sadako. 1988. *Normalization with China.* Berkeley, Calif.: Institute of East Asian Studies.

Oksenberg, Michel. 1997. "Taiwan, Tibet, and Hong Kong in Sino-American Relations." In Ezra Vogel, ed., *Living with China: US-China Relations in the Twenty-First Century.* New York: Norton.

Porter, Bruce. 1984. *The USSR in Third World Conflicts.* New York: Cambridge University Press.

Reagan, Ronald. 1990. *An American Life.* New York: Simon and Shuster.

Schaller, Michael. 1979. *The United States and China in the Twentieth Century.* New York: Oxford University Press.

Shambaugh, David. 1996. "China and Japan Towards the Twenty-First Century: Rivals for Pre-eminence or Complex Interdependence?" In Christopher Howe, ed., *China and Japan.* Oxford: Clarendon.

Shaw Yu-ming. 1985. "Taiwan: A View from Taipei, Taiwan." *Foreign Affairs* (Summer) Vol. 63.

———. 1987. *Guoji Jushi yu Zhongguo Qiantu* [The International Situation and China's Prospects for the Future]. Taipei: Liming Wenhua Shiye Gongsi.

Shen, James. 1983. *The US and Free China: How the US Sold Out Its Ally*. Washington, D.C.: Acropolis Books.

Snow, Edgar. 1968. *Red Star Over China*. New York: Grove Press.

Spence, Jonathan D. 1990. *The Search for Modern China*. New York: Norton.

Storry, Richard. 1982. *A History of Modern Japan*. New York: Penguin.

Sullivan, Roger. 1983. Testimony Before House Subcommittee on Asian and Pacific Affairs. *United States–China Relations 11 Years After the Shanghai Communique*. Washington, D.C.: Government Printing Office.

Sun Yun-hsuan (ROC minister of economic affairs, 1969–1978; prime minister, 1978–1984; subsequently, senior adviser to the president). 1989. Interview by author, Taipei, June 3.

Taiwan Relations Act. 1979. *U.S. Code*. Vol. 22, secs. 3301–16.

Teiwes, Frederick C. 1993. "The Establishment and Consolidation of the New Regime, 1949-1957." In Roderick MacFarquhar, ed., *The Politics of China, 1949–1989*. Cambridge: Cambridge University Press.

Thurston, Anne F. 1996. "The Little Island That Could." *Wilson Quarterly* (Summer) Vol. 20.

Tien Hung-mao. 1989. *The Great Transition*. Stanford: Hoover Institution Press.

——. 1991. *Brothers in Arms*. New York: Asia Society.

——. 1998. Speech at Stanford University, Stanford, Calif., May 7.

Truman, Harry S. 1955. *Years of Trial and Hope*. Garden City, N.J.: Doubleday.

Tucker, Nancy Bernkopf. 1990. "John Foster Dulles and the Taiwan Roots of the 'Two Chinas' Policy." In Richard H. Immerman, ed., *John Foster Dulles and the Diplomacy of the Cold War*. Princeton: Princeton University Press.

——. 1994. *Uncertain Friendships: Taiwan, Hong Kong, and the United States, 1945–1992*. New York: Twayne.

Ulam, Adam B. 1974. *Expansion and Coexistence*. 2nd ed. New York: Praeger.

Unger, Leonard. 1979. "Derecognition Worked." *Foreign Policy* (Autumn) Vol. 36.

United Nations Yearbook. 1969, 1970, 1971. New York: Office of Public Information.

U.S. Department of State. 1949. *United States Relations with China*. Public Document 3573. Washington, D.C.: Government Printing Office.

U.S. Senate Committee on Foreign Relations. 1980. *Taiwan: One Year After United States–China Normalization*. Washington, D.C.: Government Printing Office.

Vale, Peter. 1997. "South Africa and Taiwan: Pariahs, International Redemption, and Global Change." In Maysing H. Yang, ed., *Taiwan's Expanding Role in the International Arena*. Armonk, N.Y.: M. E. Sharpe.

Vance, Cyrus. 1983. *Hard Choices: Critical Years in America's Foreign Policy*. New York: Simon and Schuster.

Wang Gungwu. 1977. *China and the World since 1949*. New York: St. Martin's Press.

Wei Liang-Tsai. 1982. *Peking Versus Taipei in Africa*. Taipei: Asia and World Institute.

Weinberger, Casper. 1990. *Fighting for Peace*. New York: Warner Books.

Welsh, Frank. 1993. *A History of Hong Kong*. London: HarperCollins.

Werner, Roy A. 1985. "Taiwan's Trade Flows: The Underpinnings of Legitimacy?" *Asian Survey* (November) Vol. 25(2).

Wu Yuan-li. 1981. "Income Distribution in the Process of Economic Growth in Taiwan." In James C. Hsiung, ed., *Taiwan Experience*. New York: American Association for Chinese Studies.

Yahuda, Michael. 1983. *China's Foreign Policy After Mao*. London: Macmillan.

———. 1996. *Hong Kong: China's Challenge*. London: Macmillan.

Yim Kwan Ha. 1991. *China Under Deng*. New York: Facts on File.

7

The Sovereignty Script

Red Book for Russian Revolutionaries

MICHAEL McFAUL

In December 1991, Russia allegedly reacquired its sovereignty from the Soviet Union, a sovereignty that the new leaders of the Russian state claimed had been lost for almost seventy years. Compared to other transfers of sovereignty in the twentieth century, however, it was a strange event. Like dramatic moments in the history of decolonization in Africa and Asia, this transfer of sovereignty from colonizer to colonized was punctuated with the lowering of the Soviet red hammer and sickle and raising of the Russian tricolor. Yet the flag ceremony did not take place on the periphery of a former empire; it was held in the capital city of the metropole itself. For Russia to become a sovereign state, the entire empire had to be destroyed.

Moreover, the players in this decolonization drama also were not out of central casting. In most transfers of sovereignty, especially in the twentieth century, European colonizers have attended the flag ceremonies first to retire or take home their flag and then to celebrate (or at least recognize) the hoisting of the new flag of the formerly colonized non-Europeans. The multiethnic composition of most newly independent states confused the question regarding to whom sovereignty was being transferred (for instance in Nigeria, was it to Hausa, Ibo, or "Nigerians"?), but most transfers of sovereignty took place between two different ethnic groups. Usually, the colonizers were European and the colonized were not. Such was not the case in Russia's independence struggle, however, as leaders of both the Soviet Union (Mikhail Gorbachev) and the new Russian state (Boris Yeltsin) were ethnic Russians.

The event looked even more surreal when one remembered the backgrounds of the two principals. Mikhail Gorbachev, the last "imperial governor" of the Soviet empire in Russia, got his start in the Communist Party of the Soviet Union (CPSU), rising to its highest post in 1985.[1] Boris Yeltsin, the first leader of the new sovereign state of Russia, followed a similar career path, rising to the rank of candidate member of the Politburo. How can this be? Usually, the leader pulling the drawstrings on the flagpole at these events has had a long career as a protest leader or guerrilla fighter who struggled for decades to obtain national liberation. Yet Yeltsin was a senior leader in the Soviet Union, the very state that he was now in the process of dismantling as a means to secure the sovereignty of another state, Russia.

Finally, the event probably was strangest of all for the people who lived in the territory that became known as the Russian Federation after the flag ceremony. Nation and state were distinct identities in the Soviet Union, captured most vividly in the Soviet passport that identified the passport holder as a citizen of the USSR but also assigned the holder an ethnic identity, be it Russian, Ukrainian, Jewish, or German. For some ethnic groups, especially in the Baltics and Caucasus, this dual identity reconfirmed their colonized status. For them, independence from the Soviet Union resembled and probably felt like decolonization processes around the developing world. For Russians living in the Russian Soviet Federated Socialist Republic, however, the historical metaphor of decolonization was not so obvious.[2] From whom were they gaining their independence? As a young Russian told an American reporter on the eve of Russian independence, "We don't know who we are anymore. They tell me I'm a 'Russian' now. What does that mean? Does it mean that my parents, who live in Uzbekistan, are foreigners? . . . I think of myself as Soviet. I know nothing about Russia."[3]

The struggle for power that culminated in 1991 was not between colonized and colonizer, but rather between Russian and Russian. As discussed later in this essay, the existence of two or more groups with competing, irreconcilable claims to control over the same territory is what such diverse analysts as Charles Tilly, Samuel Huntington, and Leon Trotsky have labeled a revolutionary situation. So why did the revolutionary challengers in this case frame their revolutionary struggle as a contest for sovereignty, a war of national liberation, or a fight for decolonization?

The struggle for political power in the Soviet Union in 1990–1991 became a sovereignty issue because Boris Yeltsin chose to make it one. In the last year of the Soviet Union's existence, Yeltsin and his allies were locked in a political struggle for power with Mikhail Gorbachev and his backers. Yeltsin's embrace of the sovereignty script helped him to prevail in this conflict. By casting the political power struggle as a battle for Russian sovereignty, Yeltsin carved together a disparate political coalition both in Russia and the Soviet Union that may not have coalesced under a different idea or cause. Playing the sovereignty card also helped Yeltsin and his allies secure international resources at the same time that it denied his enemy, Mikhail Gorbachev, international support.

Yeltsin had other options. He could have cast his struggle as an anticommunist revolution within the Soviet Union for which Russian sovereignty would not have been essential. As president of the Soviet Union, Yeltsin could have pursued the creation of market and democratic institutions within the sovereign state of the Soviet Union. Or he could have opted to pursue a new institutional form for organizing the territory of the Soviet Union through the creation of a new federation or confederation. Ultimately, however, he selected the sovereignty script, because it served his immediate political goals and because it was most readily available.[4] This choice, in turn, had constraining consequences for Yeltsin and his allies as they sought to create a new state in an independent Russia.[5]

To develop this argument, this paper proceeds in four parts. The first section discusses why Yeltsin found it expedient to frame his political struggle in terms of sovereignty. Here, the focus is on the gains accrued by Yeltsin and his allies by selecting the sovereignty script. The end of this section, however, suggests how the sovereignty script also constrained Yeltsin and other new leaders regarding choices about institutional design after the collapse of the Soviet Union. The second section looks at the interests and actions of those that provide international legal sovereignty through recognition. Here, the focus is on how the institution of sovereignty constrained state behavior regarding the recognition of Russian sovereignty. The third section discusses a paradoxical trade-off of different kinds of sovereignty as specified by Krasner in the introductory essay to this volume. In seeking to obtain international recognition, or international legal sovereignty, Yeltsin's new Russian state had to forfeit aspects of domestic sovereignty. This section provides examples of the trade-off between different kinds of sovereignties. Section four concludes.

The Pursuit of Sovereignty as a Revolutionary Strategy

Few scholars of the Soviet Union ever considered Russia a colony of the USSR. The notion that Russia won its sovereignty back from the Soviet Union, therefore, is a recently constructed idea. The Soviet empire may have collapsed and territories called Latvia or Georgia may have won their independence from this colonizer, but Russia—the colony—did not win its independence from the Soviet empire. For most observers on both the left and right, Russia and Russians were the colonizers, not the colonized.[6]

What did occur in the Soviet Union at the end of the 1980s is still debated. For some, including this author, the metaphor and imagery of revolution most accurately captures the kind, speed, and magnitude of change that unfolded in the Soviet Union and then Russia over the last decade.[7] The breakdown of the state, the emergence of two groups claiming sovereign authority over the same territory, and the subsequent attempt by the revolutionary victors to destroy the political and economic institutions of the ancien régime and replace them with new forms of political and economic organization constitute the classic attributes of a revolution.[8] Others have preferred to call the events that transpired in the Soviet Union in the late 1980s a "transition to democracy."[9] Still others have labeled these events a "state collapse."[10] Few Western analysts, however, have employed the discourse of sovereignty or national independence or decolonization to describe the political battle between Russia and the Soviet Union.[11]

Yet Boris Yeltsin did. He and his political allies consciously and deliberately framed their struggle as one about sovereignty. Soon after his election as chairman of the Russian Congress of People's Deputies in the spring of 1990, Yeltsin declared that Russian sovereignty was a central aim of his political agenda. As he stated in May 1990, "The problems of the [Russian] republic cannot be solved without full-blooded political sovereignty. This alone can enable relations between Russia and the Union and between the autonomous territories within Russia to be harmonized. The political sovereignty of Russia is also necessary in international affairs."[12]

Two months after this speech, the Russian Congress of People's Deputies voted to declare the Russian Federation a sovereign state. The declaration implicitly underscored that this act represented a reclamation of sovereignty lost:

1. The Russian Soviet Federated Socialist Republic [RSFSR] is a sovereign state, created by the people that have historically united in it.

2. The Sovereignty of the RSFSR is the natural and essential condition for the existence of Russian statehood, which has centuries of history, culture, and accumulated traditions.[13]

Of course, these declarations of sovereignty did not translate immediately into either de facto sovereign control over political and economic activities occurring within the Russian Federation (domestic sovereignty) or de jure recognition by the international community (international legal sovereignty). The battle for sovereignty raged for another year during the "war of laws" in the fall of 1990, the battle over the referendum on sovereignty in March 1991, the "9 + 1" federal accord and the subsequent Union Treaty deliberations in the spring of 1991, the Russian presidential election in June 1991, and finally and most dramatically, the standoff between Soviet troops and Russian citizens in August 1991.[14] Yeltsin's own position on sovereignty remained ambiguous throughout this period as his definition of the concept changed over time, depending on the political circumstances of the moment.[15] Nonetheless, early on in this contest for political power, the issue of Russian sovereignty assumed center stage.

The framing of these events in the language of sovereignty demonstrates the intervening potential of the idea, institution, or script of "international legal sovereignty" in shaping political outcomes.[16] The very existence of this concept as a norm or idea of the contemporary international system changed fundamentally the way in which the revolutionary struggle unfolded in the Soviet Union in the late 1980s.[17] Given the goals of their revolution and the balance of power both domestically and internationally, Yeltsin and the revolutionary groups that allied with him aggressively sought to acquire sovereign status for Russia. Pursuit of international legal sovereignty in turn influenced their choice of revolutionary tactics and the articulation of their own revolutionary agenda.

DOMESTIC SIGNALING

Boris Yeltsin and his allies consciously framed their revolutionary challenge as a contest over sovereignty in order to obtain the domestic and international benefits accorded to those that have attained international legal sovereignty. Domestically, Yeltsin and his team believed that international recognition could serve as a *signal* to people living in Russia that the revolutionary challengers were legitimate and had a viable chance of succeeding in creating a new political system. As Krasner writes, "In an uncertain domestic political situation (a situation in which domestic sovereignty is problematic) international recognition can enhance the position of rulers by signaling to constituents that a ruler may have access to international resources like alliances and sovereign lending. Hence, international legal sovereignty can promote the interests of rulers by making it easier for them to generate domestic political support not just because they are in a better position to promote the interests of their constituents but also because recognition is a signal about the viability of a political regime and its leaders."[18]

All revolutionary movements need a clearly defined enemy and an alternative ideology to rally the troops and win domestic support. Without a coherent and viable opposition framework, it is difficult to construct an "organization of counterhegemony: collective projects for an alternative future."[19] In the Soviet/Russian context, defining the cleavage lines between opposition and ancien régime proved especially difficult given the similarities in backgrounds and objectives of leaders in these two camps.

Regarding the political institutions of the state, Mikhail Gorbachev—the leader of the ancien régime—advocated liberalization and eventually even democratization. Gorbachev—not Yeltsin—first initiated sweeping reform measures aimed at liberalizing political society.[20] His policy of glasnost, or openness, allowed for publication and discussion of previously taboo subjects while changes in the Soviet criminal code no longer punished political assembly and demonstration. In 1988, Gorbachev outlined a plan for radical institutional change by announcing that partially competitive elections for the USSR Congress of People's Deputies would be held in 1989.[21] These elections were followed by free and fair elections for soviets at the republic, regional, city, and district level the following year.

Russia's opposition found it difficult to outflank Gorbachev on the democracy debate. After all, the Russian opposition owed their very existence to Gorbachev's political reforms.[22] Toward the end of his reign, Gorbachev did make a series of decisions that allowed the Russian democratic opposition to question his democratic credentials. For instance, Gorbachev decided against holding a direct election for the office of the Soviet president in 1990; he either ordered or allowed Soviet special forces to seize control of government buildings in Latvia and Lithuania in the winter of 1991; and he tried to block a peaceful demonstration in Moscow by ordering 50,000 troops onto the streets of Moscow in the spring of 1991. Despite these authoritarian acts, few within Russia's opposition believed that they could seize power from Gorbachev using the argument that he was not a democrat. A seizure of power under this ideological banner would not have been recognized either domestically or internationally.

Different ideas regarding economic reform divided the Soviet regime and Russian opposition more distinctly. Gorbachev always had sought to reconstruct, reform, and revitalize the Soviet socialist economy.[23] In contrast, Yeltsin, Democratic Russia, and their allies eventually called for the abandonment of socialism altogether and the creation of a market economy based on free prices and private property. During the fall of 1990, these two sides attempted to negotiate an economic pact, called the 500-Day Plan, that sought to reconcile the two views. When those negotiations broke down, however, it became apparent to most radical "democrats" that a middle ground between socialism and capitalism did not exist. Yeltsin and his colleagues never articulated what kind of market economy they desired to replace the Soviet command system, nor proposed a strategy to pursue such a transformation. Nonetheless, as the Soviet economy edged toward collapse in the winter of 1991, the opposition's call for a new economic order grew increasingly militant.

And yet, the call for capitalism by itself also was not a tenable ideology of opposition. Exposed to images of the West during glasnost, most Russians preferred the lifestyles they saw in the television series *Santa Barbara* and *Dallas* to the ones they endured in Kursk or Bryansk. At the same time, capitalism was still a pejorative word in the Soviet context that did not elicit fervent support within either elite circles or the population more generally. Even within Russia's largest opposition movement at the time, Democratic Russia, a real ideological debate existed over the kind of economic system Russia should build. Whereas all within the movement knew what they were against—the Soviet communist system—they did not share a common idea of what economic system they stood for.[24] Consequently, to seize power from the Soviet regime in the name of capitalism also was not a viable option.

More obviously, power could not be seized in the name of a political leader such as Boris Yeltsin. Retrospectively, many analysts of the period have concluded that the main determinant of political struggle during the period was the personal rivalry between Gorbachev and Yeltsin. More important than developing democracy, making markets, or securing sovereignty, Yeltsin wanted to exact revenge and retribution against the man who had ended his career in the Communist Party. The only peaceful way to remove Gorbachev from power was to liquidate the office he held and the country he ruled. Without attempting to assess precisely the relative weight of this personal factor in the demise of the USSR, it is important to realize that a revolutionary challenge to the sovereign authority of the Soviet Union could not be constructed on behalf of or in the name of Boris Yeltsin.[25] Yeltsin's own political career as a Communist Party leader in the Soviet system called into question his own credentials as an opposition leader. He was not a Nelson Mandela or a Vaclav Havel. A seizure of power from one CPSU leader by another would have had little support either within Russia or abroad.

In contrast then to democracy, capitalism, or personal ambition, the call for sovereignty offered a legitimate ideology of opposition for Yeltsin and Russia's revolutionaries. Sovereignty was a cognitive construct that framed the power struggle between Gorbachev and Yeltsin or the Soviet regime and the Russian opposition in a way that advanced the opposition's cause. As noted earlier, given the historical origins of the Soviet Union and the lack of an ethnic dimension, the sovereignty card was not easily played in the Russian context. The idea actually arrived late to the Russian context and was borrowed from the Baltic popular front movements. Moreover, without the elections in 1990, in which Russian legislators were elected to the *Russian* Congress of People's Deputies, the revolutionary struggle in Russia might not have been framed in terms of sovereignty. Yeltsin's ability to obtain control of the Russian Congress offered him and his movement a symbol, physical assets, and resources from which to promote their sovereignty claims.[26]

Once sovereignty became the overriding objective of Russia's revolutionary movement, Yeltsin could forge a much larger domestic coalition than if his cause were only democracy or capitalism. At the pinnacle of its power, Democratic Russia controlled roughly three hundred of the thousand seats in the Russian Congress of People's Deputies.[27] Yet for the cause of Russian sovereignty, Yeltsin could patch together majorities within the legislative body, especially if the vote involved some direct confrontation with the Soviet authorities. Yeltsin won his own election as chairman of the Russian Congress under the sovereignty banner.

Yeltsin also employed the language of sovereignty to forge alliances with leaders of autonomous republics within the Russian Federation, urging them in the summer of 1990 to "take as much sovereignty as you can handle."[28] In promising these leaders more autonomy over their local affairs under a Russian state, Yeltsin won support from a group that was otherwise conservative on issues such as democracy and capitalism. After Soviet dissolution, this phrase would come back to haunt Yeltsin in his quest to preserve Russian territorial integrity.[29] At the time, however, Yeltsin's pledge to promote regional autonomy within the Russian Federation earned him allies who did not side with Yeltsin and Democratic Russia on other issues.

Third, Yeltsin's sovereignty script aided him in forging allies with leaders in some of the other republics within the Soviet Union who also wanted sovereignty. Baltic liberation movements and Russian democrats became staunch allies during the last years of the Soviet Union.[30] Mutual interests also motivated cooperation between Yeltsin and republican leaders in the Caucasus, Moldova, and eventually Ukraine who acted in concert with Yeltsin to diminish the influence of the Soviet center. Republican leaders in Central Asia did not embrace either Yeltsin or the idea of sovereignty during the polarized standoff between the Russian and Soviet governments in 1990–1991. After the aborted coup attempt in August 1991, when it became clear that the Soviet central government had become extremely weak, all of these leaders moved to acquire sovereign status.

UNINTENDED CONSEQUENCES OF EMBRACING THE SOVEREIGNTY SCRIPT

Yeltsin championed the idea of sovereignty as a way to build a powerful and ultimately successful coalition of political forces against the Soviet state. Although never concerned with Russian sovereignty during his decades as a Communist Party leader, Yeltsin's embrace of this issue helped him rise to power in the new conditions of pluralistic politics in the Soviet Union. In addition to serving Yeltsin's own individual interests, the language of and quest for sovereignty also shaped the political struggle between the Soviet and Russian states in ways that may or may not have served his intentions. Throughout this period of transition, his commitment to full sovereignty for Russia was ambiguous. Clarity came only when compelled by crisis.

In the spring and summer of 1991, Yeltsin and eight other republican leaders negotiated with Gorbachev to draft a new Union Treaty.[31] This document tried to carve out a middle ground between full sovereignty for nine of the republics and full subordination. Had the Union Treaty been signed and allowed to structure relations between the republics, sovereignty within the Soviet Union might have taken on a new and unique meaning in the international system of states.

Opponents of the treaty did not believe that a unique solution to the sovereignty dilemma was feasible. Rather, they believed that the treaty would lead eventually to full sovereignty for the republics and dissolution of the USSR.[32] To prevent this outcome, conservatives in Gorbachev's government orchestrated a palace coup in August 1991, days before the signing of the treaty.

Yeltsin and Russia's opposition responded to the new Soviet government, or Emergency Committee, by declaring sovereign authority over all Soviet state institutions, including the military, the KGB, and the Ministry of Internal Affairs.[33] As the new sovereign leader of Russia, Yeltsin then issued alternative military orders to the Soviet troops called into Moscow. Tank commanders received orders from the Soviet government by radio and instructions from the Russian government by leaflet and then had to make a choice concerning which orders to follow. More than any other event of the previous two years, this event crystallized the struggle for sovereignty between Russia and the Soviet Union. After three days, Russia won the struggle.

However, had the coup attempt not occurred, would Yeltsin and his allies pushed for complete sovereignty for Russia? To what extent did the sovereignty script frame decisions and actions during these moments of crisis in ways that ultimately may not have reflected the preferences of the actors involved? For Russia's elite, the dissolution of the Soviet Union was not a euphoric moment.[34] The signing of the Belovezhkaya Accords in December 1991 between Russia, Ukraine, and Belarus—the document that dissolved the USSR—was a secret and somber event.[35] In fact, similar to the Union Treaty negotiated earlier in the year, this accord sought to find a new middle ground between complete sovereignty and confederation by creating the Commonwealth of Independent States. It did not work. The Commonwealth has continued to exist as an international regime, albeit with considerable difficulty, but it did not provide a creative solution to a situation of problematic sovereignty.[36] In contrast to other cases discussed in this book, the institutional arrangements associated with the concept of sovereignty in the international system impeded the emergence of a unique resolution of the crisis of sovereignty that erupted in the Soviet Union after the August 1991 putsch attempt. Instead of engaging in negotiations over the design of a new institutional arrangement to reconstitute relations between the republics, all the members of the Commonwealth quickly became independent states recognized by the international community. Significantly, every republic (and not some subset of republics) became an independent state despite the fact that several republican leaders in Central Asia initially did not seek sovereignty.[37] The border demarcations between republics drawn decades ago by Stalin provided logical breaking points for the union, which in turn allowed the state to disintegrate peacefully.[38] Because the Soviet Union destructed along the republic cleavage lines, all republics had to become independent states. At the same time, other institutional forms such as autonomous republics like Chechnya and Tatarstan, which also desired sovereignty, were not allowed to claim domestic sovereignty and were not accorded international legal sovereignty by the international community.[39]

With time, most of Russia's elite distanced themselves from the decision to dissolve the USSR. Retrospectively, Yeltsin lamented the collapse of the Soviet Union and argued that he had no choice at the time but to guide a peaceful breakup. As he explained during the 1996 presidential campaign:

> The Belovezhkaya accords [the agreement that dissolved the USSR] were necessary mainly to turn the former republics of the collapsing union back to the center, toward the idea of a new union, to stimulate the negotiation process, and most importantly, to avoid the bloody "Yugoslav scenario" of uncontrollable collapse not only of the Soviet Union, but also of Russia itself, since already in 1991 the USSR law of 26 April 1990 was showing results in terms of the events in Tatarstan and Chechnya. Therefore it is strange to hear today that our actions were directed at the consensual collapse of the union and its immediate destruction. I know that it will not be easy to overcome this myth, but I emphasize once again: the CIS was the only possible way of preserving a united geopolitical space at that time.[40]

Likewise, the extent to which the population as a whole supported this idea of sovereignty for Russia remained ambiguous. In 1990 and 1991, disenchantment with the ancien régime was high, but acceptance of a common "alternative future" remained low. As mentioned previously, it took some real conceptual stretching for people in Russia to frame this political crisis as a struggle for Russian sovereignty, especially since no ethnic division was involved. Gorbachev and his entourage and Yeltsin and his supporters were all Russians who understood Moscow to be their capital. In March 1991, when asked on a referendum question whether they supported the preservation of the USSR, a solid 71.3 percent of Russian voters said yes, while only 26.4 voted against preservation.[41] Five years later, more than two-thirds of Russian voters thought that the dissolution of the USSR was a bad idea.[42] In sum, Yeltsin deployed the sovereignty script for immediate political goals, which in turn had long-term consequences that few anticipated or desired.

ACCESSING INTERNATIONAL RESOURCES

Another benefit of obtaining international legal sovereignty is the reduction of transaction costs in dealing with international actors and other states as well as the ability to access international resources available only to sovereign states.[43] In addition to domestic signaling, Russia's revolutionaries also pursued international legal sovereignty in order to access these international resources. Although Russia's opposition obtained most of the benefits of international legal sovereignty only *after* achieving domestic sovereignty, their pursuit of international recognition during the battle for sovereignty shaped both the aims and strategies of their revolutionary struggle.

Regarding aims, Russia's opposition articulated distinctly pro-Western goals. In sharp contrast to many revolutionary movements in the previous last two centuries, Russia's opposition did not reject the existing international community, but sought instead to integrate fully into it.[44] Communicating this position, however, proved difficult. By challenging the sovereignty of the USSR, Russia's opposition effectively breached one of the principal rules of the game of the international system, as almost all states within the international community of states had recognized the USSR as a state within their club. Yeltsin and his entourage upset the status quo. Although decolonization was a norm recognized by the international community of states, secession did not have a similar standing. As most international actors did not perceive Russia as a colony, Yeltsin's call for Russian sovereignty sounded illegitimate. As Mark Beissinger has observed, "the only unambiguous case of a successful secession since the end of World War II is Bangladesh—a fact often pointed to by those who believed that the dissolution of the USSR was unlikely."[45] Yeltsin's call for Russian sovereignty was also frightening to other states since he and his allies threatened to instigate a civil war in a country with thousands of nuclear weapons. Moreover, the leader of this recognized state, Mikhail Gorbachev, was extremely popular in the international community and was pursuing his own strategy of integration. Had their struggle for power been waged against a leader such as Stalin or even Brezhnev, Russia's opposition forces might have had an easier time gaining international recognition. Outflanking Gorbachev on the international front proved nearly impossible.

To win international recognition, Russia's opposition leaders trumpeted a revolutionary program that was even more pro-Western than Gorbachev's policies. Gorbachev advocated reformed socialism; Yeltsin and his allies pledged their allegiance to neoliberal market capitalism. Gorbachev allowed for elections of limited competition; Yeltsin called for multiparty elections and institutionalized a direct election for the Russian presidency. Gorbachev wanted to create a new Soviet federation; Yeltsin pushed for complete independence.[46] Gorbachev called for a Common European Home; Yeltsin and his allies supported (then) the expansion of NATO. Equally important were the ideas and ideological tenets absent from Yeltsin's repertoire. Above all else, Russian opposition leaders avoided language that could be associated with ethnic nationalism. Their quest for sovereignty was consciously devoid of an ethnic dimension.

The tactics of revolutionary struggle also were shaped by the desire to achieve international recognition. Most important, Russia's opposition refrained from using violence as a means for seizing power because they feared that violence would discredit their movement domestically, but even more so internationally. In making their arguments for sovereignty to the outside world, Russian leaders repeatedly assured Western states that they planned to abide by international law, not challenge it. In contrast to the Bolsheviks seventy years earlier, they also assured international lending institutions that they planned to assume responsibility for all debts of the Soviet ancien régime.[47]

The debate on these tactical issues was sometimes heated. In November 1990, during a large demonstration in downtown Moscow, Telman Gdlyan—one of Democratic Russia's more radical leaders—called for storming the Kremlin.[48] The conflict that ensued between Gdlyan and other Democratic Russia leaders over the use of violence precipitated a split in the movement. Again, in March 1991, Democratic Russia defied a Gorbachev decree banning all public demonstrations and mobilized nearly 200,000 people in Moscow to show support for an embattled Boris Yeltsin. As the columns marched toward the police barricades, a panicked debate erupted among Democratic Russia organizers as to whether it would serve their purposes to provoke violence by colliding with the armed police and soldiers. Eventually, those advocating the avoidance of violence prevailed, but several leaders within the movement lamented that a public relations opportunity had been squandered by not provoking Gorbachev's soldiers to respond violently.

Even after the collapse of the USSR, Russian revolutionaries refrained from punishing leaders from the Soviet ancien régime. The Communist Party of the Soviet Union was put on trial, but individual party members were not held personally accountable. Nor did Yeltsin's government undertake a national lustration or purge of party officials from government bureaucracies. During the initial period of seizing power, Yeltsin and his revolutionary allies wanted to demonstrate to the international world that they were not radicals, but were instead reliable and cooperative partners of the West. Given Gorbachev's international standing at the time, Yeltsin's government officials were especially careful in making sure that the Soviet leader could retire without facing retribution.[49]

In contrast, once they had obtained international recognition, Russia's leaders felt less constrained from using force in the pursuit of their revolutionary aims, be it against the Russian Congress of People's Deputies in October 1993 or against Chechnya in December 1994. Had Moscow authorities used force against Chechnya in 1991 when Chechen leaders first declared independence, the act of violence might have impaired Russia's campaign to acquire international legal sovereignty. By 1994, Russian sovereignty and the legitimacy of the Yeltsin government were no longer in question.

Despite these programmatic and tactical efforts, Russia's opposition obtained few tangible resources from external sources *before* securing domestic sovereignty. Soon after declaring Russia a sovereign state in the summer of 1990, Yeltsin created the Russian Ministry of Foreign Affairs and named a mid-level diplomat at the Soviet Foreign Ministry, Andrei Kozyrev, as Russia's first foreign minister. Kozyrev and his small staff used this institutional base to establish contacts with foreign embassies and international non-governmental organizations. Because no state recognized Russia's sovereignty, however, Kozyrev's efforts at obtaining international support, be it financial or symbolic, produced only limited success.[50]

Not constrained by the international legal sovereignty regime, international non-governmental organizations were more aggressive in recognizing and supporting Russia's opposition movement. For instance, American groups such as the National Endowment for Democracy, the National Democratic Institute, the International Republican Institute, and the AFL-CIO established working relationships with and provided limited financial assistance to leaders and organizations of Russia's opposition well before international recognition of Russia.[51] Though difficult to assess, the financial resources provided by these external actors probably had only a marginal impact on the course of Russia's internal struggle. Symbolically, however, these contacts played a role in affirming the legitimacy of Russia's opposition movement and thereby in undermining Soviet sovereignty.[52]

Russian opposition leaders did enjoy some success in raising doubts about the long-term future of Soviet sovereignty and thereby impeded the flow of external resources to the Soviet government. For instance, Russian opposition leaders worked to convince international financial institutions that Mikhail Gorbachev's economic reform plan was not viable without full participation of the Russian government. In the spring of 1991, Grigory Yavlinsky teamed with Graham Allison and Harvard economists to propose a Grand Bargain between G-7 countries and the Soviet Union, a "bargain" that aimed to supply Gorbachev and his Soviet government with billions of dollars in financial assistance.[53] Yeltsin's government countered by signing up its own group of American advisers from the Hoover Institution and then using these alliances with Western economists to discredit the Soviet plan. Well before the collapse of the Soviet Union, Russian leaders also established contacts with the World Bank and the International Monetary Fund (IMF) to ensure that no programs were negotiated with the Soviet government alone. Although Russian leaders understood that these international financial institutions would only sign an agreement with them after Russia had obtained international recognition, they wanted to thwart financial transfers to Gorbachev's government, which might prolong the Soviet Union's existence.[54]

Constraints of International Legal Sovereignty

The influence of ideas, institutions, and rules about international legal sovereignty on framing Soviet/Russian domestic politics during this period stands in sharp contrast to the passive role that the international legal sovereignty regime played in influencing international responses to the Soviet collapse. As discussed by Heller and Sofaer in this volume, international legal sovereignty usually follows changes in domestic or Westphalian sovereignty; it rarely helps to produce domestic sovereignty (Germany's recognition of Slovenia is a recent important exception). Because international legal sovereignty is a "structurally induced equilibrium,"[55] rulers do not have an incentive to defect from it, even when defection could facilitate the dissolution of a state's greatest international rival. Only after a group of rulers have obtained undisputed domestic sovereignty can it qualify for international legal sovereignty.[56]

Again, the Soviet/Russian case provides a hard test for how powerful this restraining rule or norm of international legal sovereignty can be. As stated earlier, Russia's opposition aimed to do everything programmatically that leaders in Western capitalist democracies could hope for from an opposition movement within the Soviet Union. Yeltsin and his entourage were anticommunist, pro-market, pro-West, pro-democracy, and most important, sought to dismember what Ronald Reagan once called the "evil empire." Their positions won them sympathies in many Western capitals. Some Western diplomats in Moscow at the time, including American Ambassador Jack Matlock, urged greater engagement with the Russian challengers to the Soviet state: "The Soviet Constitution explicitly gave the union republics the right to maintain diplomatic relations with other countries, and each had its own ministry of foreign affairs. Thus, the heads of union republics theoretically had greater authority than American state governors to deal with foreign governments— and our governors never hesitate to travel around the world and to meet with foreign leaders in pursuit of trade and investment, the very topics Yeltsin was most interested in talking to us about. For these reasons, I could not understand why the White House staff felt we had to make a choice between Gorbachev and Yeltsin."[57]

In fact, no state moved to grant the Russian Federation or any other republic sovereign status within the international system. Even the Baltic states had to wait until the Soviet Union dissolved to achieve international legal sovereignty, though most Western states had never formally recognized their inclusion in the Soviet Union in the first place. Only weeks before the aborted putsch attempt in Moscow, President Bush delivered his now infamous "chicken Kiev" speech in Kiev, Ukraine, in which he urged Ukrainians to go slow in their quest to obtain sovereignty: "Freedom is not the same as independence. Americans will not support those who seek independence in order to replace a far-off tyranny with a local despotism. They will not aid those who promote a suicidal nationalism based on ethnic hatred."[58] Even on the first day of the August 1991 coup, most Western states refrained from recognizing either side as the sovereign authority. Only after the coup's failure was certain did the international community denounce the Soviet Emergency Committee. Formal recognition of the newly independent states of the former Soviet Union came only after these states had secured domestic sovereignty.

As mentioned previously, by calling for the dissolution of a recognized state, Yeltsin and his "national liberation movement" challenged the rules of the game of international legal sovereignty. As Jackson has observed, "nowadays sovereign states hardly ever commit suicide, and they evidently can no longer be killed or die."[59] Even in regions, such as the African continent, where leaders agree that the sovereignty regime has locked into place states that were created by outside powers with no regard to the demarcation of nations or ethnic groups, political leaders have agreed to refrain from challenging existing sovereign states. In regions where that rule was violated, such as the former Yugoslavia, the disastrous results have reconfirmed the community of sovereign states' commitment to maintain the status quo.[60]

Like their counterparts in Yugoslavia, Biafra, or Kashmir, Yeltsin and Russia's opposition challenged this international norm. It is not surprising, therefore, that the international community was reluctant to recognize Russian sovereignty. In this case, norms and self-interest recommended the same policy prescription. Western leaders hesitated to recognize Russia because they feared the deleterious strategic consequences of dissolution. Subsequent civil wars and ethnic conflicts throughout the former Soviet Union are cited as confirming evidence by those who believe that any disruption to the international legal sovereignty regime carries with it dangerous consequences for the system as a whole.[61] The withholding of international recognition, however, was not motivated solely by interests in stability in the region. Recognition of Russia while the Soviet Union still existed would have required defection from international norms concerning sovereignty. For instance, had the United States recognized Russia before the Soviet collapse, American leaders would have signaled a challenge to other fragile federal states recognized as sovereign states by the international community. Breaking the rules of the game in this one case would have had negative repercussions for the sovereignty regime as a whole.

Trading Domestic Sovereignty for International Legal Sovereignty

At the end of 1991, Russia finally did achieve international recognition as a sovereign state. Paradoxically, however, since seizing domestic sovereignty and acquiring international legal sovereignty, Yeltsin and his allies also ceded some of Russia's Westphalian sovereignty, at least in the short run. For Russia, entry into the international system came at a steep price—the loss of Westphalian sovereignty. It gained authority over its territory in return for a loss of some control within its new borders.

In the early years after independence, Russia's loss of Westphalian sovereignty was most starkly apparent regarding economic decision making. Even before the USSR's formal dissolution, Yeltsin established a governmental commission tasked with developing relations with international financial institutions. The head of the commission, Viktor Dmitriev, immediately invited the World Bank to set up shop in his building, located in the same offices that once housed the Central Committee of the Communist Party of the Soviet Union (on *staraya ploshchad'*). Likewise, the Russian government quickly established contact with the IMF and soon thereafter became the largest recipient of IMF funds in the world.[62] These transfers, of course, did not come without constraints.[63] Although Russia has enjoyed more flexibility regarding IMF conditionality than most borrowers, the Russian government has had to conform to an array of IMF policy recommendations, from controlling spending and the printing of money to rewriting the tax code.[64] World Bank programs, though slower to be established, also have been accompanied by conditions that constrain Russian sovereignty.[65]

The task of transforming the Soviet command system into a Russian market economy is arguably the most ambitious economic reform ever attempted. To facilitate the transformation, Russia's new government not only solicited advice from international financial institutions but also invited Western economists and lawyers to work in their government agencies. At the State Property Committee (GKI), several Western advisers worked closely with their Russian counterparts to draft laws and regulations on privatization.[66] Although the presence of the (mostly American) advisers at GKI elicited a strong visceral reaction from Russian nationalists and communists, this external intervention in the internal affairs of Russia lasted for several years. Later, American consultants sponsored by the U.S. Agency for International Development (USAID) worked directly for or developed contractual arrangements with virtually every Russian government agency involved in the economic reform process, including the Central Bank, the Ministry of Finance, the Ministry of the Economy, and the Federal Securities Commission.[67]

To a lesser extent, Russian leaders also sacrificed some autonomy over political decision making in return for acceptance into the community of states. As in other postcommunist countries, Russia's first postcommunist leaders recognized that they had to construct (or create the appearance of constructing) democratic political institutions in order to integrate into the West. To this end, they allowed a flood of Western advisers on political reform to operate in Russia. For example, Western advisers were involved in drafting the Russian constitution, crafting the parliamentary and presidential electoral laws, writing the civil code (the "economic constitution" of Russia), assisting the formation of political parties, monitoring Russian elections, and instituting jury trials. Literally dozens of Russian government agencies received direct financial assistance or equipment from Western countries. In the case of the United States, most of these transfers came from USAID. Likewise, hundreds of Russian political leaders and state bureaucrats have been (re)trained in Western educational programs, schools, and universities. State-owned television networks even allowed Americans to produce and air programs about democracy that were funded by the U.S. government.[68]

Perhaps the most amazing example of external intervention in Russia is the Nunn-Lugar program. Through this program, the Russian army has been paid by the U.S. government to destroy nuclear weapons.[69] The program also has provided funds to defense enterprises to convert their production from military to civilian goods.

Such examples demonstrate the extent to which Russian leaders have been willing to forego Westphalian sovereignty in order to acquire international legal sovereignty and the benefits that are expected to come from that recognition. Such behavior, especially by leaders of the largest country in the world, challenges one of the central assumptions of the dominant paradigm in international relations theory. As Krasner writes: "Realism, however, also fails to provide an adequate explanation for intervention, because intervention in the internal affairs of another state violates one of the basic analytic assumptions of realism: namely, the assumption that all states are capable of autonomously determining their own policies. A state whose political regime—the nature of its government, the relationship between rulers and ruled, and the individuals who hold public office—is influenced or determined by external actors is not autonomous."[70] Likewise, in international affairs, Russian leaders have not followed the tenets of rational behavior as outlined by the realist approach. For instance, Russia continues to pursue integration into Western institutions at the same time that the United States and Western European states are moving to expand their alliance system, NATO, eastward. Russian leaders consciously have not sought to balance against this threat.[71] Though offered the opportunity to expand Russia's border by integrating Belarus into the Russian Federation, Russian leaders so far have resisted this potential for peaceful expansion.[72]

Some have argued that this Russian behavior, both internally and externally, simply reflects current Russian weakness. Once it has recovered, these observers argue, Russia will not allow domestic violations of sovereignty and will reassert itself as an imperial hegemon in the region and a global power in the international system.[73] It is too early to reach a final assessment, but it is wrong to characterize all decisions to acquiesce to interventions of domestic sovereignty or forego international balance-of-power politics as instances of weakness. In most of these situations, Russian leaders calculated that the benefits of integration were greater than the costs of losing some degree of Westphalian sovereignty. Westphalian sovereignty may not be as important as we once thought, while international legal sovereignty may be more important than ever before.

For Yeltsin and his allies, appropriating the sovereignty script as an ideology of opposition for their revolutionary challenge to Soviet power proved to be an expedient strategy. By framing their contest of political power as a sovereignty contest, Yeltsin and Russia's anticommunist movement widened their support within Russia, acquired important allies in other Soviet republics, and cast their quest for power in a way acceptable to the international community. Other states were reluctant to actively assist the Russian independence movement, but they also did not come to the aid of the Soviet state and did not hesitate to recognize the new Russian state once Yeltsin and his allies had secured domestic sovereignty within the Russian territory.[74]

Latching onto the sovereignty script, however, also constrained Yeltsin's range of choices and autonomy in building a new Russian state. As discussed throughout this book, cases of problematic sovereignty can persist in the international system indefinitely, but this system does privilege two institutional forms—entities that are sovereign and entities that are not. Creative forms are generally not available and rarely sustainable. In the Soviet/Russian case, the innovative treatment of sovereignty in the Union Treaty did not offer a viable alternative to either Soviet unity or Russian independence. Likewise, the next attempt at institutional innovation—the Commonwealth of Independent States—was not sustainable. Many of the actors involved in these novel institutional designs, including even Yeltsin, did not always aspire to create fully sovereign states. Rather, they hoped that the alternative arrangements might stick. The rules of the game regarding sovereignty in today's international system, however, constrained and eventually helped to suppress the alternative models.

Russia also had to pay dearly for the acquisition of international legal sovereignty. The currency was denominated in Westphalian sovereignty. To join the international community of states, Yeltsin and the new Russian government forfeited some control over their autonomy to design new domestic political and economic institutions. The new Russian government allowed international agents—be they IMF officials, USAID contractors, constitutional lawyers, or hedge fund managers—to assume real influence over decision making regarding major aspects of Russian domestic politics.

Yeltsin and his government calculated that the benefits of obtaining international legal sovereignty outweighed the costs of relinquishing parts of domestic sovereignty. Over the long run, however, other Russian leaders may rethink this trade-off, as the creation of the Russian state is still a work in progress.[75] Once granted, international legal sovereignty is difficult to lose. Consequently, the trade-offs identified previously between international legal sovereignty and Westphalian sovereignty fade, since leaders need not fear that they will lose international recognition if they move to reassume more control over their domestic affairs. Given Russia's unique size and tortured relationship with the West, the battle over the degree of Westphalian sovereignty wanted by the leaders and citizens in this new country probably has only just begun.

Notes

1.   Some scholars have written that even the idea of a Soviet empire was constructed only after its collapse. As Ronald Suny (1995:155) writes, "The Soviet Union, which a quarter century ago would have been described by most social scientists as a state and only occasionally, and usually by quite conservative scholars, as an empire, is almost universally described after its demise as an empire, since it now appears to have been an illegitimate, composite polity unable to contain the rising nations within it."

2.   Had Russia not declared independence, it is extremely doubtful that others would have broken free from the Soviet Union. Bearing this in mind, it is fundamentally wrong to think of the Soviet collapse as a classic case of decolonization in which the colonies break free of the metropole. On the contrary, it was the battle for sovereignty *within* the metropole that created the conditions for independence elsewhere.

3.   Irina Zhuravleva, quoted in the *Washington Post*, December 31, 1991. Quoted here from Beissinger 1993:102.

4.   Changes in institutional design often occur in response to a concrete political situation without regard to long-term "design" consequences. See Cain and Jones 1989:11.

5.   David 1985; North 1990; Arthur 1994; Pierson 1997.

6.   Pipes 1964; Suny 1993.

7.   Goldstone 1997; Keddie 1995; McFaul 1996; Tilly 1993; Bunce 1999.

8.   Brinton 1938; Tilly 1978; Huntington 1968; Goldstone 1991.

9.   Bova 1991; Schmitter and Karl 1994.

10.   Solnick 1998.

11.   The closest account framed this way is Dunlop 1993. Framing sovereignty struggles launched by the non-Russian republics as a process of decolonization is much more common. See Beissinger 1993.

12. Yeltsin 1995.

13. Dallin and Lapidus 1996:404.

14. Gorbachev 1992.

15. For instance, in the spring of 1991 when Yeltsin began negotiating with Gorbachev on the "9 + 1" accord, many of Yeltsin's allies in Democratic Russia felt that Yeltsin was selling out. Urban 1997. Similarly, on the referendum about whether to maintain the USSR, Democratic Russia urged its supporters to vote against the initiative, but Yeltsin refrained from taking a stand. Years later, Yeltsin claimed that he voted for preservation.

16. Meyer, Boli, and Thomas 1987; Boli 1993.

17. Klotz 1995; Sikkink 1993.

18. Krasner 1999:18.

19. Przeworski 1991:54–55.

20. Brown 1996.

21. *Materialy XIX Vsesoyuznoi konferentsii KPSS* 1988.

22. Throughout 1990 and 1991, a debate within Russia's opposition persisted regarding their relationship with Gorbachev. One group saw Gorbachev as an ally of democratic reform, while others saw him as an obstacle to further democratization. In comparative context, it is rare that the opposition has such ambiguous attitudes about the leadership of the ancien régime.

23. Gorbachev 1996.

24. McFaul and Markov 1993; Kagarlitsky 1990.

25. The counterfactual that helps control for this variable raises interesting questions. For instance, what if the sequence of elections had been reversed and republic-level elections produced more conservative parliaments while the union-level election to the Soviet Congress of People's Deputies produced the more radical legislative body and perhaps even elected Boris Yeltsin as Soviet president? Would Boris Yeltsin, armed with a popular mandate, have allowed the Soviet Union to collapse? Would he have allowed the Soviet state to collapse peacefully? Even much later in the day, think of how the trajectory of the Soviet collapse might have changed had Yeltsin become Soviet president immediately after the aborted coup attempt in August 1991.

26. Again, it is interesting to think of the counterfactual. If there had not been elections in 1990 to a Russian-level institution, where would the opposition have aggregated and what would they have defended during the August 1991 coup attempt?

27. Remington 1994.

28. Dunlop 1993:54–58.

29. Lapidus and Walker 1995.

30. Zaslavsky 1997:90.

31. *Izvestiya*, April 24, 1991.

32. Lukyanov 1993.

33. Note that Yeltsin did not dissolve these Soviet institutions or call them "Russian" institutions. The Russification of these institutions only occurred several months later. The Soviet military did not become the Russian military for several months *after*

the dissolution of the Soviet state. In this interim period, the Soviet armed forces were allegedly under the command of the Commonwealth of Independent States.

34. The author was in Moscow during this time and attended several of the parliamentary discussions as well as informal discussions among political leaders on the future of Russian sovereignty. As a student of movements of national liberation in Africa before working on the post-Soviet world, I saw that the Russian case of independence offered a stark contrast to African decolonization moments. There were no celebrations of independence in Moscow at the time and no attempts to create new symbols or myths around the event of independence. On the contrary, the only demonstrations at the time were organized by those against dissolution. The Soviet flag came down on December 25, several days before it was planned to come down, to avoid making a scene. Gorbachev gave a brief and embittered departure speech. Yeltsin never actually met with the departing "colonial governor" in a ceremonial transfer of power. Even the black box containing the nuclear codes was passed from Gorbachev to Yeltsin through an intermediary.

35. Gaidar 1999.

36. Olcott, Aslund, and Garnett 1999.

37. Olcott 1996.

38. Bunce 1999.

39. Like the other republics, Chechnya declared its independence from the Soviet Union (and Russia) immediately after the August 1991 coup and then fought a war with Russia three years later to secure independence. After winning this war, the Chechen government achieved domestic sovereignty (until the next war, which began in the summer of 1999) but never achieved international legal sovereignty. Tatarstan declared its independence in 1992 and held a referendum to confirm this status. Tatarstan did not fight a war with Russia. The republic enjoys considerable local autonomy but does not have either domestic or international legal sovereignty. Other secessionist movements in other former Soviet republics such as Abkhazia and Karabakh also have not won international legal sovereignty despite having acquired de facto domestic sovereignty through their military successes. See Walker 1998.

40. OMRI 1996.

41. Interpretations of this vote were very controversial as the phrasing of the question was ambiguous. On the ballot, voters were asked, "Do you consider it necessary to preserve the Union of Soviet Socialist Republics as a renewed federation of equal sovereign republics in which the rights and freedoms of people of all nationalities will be fully guaranteed?" The verb "preserve" seemed to contradict the notion of a "renewed" federal system. The phrase also implied that socialist republics might become sovereign republics if the referendum passed.

42. VTsIOM 1996.

43. Krasner 1999.

44. Walt 1996.

45. Beissinger 1993:94.

46. McFaul 1999.

47. In the early 1920s, one of the preconditions of American recognition of the Soviet Union was an expression of a willingness to pay Russian imperial debts. Patenaude 1996:79.

48. The author attended this meeting.

49. Yeltsin allowed Gorbachev to keep his residence and gave him a major building in downtown Moscow to house the Gorbachev Foundation. Over time, however, as the salience of Gorbachev's well-being declined in the West, Yeltsin treated the former Soviet leader with less respect and eventually took back most of the original space given to the foundation.

50. Kozyrev did not have formal relations with his American counterpart, James Baker, at the time. Informally, however, Kozyrev had established contacts with lower-level State Department officials, including Ambassador Jack Matlock, as well as several nongovernmental organizations (see Matlock 1995:509). Kozyrev used these informal relations both to communicate Yeltsin's positions and to obtain modest financial and technical assistance. For instance, Walter Mondale, in his capacity as chairman of the National Democratic Institute for International Affairs at the time, established contact with Kozyrev while in Moscow and then hosted the Russian foreign minister and facilitated these informal meetings during this trip to the United States. These kinds of meetings probably would not have taken place if Kozyrev had not been given the title *foreign minister*.

51. For instance, the AFL-CIO provided direct financial assistance to striking coal miners and later helped to establish the Independent Miners Union in Russia. Grants from the National Endowment for Democracy provided fax machines, computers, and advisers to the Russian Constitutional Commission at the time. The National Democratic Institute (NDI) usually avoided direct financial transfers at the time as it did not want to alienate the Gorbachev government. But NDI did provide technical assistance, training, and limited equipment to Democratic Russia during this period. (The author served as an adviser to NDI at the time).

52. Living in Moscow at the time and working as a representative for the National Democratic Institute, I was frequently called upon to address meetings of new political parties, NGOs, or groups affiliated with Russia's democratic opposition. Though I would try to explain that NDI was an independent, nongovernmental organization affiliated but not controlled by the U.S. Democratic Party, most of these groups treated me as a representative of the U.S. government and saw my attendance at these events as de facto recognition of their organization or objectives. The confusion reached even greater heights when former U.S. government officials such as Walter Mondale came to Russia as NDI representatives. These distinctions between the U.S. government and NDI were especially ambiguous because NDI at the time was funded by the National Endowment for Democracy, whose money came directly from the U.S. Congress. (Between Americans, relations between NDI and the U.S. Embassy in Moscow were quite tense at the time as U.S. Embassy officials quite rightly saw NDI's work as complicating their diplomatic tasks.) For Russians, the obvious parallel from their experience was the Solidarity Committee, a "nongovernmental" organization funded

by the Soviet Communist Party that supported revolutionaries in the developing world but technically was not part of the Soviet government. These kinds of organizations, whether promoting democracy or marxism-leninism, provided useful vehicles for circumventing the international sovereignty regime.

53. Aslund 1995:40.

54. In an interview with the author (July 1998), Gorbachev is interpreter and foreign policy adviser Pavel Palashchenko recalled how frustrated they were with Yeltsin's government during the G-7 meetings in July 1991, as Yeltsin's representatives succeeded in convincing the G-7 countries not to provide aid to the Soviet government.

55. Shepsle and Weingast 1981:503–19.

56. Jackson (1995:65) correctly establishes a relationship between these two kinds of sovereignty, by arguing that "[domestic] sovereignty is a necessary but not sufficient condition for membership into the community of states." He is wrong, however, to assert that "as soon as constitutional independence occurs, the international law of sovereignty and nonintervention *simultaneously* takes effect" (61). Whether international legal sovereignty follows automatically after the acquisition of domestic sovereignty depends on (1) the method by which domestic sovereignty was obtained, (2) the programmatic objectives of the new sovereign rulers, and (3) the balance of power in the neighborhood in which sovereignty has been transferred or newly acquired. For instance, regarding the first two conditions, the Bolsheviks or Islamic leaders in Afghanistan did not win recognition for their new states immediately after obtaining domestic sovereignty. Regarding the third condition, Biafra did not win international recognition after establishing, however briefly, domestic sovereignty.

57. Matlock 1995:509.

58. Bush 1991:597.

59. Jackson 1995:65. Jackson cites Zanzibar as one of the few twentieth-century states that voluntarily relinquished its international legal sovereignty. Though the options were fewer, East Germany might also qualify. Belarus also appears close to following Zanzibar's fate.

60. The objectives of the NATO military campaign against Serbia in the spring and summer of 1999 offer a vivid illustration. Even though NATO forces have openly violated Serbia's domestic sovereignty by occupying Kosovo, NATO states have reiterated that they do not plan to extend international legal sovereignty to Kosovo.

61. Derlugian 1993:76.

62. Greenhouse 1992.

63. Stone 1996.

64. The omnipresent role of the IMF and foreign forces more generally in Russian domestic politics has been remarkable to observe in a country that less than a decade ago erected mammoth barriers to insulate the state from foreign influences. In the fall of 1997, a corruption scandal threatened the career of First Deputy Prime Minister Anatoly Chubais. At the time, Yeltsin removed four of Chubais's closest colleagues from ministerial level positions. According to Chubais aides interviewed by the author in December 1997, Yeltsin allowed Chubais to remain in power because

Western officials urged him to do so. Another remarkable instance of outside influence occurred in that same month. In his first address to the Russian parliament, Yeltsin encouraged deputies to ratify his budget and warned that the "whole world is watching how you vote." Though the parliament is dominated by the Communist Party, the budget reading passed. On the IMF's most recent bailout and the conditions that accompany it, see Gordon and Sanger 1998.

65. "Russia's Economy" 1997:5.

66. My first visit to this office in 1992 reminded me very much of my visits to the State Planning Committee in Luanda, Angola, in 1987–1988, where a dozen Russians had permanent positions.

67. Office of the Coordinator of U.S. Assistance to the NIS 1998.

68. The author has been involved in many such interventions, including these television programs. Thinking about the interventions in reverse helps to underscore how radical these assaults on Russian Westphalian sovereignty have been. Imagine if Russian advisers worked in the U.S. Congress, drafted legislation for U.S. legislators with a clear set of ideological objectives, and produced propaganda films about the superior Russian way of life for American television.

69. Carter and Perry 1999, ch. 2. The initial outlay for Nunn-Lugar funds was $400 million for denuclearization in fiscal year 1993.

70. Krasner 1995:229.

71. McFaul 1997/98.

72. *New York Times*, April 3, 1997, A5.

73. Brzezinski 1994; Simes 1999.

74. After the Bolshevik revolution in 1917, the United States delayed recognition of the new regime in Moscow for sixteen years. See Gaddis 1978.

75. Breslauer and Dale 1997.

References

Arthur, Brian. 1994. *Increasing Returns and Path Dependence in the Economy.* Ann Arbor: University of Michigan Press.

Aslund, Anders. 1995. *How Russia Became a Market Economy.* Washington, D.C.: Brookings Institution Press.

Beissinger, Mark. 1993. "Demise of an Empire-State: Identity, Legitimacy, and the Deconstruction of Soviet Politics." In Crawford Young, ed., *The Rising Tide of Cultural Pluralism: The Nation-State at Bay?* 93–115. Madison: University of Wisconsin Press.

Boli, John. 1993. "Sovereignty from a World Polity Perspective." Manuscript.

Bova, Russell. 1991. "Political Dynamics of the Post-Communist Transition: A Comparative Perspective." *World Politics* 44:113–38.

Breslauer, George and Catherine Dale. 1977. "Boris Yel'tsin and the Invention of a Russian Nation-State." *Post-Soviet Affairs* 13, no. 4: 303–32.

Brinton, Crane. 1938. *The Anatomy of Revolution.* New York: Vintage.

Brown, Archie. 1996. *The Gorbachev Factor.* Oxford: Oxford University Press.

Brzezinski, Zbigniew. 1994. "The Premature Partnership." *Foreign Affairs* 73, no. 2: 67–82.

Bull, Hedley. 1997. *The Anarchical Society.* London: Macmillan.

Bunce, Valerie. 1999. *Subversive Institutions: The Design and the Destruction of Socialism and the State.* Cambridge: Cambridge University Press.

Bush, George. 1991. Remarks to the Supreme Soviet of the Ukrainian Soviet Socialist Republic, Kiev, Ukraine, August 1, 1991. In *U.S. Department of State Dispatch,* August 12, 596–98.

Cain, Bruce and W. T. Jones. 1989. "Madison's Theory of Representation." In Bernard Grofman and Donald Wittman, eds., *The Federalist Papers and the New Institutionalism,* 11–30. New York: Agathon Press.

Calvert, Peter. 1990. *Revolution and Counter-Revolution.* Minneapolis: University of Minnesota Press.

Carter, Ashton and William Perry. 1999. *Preventive Defense: A New Security Strategy for America.* Washington, D.C.: Brookings Institution Press.

Cohen, Stephen. 1999. "Russian Studies Without Russia." *Post-Soviet Affairs* 15, no. 1: 37–55.

Dallin, Alexander and Gail Lapidus, eds. 1995. *The Soviet System: From Crisis to Collapse.* Boulder, Colo.: Westview Press.

David, Paul. 1985. "Clio and the Economics of QWERTY." *American Economic Review* 75:332–37.

Derlugian, Georgi. 1993. "Ethnic Violence in the Post-Communist Periphery." *Studies in Political Economy* 41:45–81.

Dunlop, John. 1993. *The Rise of Russia and the Fall of the Soviet Empire.* Princeton: Princeton University Press.

Gaddis, John Lewis. 1978. *Russia, the Soviet Union, and the United States: An Interpretive History.* New York: Wiley.

Gaidar, Yegor. 1999. *Days of Defeat and Victory.* Seattle: University of Washington Press.

Goldgeier, James M. and Michael McFaul. 1992. "A Tale of Two Worlds: Core and Periphery in the Post-Cold War Era." *International Organization* 46, no. 2: 467–91.

Goldstone, Jack. 1991. *Revolution and Rebellion in the Early Modern World.* Berkeley: University of California Press.

———. 1997. "Theories of Revolution and the Collapse of the USSR." Manuscript.

Gorbachev, Mikhail. 1996. *Memoirs.* New York: Random House.

Gorbachev, Yeltsin: 1500 Dnei Protivostoyaniya Protivovostoyaniya. 1992. Moskva: Terra.

Gordon, Michael and David Sanger. 1998. "The Bailout of the Kremlin: How the U.S. Pressed the I.M.F." *New York Times,* July 17, 1, 6.

Greenhouse, Steven. 1992. "Bush and Kohl Unveil Plan to 7 Nations to Contribute $24 Billion in Aid for Russia." *New York Times,* April 2, 1.

Huntington, Samuel. 1968. *Political Order and Changing Societies.* New Haven: Yale University Press.

Jackson, Robert. 1995. "International Community Beyond the Cold War." In Gene Lyons and Michael Mastanduno, eds., *Beyond Westphalia?* 59–83. Baltimore: Johns Hopkins University Press.

Johnson, Chalmers. 1992. *Revolutionary Change.* Stanford: Stanford University Press.

Kagarlitsky, Boris. 1990. *Farewell Perestroika.* London: Verso.

Keddie, Nikki, ed. 1995. *Debating Revolutions.* New York: New York University Press.

Klotz, Audie. 1995. *Norms in International Relations: The Struggle Against Apartheid.* Ithaca: Cornell University Press.

Krasner, Stephen. 1995. "Sovereignty and Intervention." In Gene Lyons and Michael Mastanduno, eds., *Beyond Westphalia?* 228–49. Baltimore: Johns Hopkins University Press.

———. 1999. *Sovereignty: Organized Hypocrisy.* Princeton: Princeton University Press.

Lapidus, Gail and Edward Walker. 1995. "Nationalism, Regionalism, and Federalism: Center-Periphery Relations in Post-Communist Russia." In Gail Lapidus, ed., *The New Russia: Troubled Transformation,* 79–114. Boulder, Colo.: Westview Press.

Lukyanov, Anatoly (CPSU Politburo member, chairman of the Soviet Congress of People's Deputies, and one of the leaders of the August 1991 coup). 1993. Interview with the author, November.

March, James and Johan Olsen. 1989. *Rediscovering Institutions.* New York: Free Press.

Materialy XIX Vsesoyuznoi konferentsii KPSS: 28 yunya–1 yulya 1988. 1988. Moskva: Polizdat.

Matlock, Jack. 1995. *Autopsy on an Empire.* New York: Random House.

McFaul, Michael. 1995. "Russian Politics After Chechnya." *Foreign Policy* 99:149–165.

———. 1996. "Revolutionary Transformations in Comparative Perspective: Defining a Post-Communist Research Agenda." In David Holloway and Norman Naimark, eds., *Reexamining the Soviet Experience: Essays in Honor of Alexander Dallin,* 167–96. Boulder, Colo.: Westview Press.

———. 1997/98. "The Precarious Peace. Domestic Politics in the Making of Russian Foreign Policy." *International Security* 22, no. 3: 5–35.

———. 1999. "Lessons from Russia's Protracted Transition from Communist Rule." *Political Science Quarterly* 144:103–30.

McFaul, Michael and Sergei Markov. 1993. *The Troubled Birth of Russian Democracy.* Stanford, CA: Hoover Press.

Mearsheimer, John. 1990. "Back to the Future: Instability in Europe After the Cold War." *International Security* 15:5–56.

Meyer, John, John Boli, and George Thomas. 1987. "Ontology and Rationalization in the Western Cultural Account." In George Thomas, John Meyer, Francisco O. Ramirez, and John Boli, *Institutional Structure: Constituting State, Society, and the Individual,* 12–38. Beverly Hills: Sage.

North, Douglass. 1990. *Institutions, Institutional Change, and Economic Performance.* Cambridge: Cambridge University Press.

Office of the Coordinator of U.S. Assistance to the NIS. 1998. *U.S. Government Assistance to and Cooperative Activities with the Newly Independent States of the Former Soviet Union: FY 1997 Annual Report.* Washington, D.C.: U.S. State Department.

Olcott, Martha Brill. 1996. *Central Asia's New States: Independence, Foreign Policy, and Regional Security.* Washington, D.C.: U.S. Institute of Peace.

Olcott, Martha Brill, Anders Aslund, and Sherman Garnett. 1999. *Getting It Wrong: Regional Cooperation and the Commonwealth of Independent States.* Washington, D.C.: Carnegie Endowment for International Peace.

OMRI Russian Presidential Election Survey, No. 5. May 29, 1996 <http://www.rferl/.org>.

Palashchenko, Pavel (Gorbachev interpreter and foreign policy adviser). 1998. Interview with the author, July.

Patenaude, Bertran. 1996. "The Strange Death of Soviet Communism: The 1921 Version." In David Holloway and Norman Naimark, eds., *Reexamining the Soviet Experience: Essays in Honor of Alexander Dallin,* 77–100. Boulder, Colo.: Westview Press.

Pierson, Paul. 1997. "Path Dependence, Increasing Returns, and the Study of Politics." Manuscript.

Pipes, Richard. 1964. *The Formation of the Soviet Union: Communism and Nationalism, 1917–1923.* Cambridge: Harvard University Press.

Przeworski, Adam. 1991. *Democracy and the Market: Political and Economic Reforms in Eastern Europe and Latin America.* Cambridge: Cambridge University Press.

Remington, Thomas. 1994. "Parliamentary Elections and the Transition from Communism." Introduction to Thomas Remington, ed., *Parliaments in Transition: The New Legislative Politics in the Former USSR and Eastern Europe,* 1–27. Boulder, Colo.: Westview Press.

"Russia's Economy: World Bank Says Growth May Begin in 1998 but Reforms Are Key." 1997. *Press Backgrounder, The World Bank, Europe and Central Europe Region.* Washington, D.C.: World Bank, March.

Schmitter, Philippe with Terry Karl. 1994. "The Conceptual Travels of Transitologists and Consolidologists: How Far to the East Should They Attempt to Go?" *Slavic Review* 53, no. 1: 173–84.

Shepsle, Keneth and Barry Weingast. 1981. "Structure-Induced Equilibrium and Legislative Choice." *Public Choice* 37:503–19.

Sikkink, Kathryn. 1993. "Human Rights, Principled Issue-Networks, and Sovereignty in Latin America." *International Organization* 47:411–42.

Simes, Dmitri. 1999. *After the Collapse: Russia Seeks Its Place as a Great Power.* New York: Simon and Schuster.

Solnick, Steven. 1998. *Stealing the State: Control and Collapse in Soviet Institutions.* Cambridge: Harvard University Press.

Stanley, Alessandra. 1997. "Russia Dilutes Treaty with Belarus, Then Signs." *New York Times*, April 3, A5.

Stone, Randall. 1996. "Russia and the IMF: Reputation and Unrestricted Bargaining." Manuscript.

Suny, Ronald. 1993. *Revenge of the Past: Nationalism, Revolution, and the Collapse of the Soviet Union*. Stanford: Stanford University Press.

———. 1995. "Ambiguous Categories: States, Empires, and Nations." *Post-Soviet Affairs* 11, no. 2: 185–96.

Thomas, George, John Meyer, Francisco O. Rameriz, and John Boli. 1987. *Institutional Structure: Constituting State, Society, and the Individual*. Beverly Hills: Sage.

Tilly, Charles. 1978. *From Mobilization to Revolution*. Reading, Mass.: Addison-Wesley.

———. 1993. *European Revolutions, 1492–1992*. Oxford: Blackwell.

Urban, Michael with Vyacheslav Igrunov and Sergei Mitrokhin. 1997. *The Rebirth of Politics in Russia*. Cambridge: Cambridge University Press.

VTsIOM (All-Russian Center for the Study of Public Opinion). 1996. "Pyat Let' Reformy." Mimeo.

Walker, Edward. 1998. "No Peace, No War in the Caucasus: Secessionist Conflicts in Chechnya, Abkhazia, and Karabakh." Manuscript, Hoover Institution.

Walt, Stephen. 1996. *Revolution and War*. Ithaca: Cornell University Press.

Yeltsin, Boris. 1995. Speech to the Russian Federation Congress of People's Deputies, Moscow, May 22, 1990. Reprinted in Alexander Dallin and Gail Lapidus, eds., *The Soviet System: From Crisis to Collapse*, 410. Boulder, Colo.: Westview Press.

Zaslavsky, Viktor, 1997. "The Soviet Union." In Karen Barkey and Mark Von Hagen, eds., *After Empire: Ethnic Societies and Nation-Building*, 73–98. Boulder, Colo.: Westview Press.

8

Belarus and the Flight from Sovereignty

COIT BLACKER AND CONDOLEEZZA RICE

Given half a chance, most national communities will seek the highest degree of political autonomy and self-determination, up to and including de jure independence (or *international legal sovereignty*, to use the term employed throughout this volume). They do so in large measure on the basis of the conviction that as a unique people—ethnically, linguistically, and/or culturally distinct from all others—they have earned and thus deserve such status, and because, in the end, the only surefire way to protect themselves against oppression and exploitation at the hands of others is through self-rule.[1] Historically, few such communities, when presented with the opportunity to chart their own sovereign course, have declined to take on the challenge.[2] That many of those efforts ended disastrously should not obscure the larger point that state-seeking nationalism has been, and remains, an enormously potent force in contemporary world politics.

What are we to make, then, of Belarus, one of twelve New Independent States to emerge from the wreckage of the Soviet Union at the end of 1991, which has made political and economic union with the Russian Federation— a development that, if implemented, would surely diminish various aspects of Belarusian sovereignty—the centerpiece of its national policy?

Most new states go to elaborate lengths to imbed, affirm, and otherwise demonstrate their newly attained status as independent actors. They lower the old flag and raise the new. They field an army and begin printing their own money. They apply for membership in the United Nations and dispatch the foreign minister to Washington for "urgent consultations."

They mythologize the past—glorifying ancient triumphs and ennobling ancient defeats—and promise a future of peace, prosperity, and national renewal. Typically they seek to put as much political distance as possible between themselves and their former masters and hurry to make as many friends in as many places as possible.

Not so the Belarusians. In a referendum in 1995, the people of Belarus voted overwhelmingly to restore the Soviet-era flag and national crest, which the first postindependence government in Minsk had discarded. Belarusian schools still rely on history and social science texts published in Moscow in the 1970s and 1980s. The country's president, Alyaksandr Lukashenka, speaks in Russian when he addresses the nation, notwithstanding the fact that the national language is Belarusian. Most notably, since 1994 the Belarusian leadership has pressed the Russian government to conclude one agreement after another to accelerate the integration, or reintegration, of the two countries' economies and to forge the closest possible political ties. Minsk's efforts were rewarded in April 1997 when Lukashenka and Russian president Boris Yeltsin signed in Moscow an agreement—the so-called Union Treaty—to establish, in form if not yet in substance, a single Russian-Belarusian political and economic community.

Analysts attribute Belarus's reluctant embrace of sovereignty to a variety of factors: from a poorly developed sense of national identity and historical uniqueness and an almost disabling social conservatism to the country's overwhelming economic dependence on Russia and the Kremlin's frequent meddling in Belarusian affairs of state.

Doubtless, the existence of those factors has served to retard the development of a strong sense of national identity among the Belarusian population. The comparatively weak draw of the nationalist card in Belarus would have placed important, if mostly implicit, limits on any postindependence government in Minsk inclined to assert its nationalist credentials. And that was indeed the case, beginning with the government of Stanislau Shushkevich (1991–1994), which was careful to place the Belarusian quest for sovereignty in the context of a larger search for identity and community among all ex-Soviet republics, especially those with predominantly Slavic populations.

But Belarus is hardly unique in that regard. Most of the other Soviet successor states have encountered obstacles no less daunting in the struggle to achieve real independence, and yet each has persevered in the effort—albeit with varying degrees of success. More to the point, none has pursued a policy line vis-à-vis Russia remotely comparable to that championed by

Minsk. Some other factor, or factors, would appear to be at work in the case of Belarus, and it is the search to determine what else might be prompting the Belarusian leadership to behave as it does regarding the country's sovereignty and independence that motivates the writing of this essay.

The analysis begins with a brief review of Belarusian political history in the period since the Soviet collapse. It continues with an examination of the three explanations most often advanced to help decipher Belarusian conduct. All are judged to be necessary in some sense but not sufficient to account for the observed outcome. The essay concludes by arguing that all such path-dependent explanations fail to capture the highly contingent character of Belarusian policy between 1991 and 1997 and that the most satisfying way to think about the country's "flight from sovereignty" is as a fundamentally volitional and, taken on its own terms, entirely rational process, orchestrated by a political leadership with clear goals and objectives.

Belarus and Independence, 1991–1997

Belarus was hardly a hotbed of anti-Soviet sentiment during the late 1980s and early 1990s. In the March 1991 nationwide referendum on whether to preserve the USSR, 83 percent of those casting ballots in Belarus voted affirmatively[3]—the highest percentage of any republic in the Soviet Union. The Belarusian Communist Party (BCP) was antireformist to the core; analysts Kathleen Mihalisko and George Sanford have written that BCP leaders were among the first from the Soviet political class to break open the champagne when Moscow conservatives sought to oust Mikhail Gorbachev in the failed coup attempt of August 1991.[4]

In the confused aftermath of the August events, however, it was the hard-liners in Minsk who found themselves weakened and on the wrong side of the political divide—a somewhat surprising development that reformist elements, led by the anticommunist Belarusian Popular Front (BPF), moved quickly to exploit. In late August 1991 the country's legislature declared Belarus an independent republic and soon thereafter elected the liberal Stanislau Shushkevich parliamentary chairman and acting head of state.[5] It was in the latter capacity that Shushkevich, together with Yeltsin and Ukrainian president Leonid Kravchuk, announced the legal cessation of the USSR and the creation of the Commonwealth of Independent States (CIS) in December 1991.

The political position of Shushkevich and his parliamentary allies was never very strong, however, and between the end of 1991 and the first part of 1994, the progressives were forced to share power with a much more conservative (read: communist) government, led by Prime Minister Vyacheslau Kebich. The uneasy partnership collapsed in January 1994, when Kebich, aided by People's Deputy Alyaksandr Lukashenka, a relative newcomer to the Belarusian political scene, led a successful effort within the parliament to oust Shushkevich. With Shushkevich out of the way, Kebich pressed the docile legislature to adopt a new constitution, providing for the direct election of a president and the creation of a new, 260-member parliament, or Supreme Council.[6]

In the first round of presidential balloting in June 1994, Kebich, who by all accounts expected to win the election in a walk, polled a mere 17 percent of the vote. BPF leader Zyanon Paznyak received 13 percent of the votes cast, and Shushkevich drew 10 percent. Lukashenka, who made the fight against government corruption the centerpiece of his campaign, garnered an impressive 45 percent of the vote.[7] Kebich, desperate to regain his political footing, sought to draw the sharpest possible distinction between his status as a political "insider," on intimate terms with the Russian leadership in Moscow,[8] and that of Lukashenka, a collective farm manager with effectively no government experience. It didn't work. In the second round of balloting in July, Lukashenka won 80 percent of the vote.[9]

Beyond the sheer magnitude of Lukashenka's victory, which caught most observers by surprise, the most interesting feature of the election was the fact that relations with Russia were, in a curious way, a nonissue. Both finalists called for the restoration of the closest possible ties with Moscow, particularly in the economic sphere, which were deemed essential to the country's recovery. If the candidates differed on the issue it was only by degree, with Lukashenka calling explicitly for the merging of the Belarusian and Russian economies.[10] Whatever else might be said about the 1994 election, in other words, the contest was not a referendum on Russian-Belarusian relations. Nor was it about the precise character or dimensions of Belarusian sovereignty, except in the narrow sense that the electorate was strongly *disinclined* to support any candidate urging fewer ties with or greater distance in relations from Moscow.

Once installed as president, Lukashenka moved aggressively to enhance his personal political power, which he sought to do by eliminating rival power centers and repressing dissent. He ignored the existing, Soviet-era legislature, which, he claimed, lacked any legal authority to meet, while doing everything in his power to delay the election of a new parliament, as called for under the terms of the 1994 constitution. (Lukashenka managed, in fact, by manipulating the election laws, to prevent the convening of a new parliament for many months, during which time he ruled by decree.)[11]

Within weeks of Lukashenka's election, several opposition newspapers found themselves unable to publish because the government had suspended their printing contracts or denied them access to newsprint.[12] When antigovernment protests erupted in 1995 and 1996, Belarusian security forces, under the command of a Lukashenka loyalist, physically assaulted scores of protesters and detained and arrested hundreds more.[13] The most vocal antigovernment activist in Belarus, BPF leader Paznyak, fled to Poland in April 1996 rather than face certain arrest following an especially violent street demonstration in Minsk, originally called to mark the tenth anniversary of the Chernobyl disaster. Paznyak eventually sought, and was granted, political asylum in the United States.[14]

Regarding integration with Russia, Lukashenka sought to accelerate the process that Kebich had begun during his tenure as prime minister and that Shushkevich had sought to retard. Emboldened by the results of the May 1995 referendum, in which the majority of those casting ballots had voted for economic union with Russia (and, as noted, for the restoration of a slightly modified version of the preindependence flag and national crest), Lukashenka traveled to Moscow later that month to conclude a customs union agreement with the Russians and to announce the removal of border posts between the two countries (one effect of which was to erode the country's ability to monitor cross-border traffic of all kinds, resulting in a de facto loss of *interdependence sovereignty*). Russian prime minister Viktor Chernomyrdin pronounced the agreements a great success that had enabled a fundamental "breakthrough" in bilateral relations.[15]

The combination of political repression and economic regression during this period led to a distinct cooling of Belarusian relations with the West. Much of the assistance that international financial institutions had promised to Belarus in 1991 and 1992 was placed on hold beginning in 1994 as authorities in Minsk reimposed price controls and halted privatization.[16] Other donors, including the European Union, Germany, and the United States, also drew back.[17] In the wake of the highly irregular first- and second-round parliamentary elections in May 1995, which international election monitors termed neither free nor fair, the Council of Europe suspended Belarus's application for membership.[18]

In an effort to halt the slide and to gauge the potential for recovery, the Clinton administration in June 1995 quietly dispatched a senior National Security Council official to Belarus for consultations with the country's political leaders, including Lukashenka. The discussions did little to ease the growing tension between Washington and Minsk.[19] Relations went from bad to worse the following September when Belarusian air force units shot down a civilian hot-air balloon transiting the country's airspace, killing the two American pilots on board. Permission for the balloon to overfly Belarus had been granted by the appropriate aviation authorities in Minsk, but the military claimed that it had never gotten the word. The Belarusian government expressed regret over the incident but offered no formal apology and declined to accept full responsibility.[20]

The downward spiral continued through 1996 and 1997, as the Lukashenka government grew more repressive and the United States became more outspoken in its criticism. When Minsk expelled an American diplomat for allegedly taking part in an anti-Lukashenka demonstration in March 1997, Washington recalled the U.S. ambassador, Kenneth Yalowitz, for consultations.[21] The final phase of Yalowitz's tenure as ambassador was in fact decidedly unpleasant for the veteran and highly regarded U.S. diplomat as the Belarusian government treated him in all but name as persona non grata. Yalowitz's successor, Daniel Speckhard, fared even worse. Ten months after his installation as ambassador in September 1997, Speckhard was back in the United States, having been recalled by Washington in response to Lukashenka's heavy-handed attempts to evict the U.S. ambassador, along with several of his European counterparts, from their diplomatic compound outside Minsk, ostensibly so the residences in question could be "repaired." The real reason, it seems, was that Lukashenka wanted the land adjacent to his own residential holdings to be liberated from foreign occupation and reclaimed for the people of Belarus — most of whom wouldn't be allowed to venture within 500 yards of the place.[22]

Predictably, the ratcheting down of Western engagement with Belarus intensified Lukashenka's courting of the Russians. Less than a year after the conclusion of the bilateral customs union agreement in May 1995, Lukashenka was once again in Moscow, this time to sign a treaty establishing a Russian-Belarusian Community of Sovereign Republics.[23] Yeltsin, eager to burnish his nationalist credentials in the run-up to the first round of the 1996

Russian presidential elections, trumpeted the agreement as an important milestone in the development of relations between Moscow and Minsk.[24] Privately, however, Yeltsin's advisers downplayed the political significance of the accord, which they characterized as bereft of any real content.[25]

Domestically, the regime grew more authoritarian. The new Supreme Council, which was finally seated in January 1996 following months of wrangling between Lukashenka and his political opponents, found itself virtually at war with the president and his government from the moment of its installation. The crisis reached a fever pitch in November 1996 when the parliamentary chairman and the head of the Belarusian constitutional court threatened to initiate impeachment proceedings against Lukashenka if the president persisted with plans to hold yet another referendum—this time to extend his existing term from five to seven years, to allow him to run for a second term, and to convene elections for a new, bicameral legislature that the president would have the power to dissolve at will.[26]

Russian prime minister Chernomyrdin, together with a handful of senior advisers, flew to Minsk on November 21 to mediate the escalating conflict. Two days later they returned to Moscow, claiming that the crisis had been successfully resolved.[27] The referendum, which the parties to the dispute had agreed to regard as advisory only, took place as scheduled on November 24. When the results conformed to Lukashenka's expectations, he declared the outcome binding.[28]

Lukashenka's endless political maneuverings seemed even to exasperate the Russians, who on balance found little to oppose and much to welcome in Belarusian policy, particularly the emphasis on strong bilateral cooperation. As Lukashenka tightened the screws at home, however, a number of well-placed Russian officials expressed misgivings about drawing any closer to the regime in Minsk, which was rapidly becoming an international pariah. Economic reformers within the Russian government joined forces with those urging caution on political grounds, as any real integration of the Russian and Belarusian economies would cost the Russian treasury billions of rubles—rubles the Kremlin did not have.[29]

A showdown of sorts ensued in the first part of 1997 as plans were announced to create a federal union between the countries. With Lukashenka scheduled to travel once again to Moscow in April 1997 to sign with Yeltsin the so-called Union Treaty, Russian opponents of integration swung into action and managed to convince the president to strip the agreement of much of its content. When Lukashenka appeared for the signing ceremony, he found the agreed draft text very different from the one he had sanctioned prior to his departure from Minsk.[30] The treaty was now little more than a declaration of intent, the substance of the agreement having been transferred to the much more detailed Union Charter that Lukashenka and Yeltsin only initialed at the April ceremony.

Following several weeks of intense negotiations between Moscow and Minsk—and between rival factions in the Russian government—the two presidents met again in Moscow to sign the now-completed Union Charter. The document was immediately submitted to each country's parliament for ratification and one month later, in June 1997, the two sides exchanged instruments of ratification, thereby bringing the agreement into force.[31]

But what, exactly, had the Union Treaty and Union Charter created? A single country? A federal union? Some type of confederal arrangement? No one seemed to know, but many were more than pleased to volunteer their assessments. Russian nationalists welcomed the appearance (or reappearance) of a Russian-Belarusian "superstate."[32] At the other end of the spectrum, Ukraine's president, Leonid Kuchma, when asked for his assessment rather indelicately pronounced the entire venture "nonsense."[33] Most Russian citizens greeted the news with a shrug.

The charter itself provided for the establishment of an elaborate institutional superstructure to delimit the powers of the new union, but most of these arrangements seemed formalistic at best, ritualistic and content-free at worst. Other than the vague mandate that union institutions "oversee" the development of common foreign and defense policies (and provide the two populations with reciprocal educational and medical benefits), the actual political reach of the new entity remained obscure. Neither the Russian nor the Belarusian government formally delegated any powers to the union, and ministries in both countries behaved *after* ratification exactly as they had *before*.

A statement released by the Committee on Relations with the Commonwealth of Independent States of the Russian State Duma during the ratification debate in June sought to clarify matters by offering up a kind of depiction, if not exactly a definition, of the new entity. "The Treaty and Charter of the Union," the statement read, "as the founding documents of a new subject of international law, provide a legal basis for closer economic, political and military integration between Russia and Belarus, while preserving the sovereignty, territorial integrity and other attributes of statehood of each member-state, and reflect the present level of political will in the two countries."[34]

In reality, the Union Treaty and Union Charter meant whatever the parties wanted them to mean. To the Yeltsin government, the agreements signed in April and May 1997 served to underscore the essential dynamism of the integrative process, which they very much wanted to believe was now underway across the entire former Soviet Union. That the agreements stopped short of the outright annexation of Belarus—note the Duma committee's reaffirmation of each side's "sovereignty," "territorial integrity," and essential "statehood"—pleased many, if not most, within the Russian hierarchy, who well understood that the country could hardly afford to assume economic and financial responsibility for Belarus, which was for all practical purposes bankrupt. To the leadership in Moscow, the most appropriate analogy to invoke in trying to assess the true significance of the "union" between Moscow and Minsk was probably the European Union (or, more correctly, its antecedents), which at the time of its creation clearly constituted "a new subject of international law" but one that in no way diminished or otherwise compromised the *international legal sovereignty* of the contracting parties.

For Lukashenka, as well, the union agreements with Russia were important, and welcome, political news. Through them, he had delivered on his pledge to the Belarusian people to forge the closest possible political and economic links with Russia. The 1997 agreements, together with prior-year arrangements, also facilitated the conclusion of a number of favorable trade agreements with Moscow—to ensure the flow of Russian oil and natural gas on the most liberal of terms, for example—that made it possible for Lukashenka to postpone Belarus's day of economic reckoning, at least for a time. Finally, the treaty arrangements of 1997, which stopped just short of extending dual citizenship rights to the people of Belarus (and Russia), guaranteed Lukashenka a continuing, if ambiguous, role in Russian political affairs.[35]

To the casual observer, Lukashenka's enthusiastic support of the Union Treaty and Union Charter would seem to suggest a willingness on his part to cede a degree of *domestic* (and *interdependence) sovereignty* to the Russians in exchange for Moscow's continuing financial and material assistance, while (presumably) clinging desperately to Belarus's *international legal sovereignty*. In fact, the reverse was true. In the aftermath of the 1997 agreements with the Russians, Lukashenka sought to tighten his grip in virtually every sphere of Belarusian life even as he continued to communicate his willingness to surrender the de jure independence of his country if the Russians were prepared to meet his price.

Many of Lukashenka's counterparts elsewhere in former Soviet Union share his appetite for personal power. None, however, has sought to advance his political fortunes by raising the specter of formal union with the Russian Federation. Most, in fact, have done just the opposite, aggressively courting would-be friends and allies to offset Russia's enormous, if now mostly latent, power. How, then, to explain Lukashenka's behavior?

Maybe Belarus Just Wasn't Meant to be Independent

Those who have written on the political course of post-Soviet Belarus typically cite three sets of factors — history, geography, and economics — to explain the country's equivocal embrace of independence. All three may be thought of as "structural" in the sense that they reflect enduring or persistent features of the Belarusian political, economic, and social landscape, and the impact of each has been, and continues to be, substantial and consequential. At the same time, none is determinative in character — at least not in the judgment of the authors — and even in combination they fail to provide a fully satisfying explanation for Belarusian conduct in the period since independence.

The first set of explanations is *sociohistorical* in character. The political history of Belarus, one can fairly argue, is less about the struggle for independence than it is about the search for security and stability in a harsh and unforgiving world. The absence of a highly developed sense of national or political self-identity on the part of the people of Belarus *is* one of the more notable features of contemporary (as well as more distant) Belarusian life and an analytical staple of those seeking to explain the behavior of the country's political leadership in recent years.

Prior to 1991 Belarus had no sustained experience as an independent political actor.[36] Given this fact, it is perhaps not so surprising that the history to which the country's first postindependence leaders turned in an attempt to generate a sense of national pride and distinctiveness was that of the Grand Duchy of Lithuania — of which much of modern-day Belarus had once been a part and under whose suzerainty the area had flourished both culturally and economically for several hundred years, between the fourteenth and seventeenth centuries.[37] Unlike the three Baltic republics, which had been independent states within living memory, or Armenia and Georgia, both of which had existed for centuries in one form or another as nation-states prior to their incorporation into the Russian Empire, the Belarusians had always been a part of someone else's history rather than masters of their own.

The absence of a strong nationalist streak in Belarusian history is a product of several factors. The population of Belarus has always been small relative to that of Russia, Ukraine, and Poland, all of which have helped themselves to this or that piece of Belarusian real estate over the course of the last several centuries—a demographic and political fact of life with which the political class in Belarus has had to contend more or less continuously and about which it can do precious little. The Slavic people of Belarus do not consider themselves ethnically distinct from their Russian cousins, the existence of a separate Belarusian language and literary tradition notwithstanding. Strong religious, social, and cultural bonds also link the two peoples (intermarriage being so common as to be a nonissue, for example). Most important, beginning in the last quarter of the eighteenth century, the imperial Russian government and then its Soviet successor did everything in their power to suppress the development of a separate Belarusian sociopolitical identity—a task at which they both excelled.

More subjectively, some Belarusians speak of a kind of genetic predisposition to leave their politics to others—especially to their Slavic brothers (and sisters) to the east. In response to a question from a Western journalist to describe what distinguished Belarusians from Russians, the respondent, a young Belarusian woman, replied, "We are hardworking. And kinder. And we are more submissive."[38] Many Belarusians, when asked to explain why their country has been slow to make the most of the opportunity to establish true independence, point to Moscow's centuries-long domination of Belarusian political and economic life.

Others attribute the apparent docility of Belarusian political culture to the effects of two devastating world wars, an extremely violent civil war, and Stalin's purges, all of which combined to produce a longing for stability and order on the part of the population that is both difficult to explain to outsiders and also very difficult to satisfy.[39] The effect has been to generate a level of political and social conservatism among the populace that one very knowledgeable observer of the Belarusian scene has characterized as "crippling."[40]

It neither diminishes the uniqueness of Belarusian history nor trivializes the enormous suffering endured by the people of the country to place the Belarusian experience with independence in comparative perspective. The closest analog is probably Ukraine, which like Belarus is predominantly Slavic and Orthodox in makeup, with a rich and complicated history of association with Russia. Ukraine is considerably larger than Belarus, of course, both in size and population, and has always enjoyed a stronger sense of national identity and ethnic differentiation. It is also true that the establishment of the first Ukrainian state, Kievan Rus, predated the appearance of the Principality of Muscovy, the political antecedent to modern-day Russia, by several centuries, that culturally the two societies understand themselves to be distinct, and that as recently as the second decade of this century Ukraine existed, albeit briefly, as a sovereign entity.

It is instructive, nonetheless, to compare the Belarusian and Ukrainian attitudes toward independence as revealed, especially, through the conduct of their relations with Russia. If the Belarusian government, particularly since the advent of Lukashenka, has made political and economic union with Russia the centerpiece of national policy, Ukraine has gone to the other extreme, demonstrating in a myriad of ways that integration with the Russian Federation is, quite simply, out of the question. Ukraine—together with Azerbaijan, Georgia, and Uzbekistan—has led the campaign within the CIS to weaken Moscow's influence in the organization and to prevent it from becoming an instrument for the reestablishment of Russian dominance.[41] The irritants in relations between Moscow and Kiev are numerous, and while some have been resolved, others persist. Moreover, those that have been dealt with, such as the disposition of the Black Sea Fleet, have highlighted Ukraine's determination to stand its ground and to defend its interests.

Compared to Belarus, Ukraine has been a veritable whirling dervish on the global scene, establishing diplomatic missions in all the major capitals, seeking economic assistance from the World Bank, the International Monetary Fund (IMF), the European Union, and a host of bilateral donors, and taking an active role in as many regional and international organizations as possible. Ukrainian soldiers have served in Bosnia since the Implementation Force was first assembled in 1995.[42] In July 1997 the government in Kiev signed a bilateral agreement to promote cooperation between NATO and Ukraine that parallels in important ways the so-called NATO-Russia Founding Act of May 1997.[43] In the past five years, President Kuchma has met with President Clinton on at least five occasions, and a bilateral U.S.-Ukrainian commission, chaired by Kuchma and Vice President Al Gore, meets regularly to assess the development of political, economic, and technical relations.[44] Lukashenka, by contrast, has yet to receive an invitation to Washington, and has never had a substantive session with a top U.S. government official.

Several of the other ex-Soviet republics have decidedly weaker national traditions than those of Belarus, including at least four of the five Central Asian states. And yet each of these leaderships has gone to extraordinary lengths to generate a sense of Kazak, Uzbek, Kyrgyz, and Turkmen national identity. With the exception of the Tajik government, which has been fighting a civil war, the Central Asian countries have also been extremely active in the pursuit of political and economic ties with countries outside the CIS, including the United States, the countries of the European Union, Turkey, and China. Each has sought, in other words, to capitalize on the collapse of the Soviet Union and the relative weakness of the Russian state to create bona fide state actors, sovereign in both a *domestic* and *international legal* sense. (The attainment of true *Westphalian* sovereignty, on the other hand, has proven to be rather more elusive for a number of CIS states—including Armenia, Georgia, Tajikistan, and Turkmenistan—all of whom either welcome or tolerate the presence on their soil of Russian military units.)

The second factor that allegedly complicates the Belarusian political scene and undercuts the quest for true autonomy is *geography*. The argument has merit. The best that can be said about the geopolitics of Belarus is that they are unfortunate.

Historic Belarus—flat, poor, underpopulated, and frequently in the way— has played host to more than its share of invasions. To take but the most recent examples: Napoleon's armies traversed the area on their march toward, and their retreat from, Moscow; Imperial Germany occupied all of modern-day Belarus between 1915 and 1918; and much of the Great Patriotic War was fought on Belarusian soil. World War II was, in fact, a catastrophe for Belarus of almost unimaginable proportions. Fully one-quarter of the Belarusian population died between 1941 and 1945, an experience from which the country has never really recovered and that, as indicated, still influences its political culture.[45]

Given this tragic history, it is hardly surprising that the Belarusian leadership—any Belarusian leadership—would place a high premium on ensuring the country's physical security. Under such conditions, alliance with a more powerful neighbor makes eminent sense and is at least as compelling as, and probably easier to manage than, a policy built around balancing behavior. (It is worth noting in this context that after Poland and the Baltic states achieved independence from Moscow in 1918, all sought actively to balance Russian power by establishing and maintaining consequential political and economic relations with countries to their west; the failure of such policies to prevent the outbreak of war in 1939–1940 did not stop the four countries from effectively returning to this same strategy in 1990–1991, during and after the Soviet collapse.) But entering into an alliance with another state does not ordinarily require that the country seeking protection surrender its independence—particularly when the senior partner has made no such demand.

Kazakstan and Mongolia, both of which share long, open borders with the Russian Federation and have relatively small populations and effectively no military potential, have sought to maintain cordial, cooperative relations with Moscow. Ties between Russia and Kazakstan are especially close. Kazakstani president Nursultan Nazarbayev journeys often to the Kremlin for meetings with Russia's president; Nazarbayev's ministers, most of whom were trained in Moscow, do the same with their Russian counterparts. All things considered, it is a good relationship that the Kazaks work hard to keep on an even keel. The Mongolians, considerably more distant from the Russian metropole than the Kazaks, worry less about the sensitivities of the Moscow government, but they too mind their political p's and q's, ever cognizant of the gross disparity in power between the two countries.

To date, however, neither Kazakstan nor Mongolia has chosen to ally itself with Russia. Neither has offered up bits and pieces of its sovereignty in exchange for Moscow's protection. With the exception of Armenia, which has sought to use its historical friendship with Russia to keep presumed Turkish and Azerbaijani ambitions at bay, no ex-Soviet republic other than Belarus has assumed what might be termed a pro-Russian tilt in the conduct of foreign policy.

A country determined to safeguard its security and independence, even with geopolitical circumstances as problematic as those of Belarus, might be expected to pursue a highly nuanced foreign policy, combining elements of accommodation and defiance vis-à-vis its large and proximate neighbor. Mexican policy toward the United States comes to mind, as does Vietnamese policy toward China in the 1980s and 1990s. There is nothing very subtle, and nothing at all defiant, about the foreign and security policies of Belarus under Lukashenka.

If Lukashenka has any quarrel with the Moscow leadership, it is that the Russians have been rather more equivocal regarding the question of political and economic union than he would prefer.

The third factor limiting the Belarusian pursuit of an independent course in world politics is economics, or more precisely, the country's *economic de-*

pendence on the Russian Federation. The argument is straightforward. Whatever the political preferences of the leadership in Minsk, its freedom to maneuver—both domestically and internationally—has been, and will continue to be, severely limited by Moscow's dominant position in the Belarusian economy.

The economy of Belarus was among the most "sovietized" of the former republics of the USSR. Among its other consequences, this meant that investment decisions made in Moscow dictated what, when, and how much Belarus produced—without regard for whether any of these decisions made economic sense for a country of Belarus's size, location, and natural and human resources. The Belarusian economy was, and remains, heavily industrialized—specializing in the manufacture of transport and machine equipment and chemicals—a situation that, while perhaps unfortunate, could at least be justified as long as the country was part of a highly centralized, largely autarchic, and extraordinarily inefficient economy.[46]

That situation made little or no sense, however, once the Soviet Union had passed from the scene because Belarusian industrial goods now had to compete for market share (primarily in CIS states and in Central and Eastern Europe) against products of equal or better quality and lower cost. Thus, meaningful economic reform was bound to be painful and prolonged for Belarus under the best of circumstances and was sure to entail major political risks for any leadership bold enough to undertake such an effort. It was primarily for this reason that even the comparatively liberal Shushkevich-Kebich government moved very cautiously on the economic front between 1991 and 1994.

Compounding the problem, no one in Belarus in the early post-independence period had a sophisticated understanding of what the embrace of the market and the restoration of private property actually meant, let alone how to engineer such a transition. Teams from the IMF, the World Bank, and the European Bank for Reconstruction and Development dutifully traveled to Minsk between 1991 and 1993, reform programs and assistance offers in hand, only to discover that those in charge of the government's economic affairs had—at best—a rudimentary command of such basic concepts as supply and demand.[47] The situation improved rapidly as Belarusian officials underwent what amounted to a crash course in elementary economics, but progress was slow and uneven. At the time of Lukashenka's election in July 1994, some 90 percent of the economy remained securely in state hands.[48]

The extraordinarily slow pace of economic reform in Belarus served to increase the country's already heavy dependence on Russia. Virtually everything Belarus exported at the time of independence was dispatched to the other eleven ex-Soviet republics, and as late as 1996 well over 60 percent of what the economy generated for external consumption flowed to Minsk's CIS partners, primarily the Russian Federation.[49] Roughly the same situation obtained regarding imports. For purposes of this analysis, however, it is less the *extent* of Belarusian dependence on the Russian market (both pre- and post-1991) that warrants comment than it is the precise *form* that it takes.

Belarus produces almost no oil and gas. It relies today as it did in the past on Russian energy imports to power its industry, to keep its cars and trucks on the road, and to heat the country's households. Now, however, Russian companies charge world or near-world prices for the products they export, including oil and gas. Neither the Belarus government nor the country's minuscule private sector generates sufficient hard currency to reimburse their Russian suppliers, and the latter will not accept payment in Belarusian rubles. To keep the energy flowing and thus prevent the collapse of the country's economy, Minsk has appealed to the Russian government to subsidize its oil and gas purchases, which thus far at least the Kremlin has been willing to do, primarily in the form of credits, debt relief, and barter trade.[50] That such a relationship compounds Belarus's already considerable economic dependency on Russia is an understatement.

The degree of Russian dominance over Belarusian economic life is indeed remarkable; it is both more manifest and more consequential than in any of the other former Soviet republics. It is not, however, the inevitable outgrowth of objective economic factors. It is, rather, the result of a series of decisions, or nondecisions, undertaken by successive Belarusian leaderships, either too fearful (the Shushkevich-Kebich government) or too willful (the Lukashenka government) to introduce and then implement meaningful reforms.

In this Belarusian leaders had much in common with their counterparts elsewhere in the former Soviet Union, especially in the early years of independence. What sets Belarus apart from the other ex-Soviet republics, however, is the current leadership's manifest disinclination to use the reform process—which requires the reforming party to develop complex, consequential, and exacting arrangements with the major international financial institutions (IFIs)—to distance itself from Russia economically.

Comparison with Ukraine is once again instructive. From 1991 to 1994 the Ukrainian leadership made all the right noises regarding the central importance of economic reform but in practice did little to advance the cause. Agreements designed to achieve macroeconomic stabilization, laboriously drawn up by IMF representatives in close consultation with Ukrainian officials, were routinely suspended as the government in Kiev failed to meet the (admittedly stringent) conditions specified in the various loan and assistance agreements. Much the same pattern prevailed elsewhere in the former Soviet Union: a rush to conclude stabilization agreements with the IMF and to attract World Bank loans, followed—often within months—by the essential unraveling of the accords. (A senior U.S. Treasury Department official once remarked that he and his colleagues always knew that a stabilization program was about to come unstuck when political leaders in the recipient country began to describe the virtues of a "third way" in the reform process— something between the rapid embrace of the market and the maintenance of the existing system.)[51]

The situation in Ukraine changed, however, with the election of Leonid Kuchma as president in July 1994. With the inflation rate running at 2000 percent per year and much of the country's industry at a standstill, the new leadership in Ukraine moved aggressively to repair relations with international financial institutions.[52] It did so both to stabilize the Ukrainian economy, which by the summer of 1994 was in danger of collapsing altogether, and to strengthen its political and economic position vis-à-vis the Russian Federation.

In restoring relations with the International Monetary Fund and the World Bank, the Ukrainians were sending an important message to the West and, in particular, to the United States: To enhance the prospects for Ukraine's survival as an independent state, the Kuchma leadership was prepared to bear the considerable *short-term* costs that invariably accompany the process of macroeconomic stabilization in anticipation of *longer-term* economic and political gains. The message was received both in Washington, which in 1995 and 1996 increased bilateral assistance to Kiev in the wake of the new arrangements between Ukraine and the IFIs, and in Moscow, which once again postponed the signing of a treaty to normalize relations between the two countries.[53]

Between 1994 and 1996, most of the other New Independent States followed Ukraine's lead in economic policy. The exception was Belarus, which effectively rejected all overtures from the IMF and the World Bank to resume negotiations that could have resulted in the provision of hundreds of millions of dollars in budget support payments, loans, and outright grants. The failure to reach agreement with the IFIs also deterred all but the heartiest of foreign investors from doing business in Belarus, thereby depriving a desperately poor country of a much-needed source of capital.[54]

Thus, the economic situation of Belarus is indeed unusual, although not, as sometimes alleged, because the country is so dependent on Russia; all the New Independent States found themselves, more or less, in equally dire straits at the time of independence. What *does* make Belarus unusual is the steadfast refusal of the leadership to do anything substantial to lessen that dependence through, for example, the introduction of market reforms, the cultivation of new trading partners, or the development of good working relations with the IFIs. The real irony in this situation is that Minsk's reliance on Moscow to keep the Belarusian economy afloat directly and materially undermines the country's *domestic sovereignty*—defined here as the ability of political leaders to control developments within their own territory—in defense of which Lukashenka has repeatedly and in other circumstances demonstrated his willingness to go to extremes.

In this regard, Belarus, in many ways the least likely of the former Soviet republics to swim against the tide, constitutes a population of one. The interesting question, of course, is why.

Lukashenka as the Great Helmsman

Given the country's history, geopolitics, and economic circumstances, the Belarusian road to independence was destined, it seems, to be long and bumpy and, for the most part, unpaved. And yet other national communities—with histories no less tortured, geopolitical settings no less unfortunate, and economic challenges no less severe—have managed to survive, even to prosper, as state actors during all historical periods, including our own. In no sense, then, should Belarus be dismissed as somehow structurally unfit to be, or incapable of becoming, a fully sovereign political entity.

But if the challenge to Belarusian independence is not primarily structural in nature, what are we dealing with here? And how can we account for the behavior of the country's leadership, particularly in the period since the 1994 presidential election?

Leaders' political preferences matter, of course, in all societies at all times. Russia's story in the period since independence is also Boris Yeltsin's story, and vice versa. Elsewhere in the former Soviet Union the links between leaders, states, and national outcomes are, if anything, even more direct: Kuchma in Ukraine; Nazarbayev in Kazakstan; Aliyev in Azerbaijan, and Shevardnadze in Georgia. The same is true—both in kind and in degree—for Lukashenka and Belarus.

What distinguishes Lukashenka from his CIS confederates is not, in other words, the manner in which he wields political power or how he and others within the Belarusian system understand his role and position within society. In those respects, Lukashenka is much like every other post-Soviet leader: confident, strong willed, and very much in command. It is, rather, the particular direction in which he has chosen to take his country that sets him apart.

In advocating union with the Russian Federation, Lukashenka has given voice to a powerful longing on the part of the majority of the Belarusian people for a return to familiar ways. His electoral victory in 1994 is largely attributable, in fact, to his skill in tapping into that sentiment.[55] His populist appeal played well among an electorate that had grown resentful of the posturing and perceived excesses of the political class in Minsk. He made much of his humble beginnings and lack of formal education. He promised to end corruption and to halt the country's economic slide. It was, in other words, Lukashenka's three-part pledge—to provide strong, no-nonsense leadership, to restore social discipline, and to seek the closest possible ties with Russia—that enabled him to garner some 80 percent of the votes in the second round of the election.

Having ridden this horse to victory, one might have expected Lukashenka to change steeds. Politicians competing in open elections tailor their platforms to garner as many votes as possible; once safely installed in office, they may or may not remain faithful to that platform, depending in part on whether they believe they will ever have to face the electorate again. Given Lukashenka's open disdain for democracy, his fealty to the program that secured his 1994 election—which, carried to its logical extreme, would do him out of a job—is striking.

One might reasonably have expected Lukashenka to follow in the footsteps of his CIS counterparts, all of whom won election as social conservatives and Soviet-era insiders in the period between 1991 and 1994 but who very soon thereafter discovered the heretofore hidden virtues of nationalism. To have done otherwise—to have persisted in the pursuit of openly accommodationist policies toward Moscow—would have served to call into question their own political indispensability and to have weakened the case for strong, centralized, and disciplined leadership. It is thus no accident that two of the Soviet Union's most dedicated communists— Saparmurad Niyazov of Turkmenistan and Islam Karimov of Uzbekistan—became the most ardent and articulate of national patriots once they had claimed the top political prizes in their respective countries.

And then there is Lukashenka. During the 1994 election candidate Lukashenka was openly disdainful of those among his rivals who sought to score political points by burnishing their nationalist credentials, noting that he alone among the contenders had voted in parliament against the dissolution of the Soviet Union.[56] As noted, once in office he led the charge to do away with Belarusian national symbols and to resanctify the Russian language. More to the point, Lukashenka has never wavered in his advocacy of federal union with Russia, notwithstanding his relentless and largely successful campaign to deepen and extend his own political power as Belarusian head of state.

The key to deciphering Lukashenka's seemingly inexplicable behavior is to conceive of it in essentially self-referential terms—that is, how does *Lukashenka* understand what he is doing and why does *he* believe it makes sense? Framed in this way, mystery yields to reason—albeit reason of a particular sort.

Those in Russia and in the West who have dealt with the Belarusian leader at close range comment—virtually without exception—on the breadth and intensity of his political ambition.[57] The particular office to which Lukashenka aspires, it seems, is president of a Russian-Belarusian union or commonwealth.

Evidence that Lukashenka harbors such ambitions is circumstantial. He has been careful to keep his own counsel in the matter and has refrained from making any public statements that might serve to reinforce such speculation. The Russian political class and Lukashenka's domestic critics (many of whom have fled to the West in recent years) are convinced, however, that it is the aspiration to lead *both* Russia and Belarus at some future point in time that informs very nearly every political move that Lukashenka makes.

The idea is less absurd than it seems at first glance. Lukashenka operates from a secure, if relatively small, political base; his current term as Belarusian president expires in 2001 and the new constitution permits him to seek re-election. He maintains good working relations with Russian Communist Party officials and with right-wing nationalists, such as Vladimir Zhirinovsky, leader of the Liberal Democratic Party of Russia. He is comparatively young—45 in 1999—and can expect to remain active in CIS political affairs for decades. He has demonstrated remarkable political skill in his almost ten years in public life and has routinely outmaneuvered political figures with greater experience and better connections.

Lukashenka can have no illusions that he is electable to the office of president of the Russian Federation anytime soon, notwithstanding the highly unsettled state of Russian domestic politics at the turn of the new century. He has neither the stature nor the organization (not to mention the money) to compete successfully against leading Russian politicians. Besides, he is not even a Russian citizen. Such, however, appears not to be the focus of his ambitions. It is, rather, the more distant prospect of election to an office that does not yet exist—chief executive of some kind of federal structure linking Russia and Belarus—that seems to inform his actions, at least in the view of his (many) detractors in Minsk and Moscow.

The political jockeying between the Russian and Belarusian delegations that preceded the signing of the Union Treaty and Union Charter in 1997 provides an interesting window onto how Lukashenka appears to understand the problems confronting Belarus, as well as his own political prospects, both at home and beyond.

Russian and Belarusian negotiators found themselves at loggerheads over two major issues in 1997. The first had to do with the precise form of economic integration that the new union would entail. The team from Minsk argued in support of a specific formula to guide the integrative process, the practical effect of which would have been to saddle Moscow with billions of dollars' worth of Belarusian debt.[58] At the insistence of Anatoly Chubais, at the time Russia's first deputy prime minister and the government's leading reformer, the Russian side refused to go along with the Belarusian proposal, and the provisions in the agreements that would have resulted in such an outcome were deleted in the final phase of the negotiations.[59]

The more interesting issue, given the focus of this analysis, was the strong Belarusian push during the talks to accord dual citizenship to the people of Russia and Belarus. The Russian side again resisted. In the end the Belarusians dropped the proposal rather than precipitate the collapse of the negotiations, although under the terms of the Union Charter Belarusian citizens residing in the Russian Federation are entitled to receive Russian medical and educational benefits, and vice versa.[60]

Most Russian observers argue that the Belarusian citizenship proposal had mostly to do with preserving Lukashenka's political options and only incidentally with what one member of the Moscow political class characterized, derisively, as "the deeply felt sentiments of the Belarusian people."[61]

It is impossible to know in any definitive sense of the term what prompted the Belarusian proposal. Lukashenka has granted no interviews on the subject, nor is he likely to do so anytime in the near future. The Belarusian press has been silent on the matter.

Russian speculation on the subject is informed but impossible to substantiate. It would be surprising, however, in light of Lukashenka's tendency to conflate his own interests with those of the country he rules, if the proposal to extend Russian citizenship to Belarusian nationals were not politically motivated. (It is not as though the people of Belarus had taken to the streets during the 1997 negotiations, demanding that the government bring home an agreement awarding them Russian citizenship.)

If, as seems manifest, Lukashenka harbors political ambitions that would take him beyond Minsk, he is likely to encounter an unending series of obstacles. The reason is simple: those who populate the Russian government loathe the Belarusian leader and will go to any lengths necessary to prevent his playing a role in Russian political affairs. It is these officials who at every step in the process have frustrated Lukashenka's designs to forge meaningful links between Russian and Belarusian political, economic, and social institutions.

This is not to suggest that the Russian government is opposed to closer relations with Belarus. On the contrary, most Russian officials regard an independent Belarus as something of an oxymoron; most fully expect Belarus to rejoin the Russian fold, if not immediately then certainly within the next decade or two. The country will do so, however, on terms set by Moscow. What they object to, in other words, is not integration per se, but Lukashenka's having anything to do with the process, given what they regard as the enormity of his political ambition.

Russia's determination to control the pace of events with Belarus was once again in evidence at a year-end Yeltsin-Lukashenka summit session in 1998. At the conclusion of their meeting in Moscow on December 25, the two leaders reaffirmed their commitment to the political and economic union called for in the 1997 agreements. Determined as ever to see the "unification" glass as half full, Lukashenka expressed the hope that his latest meeting with the Russian president would enable the two countries to enter the new millennium "as one." By contrast, the Russian foreign minister, Igor Ivanov, went out of his way to describe the statement issued by the two presidents at the December 1998 meeting as a "declaration, not a treaty."[62] An unnamed Yeltsin adviser was more direct. No one on the Russian side of the negotiations, he insisted, was pressing for merging the two countries, their armies, or their budgets—not at the moment in any event, and certainly not on terms set by Lukashenka.[63]

Assuming for purposes of argument that the Kremlin leadership succeeds in keeping Lukashenka confined to the antechamber of Russian politics, one would expect to see a change in the president's attitude toward Belarusian sovereignty. Simply put, if the choice for Lukashenka devolves to one of "Belarus or nothing"—his larger ambitions having been short-circuited by his enemies in the Kremlin—the man who heretofore has had little patience with or interest in securing Belarus's long-term independence could well become its most forceful proponent.

To date, Lukashenka has undergone no such conversion. The continuing Russian interest in drawing the CIS states into a closer and more substantial kind of union may well have convinced Lukashenka that the political game between Moscow and Minsk is far from over and that his status as Belarusian head of state means the Russians have no alternative but to accommodate him and his ambitions. He may be more right than wrong on that score, although he would do well to remember that past performance is no guarantee of future success.

The larger point, in any event, is that the moment Lukashenka loses faith in that assessment—should such a moment arrive—is very likely to be the moment he becomes the most committed and most vocal of all Belarusian patriots. Any other response on Lukashenka's part would be contextually irrational and politically suicidal.

Belarus and the Issue of Sovereignty

Those interested primarily in issues of sovereignty should exercise caution in seeking to generalize from the Belarusian case. Reduced to its hard essence, the saga of post-Soviet Belarus is so intimately connected with the actions and decisions of one individual that it largely begs the questions to which students of sovereignty most want answers.

In and of itself, however, this makes the Belarusian case interesting, at least for those, like the authors, who seek to understand the degree to which choices made by political leaders during times of enormous uncertainty and unpredictability create opportunities for maneuver, departure, innovation, and change that would not otherwise exist.

In the case of Belarus, the apparent determination of Alyaksandr Lukash-enka to play out his political ambitions on a stage larger than the one afforded him from his base in Minsk explains much about the course and content of Belarusian foreign and domestic policy from 1994 to the present, including the demonstrated willingness of the leadership (albeit at Lukashenka's direc-tion) to cede important elements of the country's sovereignty to another state in anticipation of future gain. One would be hard pressed to explain the Belarusian phenomenon, in fact, without also telling the story of Lukashenka and his rise to power. Or so, at least, this analysis has sought to demonstrate.

The Belarusian case should also, and at a minimum, remind all of us interested in the study of politics that political outcomes are contingent in character—some, such as those discussed in this analysis, highly so—and that in the end it is individuals, acting alone and in groups, who make decisions. Decisions, in turn, generate actions. And actions, of course, have consequences—consequences that, in the case of nations, can and do affect the lives of millions.

Notes

The authors are grateful to Regine Spector for her assistance in the preparation of this analysis.

1.   One of the most interesting contemporary examples is the struggle of the people of Nagorno-Karabakh for independence from Azerbaijan. Karabakh, a small, predominantly Armenian enclave with a population of approximately 150,000, has fought tenaciously since 1988 against numerically superior Azerbaijani forces to secure its independence from the government in Baku. Beyond their keenly felt sense of ethnic and religious distinctiveness, Karabakh authorities underscore the need for full autonomy (de facto independence) because they have earned it, and in the end, only they—with assistance from Armenia—can be trusted to provide for their own physical security. For a general history of this conflict, see *Eastern Europe and the Common-wealth of Independent States 1999*, 4th ed. (London: Europa, 1998), 136, 158–59, 174–76. For more detailed analysis, see Shirleen T. Hunter, *The Transcaucasus in Transi-tion: Nationbuilding and Conflict* (Washington, D.C.: Center for Strategic and International Studies, 1994), 97–109; and Suzanne Goldenberg, *Pride of Small Nations: The Caucasus and Post-Soviet Disorder* (London: Zed, 1994), 152–73.

2.   There are exceptions, of course. Syria sought and achieved political union with Egypt in 1958; three years later, in 1961, the United Arab Republic collapsed in all but name as the two parties agreed to go their separate ways. On several occasions, Libyan strongman Muammar Qaddafi has called for the establishment of an Egyptian-

Libyan superstate—to be led, no doubt, by Qaddafi—a proposal in which the Egyptian leadership has evinced no interest whatsoever. Interest in such voluntary mergers, in which either or both of the parties signal their willingness to cede sovereignty to a new entity, has been quite low in the modern period, the occasional feint in that direction notwithstanding. More common (although far from routine) have been decisions on the part of various colonial and quasi-colonial entities to retain dependency status vis-à-vis the metropolitan power rather than strike out on their own. For a general history of relations between Egypt and Syria, see *The Middle East and North Africa 1999*, 45th ed. (London: Europa, 1998), 396–97, 971. For Libyan efforts to promote union, see ibid., 788. More detailed treatments of the rise and fall of the United Arab Republic may be found in S. H. Longrigg, "New Groupings Among the Arab States," *International Affairs* 34, no. 3 (1958): 305–17; and P. J. Vatikiotis, "Dilemma of Political Leadership in the Arab Middle East: The Case of the U.A.R.," *International Affairs* 47, no. 2 (1961): 189–202.

3. Kathleen J. Mihalisko, "Belarus: Retreat to Authoritarianism," in Karen Dawisha and Bruce Parrott, eds., *Democratic Changes and Authoritarian Reactions in Russia, Ukraine, Belarus, and Moldova* (Cambridge: Cambridge University Press, 1997), 242.

4. Ibid., 241–42; and George Sanford, "Belarus on the Road to Nationhood," *Survival* 38, no. 1 (1996): 144.

5. David R. Marples, *Belarus: A Denationalized Nation* (Amsterdam: Harwood Academic Publishers, 1990), 61–63.

6. Mihalisko, "Belarus: Retreat to Authoritarianism," 250; and Jan Zaprudnik and Michael Urban, "Belarus: From Statehood to Empire?" in Ian Bremmer and Ray Taras, eds., *New States, New Politics: Building the Post-Soviet Nations* (Cambridge: Cambridge University Press, 1997), 299–300.

7. Mihalisko, "Belarus: Retreat to Authoritarianism," 254.

8. Ibid., 253.

9. Ibid., 254.

10. Ibid.

11. Ibid., 265–67.

12. Ibid., 255–56.

13. Ibid., 259, 270–71.

14. Ibid., 270–71.

15. Steven Erlanger, "Yeltsin Wins Small Success at Meeting of Commonwealth," *New York Times*, May 27, 1995, A5.

16. Marples, *Belarus*, 36.

17. Ibid.

18. Mihalisko, "Belarus: Retreat to Authoritarianism," 264.

19. The National Security Council official was Coit Blacker, who was at the time special assistant to the president for national security affairs and senior director for Russian, Ukrainian, and Eurasian affairs at the National Security Council.

20.   The U.S. government sought, without success, to convince Belarusian authorities to supply both a full accounting of the incident and an unqualified apology. Initially, the Belarusians were responsive to the U.S. request. Several weeks into the formal investigation, however, Lukashenka is believed to have intervened directly on the Belarusian side to bring the matter to premature closure.

21.   Marples, *Belarus*, 102.

22.   "Return of U.S. Belarus Ambassador," U.S. Department of State, *Daily Press Briefing No. 74* (Statement by James P. Rubin), June 22, 1998. See also "Five EU Countries, U.S. Recall Ambassadors to Minsk," *Radio Free Europe/Radio Liberty Newsline* (hereafter *RFE/RL Newsline*), June 22, 1998; and K. P. Foley, "Belarus: Diplomatic Scandal Deepens," *Radio Free Europe/Radio Liberty* (hereafter *RFE/RL*), August 7, 1998.

23.   Marples, *Belarus*, 112.

24.   Ibid., 113.

25.   Blacker conversations with Russian government officials, Moscow, April 1996.

26.   Marples, *Belarus*, 90–94.

27.   Ibid., 95.

28.   Ibid., 96, 98.

29.   Andrew Meir, Rod Usher, and Douglas Waller, "It Takes Two to Tangle: Russia and Belarus Decide to Get Together," *Time* (International Edition), April 14, 1997, 28; and "Reaction to Russian-Belarusian Agreement," *RFE/RL Newsline*, April 1, 1997.

30.   Marples, *Belarus*, 114–15.

31.   "Russia-Byelorussia Treaty Enters Into Force," *ITAR/TASS*, June 11, 1997.

32.   Meir, Usher, and Waller, "It Takes Two to Tangle," 28.

33.   Ibid.

34.   Ivan Novikov, "Duma Advised to Ratify Russia-Byelorussia Union Treaty," *ITAR/TASS*, June 4, 1997.

35.   "Final, Draft Russia-Belarus Charters Compared," *Current Digest of the Post-Soviet Press* 49, no. 22 (1997): 12–13.

36.   See Marples, pp. 2–6, for an informed discussion of Belarus's confused, and confusing, political status between the February 1917 revolution in Russia that did away with Tsar Nicholas II and the Romanov dynasty and the formal incorporation of Belarus (as the Belarusian Soviet Socialist Republic) into the Union of Soviet Socialist Republics in December 1922. It is the case that at various points during that five-year period, Belarus enjoyed something akin to genuine independence, but such moments were fleeting. Except during the periods of German and later Polish occupation, Belarusian political authorities turned routinely—and reflexively—to Moscow for guidance and protection.

Nor did anything of substance change in 1945 when Soviet Belarus was admitted to the United Nations General Assembly as a founding member state. Minsk's admission was the result of a compromise between Roosevelt and Churchill, on the one hand, and Stalin, on the other, by which Moscow was awarded three UNGA seats: one each for the Soviet Union, Ukraine, and Belarus. Stalin had originally demanded fifteen seats—one for each Soviet republic.

37. Mihalisko, "Belarus: Retreat to Authoritarianism," 226–27; and Sanford, "Belarus on the Road to Nationhood," 132–33.

38. Margaret Shapiro, "Identity Crisis Pulls Many in Belarus Toward Russia," *Washington Post*, July 2, 1995, A23.

39. Sanford, "Belarus on the Road to Nationhood," 131.

40. The adjective was employed by a former Belarusian government official in an off-the-record conversation with Blacker in June 1995 in Minsk.

41. Elizabeth Fuller, "Caucasus: Interests Diverge Among the Members of GUAM States," *RFE/RL*, December 1, 1997; and Elizabeth Fuller, "1997 in Review: The CIS—Half Alive or Half Dead," *RFE/RL*, December 22, 1997. For further on Uzbekistan's accession to GUAM, see Paul Goble, "Belarus/Russia: Analysis from Washington—An Increasingly Divisive Union," *RFE/RL*, April 28, 1999.

42. Associated Press, *AP Worldstream*, December 31, 1995.

43. "President Clinton's Remarks with Prime Minister Aznar of Spain, Secretary General of NATO Solana, and President Kuchma of Ukraine in Signing Ceremony of NATO-Ukraine Charter, Madrid, Spain," White House: Office of the Press Secretary, July 9, 1997.

44. "Press Briefing by Secretary of State Warren Christopher, Secretary of the Treasury Robert Rubin, and National Security Advisor Anthony Lake, Ukraine House, Kiev, Ukraine," White House: Office of the Press Secretary, May 11, 1995; and Robert Lyle, "Ukraine: Pushing for Success with Gore-Kuchma Commission," *RFE/RL*, May 16, 1997.

45. Zaprudnik and Urban, "Belarus: From State to Empire?" 284.

46. Ibid., 285, 297–98; and Mihalisko, "Belarus: Retreat to Authoritarianism," 234–35.

47. "Belarus on the Brink of Economic Collapse," *ITAR/TASS*, November 12, 1993; and Wendy Sloane, "Clinton Visit Is Reward for Belarus," *Christian Science Monitor*, January 14, 1994, 2.

48. Mihalisko, "Belarus: Retreat to Authoritarianism," 251.

49. "Background Notes: Belarus, March 1996," Bureau of Public Affairs, U.S. Department of State, March 1996, 1.

50. Sanford, "Belarus on the Road to Nationhood," 139–40. For more recent developments, see Floiriana Fossato, "Belarus: Fate of Detained Russian Journalist Linked to Energy Talks," *RFE/RL*, October 2, 1997; "Roulette," *The Economist* 346, no. 8061 (1998): 48; and Michael Wines, " 'Bunny' Breeds Rapidly, Sinking Belarus Economy," *New York Times*, August 12, 1998, A3.

51. The comment by the Treasury Department official occurred at the start of an ad hoc meeting of senior U.S. government officials in March 1996 convened to discuss the status of Russia's economic reforms efforts. Blacker was in attendance.

52. Alexander Motyl and Bohdan Krawchenko, "Ukraine: From Empire to State-hood," in Bremmer and Taras, *New States, New Politics*, 261.

53. The economic situation in Ukraine has deteriorated significantly since 1996. The causes are many (and common to all the former Soviet republics) and interrelated: excess industrial capacity, the slow pace of privatization, the lack of investment capital, corruption, and nonsensical tax policies.

54. Robert Lyle, "Experts Say IMF Wants Faster Reforms in Belarus," *RFE/RL*, February 15, 1996; and Robert Lyle, "Former U.S.S.R.: Reform Progressing Everywhere but Belarus, Says World Bank," *RFE/RL*, September 30, 1996.

55. Zaprudnik and Urban, "Belarus: From State to Empire?" 300; and Mihalisko, "Belarus: Retreat to Authoritarianism," 253–54.

56. Mihalisko, "Belarus: Retreat to Authoritarianism," 256–57; and Marples, *Belarus*, 71.

57. Mihalisko, "Belarus: Retreat to Authoritarianism," 257. See also Michael Wines, "Yeltsin Agrees to Closer Ties with Belarus: Unified Economies but Not a Political Merger," *New York Times*, December 26, 1998, A1; and "Belarus Says Envoys Are Expected to Return," *New York Times*, December 28, 1998, A8. See also Christian Caryl, "Bellicose Belarus: President Alexander Lukashenko Preserves Soviet Republic Policy, *U.S. News and World Report*, October 26, 1998, 38; and Sergei Nikodimov, "Russian-Belarus Union Charter to be Finalized by May 15," *Kommersant Daily*, May 8, 1997, 2.

58. Michael S. Lelyveld, "Weakening of Belarus Pact Tied to Talks," *Journal of Commerce*, April 7, 1997, 1A.

59. Ibid.

60. "Key Points of Russia-Belarus Draft Union Treaty," *Reuters World Service*, March 31, 1997.

61. Russian parliamentarian in an aside to Blacker, November 1997, in Moscow.

62. Wines, "Yeltsin Agrees to Closer Ties with Belarus," A1.

63. Ibid, A4.

9

Compromised Sovereignty
to Create Sovereignty

Is Dayton Bosnia a Futile Exercise or an Emerging Model?

SUSAN L. WOODWARD

The French call it an *illusion en gaze*. The internationally negotiated framework for peace in Bosnia and Herzegovina—the
Dayton accord and its eleven operational annexes—appears to have little relation with Bosnian reality. Aiming to end a brutal war lasting nearly four
years between those who wanted an independent Bosnia and those who did
not, the peace accord's goal is to restore an image of prewar Bosnia that the
warring parties had aimed, more or less successfully, to destroy. Moreover, it
is being implemented by a massive international civilian and military operation tasked to create the attributes of domestic sovereignty that Bosnia did not
have when the major powers decided in April–May 1992 to grant the former
Yugoslav republic international legal sovereignty. To obtain a peace settlement
among the three warring Bosnian parties (and their external supporters), the
external negotiators designed a state that also does not conform to any normal
pattern of domestic sovereignty. And even after four years of international
assistance in creating that state to sustain the original international decision
on recognition that provoked the war, the operation appeared to remain an
international project with few local supporters—a continuing struggle between representatives of the international community and the Bosnians themselves.

Interference in Westphalian sovereignty is supposed to be exceptional,
interfering with the autonomy of peoples up to a limit that safeguards the
norm of nonintervention itself. The norm of international legal sovereignty is
to award recognition only after states are established and governments have

effective control over the territorial domain they claim; indeed in cases of secession, such as Bangladesh, this reluctance to recognize new states often results in a substantial hiatus between domestic and international legal sovereignty while the major powers delay until they can no longer ignore a fait accompli—the reverse of the Bosnian case. Increasingly, moreover, the essence of sovereignty is seen to be domestic legitimacy, not international decision. In Bosnia and Herzegovina, decisions regarding implementation of the peace accord, strategy and priorities in the construction of this state, and the distribution of aid are all made by outsiders: a Contact Group of the five major powers (the United States, the United Kingdom, France, Germany, and Russia) plus Italy; a Peace Implementation Council (PIC) of many states and international organizations engaged on the ground who meet annually to set policy and more frequently, as a Steering Board, to oversee its execution; and a High Representative who has the power to make decisions for elected politicians and require their implementation when the goals of the peace accord and the major powers are not being met. In the Bosnian case, the international community is defying the autonomy principle of sovereignty in order to create an autonomous state.

"Dayton Bosnia" thus appears to be a particularly blatant instance of the realist's view of international relations, where norms do not matter when they conflict with major power interests. The November 1995 peace accord's affirmation of the "sovereignty, territorial integrity, and political independence" of Bosnia and Herzegovina reflects only the recognition decision by the United States and the European Union in April 1992 and the interest of those powers to legitimate their decision by creating conditions to conform, not the reality of a land partitioned by war into three more or less nationally homogeneous enclaves whose elected leaders are using the peace to institutionalize their gains in three separate (proto) nation-states and of opinion polls suggesting that more than two-thirds of the population see Dayton as alien to their own preferences and fears. Leaders of the three parties, former coalition partners who went to war over whether Bosnia and Herzegovina should become independent and what kind of state it should have, remain the primary obstacles to this international project, having no intention of cooperating where it does not conform to their particular political and economic interests. The outside powers who supported each of the three sides in the war—the neighboring states of Croatia supporting Bosnian Croats and an emerging rump Yugoslavia supporting Bosnian Serbs, foreign powers supporting Bosnian Muslims, and international organizations attempting to protect the civilian victims of the war—continue to pursue their particular interests regardless of the effect on Dayton's implementation. Relative power in that complex of outside interests decided the war's outcome (those international supporters of Bosnian independence as against the two parties who remain opposed). The citizens of Bosnia and Herzegovina were only consulted on the eve of independence to satisfy the major powers that their decision to grant international legal sovereignty had "popular legitimacy" (a referendum that was boycotted by fully one-third of the population, one of its three nations). With the peace, refugees and internally displaced persons were expected to return to the homes from which they had been expelled or fled in order to restore the multiethnic culture and residence patterns of the prewar society that appealed to the values of the Western powers. Their refusal, in large part, during the first four postwar years to comply with this political goal of the international community was clearly a reflection of their own calculations of personal or household interest—in response not only to the outright hostility of their former neighbors or the fact that the current resident of their home had also been expelled and had nowhere to go, but also to the lack of local economic prospects, above all a job—in a country being transformed by foreign donors from a socialist regime to a market economy and political democracy, with all the initial pain and unemployment that transition entails. And the more that local parties resist the international objectives, given the massive financial and political resources expended to succeed, the more international representatives interfere with the sovereignty they are seeking to create. Thus, the "Bonn powers" of the High Representative were granted in December 1997 by the international committee in charge of the peace process (the PIC) at a meeting in Bonn, Germany (with a prelude at Sintra, Portugal, in May 1997), to impose political decisions that the parties themselves are unable or unwilling to take.

To conclude that the Bosnian case demonstrates that norms do not matter, and that sovereignty is an "organized hypocrisy" of the powerful (local or international) to cover a reality of power and interests, would be wrong, however. This unusual contest between outsiders insisting on sovereignty and locals resisting is being played by the rules of the sovereignty norm. The particular characteristics of the Bosnian state and its internationally constructed sovereignty are a consequence of the *way* that major powers and international organizations intervene in Westphalian sovereignty, which is constrained by the norm. The very intervention in Bosnia aims to preserve the norm. Thus, for example, the international community insists that the parties willingly signed the Dayton accord, and that its role is only to assist the parties. Despite its increasing assertiveness, this international mission refuses to declare Bosnia a protectorate and to act accordingly. Politicians are obliged to "cooperate with Dayton," but this obligation is treated as self-imposed. Enforcement is to be only a matter of holding local authorities accountable to their population and domestic rules. Increasing violation of Westphalian sovereignty over time is done through myriad efforts to find means of *leverage* over the parties to gain compliance, not simply to impose, and to legitimize these powers through joint committees of international and local representatives who must give their approval to each expansion of foreign authority before it is used. The initial military deployment was limited to twelve months and then extended by increments until the decision to make the deployment open-ended in June 1998 was still constrained by the goal of creating a "self-sustaining" peace. International military and civilian representatives voice greatest concern over creating a "culture of dependency" that will prevent them from leaving. Their goal in ignoring Bosnia's Westphalian sovereignty is to create a system that can be an autonomous, viable, self-sustaining country able to choose interdependence and the forms and timing of intervention in their sovereignty in the future. And those who insist that this experiment cannot survive, calling either for Bosnia's "de-recognition"[1] or for a recognition of its de facto partition,[2] do so on the grounds that the institutions of this Bosnian state do not conform to international norms or that it lacks the domestic legitimacy that is the essence of modern sovereignty.

The persistence of the major powers in pursuing the Dayton framework and goals against such local resistance and international anomaly, in fact, suggests that their interests and the norm are not in conflict. The sovereignty norm, and in this instance the Dayton accord, serves the interests of the major players individually (e.g., to stop the war because of its effects on outsiders through refugees, uncertainty about further violence and geographical spillover, and the violation of other norms such as international humanitarian law, or to respond to pressure from their own local constituencies). The norm also enables them to form an alliance and to manage their collective action. But the consequence is that the norm and its rules then constrain them.

This confusing role of the sovereignty norm—that the way it is violated is constrained by the norm, that the violation of sovereignty is done to protect the norm of sovereignty, and that the purpose of the norm is to protect the interests of the major powers—is not exclusive to Bosnia. It explains the breakup of Bosnia's parent state (Yugoslavia) and the paths that breakup took, thus the original reason for the anomaly. As more and more international intervention is aimed at increasing state capacity for autonomy, and more and more countries have internal conflicts that invite international efforts to assist in negotiating peace agreements and constructing one or more states in the aftermath of war so as to prevent the recurrence of war or further fragmentation, the Bosnian case will be part of a much larger universe. The question is, can intervention to create sovereignty actually create domestic legitimacy and autonomy? Is Dayton Bosnia a transitional status, a kind of "on-the-job training to be a state," or a new manifestation of old-fashioned imperialism? If this experiment does not work, then the constraining role that the sovereignty norm plays in the form of intervention should be recognized as among the first culprits.

The Bosnian Anomaly

While many agree that Dayton Bosnia and Herzegovina is a fragile anomaly in the world of sovereign states, they do not agree on what makes it an anomaly. There are three types of arguments.

The first is a sweeping conclusion that **nation-states are stable and multinational states are not.** Bosnia and Herzegovina is a state of three national communities—Bosniacs (formerly called Bosnian Muslims), Serbs, and Croats—each of which believes it has a right to self-determination, and who fought each other in a three-sided war over different notions of what that right to self-rule entailed. The fact that the first of the Yugoslav republics to secede, Slovenia, has been very successful—in the low number of casualties in its war for independence and its political and economic stability since (even winning a place in the first round of EU expansion)—is attributed by many to its relative ethnic homogeneity (although this is true only in the Yugoslav sense, that it does not contain large territorially concentrated minorities with a history in a different state or aspirations to statehood).

The reasons for this first argument vary. The most recent is an analysis that gained great currency in part as a result of the Bosnian war: Samuel Huntington's argument that the conflicts of the future will not be over class differences but cultural identities. States will be based on cultural identities, territorially defined, and security will be perceived in civilizational terms. The most intense conflict will be at the territorial boundaries of civilizations. These "clashes of civilization" or "fault line wars" will result because all areas where civilizations meet and mix are not viable. They are historical anomalies in a period of imperial or strategic interest, but they cannot survive in the coming period.[3] There is also a long tradition in the academic discipline of political science that views ethnic homogeneity as a precondition of stable democracy, although the empirical basis for this conclusion is rather thin.[4] The argument appears to be based on the view that states are not stable if there is not some minimal level of trust among the population, and that ethnic difference causes distrust.[5] Thus there are limits to the accommodation of ethnic minorities within one state that is also conducive to democracy and peace.[6] But there is no a priori reason why ethnic difference should be conflictual, and most countries in the world, in fact, are not ethnically homogeneous. A third version of this first argument is that there is a natural evolution of state forms in Europe, at least, toward nation-states and that the spirit of the times since 1989, marked particularly by the reunification of Germany but also by the particular character of the rebellions against the Soviet system in Eastern Europe, has been a return to this historical trend of national liberation to form national states. Those who buck this trend are simply denying reality and the greater power of nationalism over other political loyalties. By this evolutionary argument, Bosnian Croats and Bosnian Serbs belong with their kin in Croatia and Serbia, and Bosniacs should create a separate state. A fourth version is that the presence of transborder (national) minorities (diasporas) always gives an incentive to irredentism such that the borders of a multinational state are never secure and its relations with neighbors always tense. In the Bosnian case, the nationalist ambitions of its neighboring states—of Croatian president Tudjman to create a Croatian state in what he claimed to be its historical borders of 1939 (which includes much of Bosnia and Herzegovina, a portion of which is inhabited by Croats from Bosnia) and of Yugoslav president Milošević to unite all Serbs into one state (which includes one-third of the Bosnian population and almost one-half of its territory under the Dayton accord)—are an immediate and constant threat to Bosnian sovereignty. Realists will add that these two neighbors are larger, wealthier, and militarily stronger than Bosnia and will thus prevail in the long run.[7]

A second argument for the Bosnian anomaly comes closer to the simple understanding of modern sovereignty: **popular legitimacy.** The Bosnian state is being constructed under the guidance of outsiders, according to an agreement and constitution written entirely by outsiders (a delegation from one of the three Bosnian national communities was active in the negotiations at Dayton, but it made adjustments only in an American-drafted agreement, while the other two communities were represented by neighboring states). Public opinion surveys have consistently shown that the public views the Dayton accord unfavorably and as a foreign imposition, even while welcoming the end of the war and the international military presence that prevents a new war.[8] Add to this the unusually intrusive international presence in the implementation of the accord, such as the foreigners in key positions (for example, the International Monetary Fund [IMF] employee as director of the central bank or the European judges appointed to hold numerical sway in deliberations and voting on the Human Rights Commission), the governance of this process of nation building by outsiders (the PIC; the Contact Group; the Venice Commission, which determines the constitutionality—in terms of the Dayton accord—of Bosnian legislation; the International Criminal Tribunal for Former Yugoslavia [ICTY], which investigates, indicts, tries, and judges violations of international humanitarian law and conventions on war), the electoral laws and judicial and police reform designed by international civil servants on mission in Bosnia, and the authority granted by outsiders to the High Representative of the international operation to make fundamental political decisions such as the design of the currency, flag, and license plates or the laws defining citizenship that would seem to violate even the loosest concept of Westphalian sovereignty. This is not defensive Westernization, in David Strang's sense,[9] or isomorphism, in John Meyer's sense,[10] but a silent protectorate or postmodern occupation. At every turn of this operation, the only force in favor of Bosnia as a whole is the international community. While that does not mean that there are no domestic constituents of a sovereign Bosnia, the way in which this international operation is taking place gives free rein to those who are opposed. It appears to provide no sanctuary or platform for those who are committed to Bosnia.[11]

A third argument focuses on the **institutional form** being constructed by the Dayton accord, particularly its constitution. The peace agreement insists on the continuation of Bosnia and Herzegovina as one sovereign country but divides it into two entities (a Bosnian Federation and a Serb Republic), both of which are sovereign and one of which comprises two constituent nations with equal rights to self-determination. The two national communities most opposed to the country's existence control the external borders, while the constitution permits special relations with the two neighbors that sharply modify its Westphalian sovereignty. The constitution is so decentralized that few powers are left to the common state, except for foreign relations (leading the "confederalists" to refer to the government as a "thin roof," in approval, but giving greater relative influence to outside powers as a result). The country is governed by a three-person committee (the presidency) and a council of ministers and parliament that are selected on power-sharing rules based on national identity. The country contains three armies, not one, and is divided through the center by a four-kilometer zone of separation between the two entities, which is "owned" by the international military implementing forces. This does not suit the constitutional assumptions generally held about a sovereign state in the modern era, nor the central powers needed to operate effectively in a globalized economy.

This institutional argument raises the most difficult test of the normative view of sovereignty. The Dayton-designed Bosnian system has much in common with the Yugoslav system in the 1970s, which did not survive—succumbing, some say, to the natural forces of nationalism held by the first argument above, but for others, to the institutional anomalies of a multinational state that attempted to recognize national rights to sovereignty in a layered system of constitutional and individual rights under the pressures of foreign trade and financial requirements. The Dayton system also has much in common with other historical systems, such as the Philadelphian system described by Daniel Deudney, which also did not survive the challenges that led to civil war.[12]

There is no way to test these three arguments and their variants against each other because the "Bosnia" project is still in process. The origins of this case in the dissolution of Bosnia's parent state, Yugoslavia, provide some clues, however. By turning first to the Yugoslav backdrop to the Bosnian present, we can see that what looks to be an open-and-shut case for the realist position on norms is far more complicated. The outcome for Yugoslavia violated the norm of sovereignty for Yugoslavia. But that particular outcome also cannot be explained without the constraint of that norm, which gave an overwhelming advantage to those local options that won as against those that lost. Moreover, the history of the breakup has been rewritten *in terms of the sovereignty norm*. This makes it analytically far more difficult to see how influential the norm has been. Nonetheless, the Bosnian case suggests strongly that the *exercise of power* internationally is constrained not by the opposing power of local interests, but by the rules guiding that exercise of power and any choice to violate sovereignty. Those rules are set and followed by the major powers themselves.

The Yugoslav Test: Confusing Facts and Rapid Revisionism

VIOLATING THE NORM IN TERMS OF THE NORM: BORDERS

The strongest of the constitutive elements of sovereignty from the perspective of international law and policy is the territorial integrity of existing states. The sanctity of recognized state borders, a principle that gained additional armor in Europe with the Helsinki Final Act of 1975, should have protected Yugoslavia in 1991. Yet within six months of their declaration of independence on June 25, 1991, two republics of the Yugoslav federation had won recognition by European powers. Within three months, a committee of five European jurists set up by the European Community (EC) to advise it on Yugoslavia had already judged that the country was a "state in the process of dissolution," a new category with no precedent in international law. This "legal" judgment was based on the assessment that as "the SFRY [Socialist Federal Republic of Yugoslavia] no longer had an effective system of government, it could no longer be said to be a state and was therefore in the process of dissolution."[13]

This disregard for the norm of sovereignty bears strong resemblance to David Strang's analysis of nineteenth-century imperialism. He argues that Western powers respected the sovereignty of non-Western polities under two conditions: "perceptions that the indigenous polity was sufficiently vigorous to be able to maintain its integrity despite constant rounds of new conditions" and "Western powers not finding that the territory at issue was less important than their rivalries." And indeed, in the case of Yugoslavia, it was the end of those two conditions that signaled the end of Yugoslav sovereignty. The first condition disappeared more than two years before it was articulated by the Badinter Commission. In 1987–1989, the patron of Yugoslav sovereignty, the United States, decided, as David Gompert, special assistant to President Bush for national security affairs at the time, wrote later, "the prime minister wanted debt relief and a public signal of unreserved American political backing—commitments that seemed unwarranted in view of his government's apparent terminal condition . . . . the Marković government was beyond help . . . . the Bush administration could not justify putting the dying Yugoslav federal authority on life-support systems."[14]

This decision was made at the same time that events in the Soviet Union and East-West relations in Europe undercut Strang's second condition. Yugoslavia's strategic position, and thus its capacity to defend its independence militarily, no longer mattered to major power relations, as the Yugoslavs were informed beginning in 1987. Nonetheless, the sovereignty norm was strong enough to keep Yugoslavia alive four more years and to ensure that the breakup would be violent, as will be discussed below. As late as November 1990 (at the summit of the Conference on Security and Cooperation in Europe [CSCE]), the other major power with an interest in maintaining the sovereignty principle, the Soviet Union, insisted that events in Yugoslavia were an internal affair and could not justify intervention. But that country ceased to exist during the fall of 1991. The locus of major power rivalry shifted to Europe, where its largest power, Germany, took the opposite position. Pushed by a parliamentary decision in July 1991, its foreign minister, Hans Dietrich Genscher, insisted that Slovenia and Croatia be recognized as rapidly as possible. The two other European powers that continued to hold out for Yugoslav sovereignty throughout 1991, Britain and France (Italy caved by October), decided that good relations with Germany and consensus among the EC Twelve as they marched toward the Maastricht Treaty and its provision for common foreign and security policy mattered more.[15]

The abandonment of Yugoslav sovereignty picked up speed after June, when the major powers were not only reacting to events but began to initiate violations of their own. The Badinter Commission ruling, though nonbinding, and the successful stubbornness of Germany opened the way to an extraordinary invitation in December to the remaining four republics of the federation: to apply within one week's time for international legal sovereignty. Criteria for recognition were set, and just as rapidly violated. Germany took the lead again, and was followed by the EC collectively, under pressure from Greece for additional criteria. According to the EC Council of Ministers' "Guidelines on the Recognition of New States in Eastern Europe and the Soviet Union," issued the same day that Germany won its position on Croatian recognition and the invitation was issued, new states had to meet the normal criteria—territorial control, autonomy, and state viability—plus a list of additional conditions, such as respect for the UN Charter, the Helsinki Final Act, and the Charter of Paris; guarantees of the rights of ethnic and national groups and other minorities; and commitments to disarmament and nonproliferation treaties, the inviolability of frontiers, and the peaceful resolution of disputes, including those concerning succession.

Within two weeks, the Arbitration Commission issued Opinions 4 through 7, finding Slovenia and Macedonia fully qualified for immediate recognition, whereas Croatia and Bosnia and Herzegovina were *not*. The EC states, followed quickly by the United States, nonetheless recognized Slovenia *and* Croatia; imposed a referendum on Bosnia and Herzegovina as a condition

for recognition and then ignored its results and recognized anyway; and refused recognition to Macedonia on the basis of the supplementary rule demanded by Greece against "the use of 'denominations' that implied a territorial claim"—even though the commission found specifically that "the use
of the name 'Macedonia' cannot . . . imply any territorial claim against another
State."[16] Croatia, in fact, did not fulfill either the normal criteria—especially,
control of territory—or the "new" criteria of guaranteeing the rights of its
minorities (especially Serbs). The recognition of Bosnia and Herzegovina reflected no conditions of statehood, except the wish of certain powers—the
United States and some of its Middle Eastern allies, especially Turkey—that
it be so. And the legitimation given for these recognitions—the right of self-
determination—was expressly denied some other groups in the country. According to the Commission's Opinion No. 2, given at the request of Serbia,
for example, the right of Serbs in Croatia and in Bosnia and Herzegovina to
self-determination was affirmed, but unlike the Slovenes and the Croats in
Croatia, that right did not, for Serbs, mean a "right to their own countries"
but only "extensive minority and group rights."[17]

Nevertheless, further inquiry suggests that this realist picture—that norms
did not matter in the breakup of Yugoslavia—is incomplete. First, while interests seemed to prevail over the norm, there were competing interests (not
only among powers but also for actors themselves). For example, the only
foreign actors with a strong interest in maintaining the sovereignty of Yugoslavia, and the only source of consistent attention to the federal government
during the period of mounting crisis in 1986–1991, were its foreign creditors—
the multilateral and commercial bankers concerned about the country's ability
to service and repay loans. They had lent to Yugoslavia at rates based on the
capacity of the primary export-earning republics, Slovenia and Croatia. If
these republics became independent and all the republics became individually responsible for repaying their debts (as financial reforms in 1977 had made
them constitutionally), then the three southern republics—Bosnia and Herzegovina, Montenegro, and Macedonia—would surely default. Yet the conditions these creditors had set for new money in the 1980s—greater central
bank independence and discipline over the republican banks, a more efficient
federal administration, structural readjustment to Western markets, wage and
price controls, and so forth—reinforced the political and social conflicts
among the republics that were driving at the time toward disintegration. Their
demands on the federal government to ensure repayment, at least of the interest on principal, in other words, undermined their "objective interest" by

requiring a radical restructuring of Yugoslavia's domestic sovereignty that led to the country's collapse instead.

Advocates of Slovene and Croatian independence also argue that the United States was not acting in its own interests, which were said to be preventing an early-twentieth-century scenario of violence, Balkan wars, and Great Power rivalry, by holding to a conservative defense of Yugoslav sovereignty too long. Early recognition, in their view, would have prevented war. Yet, in fact, the Bush administration defense of Yugoslav sovereignty was purely rhetorical, and in that not even always consistent. It did little to support either the holders or the institutions of that sovereignty when it mattered. Its status quo defense was weak at best, and accusations against Secretary of State James Baker of having given a "green light" in June 1991 to the Yugoslav army to try to prevent Slovene secession when he reiterated that preference cannot be sustained. Like the banks, U.S. behavior undermined its stated preference, demonstrating that other interests mattered more than the sovereignty norm.

At the same time, the Yugoslav parties who wanted the norm violated—particularly Slovene nationalists—went to great lengths to frame their actions in terms of the norm. In the years preceding their declarations of independence, both Slovene and Croatian republican governments and nationalist activists spent considerable funds and time on a public relations campaign in major Western capitals to build a case for independence and to persuade major powers that their independence would not conflict with the norm but rather be in conformity with it. These arguments had power precisely because they provided the cover—the illusion—the major powers needed to protect the norm, a cover that would not have been necessary if the norm did not matter. The Slovene government referred consistently to its "disassociation" from Yugoslavia, avoiding any mention of secession, so as to persuade outsiders that there was a legal basis in the founding act of the Yugoslav federation and all subsequent constitutions for its separation, on the grounds that the "sovereignty" held by the republics (in the name of their constituent nation) gave them the right to leave, including the right to take their assets with them (rather than foregoing such claims if they were seceding).[18] One can see this reasoning in the first statement of normative standing, the resolution of the European Parliament on March 13, 1991, proposed more than three months before the declarations of independence by MEP Otto von Habsburg, in his role as a friend of the Slovene and Croatian cause: "the constituent republics and autonomous provinces of Yugoslavia must have the right freely to determine their own future in a peaceful and democratic manner and on the basis of recognized international and *internal* [emphasis added] borders."[19]

But the constitutional order of Yugoslavia gave the right of self-determination to the nations, not the republics. Where the two coincided, as in Slovenia, the argument could be made for self-determination, but the Slovenes knew—and for the Croats, it was true—that it could not be made for any of the other Yugoslav republics. As the later Badinter Commission ruling suggests, this argument had its appeal in Western capitals because Yugoslavia could be seen (and its constitution be interpreted) to be a composite of sovereign units. Giving preference to the republics as the unit of analysis rather than to the nations or to all Yugoslav citizens would apply the sovereignty norm—transferring it from Yugoslavia to subunits that also looked like states. The lengths to which the norm was active can be seen in the EC decision of December 17, 1991, to issue an invitation to each republic (but not to peoples) to request recognition. Why issue an invitation unless the norm, and the pretense of sovereign will and therefore consent, mattered? The strength of the norm is particularly blatant in the case of Bosnia and Herzegovina. The assumption that the republic was a sovereign unit, with a sovereign will expressible by the chief of the elected government, enabled President Izetbegović to meet the deadline of one week by not consulting at home, either with opposition parties or with his two coalition partners, when this was clearly the moment for an open and profound domestic political debate about the relative costs and path of choosing independence at that time.

To reinforce this interpretation for policymakers with little reason to delve into the intricacies of the Yugoslav system or its history, a second argument was made. Also originating with Slovene and Croatian campaigns to justify secession, this was that Yugoslavia was an *artificial* state. What this means remains completely unclear, since all states are human constructions, but it seems to have been extremely effective in persuading policymaker and average citizen alike that Yugoslavia was bound to collapse. Artificiality implied that it had not been sovereign, but rather held together by dictatorship rather than by popular will. It therefore did not have a fount of sovereignty, whereas those units that held referendums on sovereignty and also looked like states (yes to the Slovene and Croatian republics, no to the Serbs in Croatia and Bosnia, the Croats in Bosnia, and the Albanians in Macedonia and, for a while, in Serbia) did.[20]

To be safe, a third argument was also made that flattered the late-twentieth-century cultural project of those with the power to grant recognition, namely, that the acceptable features of a legitimate state are democracy, human rights, and a market economy. Even before the Badinter Commission mailed its questionnaire and applied its "test" for recognition to the requesting republics, between December 16, 1991, and January 17, 1992, the Slovene and Croatian nationalists made the argument that the choice for outsiders with regard to Yugoslavia was one between democracy and unity. The Slovenes made sure this was understood as a choice between Slovenia and Serbia, and the Croats, between them and Slobodan Milošević (and later, between "Europe" and the "Balkans"). Kosovar Albanian nationalists added that the choice was an issue of "communist aggression against democratic forces." Because Slovene leaders were preoccupied with joining Europe, their assessment, which was probably correct, that Kosovo—and Macedonia and perhaps also Bosnia and Herzegovina—were too poor and economically underdeveloped to win EC membership for all of Yugoslavia in the foreseeable future led them to take propaganda advantage of the federal repression of the miners' strike in Kosovo in February 1989. Slovene authorities successfully labeled this political strike against Kosovo's loss of provincial autonomy in Serbia, which had been approved by representatives of all eight constituent units of the federation, including Slovenia, as well as other Albanian grievances as an issue of "human rights."[21] Although Slovene leaders knew that human rights violations would slow the accession of Yugoslavia to the Council of Europe and the EC, they risked this characterization because they had already decided that they could get to Europe faster on their own. To achieve this required argumentation that would delegitimize Yugoslavia in the minds of recognizing powers, leaving Slovenia free to leave and join the EU as an independent state.

By the spring of 1991, European states were adopting positions on the Yugoslav domestic conflict that were in conformity with their cultural framework of sovereignty. Peculiarities of the Yugoslav constitutional and economic system were ignored. Those political alternatives that did not immediately conform to their normative image of Western nation-states (including the federal reform program) had ever less chance of getting a hearing. While their decisions and actions came to have ever greater influence, in accord with the realist's view of power over norms, the major powers appeared to go to great lengths to create the appearance that they were following their norm. Thus, crucial distinctions between Yugoslavia and the constituent republic of Serbia, between the federal prime minister, Ante Marković, and the republican president of Serbia, Slobodan Milošević, and between human rights and national rights had become lost on outsiders, successfully submerged in a rhetoric of

Serbian aggression against Albanian human rights or the threat that Milošević (or simply "Belgrade") was said to pose to the "other nations" of Yugoslavia. The European parliament resolution mentioned earlier identified the *right* of the republics to free choice. The actions of the federal army to retake control of Yugoslav customs and border posts from Slovene militia after June 25, as ordered by the prime minister and parliament and in accord with several decisions of the presidency in the preceding year, were declared acts of aggression against Slovenia, as if it were already independent. The federal army was said to be *invading* Slovenia, and then Croatia, and to make this somewhat more plausible, the federal army was quickly relabeled a Serbian army. The German campaign of July–December 1991 for rapid recognition of the two republics explicitly proposed that recognition would "internationalize" the conflict and thus make it possible to redefine the efforts of the Yugoslav army to protect the state's territorial integrity and of border-area Serbs in Croatia to express their national rights to self-determination by voting to remain in Yugoslavia as illegitimate acts, respectively, of cross-border aggression and rebellion. But the thesis that Slovenia and Croatia were democratic and tolerant of human rights whereas Serbia—or the rest of Yugoslavia—was not cannot be supported by the facts of the time.

In defense of the Slovene and Croatian perspective, one could argue that sovereignty is a complex norm and that its constitutive elements are in such cases internally contradictory. Juxtaposed to the sanctity of existing borders— supporting the territorial integrity of Yugoslavia—is the principle of self-determination and thus the right of Slovenia and Croatia, if they met the criteria of popular will through referendums, to independence. As mentioned previously, however, Opinion 2 of the Badinter Commission ruled that the right of self-determination was not necessarily a right to statehood and recognition. Many other national leaders in former Yugoslavia initiated popular referendums that the international community did not accept as legitimate. In fact, the complexity of the Yugoslav constitutional order—in which the sovereignty of each nation was lodged in a particular republic, but the borders of the republics did not conform to that of the nations or of residential patterns; in which the national rights of individuals were guaranteed equal exercise in *any* of the republics; and in which the two provinces (Vojvodina and Kosovo) did not bear sovereign rights because national minorities did not have constituent nation status—made the question of self-determination a legal nightmare. Contrary to those in Slovenia and Croatia who say that the sovereignty norm constrained the major powers from recognizing their independence early, and thus obviating the need for wars of independence, the sovereignty norm did constrain the European powers, but in a different way—by preventing them from dealing with the issues that might have made it possible to manage its dissolution peacefully and thus achieve the stability and limited violence that would have been their primary interest.

The Dutch presidency of the EC, which office it assumed in the middle of the ten-day Slovene war, made an effort in its recommendation made on July 13, 1991, in a COREU (confidential correspondence among EC foreign ministers) to the other eleven members. Based on its assumption that the country could not be saved, it proposed to initiate full consideration of the legal issues—borders, assets, debts, and monitors deployed to areas not yet at war—that are involved in the dissolution of a state.[22] As a "very tentative attempt . . . at structuring our discussion on the future of Yugoslavia, with a view to developing a common position which may serve as guidance for possible Troika involvement in the Yugoslav negotiating process," the Dutch government proposed the necessity of a "comprehensive solution which involves all republics and the federal government" and a "voluntary redrawing of internal borders as a possible solution."[23] But the member states rejected this proposal, although hindsight shows this was clearly against their own national and collective interests and would surely have prevented all of the subsequent wars. The reason was that some European powers (as well as the United States) were not yet ready to violate the norm of territorial integrity of an existing state, while those who were ready would only do so in a way that defended the norm's core—the sanctity of territorial borders. They could not accept a redrawing of borders, even to prevent war, but could reapply the principle to sovereign-appearing smaller units within Yugoslavia, the republican borders of Slovenia and Croatia. By September 7, the EC did accept the need to manage the crisis and to provide a "comprehensive solution," and convened a peace conference at The Hague. The Brussels convention that it presented to all Yugoslav parties, drafted during the month of October by EC bureaucrats, proposed what was essentially a loose confederation of independent states, joined by a customs treaty. But it insisted that the borders of those states be the boundaries of the republics as they had been in the federation. The Serbian and Albanian questions—the rights of Serbs or Albanians caught outside their motherland by these new borders of ostensibly *nation-states*—were to be addressed with provisions for special status and minority rights, not a redrawing of borders. The Badinter Commission reaffirmed this decision, in Opinion 3, when asked by Serbia to rule on the status of those boundaries.

Not only did it declare the former internal boundaries to have hardened into inviolable, international boundaries, but it also applied the *uti possidetis* rule to declare those borders legitimate. A rule first proposed by Mali and Burkina Faso to accept the status quo so as to defuse conflict—accepting the *existing* (colonially drawn but already *international*) border between them as legitimate—and used subsequently in South America, this was an opposite case from the border at issue between the federal republics of Serbia and Croatia. Their dispute was over internal borders and whether these should become international ones without any adjustment for the national identity and preferences of the population.

One might counter this argument by suggesting that the major powers were applying not the sovereignty norm but Occam's razor—that it was simply more prudent to stick with the existing borders than to complicate the diplomatic process manyfold. In light of the subsequent wars of Yugoslav succession, it is clear that a method to negotiate the borders in 1991 and to confirm popular preferences would have saved much later diplomatic complication, huge loss of life, and massive military and financial commitments to restore peace and stability (a process that remains incomplete at this writing). Border commissions set up at the time and discussions among members of the Yugoslav collective presidency in 1990–1991 also suggest that there were solutions that might have been debated without violence had the Dutch proposal been accepted. Simplicity over prudence might still be an explanation, but the fact that the republican borders appeared simpler than alternative proposals, including up-front support for the federal government or an all-Yugoslav referendum to ascertain popular preferences for or against its dissolution, can be explained only by the existence of a preconceived image of what a sovereign state is and the success of some Yugoslav parties in using that image—derived from the norm—in defense of their position. This simplicity derived from a universal rule—which does not allow for much contextual variation—may be the link that binds interest and norm: the interest of the major powers (and in 1991 of the EC) in acting collectively required them to find a rule by which they could create and maintain their coalition. As seen later in regard to Bosnia and Herzegovina and Kosovo province, territorial integrity became the overriding rule, even though its simplicity created a host of complications.

Prior to obliging certain behaviors, the sovereignty norm frames perceptions. Once framed, choices are constrained. A striking characteristic of the Yugoslav conflicts that led to dissolution in 1991 (and of the wars that ensued) is the way that outsiders redefined events in terms of categories familiar to them. The constraining role of the norm of sovereignty is particularly strong in the way in which the history of the Yugoslav crisis has already been rewritten to conform to international decisions of recognition. It is now accepted without demur that the "Serbian army" "invaded" Slovenia, then Croatia, and then Bosnia and Herzegovina; that Serbian aggression was and still is the cause of war; that the issue in Kosovo was Albanian human rights, not independence; and that it is natural that the new Yugoslavia (Serbia, including the two provinces of Vojvodina and Kosovo, and Montenegro) cannot "rejoin" the international community and obtain international legal sovereignty until it becomes democratic, guarantees the human rights of Kosovo Albanians (by restoring their rights to self-governance in the provincial boundaries of 1989),[24] and respects the sovereignty of Bosnia and Herzegovina. The consequence of this revisionist history is to obscure another significant effect of the sovereignty norm: in selecting winners and losers from among the alternatives at the time.

INTERNATIONAL (IN)TOLERANCE FOR INSTITUTIONAL ANOMALIES

Most relevant to the Bosnian anomaly that emerged from the dissolution of Yugoslavia is the shaping effect of the sovereignty norm on the path taken by that dissolution. Although definitive conclusions require an extensive counterfactual analysis, that path reveals a persistent bias against political forces that did not conform to Western notions of sovereign actors. Such a bias suggests that the Yugoslav system did not—perhaps could not in the current age—survive because both its institutions of domestic sovereignty and its foreign relations were anomalous in a world of sovereign nation-states. The similarities between the Yugoslav and the Dayton Bosnia systems are great. If Yugoslavia broke apart because it was incompatible with international norms, on what basis can Bosnia and Herzegovina survive?

The primary alternative path for Yugoslavia was the economic reform and accompanying political restructuring begun in the 1980s. Although there were many disagreements over the details of this reform and the redistribution of power and resources it required, by the late 1980s the societal consensus was behind its objectives: democracy, a market economy, and joining Europe. By late 1989, the Marković reform package showed every sign of succeeding, if given the several years needed for the anti-inflationary medicine to bring economic revival and for the democratic elections beginning in the spring of 1990 to go through several rounds, as occurred throughout much of the rest of Eastern Europe. By May 1990, after the elections in the first two of the six republics, Slovenia and Croatia, the federal policies had reduced hyperinflation to negative price growth. Public opinion surveys consistently declared the prime minister the most popular politician, alone and in paired comparisons with each of the republican leaders,[25] and more than a decade of middle-class discontent with the regime over their declining fortunes and employment opportunities was rapidly disappearing as their incomes finally began to rise. Strikes and demonstrations had begun to focus their complaints on federal authorities, such that an all-Yugoslav political space on economic issues was being revived after two decades of hyperdecentralization where all politics had revolved within the republics or provinces. The rapid growth during the late 1980s of independent trade unions, human rights groups, and independent professional groups such as those of lawyers, jurists, journalists, and accountants had their counterpart within official structures—numerous party leaders and officials in the army, courts, and administration who insisted on acting within the law, refusing political pressures to act extralegally, and beginning the formation of an accountable democratic state. Whether one looks at opposition parties in the parliaments of Slovenia and Croatia, at the sizable pro-Yugoslav opinion in Bosnia and Herzegovina, at the March 1991 opposition demonstrations in Belgrade and their success in demanding an end to media censorship in Serbia, or at the antiwar groups in Belgrade, Sarajevo, and Skopje and the thousands of draft evaders in Serbia proper, one sees a different Yugoslavia and different set of possibilities than the one portrayed by the revisionist histories after 1992.

To realize a different trajectory, there were three basic problems, none of them insurmountable. The structural problem was the 1974 Constitution and subsequent legislation, originating in the decentralizing amendments of 1967–1971, that had created republican economies and barriers to the free flow of labor, capital, and goods across republican borders. The federal government needed strengthening and the republican politicians' economic prerogatives weakened to create a market economy. But the republics with the greatest export revenues, key to the economic program, were those most opposed to any change in the 1974 Constitution.

The political problem was that those who would benefit by these reforms—the liberal reformers, urban professionals, unemployed workers, petty craftsmen, and private farmers—needed to build cross-republican political alliances if they were to win against the nationalist politicians demanding states' rights and using the media to whip up nationalist fervor and fear. The goal would have been to replace the irresponsible and spiraling rhetoric of republican competition with new countrywide political institutions in which politicians moved to compete for the center, alliances formed on real policy issues and economic interests and could shift in time, a multiparty system could develop, and there were legal channels for redress of grievances. But to achieve that, they would have to accept the republican basis of representation and decision making and then neutralize its ability to prevent change. By forming alliances across republics, they might override the Slovene veto on a countrywide referendum on the constitutional amendments scheduled for November 1988 and on federal elections that were supposed to follow the republican elections in December 1990. Even before the first elections in the four nonsecessionist republics and the scheduled federal elections, Slovenia defined the choice for the rest of the country as between a confederation of states (known to be a temporizing solution until EC membership was forthcoming) and Slovene independence. Serbian politicians responded by declaring that the political issue would then be one of borders. Slovenia and Croatia were secretly forming separate armies on the basis of their territorial defense forces, political parties in many parts of the country were forming paramilitary organizations, and violence had erupted in Croatia over the new rulings against Serbs in border areas by the new Croatian government. These developments put the economic liberals in a political bind over how to prevent escalation without giving a casus belli to the secessionists.[26] And throughout the country, the new Slovene-led agenda gave a boost to nationalists as public opinion began to face the prospect that the country might dissolve into nationally defined units.

The external problem was the difficulties over trade, security, and aid relations with Europe and the United States. Although major powers, led by the United States, were deciding that Yugoslav sovereignty was no longer necessary to an evolving European order, they continued to treat Yugoslavia as a special case. In the mid-1980s it had been left out of the East-West conventional forces in Europe reduction (CFE) talks and trade rapprochement because it was not part of the Eastern bloc (Warsaw Treaty Organization [WTO] or Council on Mutual Economic Assistance [CMEA]). But by 1989–1991 Yugoslavia faced fundamentally changed circumstances, manifested in difficulties obtaining further U.S. financial support, in renegotiating its 1982 EC agreement (which had better terms than the one negotiated with Poland, Czechoslovakia, and Hungary in 1991, but by July 1990, was simply blocked by Greece), and in persuading the EC to replace U.S. assistance in support of its macroeconomic stabilization and debt repayment reforms after 1989. The EC's aid program for Eastern Europe, set up for

Poland and Hungary in July 1989 (thus called PHARE), was extended to the rest of the former Eastern bloc in April 1990, but Yugoslavia was not included. The British blocked an EC aid package that was drafted in March 1991 at the request of EC Commission president, Jacques Delors, and when Delors first took the package to Belgrade in mid-May, his preconditions for its disbursement were all the reforms that the federal government needed the aid to promote—democratic reform, economic reform, human rights, and unity. While demanding unity, moreover, Delors and president of the EC Council of Ministers, Jacques Santer, included in their visit diplomatic conversations with the Slovene president. The Council of Europe was the first to change course in support of alternatives to nationalism when it began overtures for Yugoslav membership in February 1991, but its first condition among several was that federal parliamentary elections be held—a condition that the federal government was more than happy to fulfill but was powerless to do as long as outsiders were encouraging its opponents in Slovenia.

None of these three problems was insurmountable. A successful outcome of this reform trajectory would have conformed well to the current international requirements of sovereign states. But the obstacles that had to be surmounted were not under domestic control but lay with outsiders, suggesting an incompatibility between the domestic characteristics of a transforming Yugoslavia and international molds that stem from the sovereignty norm. The first, structural, problem arose from the nature of acceptable international intervention. Although the requirements of the IMF debt-repayment program were nearly impossible to meet in the time frame allotted, such highly intrusive programs are considered compatible with sovereignty because they are "signed." However little choice governments have when international conditions force them to resort to IMF credits, the credits and conditions are considered voluntary. But the charter of the international financial institutions forbids them from *political* action—including any attention to the constitutional consequences of their aid policies or to the political transition that would have to be supported alongside money to refinance a trade deficit if the program was to succeed. This, by their charter, would be undue interference in the internal affairs of sovereign states. Moreover, the political requirement of the sovereignty norm, that relations must be with sovereign representatives—governments and central governments—simultaneously put undue pressure on the federal authorities in relation to the republican governments that controlled the crucial resources and gave undue influence over the path of reform to political authorities. Conflicts over economic resources remained conflicts over governmental jurisdictions and rights, rather than moving toward depoliticization of economic quarrels in the direction of a market economy. Moreover, given a choice between support for the creation of a market economy and for export earnings, even the IMF and World Bank took the short-term view. But their priority on export promotion gave overwhelming advantage in the reform contest to those regions that produced export earnings, even though their political authorities were the greatest opponents of the institutional reforms of the IMF package.

External views shaped by the rules of sovereignty were also critical for the second, political, problem. When Slovenia succeeded in shaping the domestic political agenda, as a choice between Slovene independence or a confederation of states, foreign support for alternatives, such as a more effective federal government, or coalitions of groups and interests that crossed the republics in the interest of market and democratic reform, fell within the rubric of interference within the internal affairs of sovereign states. Support for the confederation alternative was weak because it proposed an institutional hybrid that few could imagine. Who would be its sovereign representatives? Who would be the appropriate counterparts for international actors? This left, by default, the Slovene choice for independence, even though many realized that support for secession was an even greater violation of the norm. The very fact that the norm gives higher value to sovereign-like representatives than to persons not in authority means that the interpreters of the conflict would be those whose interests were in state power. Aside from the IMF, outsiders seemed to accept the level of decentralization created by the 1974 Constitution as historically legitimate rather than as only a brief constitutional construction that benefited regional autocrats, not democracy or genuine local control. This general bias facilitated by the sovereignty norm gave greater influence to those who would violate that norm in the service of interest—as in the Austrian, Swiss, Vatican, and eventually German position on Slovene and later Croatian independence. And the early decision by some Western powers that Slovenes and Croats had a right to self-determination in their so-called "historical communities" reinforced the choices made by those Western leaders—excluding consideration of the primary alternative, that the citizens of Yugoslavia as a whole might also have that right. The thesis of the historical inevitability of self-determination ignores the absence of an operational definition for the principle, above all who the *people* are in each instance, or how procedurally to decide. Foreign support behind such an alternative operation to establish self-determination, leading to the insistence that federal elections be held as originally committed or that there be an all-Yugoslav referendum on the fate of the *country* prior to any external decision, would have seemed to be too interventionist, too much meddling in internal affairs in contrast to the acceptable foreign campaign to build external support for the Slovene and Croatian causes. Even before outsiders denied validity to the referendums by Serbs in Croatia, Serbs in Bosnia, Albanians in Kosovo, and Macedonians as "internal affairs" (sometimes called issues of "minority rights") of "states," the majority of the Yugoslav population was denied the option of remaining in Yugoslavia, without any choice.

As for the third problem of Yugoslavia's external position, aid and trade regimes and their enforcers insist on treating states as sovereign actors — although they operate in regional complexes and a globalized economy that can be decisive. The Yugoslav conflict cannot be understood or resolved without direct consideration of the changes in its external economic fortunes after 1979 and its foreign and security relations after 1985 (and especially 1989), yet external actors continued to insist on treating the conflict as a domestic problem (of Yugoslavia, or of the individual states that emerged). Eight years after the country's dissolution there remained a destabilizing vacuum regarding the place of its former parts in the new Europe. To the extent there were policies toward the region, they were those of the European Union, which set conditions (democracy, human rights, market economy) that had to be met by each country separately in exchange for aid and staged accession, and those of the United States, the EU, and NATO to contain refugees and violence within the peninsula — in other words, a continuation of the approach that failed so miserably in 1991.[27]

The essence of that approach was not that they felt bound by the sovereignty norm not to intervene. The very fact that there was debate over whether to act, beginning in the fall of 1990 at NATO and the CSCE, demonstrates this. It was that however each viewed the goal of intervention, from preventing violence and protecting human rights in Kosovo to gaining the cooperation of republican leaders with the market reform, their interventions were made in terms of the categories of sovereignty, seeking out "sovereigns" who they believed were responsible or could be held responsible for the particular problem. Yet it was the quarrels and competition among these government officials and politicians who appeared to exercise sovereignty or who wanted to be granted such recognition that was behind the problems they sought to address.

The result was to make choices among elements of the mixed system of socialist Yugoslavia that suggest a lack of international tolerance for such anomalies.

The clash between that system and international treatment and expectations had been going on for almost a decade. During the 1980s, the core elements of Yugoslavia's institutional anomaly faced insuperable challenges, each of which originated in external pressures and changes. The shocks hit three core anomalies: (1) a multinational federation that institutionalized the equal right to self-determination for six nations within one state by a constantly evolving constitution defining shared powers and equal rights; (2) an economic system based on socialist ownership and redistribution that was also open internationally, including membership in world trade and financial organizations, sometimes called "market socialism"; and (3) a foreign policy combining national independence with communist party rule, called "national communism," and nonalignment, in a bipolar world divided between capitalist and communist blocs.

The first shock was a balance-of-payments crisis due to changes in Yugoslavia's terms of trade and in German policy toward foreign labor, the second oil price rise by OPEC and skyrocketing interest rates on the American dollar, and *some* local difficulties such as an earthquake in tourist areas of southern Dalmatia. But the moment was also one when global pressure for economic liberalization was beginning, the U.S. Treasury and American commercial banks were mounting a harsh defense against what became called the "global debt crisis," and the IMF began to demand much stiffer conditions and targets in exchange for loans. The rules of the game were being changed and rapidly. The three-year standby conditionality facility, adopted in 1982 between the IMF and the Yugoslav government, required not only a long-term stabilization policy that induced a decade-long recession but also financial and trade sector reforms of the decentralized, socialist banking system. To attract foreign capital to the new export-promoting policy, the government was told to change the socialist property rights. It began by ending restrictions on the percentage of productive assets that foreigners could own (the limit had been 49 percent) and by 1989 had introduced a complete program of privatization, ending the rights of public sector workers and employees to self-management and income guarantees. Growing unemployment, pressures for labor "rationalization" (downsizing), and the human consequences of austerity, recession, and hyperinflation generated a major change in the social structure away from public sector (secure) toward private sector (insecure) work. Macroeconomic reform required transferring the burden of federal welfare guarantees onto republican and local budgets.

This economic policy and reform of the financial and property sectors aimed at external adjustment necessarily meant reforms in the political system. Changing the locus and manner of decision making on monetary and foreign exchange policy, and then on wage and price controls and the source of federal revenues and recipients of those tax monies—the army and the federal administration—was an extraordinary shock, effectively induced by external causes, to the complex balance of Yugoslavia's domestic sovereignty. Points of contestation in the Yugoslav system had always been over rights, in the sense of autonomy and authority—primarily rights to economic assets, the most valued of which was foreign exchange. Major quarrels therefore ensued over the rights of the republics and the writ of federal authority, and the relative balance between parliamentary and executive power. The reforms attempted clarity in a system based instead on shared jurisdictions. The package of reforms also aimed at improving the efficiency of central governmental decision making by replacing the system of elite consensus and parity or proportional distribution of monies and offices with one of majoritarian rule. But zero-sum choices mean a system where there would be losers, minorities, and exclusion. The messy combination of this legitimizing system of multiple claimants, never fully resolved disputes, time-consuming discussion to reach consensus,[28] compensating budgetary subventions to losers on a particular economic policy, and national quotas for official positions and public goods to protect the appearance of equality was to be replaced by an ideal type of Western state, under IMF and liberal reformers' guidance. The reform seemed to leave open only one question: would this state be at the federal level or for each republic as Slovenia wanted? Was the federal government or were the republic governments sovereign, now that their shared authority was not acceptable? What body or person had the final authority?

The third external shock was to Yugoslavia's foreign policy. The deepening of West European integration between 1985 and 1989, the reduction of East-West tensions and the move toward ending Europe's division into political-economic blocs, and the pressure for trade revenues from Western markets to reduce Yugoslavia's hard currency trade deficit deprived the policy of non-alignment and economic triangulation of its international context. "Europe Now!" was the 1989 party slogan of the Slovene communist party congress, aiming at membership in the EC as fast as possible. The economic buffer of bilateral trade accounts with Eastern firms and governments ended in favor of trade at world market prices and convertible currency, while the Middle Eastern buffer of cheaper oil prices in exchange for political loyalty or clearing mechanisms for payment of construction and engineering projects succumbed to the effects of the Iran-Iraq war and the hard-currency bias of the Yugoslav trade deficit.

The contest came to a head in 1988–1989, between the federal prime minister's program for "functional integration" and a more efficient federal administration, under IMF pressure and definition, on the one hand, and the antifederalists led by Slovenia (with allies in Croatia and Vojvodina), on the other. A new enterprise law ended the system of worker self-management, but few noticed, despite the insistence by liberal economists that the crux of the Yugoslav crisis was the concept of social ownership by which shared rights effectively meant no rights. By clearly delineating owners of firms, they thought one could jettison the problems they attributed to this system of shared sovereignty. The Slovene authorities proposed a solution to the constitutional quarrel, which they called *asymmetric federalism*. The republic of Slovenia would contract separately with the federal government, in essence, as an independent state linked to an otherwise continuing Yugoslavia. But the coalition that was building against the federalists required a platform that did not single Slovenia out for separate privileges. To accommodate potential allies, the Slovenes initiated a new proposal of confederation — insisting that the country be transformed into a confederation of independent states — and then, within months, calling a Slovene referendum, held December 1990, declaring total independence in six months if the other republics did not concur. Confederation suited Croatia, but the federal prime minister and international bankers negotiating debt repayment had more market-oriented federal proposals in mind. Leaders in Serbia appeared to accept that independent states were now inevitable because they tried to move the issue of borders to the top of the agenda. Macedonian president Gligorov and Bosnian president Izetbegović proposed a compromise on June 6, 1991, that mixed federal and confederal elements, but it came too late.

While international events were forcing a reduction in the anomalous elements of the Yugoslav system, proponents of confederation also struggled with a lack of receptivity to their views when they attempted to draw Western attention to the viability of confederation, based on the *difference* between the Yugoslav legacy, and for that matter that of much of Eastern Europe, and that of Western experience with and ideas regarding sovereignty. Their idea was that Eastern experience was not that of the Hobbesian notion of a sovereign order underlying Westphalian sovereignty, where political relations were hierarchical, rights exclusive, the source of sovereignty unique, the head of the hierarchy and representative of a state's sovereignty a single sovereign with a monopoly over the legitimate use of violence, and relations with neighbors were state-to-state, sovereign relations. If outsiders were willing to understand the need for an alternative approach to domestic sovereignty, however, one might save Yugoslavia.

Although many portray the constitutional contest, wrongly, as a straight-forward choice between a centralized state and confederalists (or national liberators), even that black-and-white choice leaves three grounds for serious concern. The first is the historical legacy that was later used to explain what occurred. The history of nation formation in the region was, as confederation proponents argued, different from Western state-making models. That history included the legacy of local self-government of the Byzantine system, the millet system of the Ottomans, recurring massive migrations (national as well as individual—household and transhumant), conflict between an imperial tradition (e.g., the Habsburgs, the Ottomans) and states emerging out of the nationalist struggle, the Habsburg protectorate and then annexation of Bosnia and Herzegovina in response to the end of the Ottoman empire, and the creation at Versailles of a multinational state. As Maria Todorova elucidates, the symbiosis of these historical legacies did not create a linear path toward some nationally pure outcomes but an entire region that could be characterized by "in-betweenness," liminality, and ambiguity as seen from a "Western" perspective but that was an adaptive response to its external environment.[29]

A second caution concerns the misplaced clarity with which outsiders heard (or later ascribed to) the parliamentary declarations and later referendums on sovereignty held in many parts of the country. The declarations of sovereignty by the republican legislatures of Croatia and Slovenia in July 1990 and the referendums in July on sovereignty in Kosovo (one of the two autonomous provinces of Serbia), during August in localities of Serbs in border areas of Croatia, in Slovenia at the end of the year, and in Croatia and Macedonia in 1991 were all ambiguous about the meaning of sovereignty. Was it an assertion of individuals' national identity and rights, within a larger Yugoslav state? A vote for full independence? For many voters in each of these cases, the word sovereignty did not mean full independence, only uncompromising affirmation of the *right* to sovereignty. To this day, many who voted in the Croatian referendum of May 1991 insist that the majority of the population did *not* believe that in voting in favor of Croatian sovereignty, they were voting also to leave Yugoslavia and form an independent state.

The decision to engage outsiders in this domestic contest appears to have been crucial, in swinging the victory to those who sought foreign support for their national sovereignty (Slovene and Croatian nationalist leaders) as against those who sought economic assistance for their market transformation (the federal prime minister and foreign minister). The more severe violation of Westphalian sovereignty (breaking up a state), in other words, won out over the more common violation (requiring domestic reforms in exchange for economic assistance and demanding conformity to human rights conventions, though the latter were aimed at a substate entity as well, the Serbian leadership toward ethnic Albanians in Kosovo). Even while refusing to contemplate the end of the country, let alone negotiate a peaceful breakup, EC and CSCE officials were meeting separately with republican leaders (especially from Slovenia, Croatia, and Serbia) as if they were heads of state.

The third ground for pause is Bosnia and Herzegovina. The anomaly of multinational Bosnia in the Yugoslav federation was not only viable within the Yugoslav system, its republican status was actually introduced in 1943–1945 to make the system work, creating more balance in the size of the federal units and a buffer against territorial contests (primarily between Croatia and Serbia) within the state. Yet it was an ambiguity that outsiders refused to see. The warnings that a violent war for the creation of national states out of the republic's territory would be inevitable if there were a precipitate recognition of Croatia (that is, before the whole country's dissolution had been fully managed and completed) were ignored, and commentators rapidly shifted to a description of the constitutional conflict over a Bosnian state as "ethnic conflict," "hatred," or "distrust." Like Yugoslavia before it, Bosnian alternatives to complete independence were also ignored in the pressure from the United States (now playing the role of Germany toward Croatia) to recognize Bosnian international legal sovereignty immediately. The German position was that Bosnia should remain, along with Macedonia, Montenegro, and Serbia, as a part of a smaller Yugoslavia, but German diplomats and politicians gave no justification for such an outcome nor did they lift a finger to make this happen. Yet like the Slovene proposal for confederation, there were many in Bosnia who would have supported such a policy, if only as the only route to independence in the long run that could be achieved peacefully. Popular opinion in Bosnia was also divided between supporters of the nationalist political parties (among Croats, Serbs, and Slavic-speaking Muslims in Croatia and Serbia as well as Bosnia) and the nonnationalist political parties and civic activists who had succeeded in February and March of 1992 in mobilizing huge demonstrations against the war and the nationalist party leaders (including Izetbegović). In between was a swing vote, possibly quite large, of those who voted for the nationalists in 1990 under a classic example of the security dilemma and only months after they had been opposed even to legalizing nationally defined parties. Although the EC peace conference at The Hague failed with its settlement for all of Yugoslavia, its negotiators did understand that to prevent war in Bosnia, a solution to its constitutional conflict had to be found prior to recognition, enabling all three national communities to have equal rights to self-determination and some relationship with neighbors that kept them in a Bosnian state. But the belief in popular will as the fount of sovereignty led the EC foreign ministers to require a referendum on independence, scheduled for February 28/March 1 in the midst of these EC-led negotiations, prior to granting the former republic international legal sovereignty. The EC clearly understood this referendum to mean full independence, moreover, as did President Izetbegović when he declared independence on March 4 and the leaders of the ruling Bosnian Serb political party in their decision to call a boycott of the referendum and to follow Izetbegović's declaration with their own war for independence (as a people and, given the Western concept of sovereignty, as a state territory). By the end of March, the United States had persuaded Izetbegović that he could abandon the negotiations and gain immediate recognition, on the grounds that Serb violence was an act of external aggression that sovereignty (alone) could deter.[30]

Dayton Bosnia

The breakup of Yugoslavia (and the war in Bosnia) can thus be traced to the way in which outsiders intervened in the country, violating its Westphalian sovereignty to get debt repaid and its domestic sovereignty to get its system in conformity with Western standards, and then reasserting that sovereignty in order to contain the violence and outward flow of refugees. The construction of a sovereign Bosnia and Herzegovina is following the same pattern.[31] But in sharp contrast to the former Yugoslavia, which lost any hope of sovereignty once the major powers decided that other interests took priority over its sovereignty and that the federal government was no longer capable of effective domestic sovereignty, the major powers have concluded that they have both collective interests (the survival of NATO, the credibility of European and global security organizations and norms in the post–Cold War era) and individual national interests—for some even said to be at the level of "vital"— in the sovereignty of Bosnia and Herzegovina. Indeed, that sovereignty appears to be due almost solely to a reversal in priorities among the major powers about the relation between Bosnia and their mutual relations and rivalries. The Dayton accord, which is accused of creating a nonviable state, cannot be challenged because its commitment to Bosnian sovereignty is the common denominator that holds together the international coalition that finally overcame its internal differences in mid-1995 to end the Bosnian war.

The three sets of arguments usually offered for why Dayton Bosnia is an anomaly and its durability uncertain applied as well, and were applied at the time, to the former Yugoslavia: a multinational state in a world where nation-states are believed to be the only stable state form, a country whose popular legitimacy is in question, and a set of institutional relations that do not conform to modal Western type. In the Bosnian case, the design is a deliberate act by major powers to create a sovereign state that is viable, autonomous, and relatively self-sustaining, but in ways directly shaped by the goal of protecting the sovereignty norm and its constitutive elements.

TERMS FOR INTERVENTION AND THE FAILURE OF THE MULTINATIONAL OPTION

As in former Yugoslavia, a wide range of alternatives, both before the war and in the seven explicit peace plans that preceded the Dayton accord, lost out to the requirements of the major powers, above all the United States, for intervention. The causes of war itself, and its consequences for the political future of Bosnia, cannot be separated from the early, preemptive recognition of Bosnian independence, which the United States would insist on so that it could change policy and recognize Croatia—under pressure from a Croatian lobby at home and the loss of influence over the situation after the German initiative—*without appearing to abrogate its commitment to the sovereignty norm*. The U.S. position throughout 1991 had been that Yugoslavia was sovereign, and that only if all republics chose independence could its sovereignty be seen as ended—a voluntary decision to dissolve the state as opposed to two cases of secession. Faced with a fait accompli of the EC decision to grant international legal sovereignty to those two cases, Slovenia and Croatia, the U.S. attempted to remain principled while conceding to domestic pressure. In other words, to apply recognition *as a norm*, rather than an exception, it had to accept the equal right of the other republics, in principle, to be recognized.[32] But it also supplemented this reasoning with what may have seemed a stronger argument politically, that international legal sovereignty would grant Bosnia the right to self-defense. Using the same argument that Germany made for Croatia in "internationalizing" the Yugoslav conflict, the United States asserted that those who did not accept Bosnian independence (even some of its residents) would be deterred by its new sovereign status and if they were not, would be liable for its violation and guilty of aggression. The norm thus also defined friend and foe and policies toward the parties to the conflict thereafter.

When the war began, moreover, intervention obeyed the limits of sovereignty: that no protectorate be established for Bosnia as many were urging after June 1991 because that would deny Bosnian sovereignty and hark back to no longer acceptable colonialist administration, and that there be interventions only of the kind sanctioned by higher international law—humanitarian assistance and various methods to limit the scale of war as were well established in international conventions on war (a no-fly zone, a maritime and economic embargo on Serbia and Montenegro, monitors of civilian human rights, and condemnations based on the laws of war). UN troops sent to protect international aid workers came under merciless criticism for failing to stop the war or protect Bosnian civilians, but the limits in their actions were largely imposed on them by their mandate—the official definition of their mission that defined their *right to intervene in a sovereign state* and the rules of engagement that follow, namely, consent of the parties, neutrality toward the parties, returning fire only in self-defense, and the use of force only in proportion to the provoking action.[33] This response formed the lowest common denominator of outside powers, not only because there were deep disagreements about the cause of the war and appropriate remedies but also because many continued to insist on rules that follow from the sovereignty norm.

Moreover, the type of state being constructed for Bosnia and Herzegovina since 1995 is a direct consequence of the delay in achieving a political settlement while the United States waited for, and then sought actively to create, the conditions that would allow it to send in troops on its own terms. There were two conditions: that American opponents of intervention in the internal affairs of a state be persuaded that the parties were requesting assistance and had made an agreement to settle that they would keep, and that the extreme reluctance to risk American lives on the part of both the Pentagon and the Bush and Clinton administrations be counteracted by the condition of invitation and consent. This limitation on international action of the refusal of the United States to send troops began in the early stages of the Croatian war, when the spiral of war might have been interrupted. It continued when diplomats succeeded in negotiating a full-scale peace plan to end the Bosnian war, the Vance-Owen Peace Plan of January 23, 1993, and the condition for Bosnian signatures was a sign of commitment to the plan from the major powers, first and foremost the United States, in willingness to send peacekeeping troops. In neither case was the United States convinced that there was sufficient support by local parties to guarantee consent and safety for U.S. troops, as if such support emerges ready-made after war without the reassurance that comes from external commitment. Yet the VOPP designed a state that was far less an institutional anomaly than does the Dayton accord — though also very decentralized, it composed ten regions, a balance of ethnic and nonethnic representation, no special relations with neighbors, and a reintegrated, demobilized army. Continuation of the war and the resulting population displacements to create nationally homogeneous territories for the sovereignty projects of all three warring parties thus occurred while major powers disagreed about the acceptable outcome (including even the survival of Bosnian sovereignty) and while the United States awaited and then constructed conditions (in the views of its allies and on the ground in Croatia and in Bosnia), including the use of covert arms deliveries and "technical assistance" to a Croatian invasion force, that would lead to a cease-fire and a political agreement that seemed to guarantee genuine "consent" to the entry, at last, of American troops.

The particular characteristics of Bosnian institutional arrangements considered most anomalous are a direct consequence of political agreements, written by outsiders (largely American diplomats), to obtain the cease-fires and conditions permitting consensual intervention. Indeed, it is difficult to explain the resulting characteristics of its internationally constructed domestic sovereignty without the perceptual framework of the concept of sovereignty. A war lasting almost four years over the decision of outsiders to grant Bosnia international legal sovereignty, and international insistence on retaining that sovereignty, nonetheless was ended through an American peace plan that seems to recognize the *national* character of the parties' claims. On the one hand, the two parties that rejected Bosnian sovereignty, Bosnian Croats and Bosnian Serbs, were not permitted full negotiating rights at the proximity talks in Dayton, Ohio, but were represented instead by the leaders of the two neighboring, sovereign states, Croatia and Serbia, while a single head, President

Izetbegović (still treated by outsiders as sovereign of Bosnia, although his mandate had run out in 1992), was chosen to represent the Bosnian state. On the other hand, the two-entity structure of the state, the two-nation composition of the Federation entity, the continuing existence of three armies (two supposedly joint), the power-sharing arrangements of the constitution, and the relations between international military and civilian officials in the implementation mission and the parties on the ground can be explained only by a framework that views the three armed parties as if they are contracting states in an interstate conflict, with all the characteristics, de facto, of sovereign actors. Given the extraordinary intrusiveness into domestic sovereignty of international action—for example, the structure of the state and of the Federation entity, even the territorial configuration of each entity and the border between them, and the extreme violation of Westphalian sovereignty in the confederal relations created with neighboring Croatia that were defined by the Washington Agreement of March 1994, negotiated by American diplomats (with some German assistance) to establish a cease-fire between Bosnian army (largely Muslim) and Bosnian Croat forces that could be redirected, with outside assistance, against the third party, the Bosnian Serb forces—it is striking that these outsiders did not view the Bosnian conflict in other terms such as economic conflict, cultural identity, European membership, external aggression, and other elements of the actual conflict that would have permitted state construction in a more "normal" direction.

To gain consent and cooperation of the parties, the accord is not in fact a peace agreement but a "deal"—a form of nonnegotiated elite pact drawn up by outside negotiators—among the heads of the three warring parties. Extensive decentralization was considered necessary to get an elite "deal" to stop the fighting and to allow each nation the means to defend itself—an army and state—against violations of the cease-fire. It left to the common state institutions only the minimal economic functions for internal and foreign trade (a central bank acting as a currency board for six years, hence with no independent economic role; a common currency that meets IMF standards; a customs regime providing state revenue but collected by the entity governments; and political agreements on large scale infrastructure and license plates for freedom of movement across the entire territory) and foreign relations of its citizens (passports, the part of citizenship related to other states such as rights to dual citizenship) and of the state (embassies and other forms of foreign representation). Even the continuing delays in implementing the more reintegrative elements of the Dayton accord, which many believe have doomed Bosnian sovereignty under its recognized borders, are a consequence of the international insistence that the parties themselves implement what is said to be *their* agreement. The fiction of sovereignty requires that they "cooperate" with the accord and that troops and civilian officials from the international community assume a helpmate role, not one that might require enforcement and occupation against unwilling, "sovereign-like" parties.

FOREIGN RELATIONS OF THE DAYTON STATE

The goal of obtaining signatures on an agreement that would serve as a consent to foreign military deployment while holding the parties responsible for peace is even clearer in the foreign relations established for Bosnia and Herzegovina. Despite the argument that the greatest threat to Bosnian integrity comes from neighboring Croatia and Serbia, and that the two neighbors have agreed since 1990 to partition Bosnia between them, the Dayton accord is an agreement among the three presidents of Croatia, Serbia, and Bosnia. This arrangement is ostensibly aimed at gaining the commitment of Croatia and Serbia to Bosnian integrity, supported by the accumulated knowledge that "the success of a peace settlement is inextricably tied to the interests of neighboring regional powers and their overall commitment to the peace process,"[34] but it made the two leaderships essential actors in the Bosnian political outcome. It is they who are expected to ensure that Bosnian Serbs and Bosnian Croats comply with the accord, including assistance with the work of the International Criminal Tribunal for Former Yugoslavia in The Hague. This cooperation has been purchased, moreover, with a concession to "special relationships"—between Croatia and the Bosnian Federation, on the one hand, and the Federal Republic of Yugoslavia (FRY) with Republika Srpska (RS), on the other—that can be established along the lines of the confederation provision of the Washington Agreement.[35] Bosnian Croats have dual citizenship in Croatia, vote in Croatian elections, and have twelve seats reserved for their representation in the Croatian parliament. They comply with Dayton provisions that they do not wish to implement only under pressure from party leaders in Zagreb (the ruling party of Bosnian Croats being a branch of the ruling party in Croatia), and most details of local legislation and administration in Bosnian Croat areas, such as school curricula, are designed in Zagreb. International efforts to make the border between Bosnia and Croatia a hard, sovereign border in economic transactions have been only partially successful.[36]

While confederation was the price paid to Croatian president Tudjman for agreeing to Bosnian sovereignty, the concession to Yugoslav president Milošević was to lift the main body of economic sanctions. But because the initial judgment about the war was defined in terms of state sovereignty—that Serbian actions were a case of cross-border aggression against Bosnian sovereignty while Croatian actions were friendly assistance to Croats at their request—the border relations on the Yugoslav side are less clear and more influenced by efforts at international definition. Assistance since 1995 from Zagreb is the subject of negotiation and appeal from international officials, whereas assistance since 1995 from Belgrade is viewed as illegitimate interference and the subject of verbal condemnation and punishment of Bosnian Serb politicians seen to be working closely with Serbian Serbs.

At the same time, the legitimation of neighboring "interests" in the Bosnian internal order and these special relationships facilitate interference by parties that aimed at the eventual partition of Bosnia two ways, between Croatia and Serbia. At a minimum, the arrangements facilitate interference for the strategic objectives of Croatia and FRY and could place Bosnian sovereignty under continuing threat. Whole areas of Bosnia along the two borders—the western border of Bosnia along the Dalmatian strip and the *krajina* hinterland of Croatia, inhabited largely by Bosnian Croats, and the Drina valley of eastern Bosnia alongside Serbia inhabited largely by Bosnian Serbs—can be treated as buffer zones protecting Croatian and Yugoslav territorial security. Former President Tudjman and other high Croatian officials repeatedly stated that western Bosnia (including as far east as Banja Luka, in Republika Srpska) was in the "strategic interest" of Croatia, and their actions since 1995 spoke louder than words, such as in their economic penetration of the area, planned routes (rail, road, telecommunications) linking Zagreb to Dalmatia *through* Bosnia, opening of Croatian consulates in Banja Luka and Bihać, manipulation of border closings as leverage over Bosnians in northern Bosnia, stationing troops in Bosnian territory that they decided to claim, and refusal to comply with the commitment made by Tudjman in the Dayton accord to a special arrangement for guaranteed Bosnian access to and use of the Adriatic port of Ploće. President Tudjman and Croatian ministers publicly visited Bosnian-Croat areas of Croatia without state invitation or prior notice, ignoring the diplomatic protocol of sovereignty. Croatian firms have surreptitiously set up the lines of a cellular phone network under control of the Croatian state Post and Telephone utility in Sarajevo, which covers all of Federation territory, while Croatian import-export firms take advantage of a special customs regime between Croatia and the Bosnian-Croat controlled western border to transit goods from other countries, repackaged as Croatian products, and collect customs duties for Croatian coffers that incidentally raises the price of the goods to Bosnian consumers. As James Ron argues persuasively, states act with far less restraint in frontier areas outside their borders than in the institutionally circumscribed areas occupied by national minorities *within* their sovereign borders.[37]

Equally important in the effect on Bosnia is the extent to which these arrangements require assertive international involvement in guaranteeing and defending Bosnian sovereignty against such threats. The decision of the World Bank to finance loans to Croatia for infrastructural development in Bosnia, because Croatia has a more credible economy, or the strategic partnership between the United States and Croatia that originated in Clinton administration policy on how to end the Bosnian war both send a signal to Croatia that it can continue to act with impunity in Bosnia. As long as the U.S. government views a joint Bosnian Muslim–Bosnian Croat Federation army and a military balance of power within Bosnia between its two entities as necessary to Bosnian sovereignty, this problem will remain. And as long as international officials see the primary defense of Bosnian sovereignty against Yugoslav threats to be a continuing oversight of Bosnian Serb politicians and Serbian Serb politicians and the removal of Bosnian Serbs from office or candidacy for any statements seen as challenging that sovereignty, then an international presence and interference in domestic sovereignty will remain the precondition of its international legal sovereignty.

Perhaps the most striking anomaly of the Bosnian agreement is the structural feature of three armies for one country. This might appear to be a consequence of the parties' insistence that they not demobilize until the peace had been consolidated and each felt safe—known from the well-discussed transitional role of third-party military interventions in providing a credible commitment to the peace in the first years after a civil war and the evidence that demobilization does not work until fundamental political arrangements have been settled.[38] In fact, this anomaly is the result of the wartime Washington Agreement and the follow-up at Dayton, an American-designed program, the "train and equip" program for a Federation army, deemed necessary to obtain Bosnian Muslim signatures on the peace plan and reluctant Congressional support for the original troop deployment in place of lifting the arms embargo and withdrawing UN troops.

The idea that a military balance *within* the country, between the two sides established by the Washington Agreement, was essential to deterring new war was the motivation for a semisecret side deal negotiated at Dayton. Although the program required the two parties to the Federation to create a joint defense structure before receiving training and equipment, quarrels between the two Federation partners over every issue of integrating their armies into one, including military doctrine, led the American officials behind the program to concede to a transition period, allowing command levels to unify over three years and army units to remain separate. This dispute reveals in part the changed attitude of the Bosnian Croats toward the Federation since the Washington Agreement, which they viewed only as a marriage of convenience at the time. Once a global cease-fire including Serbs had been signed, and particularly in the context of the strategic shifts on the battlefield in August–October 1995 favoring Croats, Bosnian Croats lost any incentive to cooperate with Bosniacs if the cooperation compromised their definition of national rights. Similarly, the Bosniac success in gaining an American ground presence in support of Bosnian independence, combined with the dwindling number of Croats in Bosnia, reduced their incentive to share power equally with Bosnian Croats. But the architects of the Federation and its army were not adjusting to this new, postwar situation. And although the program's officials say that, in principle, Bosnian Serbs from the RS are welcome to join the program, the conditions required in the first five years suggest that outsiders are not ready to conceive of the program differently than its origins, while donors other than the United States are unlikely to support this development (Middle Eastern donors such as Turkey, Saudi Arabia, Egypt, and the Gulf states were specifically targeted to finance this program, and they were hesitant even to contribute to a program that aided Bosnian Croats along with the Bosniacs they prefer to support alone). Critical to the "exit strategy" for American troops, a continuing military division of the country was more likely to lead eventually to renewed war between units that had been granted key traits of sovereignty without full recognition.[39]

WEAK DOMESTIC LEGITIMACY

In contrast to the anomalous institutions of the Dayton-constructed political system for Bosnia and Herzegovina, including its foreign affairs and defense, the domestic institutions being designed and tutored by outsiders for the economy and the provision of justice and human rights conform so directly to Western models that they face the opposite problem of sovereignty: no indigenous legitimacy. Although third-party mediation in ending civil wars always carries with it a heavy element of early interference with Westphalian sovereignty, the Dayton accord is on the extreme end, by imposing a design of international construction without any participation of the Bosnian people in its construction or amendment. Because the structure of guarantees for national rights built into the Dayton Constitution leaves no space for democratic politics in its implementation and possible reform, moreover, there is no clear way to generate a popular source for Bosnia's international legal sovereignty. Nonetheless, the aim of this international construction of economic institutions, an electoral system, and a system of justice (including police reform, a new judiciary, and international monitoring of human rights) is so that the international civilian and military presence can depart, leaving behind a sustainable, sovereign state.

Thus, for example, the World Bank and the European Union, as the internationally designated lead agencies for postwar reconstruction, designed a program for reconstruction and recovery to move the economy rapidly, within two years, from humanitarian assistance and reconstruction of war damage toward institutional and policy reforms aimed at cost recovery and "sustainability." Present at the Dayton negotiations, World Bank officials insisted (wrongly) that the problem of the former Yugoslavia had been over-centralization. Thus they reinforced the diplomatic process in creating a very weak central government. The International Monetary Fund, similarly, designed the central bank as a currency board for the first six years after the peace agreement so as to deprive the elected leaders of the ability to print money and spend the country into an inflationary spiral in response to the enormous needs of the economy and the population in the first period after war—even though the Bosnian leadership had maintained currency stability throughout the war and postwar peace would seem to need investment and employment as well as monetary stability. Although the technical assistance and institutional design from the IMF, World Bank, and U.S. Treasury aimed to create Western, market institutions out of the Bosnian socialist past in a manner directed throughout Eastern Europe and the former Soviet Union, the consequence was one familiar to other cases of immediate postwar construction with international assistance—setting up a conflict between the needs of the population for jobs, welfare, and a "peace dividend" and the view of donors that liberalization and privatization of the banking and tax systems, major firms and the housing sector, and a program for debt repayment should take priority.[40] Its dictate of a currency board arrangement, moreover, meant that monetary policy would be a direct translation of foreign revenues, and thus that the highest priority had to be placed on a customs regime and the transfer of customs duties to the central treasury—policies that became the greatest source of political dispute and stalemate between Bosnian Croat leaders and the Bosniac government in Sarajevo in the very same way as occurred in 1980s Yugoslavia. Although World Bank assistance becomes long-term debt for a Bosnian government, the distribution of these credits (a target of $5.5 billion over five years mobilized through pledging conferences) was decided either by program officers of the World Bank mission (and economic task forces in the Office of the High Representative in which Bosnians had no representation) or by the policy of political conditionality of the international community in rewarding those seen to be complying with specific provisions of the Dayton accord that mattered most to outsiders (cooperation with the international criminal tribunal and minority returns).[41]

Criticism of the inappropriateness of such reforms for the immediate postwar period lays the problem at the bureaucratic doorstep: that the international financial institutions (IFIs) are organized for a particular purpose and global role that cannot, for reasons of moral hazard and global responsibility as well as their founding charters, be altered and politicized as such critics are said to want. The primary operating characteristic is the IFIs make *sovereign loans*, using the authority of governments to guarantee repayment. Sovereignty for the IFIs thus reduces their risk, while it channels such assistance to governments and requires them to seek counterparts with sovereign authority who can be held accountable for the use of those credits and their eventual repayment. Accountability for loans is as important to donors as is consent to foreign militaries, and both follow directly from the legal concept of "recognition" in international legal sovereignty and thus voluntary (contractual) violations of Westphalian sovereignty. The result, however, was to reinforce the "deal" aspects of the Dayton peace accord and the "top-down" process of peace that has strengthened nationalist leaders in their goals, the resources at their command (and not flowing to rivals) to further those goals, and the anomalous characteristics of the political institutions that many view as nonviable.

Recognition of the negative consequences of this practice led the World Bank and some major single donors (followed later by the European Commission) to redirect aid away from national leaders to localities, taking great risks to innovate. Yet they did not change the essence of their procedures and charters, in seeking out authorities who could be held accountable. Thus, the redirected aid went to local officials who used the funds for projects they favored (and their political benefits) rather than what communities might have chosen.[42] Even "humanitarian agencies," Demichelis adds, "tried to deliver goods and services based on need, but became immersed in local politics and were forced to negotiate aid based on political splits."[43] Then, to get around this political bind, they distributed aid (such as housing materials in central Bosnia where both Bosnian Croats and Bosniacs live) in equal quantities— "50/50" deals between the two national groups regardless of population sizes or the extent of damage—so as to remain neutral and welcome. The mayors, in turn, had the greatest effective control over freedom of movement, the one task most critical to overcoming the results of war.[44] The European Commission took an even more radical step, in spring 1998, when criticism at the slow pace of their assistance programs (particularly in facilitating refugee return) led them to launch a major investigation of official corruption in Bosnia and to shift to the aid strategy of the U.S. Agency for International Development, namely, distributing aid through foreign, nongovernmental organization intermediaries.

Just as the norms of intervention by international financial institutions governed the construction of the Bosnian economy, so its system of justice was being reformed in conformity with Western (European or American) models and values and with the goal of reaffirming international norms of humanitarian law and the laws of war and a stronger commitment by the international community to their enforcement. Thus, the work of the International Criminal Tribunal for Former Yugoslavia, established in 1993, was a major priority of the international officials in the peace process. Originally intended to be a temporary substitute for Bosnian local courts and reliable police, the tribunal's larger goal globally made the voluntary extradition or arrest of indicted war criminals into a sine qua non of peace. Communities not cooperating with the tribunal (based on evidence that indicted war criminals were present in their midst) were deprived of economic aid, and for two years, until December 23, 1997, the U.S. government applied this condition on all of its aid and on the World Bank, through its seat on the board and its influence over the current president, to the entire RS. So important was this international agenda in the implementation of the Dayton accord in Bosnia that political disputes leading to delays and hurdles in that implementation were attributed wholly to the continuing presence in Bosnia of indictee and former president of the wartime Bosnian Serb political party, Radovan Karadžić. A Western campaign to isolate him and pressure him to go to The

Hague led during the summer of 1997 to a massive international effort, including the use of force by NATO troops in taking over TV transmitters, police stations, and holding new, special parliamentary elections in the RS, to shift the power center in the RS away from elected as well as party officials from his party to an alternative leadership and political center in Banja Luka and opposition parties in the north. Police reform and training by the International Police Task Force (a United Nations fielded mission) and bilateral training programs (particularly from the United States and Germany) required not only the downsizing of police units and their training in "community-based policing," but also the vetting of each and every certified policeman or woman to ensure that no indicted war criminal remained in police forces.

The Dayton Constitution, moreover, includes articles that allow for a substantial role of international persons in the judicial system. Article II and Annex 6 create an independent Human Rights Commission, composed of the Office of an Ombudsperson and a Human Rights Chamber. The chamber is a judicial body mirroring the European Court of Human Rights on which sit six Bosnians and eight "who may not be citizens of Bosnia and Herzegovina or of any neighbouring State, i.e., Croatia and Yugoslavia"—Europeans appointed by the Council of Europe.[45] Beginning in 1998, the Organization for Security and Co-operation in Europe (OSCE) mission was tasked to set up and reform an entirely new judiciary, and a U.S. Institute of Peace project organized the start of a Bosnian truth and reconciliation commission to take over the process of judging wartime behavior from The Hague Tribunal and hand it to Bosnians, with external support. The OSCE and the United Nations mission (UNMIBH) have human rights monitors in most towns and cities (acting under the mandate of the Dayton agreement). The Office of the High Representative and the U.S. team driving policy toward Dayton implementation chose to monitor and certify the Bosnian media, imposing rules on Bosnian Croat TV journalists, closing down Bosnian Serb television transmitters and handing control over some (and substantial financial aid) to new leaders who say they will be more cooperative, and building, with the help of George Soros, an independent television network operating largely in Bosniac areas. Much of the aid from governments and nongovernmental organizations is targeted at those who are willing to form cross-ethnic collaborations or cooperation across the Interentity Boundary Line (IEBL)—projects referred to as "multiethnic"—and at refugees and internally displaced persons willing to return to their prewar home where they would be a political minority. Rather than help to rebuild whole communities, this attempt to use aid to implant external values is implanting new sources of local tension and fragmentation.

Even the pace of change and sequencing of tasks in the construction of Bosnian sovereignty, with direct consequences for the state's uncertain viability, have been set by the conditions demanded by the United States for its military deployment. Decisions in 1996, for example, to move slowly on reintegrative projects or on the arrest of indicted war criminals were aimed at minimizing the risk to its soldiers, while the shift in pace during 1997 that amounted to a silent protectorate by the end of 1997, in which High Representative Carlos Westendorp began to assert his internationally assigned authority (called his "Bonn powers") to make any decisions for Bosnian leaders who did not meet the deadlines set by the international community, was made to enable (unsuccessfully, it turned out) the timely departure of American troops in June 1998. The distribution of ambassadorial appointments, laws on citizenship, passports, customs tariffs, and civil aerospace control, design of a flag, coat of arms, license plates, and common currency were all decided (to protect the sovereignty norm, the word used is "arbitrated") by Westendorp in order to speed the pace of Dayton's implementation and facilitate the withdrawal of foreign forces. But the consequence of this increasing foreign imposition of key aspects of domestic sovereignty was to make Bosnian politicians ever less accountable to their domestic constituents, indeed, able to bump decisions up to Westendorp that they preferred not to pay political costs to decide. And because Westendorp was not given the power to enforce these decisions, for this would violate Bosnian sovereignty, the decisions made between June and October 1997 had not yet been signed or published in the official gazette as of February 1998. The separate police forces in mixed communities of the Federation refused to integrate into single units, as required, and the ombudspersons were accused of being traitors to their people for internal criticism. And although elections were held every year, and the victory of nationalists out of favor with the international community suggested that Bosnian voters retained their autonomy, the common view locally by the third election (the second for national offices) in 1998 was that elections were being held to suit American interests, not to domesticate the Dayton accord. But instead of seeing the problem as a form of imperialism constrained by the norm of sovereignty, foreign observers insisted that Dayton was not working and that partition (into sovereign national units, of course) was the only viable and legitimate outcome.

Conclusion

Should anyone think that the Bosnian anomaly is a rare exception, international action and inaction toward the possibility of war in Serbia's Kosovo province followed the pattern established for former Yugoslavia and for Bosnia and Herzegovina. While everyone knew that the contest over this territory would eventually have to be solved, the decision that Kosovo was a part of Yugoslavia and that the territorial integrity of that state had to be respected seemed to stymie any other form of assistance to either or both parties (Belgrade or the majority Albanian population in Kosovo) to resolve a conflict that had resumed in 1981 and was at a stalemate after 1990. Indeed, the delay in acting toward a conflict that had emerged violently even before the 1991 secessions of Slovenia and Croatia was blatantly due to the sovereignty norm—that this was an internal affair of the Federal Republic of Yugoslavia (the new state of Serbia and Montenegro). Like Slovenes and Croats, Kosovo Albanians and their foreign supporters campaigned to persuade the international community that they had had sovereign rights in former Yugoslavia (although this was not the case) and that their democracy and human rights were under attack by the Belgrade regime. Even when violence had stolen the momentum, during late 1997 and early 1998, the major powers delayed another year in an active search to find a "legal" basis for intervention, such as a negotiated cease-fire that would issue the voluntary invitation to intervene. The longer they delayed, the more rapidly were alternatives being excluded by the search for negotiating partners who appeared to have sovereign characteristics, including the ability to implement agreements made. The fact that the NATO powers eventually intervened in the most extraordinary violation of sovereignty—an aerial bombing operation against Yugoslavia lasting more than eleven weeks, and an insistence on an international protectorate for this province of Serbia—does not negate the fact that the delays and choices were constrained by the norm of sovereignty or that the efforts to find a solution even during and after the military campaign were also shaped by that norm. NATO's actions in March–June 1999 provoked an international reaction to this blatant violation of sovereignty whose unintended consequences are clearly far ranging but at this writing still unknown. The UN Security Council Resolution that NATO powers finally conceded to seek, to seal the end of the campaign and the NATO victory in obtaining the withdrawal of Yugoslav security forces from the province and thus from de facto (and eventually de jure) control of part of its territory, declared a commitment to the territorial integrity and sovereignty of Yugoslavia. The resolution and the international protectorate, under United Nations mandate, insisted on yet another anomaly—full autonomy for Kosovo but no independence. While the characteristics of this outcome and its viability will provide a particularly interesting test of international tolerance for alternative arrangements, the very idea that there could be such a transition was losing ground under pressure from the United States to recognize reality and grant international legal sovereignty to Kosovo. The sole reason that its European allies were opposed to this move was its implications for the principle of sovereignty, and in the most immediate consequence, for the viability of the Bosnian accord and Bosnian sovereignty and the threat to the territorial integrity of neighboring Macedonia, where a large, territorially concentrated Albanian minority seemed ready for secession.

The cases of political and economic conflicts that evolve, with international help, into contests between or among more than one political community claiming rights to self-governance in shared territory form a potentially very large set, and according to the argument presented here, that set is getting larger as a result of the constraints of the sovereignty norm on attempts at their resolution. The fate of the Bosnian, and eventually Kosovo, cases have implications for a good part of the globe.

Notes

1. George Kenney used this term frequently in speeches and editorials during 1996–1997.

2. See Mearsheimer and Pape 1993; Kaufman 1996; Mearsheimer and Van Evera 1995. For the contrary view on partition, see Kumar 1997.

3. Huntington 1993; 1997.

4. See, for example, Dahl 1982 and Tilly 1975:3–83.

5. This argument was strong in the 1960s and 1970s in the literature generated by newly independent states and their "modernization" to explain political instability or ineffective economic development; see, for example, Pye 1962 and 1985 and Almond and Verba 1963, but it was a thesis with many critics.

6. See, for example, the discussion on page 118, of Karatnycky, "The Decline of Illiberal Democracy."

7. This realist logic is apparently behind the Mearsheimer support for Bosnian partition.

8. See the ongoing series of surveys done for the United States Information Agency throughout Bosnia since the Dayton accord.

9. Strang 1996:42.

10. Meyer 1999.

11. Efforts by the Organization for Security and Co-operation in Europe (OSCE) mission and the Office of the High Representative to reform the judiciary and their draft of the permanent electoral law—a task required by the Dayton accord—do aim at this constituency, but the rules of sovereignty require that they work through elected leaders who are not so committed.

12. Deudney 1996.

13. Szasz 1994:34–35. This was the first of ten advisory opinions by the EC's ad hoc Arbitration Commission, called the Badinter Commission after its chief judge, the distinguished French jurist Robert Badinter, which Szasz portrays as follows: "Brief, cursory and not always convincingly reasoned, they deal with many complex issues of international law in a few pages. Nevertheless, they constitute nearly all the judicial decisions we have on the subject of state dissolution" (34).

14. Gompert 1996:123.

15. On the German role, see Crawford 1996.

16. Szasz 1994:35. The full Guidelines and Opinions are published in *International Legal Materials* and also in *European Journal of International Law* 3 (1992): 182–85 and 4 (1993): 72–91.

17. Szasz 1994.

18. This constitutional claim was never definitively accepted in Yugoslav courts, legal circles, or constitutional interpretations, but a matter of ongoing dispute for over forty years.

19. Clause 8, European parliament resolution, cited by Gow 1991:308.

20. See John Boli, "Sovereignty from a World Polity Perspective," in this volume, on the critical criterion for sovereignty as the "source" of its authority, lodged in and delegated by the people.

21. The foreign minister of Slovenia after April 1990, Dimitrij Rupel, admitted at an Aspen Institute conference in Berlin in March 1992 that Slovene nationalists had "used Kosovo" to achieve their goal.

22. Discussions with Pieter de Gooijer, counselor for political-military affairs, Royal Netherlands Embassy, Washington, and Hans van den Broek's aide throughout this period; see also Owen 1995:31–33.

23. Owen 1995:32–33.

24. This article was written before the NATO air war against Yugoslavia and the changed status of the Kosovo question with international intervention. The problems created by the sovereignty norm—that the UN Security Council Resolution mandating this international intervention left Yugoslavia sovereign over Kosovo but that it was also obliged to withdraw all military, paramilitary, and police forces from the province and permit a NATO and UN transitional administration—for the international operation provide an equally compelling anomaly in support of the norm's operation to that of Bosnia and Herzegovina. It is not the subject of this article, however.

25. Given the later preoccupation with Slobodan Milošević, then president of Serbia, it is worth noting that the surveys in Serbia favored Marković over Milošević two-thirds to one-third. See Woodward 1995:128–29.

26.   The radicalizing effect of Slovenia's shift of the political agenda to the right, or more extreme options, can be analyzed with the lens of Cohen 1994.

27.   The first recognition of this problem came in the course of the Kosovo crisis of spring 1999, when the EU proposed a Stability Pact for the region that would reverse the continuing piecemeal, bilateral approach defined by the sovereignty norm that governed both international organizations like the United Nations and the World Bank and diplomats and policymakers of states. Whether the EU and its allies would be able to alter its approach so fundamentally would prove a particularly strong test of the sovereignty norm. Initial policies were not encouraging.

28.   One should not let Western standards influence judgment here, however, for studies of these "time-consuming" methods of decision making suggested greater efficiency than the system being proposed because, these studies argue, the incorporation of representatives of all "societal interests" and the deliberation to achieve consensus made decisions, once taken, far more legitimate and implementable. See, for example, Šiber 1979.

29.   Todorova 1997. This ambiguity also appears to have made outsiders nervous long before 1990–1991.

30.   There is a small problem with this argument, for Bosnian Serbs had not yet launched their war against Bosnian independence. The preceding war in Croatia, however, had already defined American official perceptions, namely, that the violence of the Yugoslav dissolution was due to Serbian aggression; distinctions among Serbian leaders in Belgrade, border Serbs in Croatia, Bosnian Serbs, and many other Serbs evaporated in the outsiders' acceptance of the nationalist discourse and tendency to see units in terms of sovereign characteristics.

31.   The following discussion is based on original field research by the author, including a period of employment as a special adviser to the head of the OSCE mission to Bosnia and Herzegovina in August–September 1998, interviews with participants in this implementation process in numerous visits to the country and in Washington, D.C., and continual following of news reporting from the country and from the international presence.

32.   In making this case for Bosnian independence, however, the United States had no difficulty ignoring principle in its policy toward Macedonia, in deference to Greece. The decision toward Bosnia and Herzegovina was also, most likely, in deference to Turkey and payback for support in Desert Storm, but American officials still made the case in terms of the principle—including the message they gave to Bosnian officials—so that one cannot say that the norm did not matter at all.

33.   Some limits were due to insufficient resources to fulfill their mandate, but these limits were secondary to the mandate itself.

34.   Hampson 1996:217.

35.   In 1996, when the representative of Republika Srpska on the trilateral presidency for Bosnia and Herzegovina negotiated the special relationship with Yugoslav authorities, the High Representative of the international community for Dayton implementation, Carl Bildt, ruled that such an agreement could be made only with the

all-Bosnian parliament, in contrast to the arrangement established in the 1994 Washington Agreement for Croatia and the other entity, the Bosnian Federation. But the extent of international direction of Bosnian domestic sovereignty is so great that the successor to Bildt in that office, Carlos Westendorp, ruled the opposite in 1998, that the nature of the special relationship had to be vetted by the international authorities but could be between the RS and Yugoslavia. Around the same time, objections from Bosnian Muslim leaders against the terms of the confederal agreement between Croatia and the Federation were ruled out of order by the same Office of the High Representative.

36.   It is possible that the new government in Zagreb elected January 2000 could change Croatian policies toward Bosnia-Herzegovina fundamentally and thereby transform the Dayton provision from a threat to a guarantee of Bosnian sovereignty. It is too soon to say, at the time of publication. Any provision so vulnerable to the party (or coalition) in power in Zagreb, however, can scarcely be a credible guarantee.

37.   See Ron 1999. While Ron focuses on Serbia's role toward Bosnia during the war, there is less evidence currently about Serbian intentions and penetration of eastern Bosnia since the Dayton accord than the massive evidence about Croatian penetration.

38.   See Walter 1994 and 1997; Berdal 1996; and Hampson 1996.

39.   The possibility of war, in the interest of Bosniacs, after international forces depart is the subject of frequent commentary in the Bosnian media. One particularly explicit scenario is described in "Bosnia-Herzegovina" 1997.

40.   This sets up a conflict between the strategy for peacekeeping, demobilization, and political and social reconciliation, on the one hand, and the IMF–World Bank group program for economic reform, on the other, that has been seen as an obstacle to peace in a number of other postconflict cases. See, for example, de Soto and del Castillo 1994 on El Salvador and Plan 1993 on Mozambique.

41.   It should be noted, however, that the World Bank officials did not favor political conditionality and fought the use of its assistance program as political leverage until it lost in May 1997.

42.   See the extremely interesting report from the field by Julia Demichelis 1997 for the U.S. Institute of Peace.

43.   Demichelis 1997:4.

44.   Demichelis praises the UN Development Program and the local initiatives program created by the World Bank as finding ways around this politically controlled distribution of aid.

45.   Aybay 1997.

References

Almond, Gabriel and Sidney Verba. 1963. *The Civic Culture: Political Attitudes and Democracy in Five Nations, an Analytic Study.* Princeton: Princeton University Press.

Aybay, Rona. 1997. "Appendix I: A New Institution in the Field: The Human Rights Chamber of Bosnia and Herzegovina." *Netherlands Quarterly of Human Rights* 15, no. 4: 529–58.

Berdal, Mats. 1996. *Disarmament and Demobilisation After Civil Wars: Arms, Soldiers, and the Termination of Armed Conflicts*. Adelphi Paper 303. London: IISS, Oxford University Press, August.

"Bosnia-Herzegovina: Article Says Bosniaks Preparing for War." *Slobodna Bosna* (a Sarajevo weekly), September 21, 1997, 19–21, in FBIS-EEU-97-267 (September 24, 1997).

Cohen, Youssef. 1994. *Radicals, Reformers, and Reactionaries: The Prisoner's Dilemma and the Collapse of Democracy in Latin America*. Chicago: University of Chicago Press.

Crawford, Beverly. 1996. "Explaining Defection from International Cooperation: Germany's Unilateral Recognition of Croatia." *World Politics* 48 (July): 482–521.

Dahl, Robert. 1982. *Dilemmas of Pluralist Democracy: Autonomy vs. Control*. New Haven: Yale University Press.

Demichelis, Julie. 1997. "Civilians Reaching Across Political Divides in Bosnia: Lessons Learned at the Grassroots Level and a Strategy of Institutionalization." October. Issued as a Special Report of the United States Institute of Peace in June 1998 as *NGOs and Peacebuilding in Bosnia's Ethnically Divided Cities*.

de Soto, Alvaro and Graciana del Castillo. 1994. "Obstacles to Peacebuilding." *Foreign Policy* 94 (Spring): 69–83.

Deudney, David. 1996. "Binding Sovereigns: Authorities, Structures, and Geopolitics in Philadelphian Systems." In Thomas J. Biersteker and Cynthia Weber, eds., *State Sovereignty as Social Construct*, 190–239. Cambridge: Cambridge University Press.

Gompert, David C. 1996. "The United States and Yugoslavia's Wars." In Richard H. Ullman, ed., *The World and Yugoslavia's Wars*, 122–44. New York: Council on Foreign Relations.

Gow, James. 1991. "Deconstructing Yugoslavia." *Survival* 33, no. 4 (July/August): 291–311.

Hampson, Fen Osler. 1996. *Nurturing Peace: Why Peace Settlements Succeed or Fail*. Washington: United States Institute of Peace.

Huntington, Samuel P. 1993. "The Clash of Civilizations?" *Foreign Affairs* 72, no. 3 (Summer): 22–49.

———. 1997. *The Clash of Civilizations and the Remaking of World Order*. London: Simon and Schuster.

Kaufman, Chaim. 1996. "Possible and Impossible Solutions to Ethnic Civil Wars." *International Security* 20, no. 4: 136–75.

Kumar, Radha. 1997. *Divide and Fall? Bosnia in the Annals of Partition*. London: Verso.

Mearsheimer, John J. and Robert A. Pape. 1993. "The Answer: A Three-Way Partition Plan for Bosnia and How the U.S. Can Enforce It." *New Republic*, June 14, 22–28.

Mearsheimer, John J. and Stephen W. Van Evera. 1995. "When Peace Means War." *New Republic*, December 18, 16–21.

Meyer, John. 1999. "The Changing Culture Content of the Nation-State: A World Society Perspective." In George Steinmetz, ed., *State/Culture: State Formation After the Culture Turn*, 123–43. Ithaca: Cornell University Press.

Owen, David. 1995. *Balkan Odyssey*. London: Victor Gollancz.

Plan, David N. 1993. "Aid, Debt, and the End of Sovereignty: Mozambique and Its Donors." *Journal of Modern African Studies* 31, no. 3: 407–30.

Pye, Lucian W. 1962. *Politics, Personality, and Nation-Building: Burma's Search for Identity*. New Haven: Yale University Press.

——. 1985. *Asian Power and Politics: The Cultural Dimensions of Authority*. Cambridge, Mass.: Belknap Press.

Ron, James. 1999. "Ghettos and Frontiers: Alternate Forms of State Violence in Bosnia and Palestine." Ph.D. diss., University of California at Berkeley, Department of Sociology.

Šiber, Ivan. 1979. *Delegatski Sistem i Izborni Procesi-Istraživanje*. Zagreb: Institut za Političke Nauke, Fakulteta Političkih Nauka.

Strang, David. 1996. "Contested Sovereignty: The Social Construction of Colonial Imperialism." In Thomas J. Biersteker and Cynthia Weber, eds., *State Sovereignty as Social Construct.*, 22–49 Cambridge: Cambridge University Press.

Szasz, Paul. 1994. "The Fragmentation of Yugoslavia." In *Proceedings of the 88th Annual Meeting of the American Society of International Law: The Transformation of Sovereignty*, 34–35. Washington, D.C., April 6–9.

Tilly, Charles. 1975. "Reflections on the History of European State-Making." In Charles Tilly, ed., *The Formation of National States in Western Europe*, 3–83. Princeton: Princeton University Press.

Todorova, Maria. 1997. *Imagining the Balkans*. New York: Oxford University Press.

Walter, Barbara. 1994. "The Resolution of Civil Wars: Why Negotiations Fail." Ph.D. diss., University of Chicago.

——. 1997. "The Critical Barrier to Civil War Settlement." *International Organization* 51, no. 3: 335–64.

Woodward, Susan L. 1995. *Balkan Tragedy: Chaos and Dissolution After the Cold War*. Washington, D.C.: Brookings Press.

10

The Road to Palestinian Sovereignty

Problematic Structures or Conventional Obstacles?

SHIBLEY TELHAMI

The perception that a future Palestinian state will have "problematic" sovereignty is justified for a number of reasons. But
that the Palestine case is selected as the problematic case in the Middle East
over, say, Lebanon indicates the obvious bias in favor of legal sovereignty over
the other forms of sovereignty: whereas Lebanon has full international legal
sovereignty, it has neither full Westphalian nor full domestic sovereignty. Indeed, in the limited territories that the less-than-sovereign Palestinian Authority controlled following the Oslo accords, it maintained more Westphalian
and domestic authority than did Lebanon; despite international law, Israel was
more likely to intrude into Lebanese territories than into the Palestinian ones.
The very sovereign order in the Middle East, set up by departing colonial
powers, witnessed a significant gap in the past half century between the full
legal status bestowed on the states and the degree of Westphalian and domestic
sovereignty they in fact held.

Nonetheless, the Palestinian case has been seen as problematic from the
inception of the current state system in the Middle East. Unlike what they
did with other territories they controlled, the British Mandate authorities de-
ferred final status for Palestine to the United Nations and withdrew from it
without leaving a new state in place. The United Nations' vision for Palestine
was not conventional: the 1947 partition plan (UN General Assembly Resolution 181), which envisioned the division of Palestine into one Arab and one
Jewish state, saw the need not only for a separate and unprecedented international status for Jerusalem but also for an "economic union" to be run by

a "joint economic board" whose membership would consist not only of representatives of each state but also of an equal number of foreign members appointed by the Economic and Social Council of the United Nations.

The problematic aspects of this case have historically emanated from four sets of factors: material factors, concerning disputes over limited territory and economic resources and concerning overlapping populations (issues of interdependence sovereignty); ambiguous and competing notions of Palestinian identity (Do the Palestinians constitute a "people" with a right to self-determination?); ambiguities about leadership (Who represents the Palestinians?); and opposition by important states, especially Israel, to a fully sovereign Palestinian state (thus preventing international law sovereignty). Throughout the history of the Arab-Israeli conflict, the Palestinians have lacked full international legal sovereignty, full domestic sovereignty, and full Westphalian sovereignty. Yet at least since 1974, the Palestinians have gradually, but with some setbacks, acquired more international legal sovereignty, reaching a new status at the United Nations in 1998 that is just short of that given to states; and since 1994, the Palestinians have acquired increasing domestic and Westphalian sovereignty. What are the sources of future obstacles to conventional Palestinian sovereignty?

My aim in this paper is to address these questions by examining the key junctures of change in the Palestinian status over time, as a way of gaining an understanding of the trade-offs that face a people, their aspiring leadership, and other states over the issue of sovereignty. At each juncture of change toward or away from fuller sovereignty, I will examine the causes and the consequences of change. In particular, change in five issues related to the evolution of Palestinian sovereignty will be explored: identity, leadership, territory, constituency, and international legitimacy.

Identity. How do Palestinians view themselves, and how does the world view them? Here, the Palestinians have moved from a homeless Arab people whose primary drive is the attainment of return to their homes to a differentiated national community whose primary drive is to achieve sovereignty on part of its territory.

Leadership. Who is recognized by the outside world as a leader, and who asserts some effective control over parts of the community? Here, claimants were numerous before 1967, ranging from Jordan to Egypt to Palestinian organizations that were subservient to Arab governments. The Palestine Liberation Organization (PLO) began to emerge as the primary leader in 1968 and was firmly established in 1974. In 1988, the Jordanians officially gave up claims to the West Bank, and in 1993, the PLO achieved the ultimate recognition when its foe, Israel, recognized it as the representative of the Palestinian people.

Territory. On what territory does leadership assert relative autonomy? Here, Palestinians had no autonomy before 1967; achieved some autonomy in Jordan (1968–1970) that challenged Jordanian sovereignty; achieved formalized autonomy, almost a state within a state, in Lebanon, which began in 1969 and climaxed just before the Israeli invasion of Lebanon in 1982; and achieved relative domestic and Westphalian sovereignty in parts of Gaza and the West Bank after the Oslo accords.

Constituency. What is the primary constituency for leadership? Since Palestinians were dispersed, the center of power has not been constant, moving from Egypt to Jordan to Lebanon to the West Bank and Gaza. Typically, territory and constituency overlap, but not always: while headquartered in Tunis from 1982 to 1993, the PLO turned to the West Bank and Gaza as its primary constituency.

International Legitimacy. Here, the Palestinian issue changed from a refugee question to a national self-determination question, with 1974 being the key juncture of change.

Three central arguments are made in this article: (1) The transformation of the Palestinian movement from one of refugees in 1948 to a national movement after 1967 was in part a result of the collapse of pan-Arabist norms and the rise of statist norms. The primary drive for the Palestinian movement following the 1948 *nakba* (catastrophe) was neither nationalism nor statehood, but the "right of return." The primary vehicle in the 1950s and 1960s was the pan-Arab movement that championed the Palestinian cause and offered the best potential for aiding it. By 1967, following a major Israeli victory over Arab forces, it had become clear that states were the primary actors in the Arab world, that the state of Israel was there to stay, and that pan-Arabism was a myth that delivered more Palestinian homelessness.[1] Those changes helped crystallize new Palestinian national aspirations focused on a distinct Palestinian national identity and on establishing a state. They also opened new opportunities for leadership competition. (2) The external responses to the Palestinian movement at every major juncture after the Israeli capture of Gaza and the West Bank in 1967, and the success of the PLO in establishing itself as the representative of the Palestinians, are best understood by examining the exchange between the PLO and key international actors: the PLO's demonstrated ability to assert increasing "domestic sovereignty" in return for a degree of international legal sovereignty, with some limitation on Westphalian sovereignty. That exchange was also the basis of the deal at Oslo in 1993. At every juncture of change, the "international" response to the Palestinian movement was determined by the interests of the powerful states. (3) The problems arising from the status of the Palestinian territories during the interim period following the Oslo accords were largely due to the absence of legal Palestinian sovereignty, and with important exceptions the status of Palestinian territories is likely to become less problematic with a final settlement. The primary obstacle to a conventional sovereignty outcome has been a more classic dispute over land.

The Palestinian Road to Sovereignty

The most dramatic breakthrough on the Palestinian road to sovereignty came in 1974 at an Arab summit conference in Rabat, Morocco, when Arab leaders unanimously agreed to designate the Palestine Liberation Organization as the "sole legitimate representative" of the Palestinian people. The deal struck at that conference exemplifies the typical exchange: the claimant (in this case the PLO) demonstrates and offers increasing degrees of domestic sovereignty in exchange for greater degrees of international law sovereignty; key international actors are more likely to accept the deal if there are practical constraints on the claimant's Westphalian sovereignty, since that translates into having influence with the claimant.

An analysis of both the causes and the consequences of this move is a good starting point for understanding the evolution of Palestinian nationalism. First, the move by the Arab states was a precondition for the subsequent admission of the PLO as an observer at the United Nations, a status that was eventually elevated in 1998 to a new status just short of membership; in other words, this was a milestone on the road to international law sovereignty. Second, the Rabat agreement resolved the issue of Palestinian representation. Jordan, which had annexed the West Bank in 1950, had maintained claims to Palestinian representation. And Egypt, during the pan-Arab era of Gamal Abd al-Nasser, had insisted on speaking for the Palestinians as leader of the Arab cause. Significantly, in 1974 the main PLO operations were neither in Egypt nor in Jordan, but in weak Lebanon, where the PLO maintained relative autonomy. In other words, this was the first unanimous Arab acknowledgment that the Palestinians, as a separate portion of the Arab world, have a right to represent themselves. Third, by virtue of designating the PLO as the representative of the Palestinians, Arab governments, and in particular Egypt, freed themselves to base their respective foreign policies primarily on their own national interest with minimal regard to the question of Palestine. In this regard, the Rabat resolution was a precondition for Egypt's separate peace with Israel in 1978. Ten years before, in 1964, Nasser's Egypt had backed the establishment of the PLO as a way of preventing other Palestinians from drawing Egypt into a confrontation with Israel, at a time when the PLO leadership was closely allied with Nasser and the Palestine Liberation Army was under Egyptian command.[2]

The significance of the episode in 1974 deserves further examination. Two questions are central: Why did Arab states agree to give up any claims to representation of the Palestinians? And, why was the PLO their choice? To be sure Jordan was reluctant to support the Rabat summit resolution. In fact, the Jordanians did not support a similar resolution in November 1973 at an Arab summit in Algiers and worked hard for months to prevent it. Jordan, which had annexed the West Bank in 1950 and controlled it until 1967, continued to pay salaries to former state employees and to recognize West Bankers as Jordanian citizens even after the Israeli occupation.[3] Jordan's support for the Rabat resolution was halfhearted; only in 1988, following the beginning of the Palestinian uprising (*intifada*), did Jordan officially give up its claims to the West Bank. But Jordan's position was weak. As former Egyptian foreign minister Ismail Fahmy put it: "After the October war, King Hussein's authority to speak for the Palestinians was being questioned. His prestige had reached its lowest ebb, because he had sat on the sidelines while Egypt and Syria fought."[4] Jordan was facing several important players in its attempt to legitimize its claims to represent the Palestinians: Egypt and Syria, the two combatants; Saudi Arabia, whose role in the Arab oil embargo was central and whose coffers were growing by the day, following the dramatic increases in oil prices; and also Algeria, whose financial contributions to the war effort gave it clout. In other words, once the others supported the resolution, it became impossible for Jordan to abstain. The key players were Egypt and Saudi Arabia.

For Egypt, this was an opportune moment to try to clinch a favorable deal with Israel. Its strategic position had dramatically improved following the war, and the position of President Anwar Sadat was enhanced at home and in the Arab world. Having given up on pan-Arab aspirations, Egypt did not want the Palestinians to jeopardize its deals with Israel.[5] For Saudi Arabia, whose stakes in regional stability were growing with its oil wealth, designating a single Palestinian representative who, with the help of substantial Saudi aid, could control the actions of other groups was in its interest. These key decisions by Egypt and Saudi Arabia were a precondition for the Rabat resolution, and the Rabat resolution was a precondition for the UN admittance of the PLO as an observer later that year.

The Rabat summit brought to the forefront two important sets of variables affecting the behavior of Arab states, and both involved the Palestinian issue. The first set involved norms of Arab identity; the second, particular interests of Arab states. Rabat was a meeting of members of the Arab League to address collective issues, a meeting at which they viewed their relations with the rest of the world partly from a collective perspective, which was enhanced by the impressive performance of Arab armies in the 1973 war and by the unprecedented coordination among several Arab states. Historically, the issue of Palestine (and earlier the issue of anti-imperialism) has been the most visible stick with which to measure Arab identity, because it was the first post–World War II issue that Arabs collectively faced (the defeat in the 1948 war), because it was the issue that the pan-Arabist movement of Gamal Abd al-Nasser championed, and because it was one of the few issues over which Arabs broadly agreed. In this spirit, the speeches at the Rabat summit reflected pride in the accomplishments of Arab armies in the October war but also a sense that the international community, as a consequence, was more responsive to Arab issues. The singular example invoked for this international responsiveness was the increasing acceptance of the PLO.[6] This was in no small part due to the PLO's success in creating in only a few years an almost automatic association in the minds of most Arabs between itself and the Palestinian cause, broadly speaking. So, to the extent that a dominant Arab norm existed at the time of the Rabat conference, that norm favored the PLO over Jordan.

But despite the collective Arab pride over the 1973 war, Arab nationalism had been on the decline since the 1967 war, and statist interests had been increasingly the driving force. Strictly from the point of view of state interests, the calculations of Arab governments on the issue of the PLO were not identical. While Syria, which was above all against Jordanian representation of the Palestinians,[7] saw that the most important Arab issue was Israeli withdrawal from Arab territories, not the choice between Jordan and the PLO, President Houari Boumedienne of Algeria declared that "Arab trusteeship over the Palestinians had to be lifted and . . . the sons of Palestine allowed to bear their historical responsibilities."[8]

Two critical states were Egypt and Saudi Arabia. Their calculations about the PLO came in the midst of heavy campaigning by the United States, Israel, and Jordan to prevent the designation of the PLO as the Palestinian representative. Jordan's calculations were obvious. Not only did Jordan aspire to regain control of the West Bank, but half its citizens were Palestinian. The designation would have significant consequences for both its identity and its security. Indeed, once the king of Jordan sensed that the PLO was the popular choice among Arab states, he sought to minimize the damage by persuading Egyptian president Sadat to issue a statement recognizing the PLO as the representative of the Palestinians outside Jordan. Bolstering Jordan's efforts were Henry Kissinger's lobbying on its behalf and its threat to stay out of the Geneva conference negotiations between Israel and its Arab neighbors that Sadat badly wanted.[9] Israel's insistence on keeping the PLO out of the negotiations and its preference to deal with Jordan on the issue of the West Bank were also an asset for Jordan's case.[10]

As for Saudi Arabia, it was emerging as a powerful player in Arab politics because of large increases of oil revenues that it was now willing to employ politically, and it was less vulnerable to U.S. pressure than at any time before. In its relation with Saudi Arabia, the United States was more concerned about oil embargoes than PLO recognition. Aside from the Saudi lack of trust in Jordan's King Hussein, they simply had few levers with him, and in practice he wielded less influence with the Palestinian people than did the PLO. The PLO controlled guerrilla action more than Jordan, and the Saudis were conscious of that fact. Through their financial support, the Saudis stood to gain more influence with the PLO than with Jordan. Normatively, their position would also garner broader Arab support. This left the key position of Egypt.

On the one hand, Egyptian calculations strongly favored the PLO. Egypt had been one of the stronger supporters of the Palestinians, had backed the establishment of the PLO, and had had a rocky relationship with Jordan. The Egyptian foreign ministry was clear in its assessment of the issue of representation. Former Egyptian minister Ismail Fahmy described Egypt's strategy concerning the convening of the Geneva conference in December 1973 this way: "In stage one we should put an end to the Jordanians' claim that they speak for the Palestinians. In stage two we should give official recognition to the legitimacy of the PLO and its political role. In stage three we should prepare a framework for the recognition of the Palestinians' right to statehood. In stage four we should help negotiate and formalize the relationship between the Jordanians and Palestinian state, if they so desired."[11] Fahmy also suggests that the absence of a Jordanian-Israeli agreement was to due to Egypt's "veto," as Egypt warned Secretary of State Henry Kissinger that "any move on the Jordanian front made without legitimate Palestinian representatives would adversely affect Egyptian-American relations."[12]

But Egypt was also anxious to exploit the leverage of the 1973 war to conclude a quick deal, and it was realistic about Israel's positions. Moreover, Sadat was trying to forge a new relationship with the United States and to be responsive, to the extent possible, to Henry Kissinger's lobbying on behalf of Jordan by at least making the decisions at Rabat ambiguous.[13] Hermann Eilts, former U.S. ambassador to Egypt, revealed (at the Middle East Institute conference on the 1973 war, Washington, D.C., October 11, 1998) that Sadat told him on the eve of his departure to the Rabat summit that Jordan would be the one to represent the Palestinians. He later received a call from Egyptian officials trying to assure him that President Sadat was not trying to mislead him, but that "things went in a different direction." In his own speech at the Rabat conference, however, "Sadat proposed the establishment of a Palestinian government in exile."[14] Sadat's proposal came after two important allies at the conference took the lead: President Boumedienne of Algeria declared, "Algeria does not recognize anybody to speak for the Palestinians except the PLO." The next speaker was King Faisal of Saudi Arabia, who expressed support for Boumedienne's stand.[15]

The mutual benefits of the Rabat deal—offering the PLO more internal legal legitimacy in exchange for increasing PLO enforcement of domestic sovereignty—were quickly clear: the PLO, now a key independent Arab actor, was the recipient with Egypt, Syria, and Jordan of a significant financial package from the oil states totaling $2.3 billion. Within a month, on November 23, 1974, the UN General Assembly granted the PLO permanent observer status by a vote of 95 to 17 with 10 abstentions. On the other hand, for Arab states seeking more regional peace, the PLO moved to prove its ability and willingness to deliver: on November 27, the PLO announced the arrest of twenty-six Palestinians in connection with the hijacking of a British airliner the prior week, stating that the PLO bears its responsibility more and more in putting an end to such kinds of operations.

The Rabat deal may have resolved the issue of Palestinian representation once and for all if it weren't for two significant players: Israel and the United States. Israel preferred Jordan to the PLO not only because of long-standing cooperation behind the scenes with Jordan and public Israeli views of the PLO, but also for practical reasons: dealing with Jordan over the West Bank meant that Israel did not have to address the issue of "Palestinian return" or any questions that would come from identifying the Palestinian issue as a "national" issue; it would also enable Israel to retain bigger parts of the West Bank, since the issue of "viability" of an independent Palestinian state would not come up. Israel certainly had more influence with Jordan than with the PLO and still believed in 1974 that Palestinian support for the PLO in the West Bank and Gaza was not solid and that it could tip the balance in favor of Jordan there. The U.S. position was bound to Israel, since the United States needed Israeli cooperation in the negotiations. Thus, the Israelis extracted a price from the United States over their acceptance of a disengagement-of-forces agreement with Egypt a few months after Rabat: a secret U.S. commitment not to recognize or negotiate with the PLO before the latter recognized Israel and accepted UN Resolutions 242 and 338.[16] That deal stood until 1988, when the PLO was seen to meet U.S. conditions for the start of a dialogue.[17]

Why the PLO? The Emergence of the PLO and Palestinian Nationalism

That Arab states designated the PLO specifically as the Palestinian representative was not a coincidence, of course. By 1974, the PLO had established itself as the dominant player among Palestinians and had acquired some "domestic sovereignty" in parts of Lebanon, where it had a civilian constituency of about 300,000. By then, most Palestinians had also given up on pan-Arabism, and Palestinian nationalism was emerging as the dominant identity.

Before the 1967 war, the Palestinians lacked effective independent leadership and heavily relied on Arab states, especially Egypt, for help with their cause. Even the PLO, which was established in Cairo in 1964, was neither effective nor independent under the leadership of Ahmad Shukairi. Most important, Palestinians lacked autonomy on a single piece of land. A key turning point for the PLO, and especially its main faction, Fatah, was the battle of Karameh in March 1968. Coming on the heals of the devastating Arab defeat in the 1967 war, which resulted in Israeli control of the rest of Palestine and in a new wave of refugees, the battle of Karameh became an instant legend of the Palestinian movement. Although many of its details are disputed, the battle involved about fifteen hundred Israeli soldiers raiding PLO bases in the town of Karameh, Jordan, where approximately three hundred Palestinian commandos were stationed. The Palestinians were able to engage the Israeli forces in a bloody battle that resulted in the deaths of twenty-eight Israelis and the wounding of ninety. But word quickly spread of Palestinian heroics with claims of much bigger Israeli losses, and comparing the relative success of the PLO to the collective failure of Arab states in the 1967 war. Karameh, which means "dignity" in Arabic, became a metaphor for Palestinian self-reliance. Within twenty-four hours, five thousand volunteers applied to join Fatah forces.[18] Armed with its new popularity among the Palestinians and in many parts of the Arab world, Fatah turned to challenge the traditional PLO leadership, which was seen to be subservient to Arab governments. The Fatah central committee appointed Yassir Arafat as its representative at the Fourth Palestine National Council (PNC) meeting in Cairo, in July, and he was subsequently elected chairman of the PLO Executive Committee. The Fourth PNC also passed a revised National Charter that rejected the language of UN Resolution 242, passed after the 1967 war, which had addressed the Palestinians as "refugees." The charter declared that "the Palestinian Arab people assert . . . their right to normal life in Palestine and to exercise their right to self-determination and sovereignty over it" and that "the Palestine Liberation Organization, the representative of the Palestinian revolutionary forces, is responsible for the Palestinian Arab people's movement in its struggle to retrieve its homeland . . . and exercise the right of self-determination in it."[19]

Between 1968 and 1970, the new support for the PLO, especially among new refugees but also among other Arabs looking for signs of action to avenge the 1967 defeat, emboldened Palestinians to the point of challenging Jordanian sovereignty. The PLO came to have a significant constituency, to establish a police force and a radio station, and to organize public demonstrations. A series of dramatic airplane hijackings in 1970 by the Popular Front for the Liberation of Palestine (which was denounced and suspended by the PLO), three of which ended in aircraft being blown up on Jordanian territory, finally dragged the PLO and the Jordanian army into a bloody war that did not spare civilians. In what became known as Black September, the Jordanian army defeated the PLO forces and forced many out, mostly to Lebanon. This was another example of Palestinian abandonment: with the exception of a limited and failed Syrian effort, the primary Arab intervention, including that by Egypt's popular President Nasser, was diplomatic. To add to the end-of-Arabism gloom among the Palestinians, Nasser died only one day after his mediation effort.

For the next decade and up until the Israeli invasion of Lebanon in 1982, the PLO turned parts of Lebanon into a state within a state. The Palestinians were helped by an agreement with the Lebanese government in 1969, brokered by Nasser, that gave the PLO the rights to administer and police Palestinian camps in Lebanon and to carry out operations against Israel from Lebanese territories. This gave Palestinian leaders for the first time relative territorial autonomy and a sizable immediate constituency. The new international legitimacy bestowed on the PLO in 1974 also brought significant new resources, mostly from the oil-rich states. Despite the 1975–1976 Lebanese civil war in which the PLO took part, its autonomy in south Lebanon reached a climax in 1981–1982.

Between Leadership and the Public

As noted, the PLO successfully established itself as a representative of the Palestinians by appearing more effective than Arab governments (as in Karameh), as an administrator in Palestinian camps where a vacuum of power existed (as in Lebanon), and as a fund generator (for the West Bank and Gaza); however, there is another side to the story. The breakthrough after the 1967 war was not merely one of replacing one set of representatives with another but also involved a transformation in community aspirations and priorities— in communal identity. The new PLO represented these aspirations well, and its success at securing international recognition for the Palestinian people was a measure of its success at garnering public support, even among Palestinians who were not under its direct control.

On this issue, I take the view that modern Palestinian nationalism, which placed priority on an attainment of an independent Palestinian state, was a product of the Palestinian experience of the second half of the twentieth century, during which the pursuit of the return to all of Palestine and dreams of Arab unity ran against the reality of Middle East politics: the Middle East is a world made of state actors, and Palestinian interests had no chance of being met without a state of their own. As Rashid Khalidi put it: "The quintessential Palestinian experience, which illustrates some of the most basic issues raised by Palestinian identity, takes place at a border, an airport, a checkpoint: in short, at any one of those many modern barriers where identities are checked and verified. What happens to Palestinians at these crossing points brings home to them how much they share in common as a people. For it is at these borders and barriers that the six million Palestinians are singled out for 'special treatment,' and are forcefully reminded of their identity: of who they are, and of why they are different from others."[20]

This is not to say that Palestinian identity had no older roots or that other forms of identity did not continue to compete, especially Islamic ones. More-over, ambiguities remained. A telling example was the Palestinian predica-ment immediately after PLO forces were pushed out of Lebanon by Israeli forces, without much intervention from Arab states with the exception of a partial Syrian engagement. Although frustrated Palestinians sought to distance themselves more from Arab governments, such a move would result in iso-lation from Arab governments but also could result in the erosion of support among Arab masses as well. If Palestine is strictly a Palestinian issue, then how can other Arabs be expected to make it a major concern? This dilemma for Arabs at large can be seen in a Saudi student's letter to the editor of *Falastine Althawra*, the central organ of the PLO, requesting an explanation for the choice of Cyprus as the center for Palestinian publications. "Why," asked the student, "did you not choose an Arab state as your center, as we all would have expected? . . . I had not expected that the PLO would be so ungrateful to all the aid provided to it by the Arabs . . . especially since the Liberation of Palestine is the primary Arab concern." The editor's reply was also telling. "The PLO is not ungrateful," the editor replied. "The deposits of one Arab state in the United States provide a sufficient budget for the Liberation of Palestine in a year. Payment in blood cannot be compared with monetary payments. This revolution is indeed Arab, *but* Palestinian decisions shall re-main independent regardless of the cost." Yet the same *Falastine Althawra*, in considering the debate on *qawmiyya* (Arab nationalism) versus *qataniyya* (statism) concluded in its leading article that the Palestinian considers himself "first Arab, second Arab and third Palestinian." In practice, however, Palestin-ian behavior more closely resembled the editorial response to the Saudi student.

Given rising Palestinian aspirations for statehood, which took precedence over the issues of justice, return, and Arab nationalism, public support for the PLO grew as its international legitimacy grew.

Bestowing International Legitimacy and Getting Peace

The international legitimacy the PLO attained between 1974 and 1982 is un-precedented for a nonstate actor. Besides its special UN status, its representatives kept offices in more than a hundred states worldwide. This drive for legitimacy was accelerated in 1981 and 1982 with great success. States from Malaysia to the Soviet Union elevated PLO representation to full diplomatic levels. A similar trend was evident in Western Europe, though to a lesser extent. Greece granted diplomatic status to the PLO during Arafat's visit there. Austrian chancellor Bruno Kreisky received Arafat as if he were a head of state. The foreign minister of France met with Arafat in Beirut. Even in the United States there were signs of more receptiveness toward the PLO. First, former National Security Adviser Zbigniew Brzezinski urged "some form of dialogue" with the PLO. Then a joint statement by former presidents Gerald Ford and Jimmy Carter echoed the same advice. Two days later President Ronald Reagan was quoted as saying, "there has never been any refusal to talk with the PLO," only a condition that it recognize Israel. Representatives of the PLO were participating in an increasing number of international organizations. Even the World Bank annual meeting called on its executive directors to review the issue of granting observer status to the PLO.

As this trend continued, it was becoming clear that PLO support among Palestinians was growing even in areas not directly under its control. The first indicator came in 1976, in the municipal elections held in the Israeli-controlled West Bank. PLO-supported candidates defeated incumbents, despite Israeli and Jordanian roles in the elections. By May 1982, a poll taken by *Time* (May 24, 1982) showed that 86 percent of Palestinians in the West Bank saw the PLO as their representative. PLO-supported demonstrations in the West Bank and Gaza, which led to bloody confrontations with Israeli forces, made international headlines in 1981 and 1982.

Perhaps the most important recognition of PLO power came from the Likud government in Israel when it entered into a cease-fire arrangement with the PLO in 1981, arranged by American envoy Philip Habib. The Israeli and Palestinian calculations during that episode and the subsequent Israeli invasion of Lebanon in 1982 are informative for the issues at hand.

Between International Legitimacy, Domestic Sovereignty, and International Peace

If international actors bestow international legitimacy on national actors in exchange for relative peace, the evidence is that it works. Between 1968 and 1974, the annual average of reported "commando" operations by all Palestinian groups appearing in the daily chronology of the *Middle East Journal* was 29.4. That annual average dropped to 18.0 in the 1975–1981 period. Many of the operations were conducted by non-PLO groups, but the PLO was in a better position to enforce discipline. Indeed, the PLO found itself in a unique dilemma in Lebanon, which ultimately led to its cease-fire agreement with Israel—despite the contradiction inherent in a "liberation" organization accepting the status quo. Although this move was partly intended to generate more international support, there were other important reasons for the Israeli-Palestinian cease-fire.

The PLO dilemma in Lebanon was this: although it had accumulated significant forces with a good amount of military hardware, those forces did not constitute an army in the conventional sense. Nor could it be imagined that the PLO, in the Lebanese arena, was in a position to build an army that could confront the Israeli army *conventionally*. The Palestinian forces were capable of guerrilla operations against Israel, not more. Effective guerrilla operations require neither thousands of troops nor tons of heavy military hardware. They require dispersion of forces, not centralization. Consequently, the centralized deployment of the PLO's forces in southern Lebanon retarded its only viable military options. Centralization helped the PLO politically, but at the expense of its military effectiveness. For any small guerrilla operation it could undertake, Israel could hit hard where it hurts most. There was no place to hide. The costs outweighed the benefits. This military dilemma partially accounts for the PLO's willingness to enter an indefinite cease-fire agreement with Israel.

But centralization also meant the ability to enforce discipline. Within the PLO, the stronger groups could control the smaller ones without outside interference. Arafat and Fatah, therefore, were able to control the smaller, more extremist organizations and punish them when they violated the rules. This was manifested in the fact that for nearly a year, contrary to the expectations of many, the extremist groups were successfully prevented from breaking the cease-fire agreement with Israel.

From the Lebanon Invasion to the Intifada

This is not a place to address the Israeli calculations in invading Lebanon despite the relative success of the cease-fire with the PLO or to discount the domestic Israeli concerns about the growing military power of the PLO in

Lebanon. But there is little doubt that one aim of the strategy was the West Bank, not Lebanon. The growing power and legitimacy of the PLO inspired Palestinian nationalism and resistance in the West Bank, making the Likud government's aims of attaining eventual sovereignty there more difficult to achieve.

Until the Palestinian *intifada* in 1987, relative Israeli power allowed Israel to oscillate between two visions: one less religious, less territorial, and more pragmatic; the other more ideological, more linked to historical symbols, and more expansionist with claims to the West Bank. As the first vision prevailed in the early days of the state, through Labor Party dominance, the primary Palestinian objectives of return to the homeland were incompatible with any Jewish state; the game was zero-sum. As Palestinian nationalism crystallized in the mid-1970s with the aim of establishing a state on part of Palestine, thus opening the door for territorial compromise, the second vision took hold in Israel, through the ascension of Likud to power in 1977. The problem was not that there was no room for a conventional solution to the sovereignty problems of both, but that there was a conventional fight over how, or even if, to divide the land. It was not a coincidence that Oslo occurred on the first occasion of the Labor Party's return to power: between then and the Israeli election in 1992, Labor saw only partial power through a coalition government with Likud.

The Likud government strategy nearly worked. The PLO headquarters after 1982 moved to Tunis—far from the front with Israel and from major Palestinian populations. Their relevance was further marginalized by the Iran-Iraq war (1980–1988), which became the primary issue of concern to Persian Gulf states in the mid-1980s. The PLO still held two important levers: it maintained international political support, and it used financial support from the gulf to affect politics in the West Bank and Gaza.

The tide shifted with the advent of the Palestinian *intifada* in 1987, a spontaneous uprising supported and later orchestrated by the PLO. The costs to Israel made the status quo uncomfortable. And it forced the PLO into diplomatic initiatives in 1988, including accepting the American conditions for recognizing Israel and renouncing terrorism, in exchange for a limited dialogue with the United States. Although the PLO also declared "statehood," the absence of territorial autonomy and of any real strategy to push it through international organizations diminished its significance. In any case, these actions were superseded by the Oslo accords.

The Deal at Oslo: International Law Sovereignty for Domestic Sovereignty

After the Iraq-Kuwait war of 1991, the PLO reached perhaps its lowest point since 1974. Stranded in remote Tunis and increasingly losing support in the West Bank and Gaza to rising Islamist groups, it managed to take a position that alienated not only the remaining superpower but also its key Arab allies, Saudi Arabia and Egypt. Perhaps more important, it lost its major source of income from the Arab gulf states, which had enabled it to maintain influence in the West Bank and Gaza. Yet within three years, it was well on its way to establishing its first foothold in Palestine. Examining this deal reveals what other junctures of the Palestinian drive toward sovereignty have revealed: an exchange occurs between the key international actors, in this case especially Israel and the PLO—increasing domestic sovereignty for increasing international legal sovereignty and limitations on Westphalian sovereignty. No alternative to the PLO could deliver such a deal.

From the point of view of Palestinian critics of the Oslo accords, that's just the point: the Declaration of Principles agreement (DOP), which gave the Palestinians minimal territorial control and postponed the major issues that had presented obstacles to a Palestinian-Israeli agreement in the past (Palestinian sovereignty, Jewish settlements, the status of Jerusalem, the return of Palestinian refugees), resulted strictly from "capitulation" by a PLO on the verge of collapse. In this view, it is telling that the DOP came about without the U.S. pressure on Israel that Arabs traditionally believed was required—perhaps even despite the reluctance of the United States to deal directly with the PLO. In short, Israel did not need to be pressured by anyone because what the PLO offered Israel was too good to be turned down.

The assassination of Israeli prime minister Yitzhak Rabin and the subsequent position of the Likud-led Israeli government after the 1996 elections made clear the deal was not good enough for many Israelis. But it is important to understand what sort of concessions each side made. While it is true that most of the concessions leading to the breakthrough came from the Palestinian side and that those concessions were largely driven by a weakened Palestinian position, it is not obvious that Israel had no other option to this agreement. (If it were so obvious why did no one predict it?) Nor is it obvious that the Palestinians saw the terms of the DOP as inferior to the terms of the Camp David Accords, which they had rejected many years earlier.

A comparison of the DOP and the Palestinian autonomy component of the Camp David Accords reveals two significant differences that made the DOP appear more favorable to the Palestinians. First, the central issue of territorial control was addressed differently. In the vision of former Israeli prime minister Menachim Begin, Palestinian autonomy related largely to affairs of the people of the West Bank and Gaza (Judea and Samaria), not to territorial control. In this vision, derived not only from security concerns but also from principled claims, Israel intended to control the land in the autonomous areas with the continued ability to build and expand Jewish settlements. In contrast, the vision in the Declaration of Principles Agreement grants authority over land in autonomous areas to the Palestinian Authority. Since land has been one of the core issues of conflict between Israel and the Palestinians, this difference between the Camp David Accords and the DOP should not be underestimated, and it is unlikely that a Likud-led government would have readily agreed to the terms of the DOP on this issue. In essence, even during the transitional period of autonomy, the PLO was offered Westphalian sovereignty over the territories fully under its control, in exchange for being held responsible as the domestic sovereign.

Second, the two agreements differed on the question of Palestinian "peoplehood." Although the term *Palestinian people* is employed in the text of the Camp David Accords, a letter from President Carter to Prime Minister Begin, written at the urging of Begin and later appended to the accords, stated that Carter acknowledged that "in each paragraph of the agreed framework document, the expressions 'Palestinians' or 'Palestinian People' are being and will be construed and understood by you as 'Palestinian Arabs' " and that "in each paragraph in which the expression 'West Bank' appears, it is being and will be understood by the Government of Israel as Judea and Samaria." This interpretation continued to be held by the Likud-led government of Prime Minister Yitzhak Shamir, which sought to differentiate between "residents of Judea and Samaria" and Palestinians residing outside those territories. Even after the Gulf War, while facing an administration (that of President George Bush) that it considered antagonistic, the Shamir government managed to prevail on this question by excluding any Palestinians from the "outside" from the Palestinian delegation in the U.S.-arranged negotiations inaugurated in Madrid, Spain. In contrast, the DOP was signed not by the Palestinian negotiation team from Madrid but by the PLO, most of whose leadership came from outside the West Bank and Gaza. Moreover, the signing of the agreement was preceded by a letter from Israeli prime minister Yitzak Rabin to PLO chairman Yassir Arafat declaring that the Israeli government recognized the PLO as the representative of the Palestinian people. In addition, the Israelis agreed that concerns such as sovereignty, the return of refugees, and the status of settlements were legitimate issues in the negotiations although their discussion would be postponed. Given the centrality of the issues of "peoplehood" and "unity" of the Palestinians, this shift in the Israeli position is significant. It is unlikely that any representatives of the Palestinians would have been willing to accept an agreement that did not contain this component. In essence, the Palestinians saw this as a promise of legal sovereignty upon final settlement.

What did Israel get in return? Israel faced the following situation. It confronted an escalating *intifada*, especially in Gaza, which had demonstrated that Israel itself could not assert domestic sovereignty over the Palestinian territories. Jordan was no longer a viable contender for representing the Palestinians, having formally renounced its claims in 1988. There were only two other alternatives to the PLO: Hamas, the militant Islamist organization that did not recognize Israel and engaged in bloody attacks, and local Palestinians from the West Bank and Gaza, who had been participating in the Madrid-process negotiations. Needless to say, the first option was not an Israeli preference, but the second was Israel's hope. By the end of 1992, however, as Israel became anxious to disengage from Gaza, it was becoming clear that the local leaders could not deliver and had no effective local control. As former Israeli negotiator Uri Savir points out, the local Palestinians were simply receiving orders from the PLO anyway: "we were actually negotiating with Yasser Arafat by fax" at the same time that the PLO weakness after the Gulf War made it more willing to compromise.[21] Only the PLO could deliver a deal that offered the Palestinians as little as Israel was willing the accept.

The contours of the deal began emerging in March 1993 in Rome. It came as attacks against Israelis by Islamist groups escalated, especially in Gaza, during the Labor Party's first year in office, and progress in the Madrid process was slow. Some Labor leaders, pessimistic about immediate prospects for an agreement with the Palestinians, were considering a unilateral Israeli withdrawal from Gaza. One of the groups that brought PLO officials and Israelis together behind the scenes, a study group of the American Academy of Arts and Sciences, met in Rome in March 1993 (a meeting I attended). A leading Israeli, General Shlomo Gazit, brought a proposal for unilateral Israeli pullout for the group to discuss, because Israel was anxious to exit Gaza even in the absence of agreement but was fearful of the rise of Hamas or of complete disorder. The agenda was preempted by a surprise announcement by the PLO official present. The PLO, he announced, was now ready for a "Gaza-first" agreement with Israel on two conditions: the PLO would take over directly in areas evacuated by Israel, and "concrete" gestures would be made to indicate that there would be an eventual link between Gaza and the West Bank, so that a "Gaza-first" would not be a "Gaza-only" agreement. He explained that he was as anxious as the Israelis to control the rising power of Hamas before it was too late. The mutual advantages of such an exchange became instantly clear.

Ultimately, the deal offered Israel an end to the *intifada*, which was weighing most heavily on Israel, and the end to the job that the Israeli military had not cherished: policing civilian populations. Second, Israel expected the Palestinians to contain the rising Islamist movements and prevent attacks on Israel. The deal was simple: PLO responsibility for domestic sovereignty and some Westphalian sovereignty, in exchange for more legal sovereignty and some limitation on Westphalian sovereignty.

Some of the problems in implementing the Oslo accords and in gaining broader Israeli and Palestinian support for them were due to the absence of "interdependence sovereignty," especially in the case of the terrorist bombings. Although each blamed the other for not doing enough or doing too much, the phenomenon was not fully under the control of either side, given the proximity of Palestinian and Israeli towns. But there were two bigger obstacles, however. First, the absence of Palestinian legal sovereignty on contiguous territories led to a situation where Israeli security-related measures (which were often more responsive to domestic politics than to real security needs), such as the closure of the territories, significantly weakened the Palestinian economy, thus undermining the PLO's domestic sovereignty. Because the Palestinian territories had no international law sovereignty, these closures meant closure to the outside world and closure between noncontiguous portions of the territories. This structure made it difficult for both sides to make concessions in the negotiations. Second, the interim arrangement itself became a factor in the negotiations. The dilemma for the Palestinians, who lacked levers in the negotiations with Israel, was this: if the PLO delivers domestic sovereignty (full control of Hamas and prevention of *intifada*), Israel's incentives to make further concessions become minimal; if the PLO doesn't deliver, Israel's strategic needs to make further concessions increase, but the short-term political pressures prevent this from happening. Thus Arafat's dilemma in sometimes "threatening" to unleash the *intifada* has been a double-edged sword. This became even more problematic with the outcome of the Israeli elections in 1996, which brought Prime Minister Netanyahu to power, an opponent of the Oslo accords who diminished Arafat's incentives by seeking to undermine his international legitimacy.

The more important question in the end pertains not to the problematic nature of the Palestinian authority in its transitional state of affairs, but to whether the final status of the Palestinian territories will also be problematic because of some unusual features of the Israeli-Palestinian conflict. Here, the primary obstacles are conventional, distributional issues, with some exceptions.

The exceptions are important ones: Jerusalem and a passageway from Gaza to the West Bank. The issue of Jewish settlements in the West Bank will be difficult, even though 80 percent of the settlers are concentrated in 10 percent of the land. Will the others have extraterritorial status, be citizens of Palestine, or will they move?

But the biggest issue for Israel regarding a legally sovereign Palestinian state is security. Here, most analysts agree that any Palestinian state will have significant limitations placed on its military forces and on its ability to forge military alliances with other states. In theory, this concession undermines the very concept of legal sovereignty; in practice it makes little difference. Limitations can be handled through bilateral "arms control agreements" that address the issue without undermining the state's legal status in international institutions. In any case, a small Palestinian state could not compete with Israel militarily, even if it wanted to, and there is something to learn from the complaints of many in the small gulf states who oppose their government's huge military expenditures, knowing that they will never make a serious difference in war.

The biggest security threat to Israel from a Palestinian state will not be a conventional one, but the threat of terrorism. Here the best formula remains the conventional formula: full legal sovereignty for domestic sovereignty, with someone to hold responsible.

Notes

1. In an earlier work (Telhami 1990), I argued that this shift away from pan-Arabist norms was itself a function of change in the distribution of power in the Arab world.
2. Smith 1988:188–89.

3. Jordan was the only state to offer Palestinians citizenship. This came back to haunt Jordan in its conflict with Israel when Israelis began describing Jordan as a Palestinian state by virtue of its large Palestinian population. Even after the 1991 Gulf War, with Jordan having renounced its claims to the West Bank, it readily accepted tens of thousands of new Palestinian refugees expelled from Kuwait.

4. Fahmy 1983:96.

5. For a detailed explanation of the decline of Egypt's pan-Arab aspirations, see Telhami 1990, ch. 4.

6. Fahmy 1983:96–101; Riad 1982:282–84.

7. Syria's stance was partly due to its own ambitions: as an aspiring pan-Arab leader, Syria wanted to have a say on the Palestinian issue, and historically many Syrians viewed Palestine as being part of greater Syria. Syria was the only state to send its army across the border with Jordan to help the PLO forces battling King Hussein's army in 1970.

8. Riad 1982:282.

9. Quandt 1986:226.

10. Although Israel ultimately made its position clear on this issue when Prime Minister Yitzhak Rabin declared that "the only party with whom a solution of this [Palestinian] problem could be reached is Jordan" (*New York Times*, July 13, 1994), there were some ambiguities in the Israeli position in the previous weeks. Even the day before Rabin's statement, Israeli information minister Aharon Yariv said that negotiations between Israel and the PLO could be held if the PLO would acknowledge the existence of Israel as a Jewish state and terminate hostile action against it.

11. Fahmy 1983:97.

12. Fahmy 1983:98.

13. Quandt 1986:226.

14. Riad 1982:282–83.

15. Fahmy 1983:100.

16. Quandt 1986:242.

17. Harold Saunders points out that the secret deal was not intended to prevent the United States from talking with the PLO and that the United States rejected Israeli wording to that extent. Instead, Kissinger believed that it prevented formal negotiations and formal recognition by the United States (Saunders's comments at conference of Middle East Institute on the 1973 war, Washington, October 11, 1998).

18. Tessler 1994:426.

19. Tessler 1994:434.

20. Khalidi 1997:1.

21. Savir 1998:5.

References

Fahmy, Ismail. 1983. *Negotiating for Peace in the Middle East.* Baltimore: Johns Hopkins University Press.

Khalidi, Rashid. 1997. *Palestinian Identity: The Construction of Modern National Consciousness.* New York: Columbia University Press.

Quandt, William. 1986. *Camp David: Peacemaking and Politics.* Washington, D.C.: Brookings Institution.

Riad, Mahmoud. 1982. *The Struggle for Peace in the Middle East.* London: Quartet Books.

Savir, Uri. 1998. *The Process: 1,100 Days That Changed the Middle East.* New York: Random House.

Smith, Charles D. 1988. *Palestine and the Arab-Israeli Conflict.* New York: St. Martin's Press.

Telhami, Shibley. 1990. *Power and Leadership in International Bargaining: The Path to the Camp David Accords.* New York: Columbia University Press.

Tessler, Mark. 1994. *A History of the Israeli-Palestinian Conflict.* Bloomington: Indiana University Press.

11

Explaining Variation: Defaults, Coercion, Commitments

STEPHEN D. KRASNER

How constraining are conventional rules of sovereignty such as recognition of juridically independent territorial entities, nonintervention in the internal affairs of other states, and de facto autonomy for sovereign entities? Some of the cases in this volume, especially the breakup of the Soviet Union, suggest that these rules are highly salient and constraining, leaving actors with limited options and making some outcomes far more likely than others. Others, such as Hong Kong and Taiwan, indicate that there is more flexibility. New rules can be defined for new situations. Still others, notably Bosnia, suggest that the rules of sovereignty are salient, offering the most obvious way to organize political life, but that such rules can be ignored at least in the short and medium term in an effort to make conventional sovereignty more viable over the longer run.

What explains this variation? The standard approaches to the study of international relations, and politics more generally, suggest three general kinds of explanatory variables—power, interests, and ideas—suitably defined and elaborated of course to deal with specific issues. In the extreme, constructivist arguments suggest that only ideas matter, realist arguments that only power matters, and liberal arguments that only interests matter. No one of these explanatory variables can by itself provide an account of the conditions under which sovereignty is more or less consequential. But they do suggest three possibilities regarding the salience of widespread rules, such as those associated with sovereignty.

1. If rulers cannot make voluntary commitments to honor alternative rules and if the more powerful judge that the cost of coercion would outweigh the benefits, then the conventional rules of sovereignty are a default or focal point. They become highly consequential. Ideas matter and shape the conception that actors have of their own interests. In this volume the breakup of the Soviet Union into units that conformed with the rules of international legal sovereignty, Palestinian demands for sovereignty, efforts to create a Bosnian state that has the conventional attributes of domestic and Westphalian sovereignty, and the Chinese refusal to grant autonomy to Tibet offer examples.

2. More powerful states may use coercion to impose an alternative institutional arrangement on weaker actors. Such an initiative can be viable, but only if the more powerful decide that the benefits of coercion outweigh the costs, a calculation that will be affected by interests, by material capabilities, and by conventional sovereignty rules that can affect the behavior and level of resistance of the targets of coercion. In this volume, the 1995 arrangements for Bosnia, and even more clearly the occupation of Kosovo, offer examples. Ideas are not irrelevant, but power determines outcomes.

3. If rulers can make voluntary commitments, that is, create an equilibrium outcome from which no critical player has an incentive to defect either through unilateral initiatives or by contracting with other states, then anything is possible. As the conventional understanding of sovereignty provided by international lawyers suggests, no contractual arrangement between states is illicit. States are free to do whatever they choose. That is why Heller and Sofaer emphasize the flexible nature of sovereignty, its ability to conform to the various needs and situations of many different states. In the contemporary environment the European Union, a case not covered in this book, and Hong Kong are examples of situations in which states have made voluntary commitments, used their international legal sovereignty to undermine their Westphalian sovereignty, and in so doing created internationally recognized entities, the European Union itself and Hong Kong, which violate the rule that recognition should be extended to juridically independent territorial entities. The EU does not have a territory and Hong Kong is not juridically independent, yet both are recognized. In these situations interests trump ideas.

Sovereignty as a Default

The defining characteristic of international politics is anarchy, a situation in which no hierarchical authority is recognized as having the legitimate right to set rules and resolve conflicts. But given the condition of anarchy, many different sets of rules and norms are possible. The traditional Chinese system, as Oksenberg and Madsen note, relied on the concept of a tributary state. Tributary states symbolically recognized the imperial center, but the degree of control actually exercised by the center varied. Medieval Europe was characterized by overlapping claims of authority within the same territory. Prior to the sixteenth century, the Ottoman Empire made a distinction between relations conducted among Islamic states and those conducted with infidels, including an at least formal refusal to treat non-Muslim states as equals.[1] During the nineteenth century some political entities were formally established as protectorates with their foreign policy controlled by one of the major European states, while their internal affairs were governed by local decisions. In the contemporary international system, the concepts of tributary states, protectorates, and infidel states are not widely recognized. They are not readily available constructs that can be easily understood by either political leaders or their constituents. (This is not to say that functional equivalents do not exist. Micronesia and the Marshall Islands, both formerly American trust territories, are recognized as independent states, but the United States has established what is in effect a protectorate relationship with them.)[2] The rules of sovereignty including autonomy, nonintervention, territoriality, and mutual recognition are the most widely available in the contemporary international system. If states are unable to voluntarily commit to different rules or are unwilling to use coercion to establish such alternatives, then the conventional rules of sovereignty will strongly influence outcomes because they provide a widely understood script that political leaders can use to appeal to their constituents.

   In the Sinocentric world, Oksenberg notes, solutions that were readily available to China in the nineteenth century no longer have much salience. The concept of a tributary state provided traditional China with an institutional structure that allowed Beijing to claim some authority over far-flung areas that it could not govern effectively on an ongoing basis. The European dominance of China in the nineteenth century introduced the sovereign state system with its claim to formal equality and mutual recognition for all states. Territories were usually either states themselves or parts of some other state, such as colonies. Churchill and Chiang Kai-shek declared at the end of the Second World War that Taiwan was a part of China, a position that was endorsed by the three major powers at Potsdam and accepted by Japan. As Madsen argues, once the situation of Taiwan was clarified "neither the KMT nor the CCP could abjure it without jeopardizing their nationalistic credentials." While the tributary state concept echoes in the idea of "one country, two systems," which has been floated by Beijing, Hong Kong and Taiwan cannot simply be designated as tributary states of China since neither other states nor major groups within China would understand what that means.

The absence of the concept of a tributary state has made a mutually acceptable settlement of the situation of Tibet, and Taiwan as well, more difficult than it would have been in the traditional Sinocentric world. Oksenberg argues that "the Tibet issue is perhaps the clearest case where the repertoire of solutions drawn from the sovereignty medicinal kit seems inadequate to the challenge at hand; indeed by introducing concepts of independence and autonomy, the kit has probably compounded the problems." In the past leaders in Beijing and Lhasa would have been satisfied with an ambiguous set of relations provided that the Tibetan rulers paid at least symbolic obeisance to the imperial center. In the contemporary world, Tibetan and Chinese nationalists would find the ambivalence of tributary state status unacceptable—Tibetans because they would want to be recognized as a fully sovereign entity, and Chinese because they would want complete control and authority. Compromising on these objectives could be problematic for rulers because they could not secure adequate support from some of their own constituents. They could be accused of betraying their own national cause. In an environment in which sovereign equality, autonomy, and recognition were not as widely understood, such accusations could not be made. A different range of options would be available to political leaders. A mutually satisfactory solution might be more easily arrived at—for instance, a confederal structure that would give Tibet more autonomy but still provide Beijing with adequate levels of authority and control.[3]

In her analysis of developments in the Balkans, Susan Woodward also suggests that traditional institutional arrangements that were available in the past, different from formally equal, autonomous, mutually recognized sovereign states, could have provided a more satisfactory outcome in the Balkans. She writes that the history of the area includes "the legacy of local self-government of the Byzantine system, the millet system of the Ottomans, recurring massive migrations (national as well as individual—household and transhumant), conflict between an imperial tradition (e.g., the Habs-burgs, the Ottomans) and states emerging out of the nationalist struggle, the Habsburg protectorate and then annexation of Bosnia and Herzegovina in response to the end of the Ottoman empire, and the creation at Ver-sailles of a multinational state." These legacies did not establish a linear path to purely national outcomes, but rather a situation in which ambiguity was expected.

Telhami's discussion of Palestine also suggests that the conventional norms of sovereignty have been constraining and that the availability of some alternative conceptualization might have made a mutually acceptable agree-ment more likely. Palestinian nationalism, Telhami avers, grew out of the collapse of pan-Arabism. When pan-Arabism failed, the Palestinian leadership and its followers saw sovereignty—at least international legal sovereignty and some elements of Westphalian sovereignty—as the only available option. Be-fore the 1967 war, a Palestinian entity on the West Bank and Gaza might have been possible in a pan-Arab world, but it was not tenable in an environment in which sovereign states were the default option.

Finally, the conventional rules of sovereignty—at least the rules associated with international legal sovereignty—were also highly salient for the breakup of the Soviet Union. The rulers of the Soviet Union, including its constituent parts, did not see sovereignty as the only available option, but it was the most attractive and available script for some major players. In 1990 Yeltsin, as chair-man of the Russian Congress of People's Deputies, had a number of different strategies that he could have pursued to enhance his position vis-à-vis that of Gorbachev, who governed the Soviet Union. As McFaul argues, Yeltsin could have called for economic and political reforms within the Soviet Union, but in the early 1990s capitalism was too discredited for such a program to have much appeal.

The most significant attempt to secure some alternative arrangement was undermined not directly by Yeltsin but by conservatives in the Gorbachev government for whom the conventional rules of sovereignty were highly sa-lient. McFaul writes that in "the spring and summer of 1991, Yeltsin and eight other republican leaders negotiated with Gorbachev to draft a new Union Treaty. This document tried to carve out a middle ground between full sov-ereignty for nine of the republics and full subordination. Had the Union Treaty been signed and allowed to structure relations between the republics, sovereignty within the Soviet Union might have taken on a new and unique meaning in the international system of states." The treaty was, however, never signed—not only because Yeltsin was not so enthusiastic but because conservatives within the Gorbachev government were skeptical about the viability of any new institutional arrangement. They feared that the treaty would be the first step toward the breakup of the Soviet Union and staged a palace coup, one which ultimately failed, precipitating the outcome they had tried to avoid.

Yeltsin then pushed for Russian sovereignty. Sovereignty was a readily available script. It was understood both by political leaders and their potential supporters. It would serve Yeltsin's goal of becoming a head of state although the state would be Russia and not the Soviet Union.

China and Bosnia have seen historical forms of organization—the tributary state and decentralized imperial structures such as the millet system— that differed from the conventional rules of sovereignty. In Palestine and the former Soviet Union, political leaders explored alternative structures: in the case of Palestine, pan-Arabism; in the case of the former Soviet Union, confederation. The existence of such possibilities shows that conventional rules were not taken for granted. Political leaders did not see themselves as having no options. They were capable of inventing new institutional arrangements, even though in the case of Palestine and the former Soviet Union they did not work.

But in the end conventional sovereignty more or less triumphed. International legal sovereignty has been embraced by Palestinian, Bosnian, Tibetan, Chinese, and Russian leaders. Westphalian sovereignty, especially for Palestine, Bosnia, and parts of the Soviet Union, has been more problematic. The relevant actors were not able to agree on alternative institutional arrangements, nor did any set of actors have the power to coerce the others, even though such arrangements might have better served the material and political goals of all the parties.

The attractiveness of different rules is most apparent in the case of Tibet. The most likely outcome for Tibet is continued repression from the central government in Beijing. Independence is a remote possibility, but it would involve either a breakup of China itself or a radical change in its central regime. In the present situation, China incurs substantial governance costs and Tibet has very limited autonomy. Were traditional Sinocentric institutions widely understood and accepted, both Tibetan and Chinese leaders might have found tributary state status more satisfactory, but given the salience of conventional sovereignty rules, neither party could compromise without risking support from important groups among their own constituents. For China, there is the additional anxiety that granting Tibet substantial autonomy might lead to similar demands from other regions.

Hence, in the former Soviet Union, parts of China, Palestine, and Bosnia the conventional script of sovereignty—autonomy, mutual recognition, and territory—has played a significant role. Recognition as an independent state has been particularly compelling. Alternative institutional arrangements could be imagined, and in some cases were even tried, but they have been discarded. Absent voluntary action or coercion, sovereignty was the default.

Coercion and Alternative Institutional Arrangements

While conventional conceptions of appropriate structures for sovereign states provide a reasonably accurate description of developments in some of the areas discussed in this volume, most notably Tibet and most aspects of developments in the states that formerly made up the Soviet Union, such conventional constructs fail to capture developments in other cases. In some instances innovative arrangements have been the result of voluntary contracting, but in others they have resulted from coercion.

The clearest case of coercion discussed in this volume is Bosnia. The settlement resulting from the Dayton accord has been coercive. It would not be viable absent the presence of large numbers of NATO troops. The troops are not there simply to prevent an escalation of violence that might result from misperception—one party identifying as a violation a move that the initiating party regarded as benign. Rather the troops are there because one or more of the local actors would opt for a different solution if the threat of external military intervention was removed.

In her analysis Woodward astutely observes that the major Western states have violated the rules of sovereignty, especially Westphalian sovereignty, in an effort to create a political entity that would ultimately conform with those rules. Ultimately what the major Western powers want is a stable situation in the Balkans. There are no material gains to be had by violating the Westphalian sovereignty of Bosnia and other Balkan states. The problem confronted by the members of NATO is that ethnic conflict in the Balkans can precipitate instability in a larger area that could draw in the major powers. This is not a new story. External actors want a set of fully sovereign status quo Balkan countries—polities where indigenous governments are able to maintain effective domestic order and eschew external expansion—because this would avoid any threat to the larger security of Europe and would not entail any governance costs.

The Dayton accord and subsequent developments have trampled on Bosnia's Westphalian sovereignty. Woodward's paper elaborates these measures. International persons play an extensive role in the judicial system. There is an independent Human Rights Commission, a majority of whose members are appointed by the Council of Europe. The Organization for Security and Co-operation in Europe and the UN mission have human rights monitors in most of the major towns and cities. The International Criminal Tribunal for the Former Yugoslavia investigates, indicts, and tries violations of humanitarian law. The director of the Central Bank is an employee of the International Monetary Fund. The electoral laws, judicial reforms, and police procedures were designed by international civil servants on mission in Bosnia. The High Representative is empowered to make decisions for locally elected politicians when they act in ways that are inconsistent with the peace agreement, and he has made decisions about the symbolic representation of the country including the layout of the currency, the flag, and automobile license plates. The High Representative's office has monitored Bosnian media, closed down some Bosnian Serb television transmitters, and promoted, with the aid of George Soros, an independent television network.

The level of external involvement in constructing and implementing basic constitutional structures in Bosnia has been intrusive, comprehensive, and sustained. Nothing about these arrangements is consistent with conventional notions of Westphalian sovereignty. Nevertheless, they have been put in place despite local dissent, because of the coercive power of the major Western states.

These recent developments in the Balkans echo earlier policies by the great powers. The recognition of every state that emerged from the Ottoman Empire was conditioned on provisions guaranteeing the civil and political rights of religious minorities, and often the major states of Europe intervened in even more intrusive ways. When Greece was recognized as an independent state in 1832 (largely as a result of external military intervention at Navarino in 1828, when a combined British, French, and Russian fleet defeated an Egyptian armada), the major powers insisted on provisions for minority rights in Greek law. In addition the head of state, Otto, the second son of the king of Bavaria, was appointed by the major European states. During the 1930s the military was commanded by European, not Greek, officers. The Treaty of Paris following the Crimean War gave Moldavia and Wallachia (later to become Romania) a very high level of self-government within the Ottoman Empire although not international legal sovereignty, but the major powers again insisted on equal treatment for all religious groups. Following the Balkan Wars of the 1870s, the major powers met at Berlin in 1878. Serbia, Montenegro, and Romania were recognized as independent states, and Bulgaria as a tributary state of the Ottoman Empire; but again the major European powers conditioned their grant of international legal sovereignty on provisions for the equal treatment of members of all faiths. External actors sought religious toleration primarily to stabilize the Balkans. Orthodox religious concerns had provided a pretext for Russian intervention in the Balkans and Anatolia, which threatened British interests in the eastern Mediterranean. The Habsburgs were apprehensive about ethnic nationalism that might spill over into the Dual Monarchy. This fear had prompted the occupation and later annexation of Bosnia and Herzegovina, hardly the best solution for the empire since it brought more Slavs under Habsburg rule. Bismarck was anxious to maintain Germany's alliance with both Austria-Hungary and Russia, an alliance strained by conflict in the Balkans. Albania was recognized as an independent state in 1912, but its constitution was then drafted by an International Control Commission that had only one Albanian member. Like other states in the Balkans, Albania was supposed to provide for civic and political equality for all religious groups. The new country's king, a German prince, was appointed by the major powers. Albania was declared to be a neutral state.

All these violations of Westphalian sovereignty in the Balkans from the 1820s to the outbreak of the First World War were designed to establish stable and status quo states. The major European powers had their ambitions in the Balkans, especially Russia. But at the same time they all feared that they would be drawn into a cauldron of instability in the area. In the summer of 1914 these anxieties proved all too true.

Similar efforts to contain ethnic conflicts were made in the Balkans and elsewhere after the First World War. The vision for the postwar world as embodied in many parts of the Versailles settlement was that a system of collective security would replace balance of power. Peace-loving states would join together to oppose an aggressor. This could only happen, Woodrow Wilson and his supporters believed, with democratic political regimes. International peace depended on national self-determination. At the same time decision makers realized that it would be impossible to create ethnically homogenous states in Europe. The goal was to reconcile ethnic minorities to the polities within which they found themselves. To accomplish this objective, the major powers insisted on minority rights protections as a condition of international recognition or membership in the League of Nations. Some thirty-three smaller states accepted such conditions. Most of these arrangements were the result of coercion. The political leaders of these weaker entities, some of whom had never been accepted as international legal sovereigns, needed international recognition, without which the states they hoped to rule might not exist. They would have preferred, however, to establish their own domestic rules regarding the treatment of minorities. Only a few countries—notably Hungary, which had few minorities within its own borders but many Hungarians in others states, and Czechoslovakia, which hoped to mollify its own large German minority—embraced the minority rights regime that emerged from Versailles and that was institutionally embedded in the League of Nations, where a Minorities Section was created in the Secretariat.[4] Individuals as well as official organizations could bring complaints to the league. If the league's elaborate procedures proved inadequate, cases could be taken to the International Court of Justice. In the interwar period, as in the nineteenth century, the primary objective of the major powers when they violated the Westphalian sovereignty of their weaker counterparts was to enhance international security. They feared that domestic instability would threaten international security.[5]

Thus the motivations, policies, and objectives that Woodward describes in her discussion of Bosnian developments in the late 1990s are similar to developments in earlier periods. Major powers violated the Westphalian sovereignty of weaker states primarily because they wanted to enhance international stability. These earlier efforts accomplished little in large part because rulers judged that the governance costs associated with sustained attempts at intervention were prohibitive. The leverage of the major powers was greatest at the moments when the leaders of would-be states sought international legal sovereignty. Recognition could be extended in exchange for protections of minority rights. Once recognition was bestowed, however, it could not easily be withdrawn, and the leverage of the major powers eroded. Absent recognition, the reversion point for the leader of a national movement could be nonexistence. Once recognition had been given, the reversion point was not so dire. A leader could decide, as Pilsudski did in 1934 when Poland abrogated its minorities treaty, that assertions of Westphalian sovereignty were preferable to the status quo.

What is different about recent developments in Bosnia and Kosovo is not the motivation of more powerful states, but rather the implementation of their policies. The extensive military occupation of Bosnia and later Kosovo is a departure from past practices in the Balkans, although there have been sustained American military occupations in Central America and the Caribbean and Soviet occupations in Eastern Europe, both aimed at altering the constitutional structures of weaker states such as Haiti, Nicaragua, Poland, and Czechoslovakia.

The necessary condition for intervention with or without the use of military force has been the absence of opposition from a major power. Interventions aimed at compromising the Westphalian sovereignty of target states have taken place only in situations where one major power exercised control over a mutually recognized sphere of influence, as was the case for the Soviet Union in Eastern Europe from 1945 until 1990 and for the United States in most of the Caribbean and Central America since the Spanish American War, or when there has been an agreement among the major powers, as was the case in the Balkans for decisions regarding Greek independence, Romanian autonomy after the Crimean War, and at the Congress of Berlin in 1878. Intervention in the face of opposition from another major power has not occurred because the costs of imposing institutional arrangements on a resistant local elite and its constituents coupled with opposition, possibly military, from another major power have outweighed the expected benefits.

The deployment of occupying troops, which occurred in both the American and Soviet spheres of influence, did not take place in the Balkans before the 1990s, with the possible exception of Bavarian officers in Greece in the 1830s. What accounts for this new development?

In Bosnia and Kosovo there was, if not consensus, at least no active opposition from any of the major powers. It is not likely that NATO involvement could have been sustained in the face of significant military costs. Clinton's announcement at the beginning of the Kosovo campaign that ground forces would not be used and the extreme caution with which the air campaign was carried out were indicative of the fragility of domestic support. Nevertheless, the deployment of a large occupying force outside of a recognized sphere of influence is something new. It cannot be attributed to security concerns, which were less compelling than has been the case in the past. Even under the worst scenarios—large-scale refugee flows and the spread of conflict to neighboring countries—there is no equivalent to the pre–World War I situation in which both Austria-Hungary and Russia were inevitably drawn into local conflicts in the Balkans.

Rather, the large occupying force is better explained by the increased salience of humanitarian concerns at the end of the twentieth century, a phenomenon reflecting the change in domestic political structures within the major powers, and by the existence of multilateral structures that reduced transactions costs. Democracy has increased the importance of humanitarian groups. The influence of such groups is always contingent on the domestic political environment wherein they are pursuing their objectives.[6] The majority of any electorate may be indifferent to humanitarian issues, but a committed minority can still be electorally significant. Any political leader, regardless of his or her own convictions, must weigh the electoral costs resulting from public criticism for failing to intervene against the costs that might be incurred if an intervention failed to stop bloodshed or resulted in casualties for the intervening power. Clinton yanked American troops out of Somalia after eighteen soldiers were killed in October 1993, did not intervene in Rwanda, but deployed thousands of troops in Bosnia and Kosovo. With the spread of democracy and the rising salience of human rights concerns among some groups within democratic countries, the electoral costs of not intervening have grown.

Intervention in the Balkans was also facilitated by the existence of NATO. At least one reason that long-term military occupations have taken place in spheres of influence but not elsewhere is that unilateral intervention is easier than multilateral. If several states are involved, they must agree not only on their objectives but also on the distribution of costs. Collective action problems are unavoidable. Moreover, the possibility of organizational mishaps is higher. Even among military forces from the same country, snafus are more than possible. During the 1983 invasion of Grenada, for instance, contingents from the U.S. Army and Navy had difficulty communicating with each other, a kind of problem that is much more likely to occur among units from different countries. NATO provided a framework that made it easier to allocate costs and minimize organizational failures. The involvement of Russian troops, notably their seizure of the airport in Priština, was more problematic.

In sum, the conventional rules associated with Westphalian sovereignty can be violated through coercion, and there is a long history of such efforts in the Balkans. The goal of those interventions has been, as Woodward emphasizes, to establish a stable polity that would, in the long run, conform with these very same rules. What is unique about recent developments is not the violation of domestic autonomy, but rather the extensive use of occupying military forces, a change that is most persuasively explained by increased concern for humanitarian issues among democratic electorates and the existence of NATO, which facilitated multilateral coordination.

Voluntary Initiatives and Alternative Institutional Arrangements

No legitimate hierarchical structure of authority exists in the international system. Political leaders can make up any rules they please. Whether such rules will be viable, however, depends on the leaders' ability to reach agreement with their counterparts in other countries, to secure the support of their own constituents, or to coerce compliance from resistant targets. Bosnia, and indeed the history of the Balkan states since the 1820s, provides many examples of the use of coercive power to violate the rules of Westphalian sovereignty. Coercion is, however, not the only way in which alternatives to conventional rules can be developed. Political leaders may also be able to voluntarily reach an equilibrium outcome that violates Westphalian or international legal sovereignty.

In the contemporary world the European Union provides the most obvious example of a contractual arrangement that has established institutional structures inconsistent with conventional sovereignty rules. The major treaties that have created the EU do not violate international legal sovereignty; indeed, they are a manifestation of the right of mutually recognized states to make voluntary agreements. But many of the rules themselves, and the subsequent development of European institutions, are inconsistent with Westphalian sovereignty.

Beginning in the early 1960s, the European Court of Justice (ECJ) elaborated doctrines that have compromised the autonomy of member states. The ECJ held that its decisions had direct effect in national courts and asserted that community law, including administrative law, trumped national law. In 1971 the court ruled that the European Community itself had the right to enter into treaties. The member states of the EU have accepted procedures that allow their own domestic authority structures to be changed by the rulings of a supranational judicial body, even though the doctrines of direct effect, supremacy, and implied powers were not explicitly agreed to in the Treaty of Rome or other founding documents of the European Community. The Maastricht Treaty created pooled sovereignty. It provided for qualified majority voting in the Council of Europe in a number of issue areas. Individual member states could be bound by policies that they themselves had not agreed to.[7]

While the practices of the European Union that compromise the West-phalian sovereignty of its members are entirely consistent with international legal sovereignty because they have been the result of voluntary agreements among the member states, the EU itself has also challenged international legal sovereignty. The standard rule for international legal sovereignty is that mutual recognition is extended to juridically independent territorial entities. The EU has been recognized, but it does not have territory and its actions are to varying degrees subject to control by its members. Nevertheless, the union has entered into treaties with other states. Usually the EU has only observer status in international organizations, but it is a full member of the United Nations Food and Agriculture Organization, as are its individual member states. The union has diplomatic representation in a number of countries.[8] The union is a sovereign person. But so are its member states. Although not discussed in any of the cases in this volume, the European Union is a clear example of the ability of political leaders to reach voluntary agreements on rules that differ from those that define conventional sovereignty.

In the cases discussed in this volume, issues associated with Palestine, Taiwan, and especially Hong Kong provide further illustrations. All these ex-amples involve the development of alternatives to international legal sover-eignty, and for Palestine and Hong Kong Westphalian sovereignty as well. With regard to new criteria for international recognition, all required volun-tary agreement among a number of states; with regard to domestic autonomy, departures were the result of both international agreements and, for Hong Kong, unilateral initiatives.

The Palestine Liberation Organization (PLO) emerged as the primary representative of Palestinian aspirations during the 1970s. Its constituents lived in a number of different countries—Israel, Jordan, Lebanon. It did not have juridical independence. But the PLO was endorsed by some of the more important states in the Arab world including Algeria, Saudi Arabia, and Egypt. As Telhami points out, the PLO also received financial resources, especially from oil-rich states. It was supported by many third-world states. Within a month after the 1974 Arab summit conference in Rabat, which recognized the PLO as the representative of the Palestinian people, the organization was granted permanent observer status in the United Nations by a vote of 95 to 17 with 10 abstentions. This was not a direct violation of the conventional rule for international legal sovereignty because the PLO was not given full mem-bership, but it did give the organization international standing. Before 1974 permanent observer status had been accorded only to regional organizations and to states, such as Switzerland, that were not members of the United Nations. In 1988 the PLO's status was upgraded to that of an observer mission. During the 1970s the PLO established representative offices in more than a hundred states, and in the early 1980s, in direct violation of conventional rules, a number of states, including the Soviet Union, accorded the PLO full diplomatic status.

Taiwan offers a more intriguing case than Palestine. Granting the PLO a status not quite that of a state was part of a political program designed to enhance the possibility that Palestine would secure international legal sovereignty even though, as Telhami notes, the security options of any Palestinian state would almost certainly be formally constrained. Diplomatic recognition of one kind or another has been a policy tool; recognition, especially of governments, has not been automatic. In the case of China, the United States and other leading capitalist states refused to recognize the Communist government in Beijing for more than twenty years after it had clearly established effective control. In the 1970s that policy changed, culminating with the American decision to formally recognize the People's Republic as the government of China, thereby withdrawing that status from the regime that governed Taiwan. The problem for the Americans and others was how to deal with Taiwan. The Nationalist government exercised effective domestic and interdependence sovereignty. It also had Westphalian sovereignty even though it did not claim to be an independent state. What the Taiwan regime did not have was international legal sovereignty. This was a problem not only for the government in Taiwan but also for its supporters, most importantly, the United States.

Despite not being recognized as a sovereign state or as the government of a sovereign state, Taiwan has not only thrived economically but has also maintained extensive relations with other states. As Madsen points out, Taiwan and the other entities with which it was dealing devised a number of nongovernmental institutions that served as the functional equivalent of diplomatic missions. The earliest examples were the Interchange Association that Tokyo established to conduct relations with Taipei and the East Asia Relations Association that Taipei established in Tokyo. The United States enacted a new set of rules for relations with the Nationalist regime. When the United States recognized the People's Republic of China as the legitimate government of China in 1979 and withdrew recognition from the Republic of China, it established a special status for Taiwan by passing the Taiwan Relations Act. Taiwan was given legal standing in American courts even though conventional

338 STEPHEN D. KRASNER

practice restricted such status to international legal sovereigns. Taiwan was allowed to keep commercial property that had been acquired after 1949, a policy also followed by other states, even though standard procedures would have invested ownership with the newly recognized regime in Beijing. Any American law referring to foreign countries was also applied to Taiwan. International diplomacy was conducted through a new organization, the American Institute in Taiwan, and a counterpart entity established by Taiwan in the United States. American officials could be seconded to the institute and returned to "an appropriate position with the attendant rights, privileges, and benefits which the officer or employee would have had or acquired had he or she not been so separated."[9] At the same time, to conform with the requirement that the United States not have formal relations with Taiwan, employees of the institute were declared to not be employees of the United States, and the act stated that "no requirement, whether expressed or implied, under the laws of the United States with respect to maintenance of diplomatic relations or recognition shall be applicable with respect to Taiwan."[10] Essentially, the United States needed to recognize the People's Republic but at the same time maintain ties with Taiwan, and it succeeded by giving Taiwan a special status more or less comparable to that of a recognized state.

The Taiwan Relations Act also formally declared America's commitment to the defense of the island. The United States asserted the right to provide military assistance to Taiwan without regard to the views of Beijing and unilaterally committed itself to maintain the capacity to "resist any resort to force or other forms of coercion that would jeopardize the security, or the social or economic system, of the people on Taiwan."[11] In sum the United States recognized the PRC as the government of China, accepted the fact that there was only one China, created an institutional structure to maintain routine interaction with Taiwan, and committed itself to defend Taiwan. Did this set of commitments conform with conventional notions of sovereignty? Not exactly. Did it offer a way to maximize the objectives of the United States, which wanted to normalize relations with Beijing while at the same time guaranteeing the de facto independence of Taiwan? Yes. These arrangements required the formal agreement of both the United States and Taiwan and the tacit acceptance of China.

As Madsen notes, the loss of diplomatic recognition did have costs for Taiwan. In the early 1970s Japanese and European investments fell sharply. The absence of formal ties made it more difficult to assess sentiments in some other countries. Taiwan was subject to trade restrictions, especially by the

European Union, because unlike members of the General Agreement on Tariffs and Trade, it could not make formal protests. It was more difficult for Taiwanese businessmen to travel. In some countries, Taiwanese companies were more exposed to criminal gangs because the Taipei government did not have standing to bring complaints.

Taiwan has tried to enhance its formal standing. It has used its economic resources to secure formal recognition from smaller states. It has encouraged unofficial ties. Perhaps most important, as Madsen argues, Taiwan has improved its international standing as a result of its adoption in the 1990s of democratic political institutions. Taiwan has become more appealing, more legitimate, as a political entity because its domestic reforms have made it more attractive to constituencies in many Western states. Hence, as a result of voluntary arrangements, most notably those engaged in by the United States, Taiwan has secured something that is close to international legal sovereignty while being recognized as an international legal sovereign by only a scattering of smaller states, and it has enhanced its status and the support it might receive by altering the character of its domestic sovereignty.

Hong Kong offers a second example of a set of institutional arrangements, inconsistent with both international legal and Westphalian sovereignty, that have been developed through voluntary arrangements, both unilateral and multilateral. The Beijing regime wanted formal control over Hong Kong, but at the same time, it did not want to undermine Hong Kong's economic dynamism. These objectives could not be achieved by applying the conventional rules associated with Westphalian and international legal sovereignty.

China, as James Smith points out, had various options. Simply incorporating Hong Kong as, for instance, a province of China would have weakened the confidence of both local and foreign economic interests. China could have established Hong Kong as a distinct part of China governed by different rules, part of a federal system, but without any special international or transnational ties. Such an arrangement would have been perfectly consistent with international legal and Westphalian sovereignty but would not have assuaged the anxiety of commercial interests. China could have accepted the continuation of British administration or agreed to some supranational enforcement mechanism, an international court, for instance, a majority of whose judges were not appointed by Beijing, but such options would have been incompatible with China's nationalist aspirations and the desire of its leaders to expunge the legacy of colonialism.

Instead China opted for an arrangement that gave Hong Kong a distinct status that was reinforced by the involvement of external actors. China's commitments to Hong Kong were enshrined in the Joint Declaration concluded with Britain and in the Basic Law promulgated for Hong Kong. Hong Kong was given the right to participate in international organizations. It is a full member of eight organizations including the World Trade Organization, the Asian Development Bank, and the World Health Organization. It is an associate member of another six and participates in another nineteen as part of the Chinese delegation. In addition Beijing gave Hong Kong the right to issue passports, to enforce its own customs procedures, to conclude visa agreements with other states, and to establish foreign economic missions. All these activities required the explicit agreement of other states. Passports are worthless unless they are recognized. An entity cannot join an international organization unless its members agree. Hong Kong is not juridically independent, but it has been given international legal sovereignty.

In addition, the judicial arrangements for Hong Kong legitimate external authority sources. These arrangements, as Smith emphasizes, were constructed by the regime in Beijing, but their salience was reinforced because they emerged from the negotiations with Britain and were explicitly spelled out in the 1984 Joint Declaration describing the conditions under which the British would relinquish their authority claims. The Joint Declaration and the Basic Law stated that the common law of Britain as applied in Hong Kong would remain in force after the turnover. The Hong Kong Court of Final Appeal could call on foreign judges from common law countries to sit with the court and could refer to precedents from common law countries in reaching decisions. In the first two years of the court's existence, the fifth position on the bench was always occupied by a Commonwealth judge. The annex to the Joint Declaration also states that the provisions of the International Covenants on Civil and Political Rights and on Economic, Social, and Cultural Rights would remain in force for Hong Kong.

As Smith astutely notes, China did not "fully lash itself to the mast of Hong Kong's autonomy." No supranational adjudicating mechanism was created. The Basic Law distinguishes between the power to interpret and the power to adjudicate, giving the power to interpret the Basic Law to the Standing Committee of the National People's Congress in Beijing. Beijing could unilaterally revise the institutional arrangements for Hong Kong. However, if changes were made, they would be a clear signal that the Chinese government was altering its policies. This in turn could lead actors with economic resources to withdraw from Hong Kong. Knowing this, China will be reluctant to unambiguously shift its stance. There is, Smith argues, no guarantee that China will not change the rules for Hong Kong. The leadership in Beijing will calculate the economic benefits, which might diminish, for instance, if other parts of south China became dominant, against the possible political costs, which could increase if, for instance, practices in Hong Kong lead to increased dissent in China itself. Nevertheless, in agreeing to the use of common law, to foreign judges, and to universal human rights declarations, China compromised its own Westphalian sovereignty by legitimating external sources of authority.

Conventional rules are a default if leaders cannot voluntarily agree to, or use coercion to impose, alternatives. The Soviet Union and Yugoslavia split into separate entities that claimed international legal sovereignty and to some extent secured Westphalian sovereignty as well. For Yeltsin and Milošević, division of the existing political entity was a path to power. Claims for international recognition and autonomy were widely understood scripts that could readily be appreciated by potential supporters. Failure to make sovereignty claims could enhance the position of rival elites who could rally support by arguing that the nation's patrimony had been betrayed.

To note that conventional rules are a default acknowledges that they are constraining but does not imply that they are determinative. Decision makers can devise different rules. In some cases, Bosnia being the most telling example in this volume, coercion has been used to impose such alternatives on reluctant targets. In others, most notably Hong Kong, voluntary arrangements can be contrived either unilaterally—for example, China's acceptance of foreign judges on the Court of Final Appeal—or through multilateral agreement—for example, Hong Kong's continued membership in international organizations despite its lack of juridical independence.

The degree to which any rules are constricting will depend on their congruence with the material interests of actors, the extent to which individuals are socialized to embrace them, the available alternatives, and relevant enforcement mechanisms. In deeply institutionalized and well-ordered domestic polities, rules matter. Individuals are taught to obey them. Enforcement mechanisms, including police and courts, are elaborate. Alternatives may be limited. Material interests are promoted. In the international system, any international system, conventional rules will be less compelling, even those that are widely understood. Political decision makers are subject to many different sources of socialization, and domestic ones are likely to be the most compelling.[12] Different rules are available sometimes from the international environment and sometimes from a polity's own past. The success of the European Union, for instance, and especially its explicit linking of an economic common market with political democratization was an inspiration for the development of Mercusor for the southern part of South America. The availability of practices from the traditional Sinocentric world might have made it easier for China's leaders to develop formulas like "one country, two systems." Whatever the prevailing rules, they are likely to promote the economic interests of some actors while being less attractive to others. In the international environment there is no authoritative mechanism for resolving conflicts among competing rules.

The rules of sovereignty, like the rules that have existed in any international environment, do matter, especially if political leaders cannot agree, or use coercion, to create alternatives. Prevailing rules make it easier to do some things and harder to do others. But they are not determinative. New rules can be invented. And new rules can work, especially if they are the product of an equilibrium outcome arrived at through voluntary decisions rather than coercion, which inevitably involves governance costs. Conventional rules do not necessarily make the resolution of unconventional situations more problematic.

Notes

1. Lewis 1995: 120, 273.
2. Lake 1996.
3. These arguments are developed fully in Oksenberg's paper in this volume.
4. Bartsch 1995: 81–82, 84–85.
5. In many instances, humanitarian concerns were also present. More than a thousand volunteers from all parts of Europe, including Byron, fought for Greek independence. Gladstone was returned as prime minister in 1880 in part because of his writings against Turkish atrocities in the Balkans. Some European leaders as well as Jewish groups expressed concern for the repression of Jews in Romania during the nineteenth century.
6. For an illuminating discussion of the domestic politics associated with the abolition of the slave trade and slavery in the British empire during the first part of the nineteenth century, see Kaufmann and Pape 1999.
7. Moravcsik 1994: 51; Burley and Mattli 1993; Weiler 1991: 2413–27.

8. See <http://europa.eu.int/commdg1a/index.html> for a listing of the international activities of the European Union.

9. *Taiwan Relations Act* 1979, sec. 3310 (a).

10. *Taiwan Relations Act* 1979, sec. 3303 (b)(8).

11. *Taiwan Relations Act* 1979, sec. 3301 (b)(6).

12. As John Meyer and his collaborators have pointed out, however, this is not so much the case for weaker and less developed polities that are anxious to pursue the script of modernity. For such states international influences can be, in some issue areas, more consequential than domestic ones. See, for example, Meyer et al. 1977.

References

Bartsch, Sebastian. 1995. *Minderheitenschutz in der internationalen Politik: Völkerbund und KSZE/OSZE in neuer Perspektive.* Oplanden, Germany: Westdeutscher Verlag.

Burley, Ann Marie and Walter Mattli. 1993. "Europe Before the Court: A Political Theory of Legal Integration." *International Organization* 47, no. 1: 177–210.

Kaufmann, Chaim D. and Robert A. Pape. 1999. "Explaining Costly International Moral Action: Britain's Sixty-Year Campaign Against the Atlantic Trade." *International Organization* 53, no. 4: 631–68.

Lake, David A. 1996. "Anarchy, Hierarchy, and the Variety of International Relations." *International Organization* 50, no. 1: 1–33.

Lewis, Bernard. 1995. *The Middle East: A Brief History of the Last 2,000 Years.* New York: Scribners.

Meyer, John W., John Boli, George M. Thomas, and Francisco O. Ramirez. 1997. "World Society and the Nation-State." *American Journal of Sociology* 103, no. 1: 144–81.

Moravcsik, Andrew. 1994. "Lessons from the European Human Rights Regime." In *Inter-American Dialogue, Advancing Democracy and Human Rights in the Americas: What Role of the OAS?* An Inter-American Dialogue Conference report. Washington, D.C.: Inter-American Dialogue.

Taiwan Relations Act. 1979. *U.S. Code.* Title 22, ch. 48, secs. 3301–16.

Weiler, Joseph H. H. 1991. "The Transformation of Europe." *Yale Law Journal* 100, no. 8: 2403–83.

Index